# THE MAN
# WHO WOULD
# BE KING

# THE MAN
# WHO WOULD BE
# ❧ KING ❧

## THE LIFE OF PHILIPPE D'ORLÉANS
## REGENT OF FRANCE 1674–1723

*Christine Pevitt*

Weidenfeld and Nicolson
LONDON

First published in Great Britain in 1997
by Weidenfeld & Nicolson

© 1997 Christine Pevitt

A CIP catalogue record for this book is
available from the British Library

ISBN 0 297 81317 X

Typeset by Selwood Systems, Midsomer Norton

Set in Garamond (Adobe)

Printed in Great Britain by
Butler & Tanner Ltd, Frome and London

Weidenfeld & Nicolson

The Orion Publishing Group Ltd
Orion House
5 Upper Saint Martin's Lane
London, WC2H 9EA

*To my parents*

# CONTENTS

# ILLUSTRATIONS

*Return from the Ball*, 1712–14, Antoine Watteau (Château de Versailles, France/Giraudon/Bridgeman Art Library)

*The Council of Regency for the Minority of Louis XV*, French School (Château de Versailles, France/Giraudon/Bridgeman Art Library)

Philippe II d'Orléans and Madame de Parabère as Minerva, Jean Baptiste Santerre (Château de Versailles, France/Giraudon/Bridgeman Art Library, London)

*Embarkation for Cythera*, 1717, Antoine Watteau (National Gallery of Scotland, Edinburgh/Bridgeman Art Library, London)

*Fêtes Vénitiennes*, 1718–19, Antoine Watteau (National Gallery of Scotland, Edinburgh/Bridgeman Art Library, London)

The Palace of Versailles in 1722, Pierre-Denis Martin (Château de Versailles, France/Giraudon/Bridgeman Art Library, London)

General view of the Château and the pavilions at Marly, Pierre-Denis Martin (Château du Grand Trianon, Versailles, France/Giraudon/Bridgeman Art Library, London)

*L'Enseigne de Gersaint*, 1721, Antoine Watteau (Schloss Charlottenburg, Berlin/Giraudon/Bridgeman Art Library, London)

*The Lit de Justice held in the Parlement on the Majority of Louis XV*, 1722, Nicolas Lancret (Louvre, Paris, France/Giraudon/Bridgeman Art Library, London)

*The Queen with her Stepsons*, c. 1723, Jean Ranc (Prado, Madrid/Bridgeman Art Library, London)

Voltaire, aged 23, Largillière (Private Collection/Giraudon/Bridgeman Art Library, London)

Antoine Watteau, c. 1722, Rosalba Giovanni Carriera (Museo Civico, Treviso/Giraudon/Bridgeman Art Library, London)

The Tomb of Cardinal Guillaume Dubois, 1705, Guillaume I Coustou (St Roch, Paris/Giraudon/Bridgeman Art Library, London)

# CAST OF CHARACTERS

PHILIPPE, duc d'Orléans, the Regent

MONSIEUR, Philippe de BOURBON, duc d'Orléans, his father

MADAME, Elisabeth-Charlotte, duchesse d'ORLÉANS, his mother

Françoise-Marie, duchesse d'Orléans, his wife

LOUIS XIV, King of France, his uncle

Mme de MAINTENON, secret wife of Louis XIV

MONSEIGNEUR, the Dauphin, son of Louis XIV

The duc de BOURGOGNE, eldest son of Monseigneur

The duchesse de BOURGOGNE, Marie-Adélaïde of Savoy, his wife

The duc d'Anjou (later King PHILIP V of Spain), second son
  of Monseigneur

The duc de BERRY, third son
  of Monseigneur

The duchesse de BERRY, Marie-Louise-Elisabeth d'Orléans, eldest
  daughter of the Regent

The duc du MAINE, son of Louis XIV and Mme de Montespan

The duchesse du MAINE, Anne-Louise-Bénédicte de Bourbon-Condé,
  his wife

The comte de TOULOUSE, younger son of Louis XIV and Mme
  de Montespan

MADAME LA DUCHESSE, Louise-Françoise de Bourbon, daughter of Louis
  XIV and Mme de Montespan

MONSIEUR LE DUC, Louis de Bourbon-Condé, her husband, Prince
  of the Blood

MONSIEUR LE DUC, Louis-Henri de Bourbon-Condé, her son

The prince de CONTI, Prince of the Blood

The Regent's other children: Louise-Adélaïde, abbesse de Chelles
Charlotte-Aglaé, Mlle de Valois
Louis, duc de Chartres
Louise-Elisabeth, Mlle de Montpensier
Philippe-Elisabeth, Mlle de Beaujolais
Louise-Diane, Mlle de Chartres

His illegitimate children;  Jean-Philippe, chevalier d'Orléans
Charles, abbé de Saint-Albin
Philippe-Angélique, Mlle de Froissy

# NOTE

*Dates:* In 1582 the French adopted the Gregorian calendar, which was eleven days ahead of the Julian calendar used by Great Britain until 1752. Thus 15 September 1715 in London was 26 September 1715 in Paris. I have adopted the French usage.

# FAMILY TREE

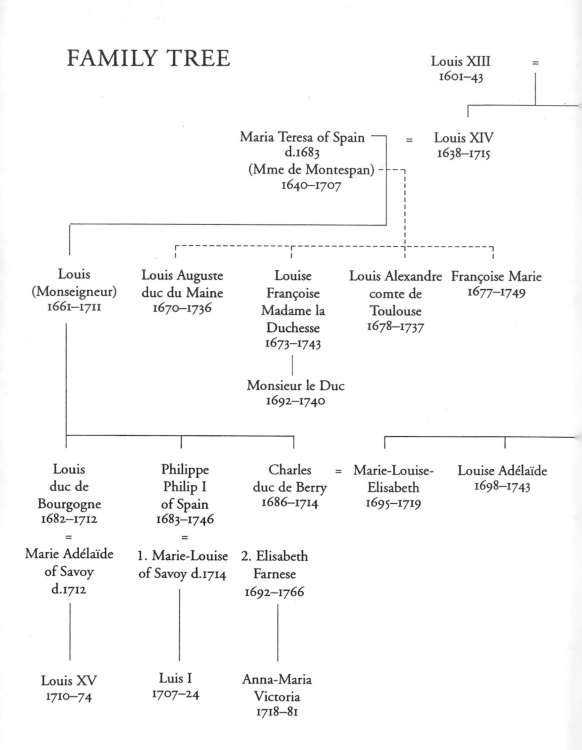

Louis XIII
1601–43
=

Maria Teresa of Spain ¬
d.1683
(Mme de Montespan) ¬ ¬ ¬
1640–1707

= Louis XIV
1638–1715

Louis
(Monseigneur)
1661–1711

Louis Auguste
duc du Maine
1670–1736

Louise
Françoise
Madame la
Duchesse
1673–1743

Louis Alexandre
comte de
Toulouse
1678–1737

Françoise Marie
1677–1749

Monsieur le Duc
1692–1740

Louis
duc de
Bourgogne
1682–1712
=
Marie Adélaïde
of Savoy
d.1712

Philippe
Philip I
of Spain
1683–1746
=
1. Marie-Louise
of Savoy d.1714

Charles
duc de Berry
1686–1714

= Marie-Louise-
Elisabeth
1695–1719

Louise Adélaïde
1698–1743

2. Elisabeth
Farnese
1692–1766

Louis XV
1710–74

Luis I
1707–24

Anna-Maria
Victoria
1718–81

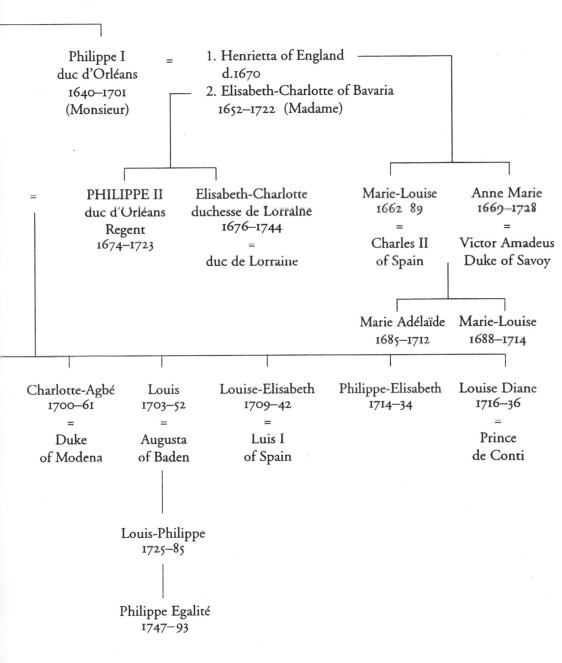

Anne of Austria
1601–66

Philippe I          =    1. Henrietta of England
duc d'Orléans                 d.1670
1640–1701                2. Elisabeth-Charlotte of Bavaria
(Monsieur)                    1652–1722  (Madame)

=     PHILIPPE II          Elisabeth-Charlotte          Marie-Louise          Anne Marie
      duc d'Orléans        duchesse de Lorraine          1662 89              1669–1728
      Regent               1676–1744                       =                     =
      1674–1723               =                         Charles II           Victor Amadeus
                           duc de Lorraine              of Spain             Duke of Savoy

                                                        Marie Adélaïde       Marie-Louise
                                                        1685–1712            1688–1714

Charlotte-Agbé     Louis          Louise-Elisabeth     Philippe-Elisabeth   Louise Diane
1700–61            1703–52        1709–42              1714–34              1716–36
    =                 =               =                                         =
Duke              Augusta         Luis I                                    Prince
of Modena         of Baden        of Spain                                  de Conti

Louis-Philippe
1725–85

Philippe Egalité
1747–93

# PREFACE

How does one become so involved with a person long dead? I had reason to wonder. I was aboard a plane to Paris on a trail three hundred years old. I was following a path deep into the past, a path which led to a man born in France in 1674, a man who had played an important part in the great affairs of his time, but who remained an enigma, his name now forgotten. I recognise that the persistence of a biographer pursuing a subject who left such a faint scent is close to obsession. Obsession is irrational, but it is nothing if it is not tenacious. And so there I was, aboard a flight to Paris.

The subject of my obsession was Philippe d'Orléans, nephew of Louis XIV. He can be seen in the portraits of Versailles in its heyday, one of the periwigged princes standing respectfully by the King. When Louis XIV died in 1715, after a reign of over seventy years, it was Philippe who took power in France, as Regent for the five-year-old boy King Louis XV, great-grandson of Louis XIV. Philippe d'Orléans ruled France for eight years, until his death at the age of forty-nine.

His Regency was the time of Watteau, the young Voltaire, the Mississippi Bubble, the founding of New Orléans, the plays of Marivaux, the perfection of the Paris town house, and the Boulle commode. Manon Lescaut is its enduring symbol. The period has been condemned for 'stupre, lucre et cruauté', and glamorised for its demonstration of the art of *douceur de vivre*. The man who presided over it has been dismissed as a rake, an idler, *a débauché*, and hailed as a dedicated worker for the good of the state, a statesman of vision, a wit and a hero, a modern man in his tolerance and freedom from bigotry. As he looks out from his portraits he has a sardonic air. Try and fathom me, he seems to say. And now I was in pursuit.

I had rented an apartment in Paris at a very grand address on the avenue Gabriel, which borders the gardens at the place de la Concorde end of the Champs-Elysées. The handsome building faces the bi-weekly stamp market and the Théâtre Marigny, right next door to the President of the Republic at the Palais d'Elysée. I had found the place through a network of distant, rich friends and was paying as much as for a room in a small hotel, but gaining incalculable benefits. The rambling building was divided up, most of the apartments belonging to some branch or other of an old family complete with the particule, the desirable *de*, which signifies some tinge of nobility, however slight. My apartment was the grandest, at the front, on the *étage noble*, full of dusty Belle Epoque furnishings and portraits of various particuled ancestors on the walls. There was a piano, mirrors in gilded frames, glass-fronted armoires, volumes of the sermons of seventeenth-century bishops, a hint of Catholic, Royalist *bienséance*. In contrast, the kitchen and bathroom were resolutely ugly, decorated in the manner of the 1950s, with bamboo furniture and garish wallpaper. There was a bath but no shower, no television, no microwave. It suited me perfectly.

Barely arrived, and turning my back on all the temptations of Paris, my first destination was Saint-Cloud, just west of the city, where Philippe was born in 1674 in his father's palace on the banks of the Seine. As if fate had ordained it, the 52 bus to the pont Saint-Cloud stopped right outside my apartment. It was a sparkling Sunday morning; the bus hastened through the wide empty avenues to the Etoile, unhindered by weekday traffic. Then it twisted and turned through the narrower streets of Boulogne-Billancourt, full of people carrying pastries and tartes tatins for Sunday lunch. After living in New York for ten years, I was amazed that a bus could swing so nimbly around corners and pursue such a sinuous route. And I drank in the overwhelmingly Parisian atmosphere of it all.

Past the porte Saint-Cloud and over the river, we came to rest at a remarkably ugly concrete pen, an island in the middle of converging motorways. There seemed no possibility that a palace known for its tranquil beauty could have existed anywhere near here. But a sign pointed to the parc de Saint-Cloud and, having careered across the intersecting junctions, I came upon a long, flat, grassy plain, once the *bas-parc* of the château, where people strolled down broad gravelled paths, between flowered terraces, and groves of trees studded with statues and urns, where fountains played into stone basins. On this day there was no sign of life, no evidence of past or present animation; but suddenly I came upon a noble stone staircase rising to the sky, the steps overgrown with moss and lichen. Here, I realised, were the remains of the Grande Cascade, forlorn now without the splash and sparkle of rushing water. The ground rose steeply behind it; up there had been the château itself.

I climbed the slope and came out into a scene of the utmost charm, a clearing with tall wrought-iron gates framing the avenue of approach and, delightfully and unexpectedly, for this was February, an open-air café serving lunch. On the menu were gigot and haricots verts, pommes frites, wine and espresso. Robins hopped around, laughter and cigarette smoke were in the air. I was happy, that state of equilibrium between pleasure just experienced and pleasure to come. I prolonged my lunch in preparation for the visit to what I considered almost a holy place. It was the first step in my search.

Finally I rose and walked down the wide avenue. To the right the ground fell away to the cascade and the vanished Grand Jet, a forty-foot spray of water which had dazzled the château's guests. Straight ahead would have been the south façade, a large horseshoe-shaped expanse of water before it. I climbed the steps to the site. It is today a bare, flat square, the corners of the vanished building marked by yew trees. To the west, a series of stone basins, now overgrown and mossy, stretch to the horizon; these basins, where fountains had played and carp swam, march in line past parterres and groves. Balustrades and carved stone seats dot the landscape. Long avenues extend to the south, bordered with tall old trees, one leading to Versailles, others to Sèvres, La Celle, Saint-Germain-en-Laye. The Seine still flows past the lower park, there is still a bridge where the old wooden one used to cross the river. The road to the *cour d'honneur* still runs up a steep incline from the bridge; the gatehouses and some humble dependencies are still standing. But the great château, the Orangerie, the maze, the trellised walks, have all vanished as if they had never been.

I closed my eyes in a vain attempt to summon up the spirits of the place. But if there was a *genius loci* I failed to find it. The autoroute to Normandy runs close by the site, cars appearing with terrifying speed and noise right by the old stables. The sounds and smells of engines dominate the landscape; the birdsong, the crunch of carriage wheels on gravel, the splashing of water, the laughter and the life were all gone.

As so often, the physical remains were frustratingly deceptive. The link between past and present was fragile here, almost broken. But it was a beginning. The task was to connect by other means and with that in mind my next recourse was the Musée, where different kinds of evidence might be available. Here, in a former dependency of the château, I found the directrice about to take a group of rather hangdog visitors on a tour. Madame was of a certain age, handsome and imposing, her abundant grey hair tied back but escaping all around her face. The museum over which she presided had only a couple of rooms, in which were displayed paintings of the château from its earliest days – when it was the palace of Gondi, chancellor to Catherine de Medici – to the poignant photographs of the smouldering ruins after the fire of 1870, which razed it to the ground. There were portraits of the owners, the family of Orléans, the cadet line of the ruling Bourbons of France, from 'Monsieur', brother of Louis XIV, father of my Philippe, to his great-great-great-grandson, Louis-Philippe, King of the French (1773–1850).

Madame la Directrice clearly loved her subject and soon had her unpromising group of captive listeners obediently following her from room to room and nodding receptively. There were even a few questions, although most of them betrayed a certain lack of familiarity with French history. Madame was authoritative. At the end of the tour, which culminated in a scale model of the château and its park, she dismissed her class. Rather timidly, I followed her to the tiny bookstall where a few postcards and guidebooks were on display. I was her only customer.

Picking up a postcard of a gawky-looking woman dressed in the height of seventeenth-century fashion, I ventured a remark about the lady, Madame Henriette, the first wife of Monsieur, daughter of Charles I of England, who collapsed on the terrace at Saint-Cloud on a summer evening in 1670 and died in agony a few hours later, perhaps poisoned by her husband's lover. Her sudden death was the subject of a celebrated funeral oration which began sonorously, 'Madame se meurt! Madame est morte!' Quoting these famous words gained me the approval of Madame la Directrice. Emboldened, I moved on to my Philippe, the son of Monsieur and his second wife. I had struck a chord; 'Ah oui! Un homme très intelligent, grand travailleur. Les Orléans étaient toujours plus intelligents que les autres Bourbons. Le Régent Philippe d'Orléans était un homme courageux, très doué' (A most intelligent man, very hard working. The Orléans were always more intelligent than the other Bourbons. The Regent d'Orléans was a brave man, very gifted). But of course, I remarked, he was also a libertine, a philanderer, a rake. And didn't he die in the arms of his mistress? Madame regarded me coldly; after a pause she stated with a certain finality, 'Mais, un grand travailleur, alors,' and turned away. To placate her, I hastily bought a postcard, the beautiful bird's-eye view of Saint-Cloud painted by Allegrain in 1677, and left.

On the bus back to my apartment, winding my way through the Sunday-afternoon suspended animation of the city, I considered the afternoon. It was a symbol of my search for a man dead more than two hundred years, a man who clearly still aroused passion, perhaps particularly in women, and whose surroundings, the places he knew, were as vanished as Atlantis.

Apart from the physical remains, and far more accessible today, are two monumental contemporary sources. How lucky to be the occasional subject of two works of genius, of some of the liveliest, funniest letters and memoirs ever written. Did Philippe know that his mother's voluminous correspondence would become so widely read? Had he any idea that his friend, the duc de Saint-Simon, was scribbling away with his recollections of life at the court of Louis XIV and during the Regency? He would no doubt have been astonished that so much could be found out about his life; and gratified that, despite it all, he remained so mysterious.

These memoirs and letters were the twin beacons which illuminated my path. Madame Palatine, Philippe's mother, was a German princess from the Rhineland. She had arrived in France in 1671 at the age of nineteen and spent much of the next fifty years writing long letters to her relatives in Germany and England and to old friends and family all over Europe. It is estimated that she wrote sixty thousand letters, two-thirds in German, one-third in French, of which scarcely a tenth are conserved. She wrote from her rooms at Versailles, Trianon or Fontainebleau, Saint-Cloud or the Palais-Royal. Many of these letters have disappeared, many are still unpublished; what remains is an incomparable record. Madame was a keen observer, with a robust wit and a passionate, partisan character. She admired Louis XIV immensely, was possibly in love with him, certainly fascinated by him. She hated with venom Madame de Maintenon, whom she would never acknowledge as his secret wife. The pungent essence of the seventeenth century rises unfiltered from her letters. Naturally, she was not an objective observer of her beloved son; but her descriptions of him and his family and activities are so piercing and uninhibited that they are irresistible.

The duc de Saint-Simon was brought up with Philippe and came to court in 1691 at the moment of his friend's marriage. He remained close to Philippe all his life and later wrote his scathing, malicious, brilliant memoirs of those thirty years. No two men could be more different than Philippe and Saint-Simon; but their vices and virtues neatly complemented each other and their friendship, although severely tested, was never sundered. That did not mean that Saint-Simon understood his friend any better than his contemporaries did; he often misunderstood him completely. But his dazzling pages are another precious resource.

These two pillars take the thrust of the work, but there are other supports: the memoirs of the Parisian lawyer Mathieu Marais; of other contemporaries, the marquis d'Argenson, Duclos, Barbier and Buvat. Rare letters and documents from Philippe himself repose in the archives of Paris. The plays and operas he saw, the composers he heard, from Lully and Molière to Couperin and Marivaux, exist, as does Voltaire's first play, *Oedipus*, of which he attended the opening night. Montesquieu's *Persian Letters*, Lesage's *Turcaret* can still be read, Watteau's *L'Enseigne de Gersaint* admired, the place de Vendôme and the Hôtel de Matignon still stand.

French historians have recently turned a favourable regard on the Regent; he has been the subject of several biographies, some of which portray him as a liberal, some as an early socialist, some as an eighteenth-century New Dealer. All of them recognise his allure. It seems time to show Philippe d'Orléans and his age to English readers. Perhaps they have missed this dynamic, glamorous, pivotal slice of French history, quite unlike the years before or after, a uniquely Parisian period, when the King of France, for the only time in a hundred years, lived in his capital, with the court and government, the nobility and bourgeoisie, intertwined.

But the story starts at Saint-Cloud.

# PART ONE
*Grandson of France*

# ✼ I ✼

# THE SON OF MONSIEUR
# AND MADAME

Philippe d'Orléans was born on 2 August 1674 at Saint-Cloud, the home of his parents, the duc and duchesse d'Orléans, known at court simply as Monsieur and Madame, brother and sister-in-law of King Louis XIV. The birth of a nephew to the King of France was a noteworthy event. But the court of France scarcely noticed; their eyes were fixed on the King himself, who at that very moment was staging a series of spectacular parties at Versailles.

Louis XIV was at the height of his glory, his armies victorious abroad, his authority unchallenged at home. Throughout July and August of 1674 he showed off his new gardens and attractions at Versailles, nominally in honour of the French conquest of the Franche-Comté, actually to celebrate himself and his new mistress, the marquise de Montespan. All the court was busy recalling the last party and awaiting the next; and so, from the very beginning, Philippe was merely a footnote to the overwhelming epic of the glory of his uncle, the Sun King.

That summer, Versailles still conserved some of its original charm as a hunting lodge and summer pavilion. There was as yet no Hall of Mirrors or long stone façades on the garden. Its main beauties were the gardens, laid out in parterres and terraces, studded with pools and fountains, its dense woods arranged into patterns of groves, quincunxes, *cabinets de verdure*. The Grand Canal stretched to the western horizon, past the Porcelain Trianon and the Ménagerie. The air was scented with the perfume of hundreds of orange trees planted in tubs in the new Orangerie. Within the palace, the Grands Appartements were just completed, with their breathtaking décor of coloured marble, their ceilings painted with scenes of gods and goddesses, the walls hung with rich tapestries, the furniture silver and gold. Everything was sparkling and new.

The summer of parties began on 11 July in the gardens of the new

Porcelain Trianon, the exquisite blue and white tiled pavilion built for Mme de Montespan. Lully directed a performance of his *Eclogue de Versailles* under a pergola decorated with flowers. Supper was taken in the new *bosquet* of the Salle des Festins, marvellously illuminated. A week later there was a collation in the Ménagerie and a promenade on the Canal; the King's gondola preceded a miniature galleon, on which musicians and singers gave a concert. Molière's *Malade imaginaire* was presented in the Grotto of Thetis. On 28 July Lully's *Fêtes de l'Amour et de Bacchus* was performed in a theatre designed by Bérain at the end of the allée du Dragon. After a torchlight promenade in carriages there were fireworks at the Canal, and an open-air supper in the Cour de Marbre.

Philippe had the tact to present himself between parties; the next fête did not take place until 18 August: a collation in a *bosquet* near Latona, perhaps the Girandole, then, in a theatre improvised in the Orangerie, Racine's *Iphigeneia*, followed by fireworks over the Canal.

Finally, on 31 August, there took place the last and perhaps most beautiful party of them all. The King and his court rode to the Grand Canal through the illuminated park, then embarked on gilded boats. 'Their Majesties boarded richly decorated gondolas,' cooed the diarist Félibien, 'followed by the court, also travelling in beautifully ornamented vessels. Then we saw the water in the canal, calm and unruffled, but seemingly swelling with pride at being privileged to bear the most great and august the world has to offer.'*

At thirty-five, the King was in his prime, handsome and vigorous, the centre of everything. He was determined to be the most glorious monarch of his era, and to that end was imposing his authority over almost every aspect of national life. Artists, musicians, writers and architects were called upon to celebrate his magnificence. Idolised, seductive and adored, Louis could regard his handiwork at Versailles with satisfaction. And he could take pleasure in his very public private life. Queen Marie-Thérèse, a Spanish princess, was submissive and obedient and had done her dynastic duty. Louis had fathered a male heir, a boy thirteen years old in 1674, who,

---

* There were originally nine vessels in the miniature fleet. A brigantine decorated with blue, gold and silver brocade; three chaloupes, each fitted out in a differently coloured damask, green, yellow and blue; a Neapolitan felucca in violet damask; a chaloupe biscayenne in red damask; a little green and white chaloupe with silver brocade; a little red chaloupe, in red damask embroidered with gold; and a little barge for Monsieur and Madame with their monograms embroidered on the velvet fittings. There was also a miniature warship, carved and gilded, with little guns, pavilions, pennants, streamers; the fourteen little windows and the three doors were decorated with rich crimson stuff; the folding table, three armchairs, and twelve tabourets were covered with gold and silver brocade. In 1674 four gondoliers arrived from Venice with two gilded gondolas, joining the French sailors at their lodgings in the park of Versailles, part of which exist under the name of 'Petite-Venise'.

despite his lack of promise, was the only direct heir to the throne. The King continued to honour the Queen with his presence in her bed; but increasingly he visited elsewhere.

The mistress for whom the fête was being given, Athénaïs de Rochech-ouart-Mortemart, marquise de Montespan, although already thirty-four, was still a radiant beauty. She had displaced Louise de La Vallière as royal mistress in 1669, and in 1674 the relationship between her and the King was as passionate as ever. Mme de Sévigné has left a description of Mme de Montespan on a summer day at Versailles at about this time. She was playing cards with the King, resplendent 'in a gown of French needlepoint lace. Her hair was all done up in curls, black ribbons in her hair, pearls and diamonds all about her person, in a word a triumphant beauty to make all the ambassadors gasp.' And Mme de Montespan was as fertile as she was dazzling. She had already presented the King with three children, who lived at court, looked after by the modest widow Françoise Scarron, newly created marquise de Maintenon.

At no time would Louise XIV be closer to the dazzling, self-selected image of Apollo, the God of the Sun, than he was that summer.

If he turned away from his own magnificence, Louis might observe the only other person in his Kingdom with whom he might entertain the notion, if not of equality, then at least of proximity. That was his only brother Philippe, duc d'Orléans, known at court simply as Monsieur. But Monsieur, two years younger than Louis, was condemned to the shadows. A brave soldier, he had rarely been given the chance to shine; he was never included in the councils of state and had no influence at all on the government of the Kingdom. As a foil to his glorious brother he was perfect. Dependent upon Louis in every way, Monsieur revenged himself in the only way he knew: he flaunted his homosexuality. Perfumed, bejewelled and extravagantly clothed in lace and silk, Monsieur made no secret of his femininity, or his preference for male companions and lovers. Whether through strategy or heredity, Monsieur had developed into a man whose opinions were sought only on matters of ceremony, clothes and gardens. His palace of Saint-Cloud on the banks of the Seine was his passion. If he had not been a royal personage, perhaps he could have pursued his interests untroubled by the duties of marriage and procreation. But, as a member of the semi-divine royal family, he had to marry and attempt to provide children; France needed as many demi-gods as possible.

He and his second wife, Elisabeth-Charlotte of Bavaria, had been married for almost three years; his first wife, Henrietta of England, daughter of the executed Charles I, had died dramatically in 1670 at the age of twenty-seven, collapsing on the terrace of Saint-Cloud. She left Monsieur with two young daughters, Marie-Louise, aged eight, and Anne-Marie, not yet one, and the necessity to marry again in order to provide the required male heir. His new bride was a robust and tomboyish German princess; she it was who had accomplished the bringing forth of a male child.

In fact Philippe was their second son. At his birth he had an elder brother, Alexandre, duc de Valois, who was just over a year old. This was significant, for second sons were traditionally destined for the Church, in order not to spoil the inheritance of the elder. If Alexandre had lived, Philippe might have become a cardinal, a prince of the Church; but the little duc de Valois died before his third birthday, to the intense and prolonged grief of his mother, who never trusted French doctors again, and Philippe, at the age of eighteen months, came into a different birthright, the fortune of the house of Orléans.

Philippe was a very grand personage from birth. He was given the title of duc de Chartres. He was nephew to the King, a Royal Highness, with the exalted rank of Grandson of France, or in other words of Louis XIII.

One's rank determined whether one had to stand at all times or could occasionally sit, and if so whether in an armchair or on a stool; whether one could wear one's hat or was obliged to take it off; whether one could approach the King in his bedroom or only in the antechambers. The hierarchy at court was, after the King, his son, then his brother Monsieur. All these were Sons of France. Then came Philippe, a Grandson of France; then the Princes of the Blood, cousins of the royal family; then the dukes; then the rest of the nobility and so on. Philippe was at the top of the pyramid, but, and it was an important but, he was not of the direct line, merely the junior branch, and with every birth in Louis' own family he would take a step down in precedence. His position was thus from birth subject to change and, despite the sonorous titles, peripheral to the real royal family.

That August there was only rejoicing. Saint-Cloud, so perfect for a summer party, celebrated the newborn boy with fireworks and balls and banquets. The maleness was important; as a general rule, only boys could inherit property and titles. Now Monsieur and Madame had two sons, the proverbial heir and a spare, and that was cause for joy, particularly in view of Monsieur's personality, habits and approach to lovemaking.

After the exciting events of the summer the family at Saint-Cloud settled back. Monsieur, the proud father, was still a good-looking man, although now a little stout. He was short with fine legs and a large nose. He was always enveloped in a huge black wig, his clothes the most gorgeous at court at a time when all the men there were decked out in silk and brocade, lace jabots and plumed hats. He was a passionate gambler, party-giver and gossip. He loved to discuss clothes and jewels and questions of etiquette with women; but for sex he preferred men.

It was said that Monsieur had been perverted for reasons of state so as to render no effective opposition to his elder brother. His mother Anne of Austria (she was not Austrian, but Spanish, a princess of the Hapsburg dynasty who ruled in Spain) is said to have encouraged him to dress as a girl and follow feminine pursuits. She and Cardinal Mazarin were determined to avoid a repetition of the bloody civil wars of the Fronde in which, from 1648, the nobles and princes of the Blood, including Louis' uncle Gaston, brother of Louis XIII, made war on the crown. Philippe, brother of Louis XIV, would not be allowed to become another Gaston. He had to be rendered ineffectual. Perhaps. But Monsieur's tastes needed little encouraging; and later on it was Louis XIV himself who kept his brother subjugated and humiliatingly dependent upon him. He himself made this chillingly clear; 'it can be useful for rulers to see their relatives very much opposite in character. The grandeur and constancy of soul which a king should have shown to better effect in contrast to their softness; and his love of duty and true glory is made infinitely more brilliant when one compares it to the idleness and frivolity of others.' Louis had learnt from the Fronde: one could not trust one's own family. Monsieur would suffer from this perception all his life, and his son after him.

Monsieur had found his great love in Philippe de Lorraine-Armagnac, chevalier de Lorraine. The chevalier was beautiful, 'fait comme on peint les anges', utterly corrupt, and had ruled Monsieur from the late 1660s. At the Palais-Royal Monsieur appeared in public dressed as a woman, in décolletage and earrings, led out to the minuet by the chevalier. The chevalier de Lorraine controlled Monsieur and his favours; the two Philippes would be a couple until death.

While Monsieur danced, Madame, too, was very much a part of the glamorous life at court. Arriving from Heidelberg four years earlier, gauche and provincial, she had conquered the King by her sense of humour, her enthusiasm and her love of the chase. She plunged into everything with gusto, was infatuated by the theatre and the King. She was no beauty and ran no risk of embarrassing her husband by flirting with Louis as Madame Henriette had done; but she was young and vital and made sure everyone had fun. Madame was at the centre of things. Her son would inherit her humour, intelligence and devouring curiosity.

Her arrival in November 1671 came just over a year after the death of Monsieur's first wife, Henrietta. The rumours that she had been poisoned by Monsieur's jealous lovers singled out the chevalier de Lorraine, exiled to Rome at Henriette's request. The court shuddered at the spectacle of royal mortality. They then turned their attention to the search for a new bride for Monsieur, a somewhat perfunctory procedure which quickly led to the Princess of the Rhine. On the face of it she seemed an inadequate match; she was poor, Protestant and not pretty, but she was promoted by Monsieur's close friend, the formidable Anne of Gonzaga, aunt by marriage to Elisabeth-Charlotte.

And perhaps there was another reason for this marriage. The lands of the Elector Palatine, Elisabeth-Charlotte's father, lay along the Rhine, encompassing the cities of Heidelberg, Mannheim and Karlsruhe; these lands were of the greatest strategic importance to France in case of war with the Holy Roman Emperor, suzerain of the German states. (The Emperor was a Hapsburg; for decades Bourbons and Hapsburgs had divided Europe between them.) Perhaps Louis XIV had already concocted the Macchiavellian plot later attributed to him: to use the excuse of the unpaid dowry of the poor Princess to invade and occupy her country when he deemed it convenient. After all, he had done it before; in 1667 Louis had invaded the Spanish Netherlands, using as pretext the unpaid dowry of his wife, Marie-Thérèse of Spain. Louis was adept at laying long-term plans; but plotting the marriage of Elisabeth-Charlotte seems too much even for him. Whether or not he planned it, however, it paved the way for the later French destruction of the Rhineland, not just once but twice.

Liselotte, as her family called her, endured a long and miserable journey to France in 1671, along cold and bumpy roads from Heidelberg to Strasbourg. Here she bade farewell to her father, whom she would never see again, and to the person she loved most in the world, her aunt Sophie, her father's sister, the Electress of Hanover.

Liselotte was not ill prepared for domestic controversy. Her father, a cold, studious, arbitrary man, repudiated her mother, a princess of Hesse-Cassel, and sent her back to her own father. He had, even before his wife departed, proclaimed his union with his mistress, the red-haired and submissive Luise von Degenfeld. He eventually gave Luise thirteen children whose rank, since they were the product of bigamy, was very hard to establish. In order to avoid this odd situation, Liselotte, aged seven, was sent to live with her aunt Sophie, who lived in Hanover, and her husband the Elector. She stayed there for four years, returning to Heidelberg as soon as her mother had left. These were happy years in Hanover; Liselotte would love Sophie all her life and write her thousands of letters over the next thirty years.

Liselotte was nineteen, a robust, intelligent girl with few pretensions to beauty and none to elegance. But 'she had an open and easy air, a face which, without being regularly beautiful, was not unattractive in its nobility and gentleness'. She also had untameable curly hair, a large nose and a flat forehead, wit, a sense of humour and a lively curiosity. She was noisy, plump and freckled; she preferred playing with toy guns to doing needlework. She was not at all a conventional princess.

Destined for the most luxurious court in Europe and the most fashionable Prince in the world, she brought a trousseau of six gowns. Anne of Gonzaga, arriving in Strasbourg to organise everyone, found the pale-blue taffeta gown she would wear for her proxy marriage in Metz not only unsuitable but embarrassing. In a hurry, she sent out for dressmakers and velvet and brocade. Liselotte was weeping too much to care; she watched her father return home and, even though her childhood in Heidelberg had been difficult, she would always remember it with nostalgia.

Liselotte struggled through interminable services in the cathedral at Metz, where she gave up her Protestant faith and was received into the Catholic Church; through the wedding by proxy, at which the aged maréchal Du Plessis-Praslin stood in for her husband; through speeches and fireworks and more travelling to meet her groom at Châlons. When she arrived there she had been on the road for over a month, had changed her faith and become the second lady in France, the bride of a man she had never met.

Monsieur meanwhile had arrived in Châlons in a very different procession. A magnificent entourage, all in splendid new outfits, cheering crowds, fireworks, declarations of loyalty, had all followed him. There were moving references to his recent widowerhood and to his hopes of a son for France. Trumpets sounded, wine ran from fountains, bishops delivered homilies, magistrates presented the keys to their cities, triumphal arches sprang up along the way. Monsieur was enjoying it all immensely. And there was another, more questionable reason for his good temper. On the very day on which Liselotte arrived at Strasbourg, Louis XIV had given his permission for the chevalier de Lorraine to return to court from his exile in Italy. When Monsieur heard the news, he threw himself at his brother's feet and kissed his hand in an ecstasy of joy. It was not a gallant act towards the unsuspecting new wife.

And so they met, the fresh and the faded, innocence and disillusion. Philippe was covered in jewels, balanced on high-heeled shoes, a huge black wig obscuring his face. It appeared that he was wearing rouge. Liselotte, rising from her curtsy, was speechless; Monsieur, it is said, turned to his entourage and whispered, 'Oh! comment pourrai-je coucher avec elle?'

The couple entered the town of Châlons, stopping on the way to listen to a concert (which must have been torture for Monsieur, who had no ear for music) and then heard a nuptial blessing from the Bishop. Afterwards there was no help for it; the couple had to enter their apartment at the Bishop's palace and into the mystery of intimacy.

Perhaps because his new partner was a robust, rather masculine woman, Monsieur managed to procreate. With Madame Henriette, very feminine and a flirt, it had been harder. Even so, the fact that the second marriage produced three children was rather remarkable. Monsieur clearly found sexual intercourse with women difficult and had to resort to the mediation of higher powers to accomplish his aim. Madame confided much later that Monsieur always brought to bed a rosary hung with holy medals, in order to say his prayers. One night she heard a great rattling of medals under the blanket and asked what he was doing; on his refusal to tell her she got up and shone the nightlight into the bed. Monsieur was clutching his rosary to his private parts. 'You do not persuade me at all, Monsieur,' she said, 'that you are honouring the Virgin by placing her image on those parts destined to relieve virginity.' Monsieur had the grace to laugh and begged her not to tell anyone; she apparently kept her word for forty years.

There is an air of affectionate complicity about this story; and at the beginning, despite the obvious difficulties, Monsieur and Madame did not get along too badly. There was one more child after Philippe, a girl born in 1676, named Elisabeth-Charlotte. Then the couple retired to separate beds, much to the relief of both parties. 'When Monsieur slept in my bed,' Madame wrote to Sophie many years later, 'I was always obliged to lie on the very edge, and often fell out in my sleep. Monsieur couldn't bear to be touched, and if I stretched out my foot and accidentally brushed against him in my sleep he would wake me up and berate me for half an hour. Really, I was very glad when he decided to sleep in his own room and let me lie peacefully without fear of falling out or being scolded.' Monsieur renewed his pursuit of virile young men, while remaining the slave of the chevalier de Lorraine.

Philippe, consigned to the care of nursemaids, was too young to understand the oddity of his parentage. Rank meant that, however bizarre Monsieur and Madame might be, no one would regard them with any less deference. They were royal, which in those days meant semi-divine. Unusual behaviour did not make them less so. Madame, having done her dynastic duty, enjoyed the pleasures of the hunt and the beauty of her surroundings, and lavished affection on her little boy. In this he was fortunate: most princes and noblemen sent their children off to a wet-nurse, and ignored them until they were old enough to be presentable in society. Motherhood was not considered a duty; the bond between parent and child was a fragile one. Children were seen as pieces of property or assets to be managed for the profit of the house. Boys were much more valuable because they carried on the family name; but younger brothers would be sent into the Church or to make their own way. Girls would disappear into convents unless they could be well married. In this environment Madame's enjoyment of her children was unusual.

Madame first mentions her son in a letter to Sophie. The boy was three months old when his mother informed her aunt that a horoscope had been cast for him which predicted he would be Pope. Madame found this most amusing: 'I'm very much afraid that he's more likely to be the Antichrist.' The little duc de Chartres was given a governess of noble birth and a household of maids and footmen. The post of governess, like all other posts in the *ancien régime*, was hereditary. Every post, even those of ministers of state, was handed down from father to son or mother to daughter. Only if the next generation was hopelessly incapable would the post be sold. Thus Philippe's first governess was Mme de Clérambault, who had been governess to the daughters of Madame Henriette; she was a widow, a woman who loved to gamble and always wore a mask of black velvet to protect her fine complexion. She had no discernible talent in handling young children, and in fact neglected her own children completely, but Madame liked her, as did Saint-Simon, who praised her for 'un tour, un sel, une finesse, etc ... un naturel inimitable' ('her turns of phrase, salty wit, finesse ... and lack of affectation'). She had very little to do with her new charge.

Philippe was too young to know of his father's last appearance on the field of battle, at Cassel in April 1677. Monsieur had spent the spring and summer of the previous years serving in the army in Flanders and the Netherlands. At Cassel, he won a significant victory over William of Orange and showed great personal bravery; but after this success he never served again. Louis XIV did not want a rival in any sphere; his brother had to go back to his houses and gardens.

Monsieur turned his energies to the transformation and embellishment of his château at Saint-Cloud. Following the advice of his chancellor, the artistic Béchamel (a great gourmet after whom the sauce was named), Monsieur hired his own team of artists and architects, preferring Giraud, Le Pautre, Nocret and Mignard to the King's team of Le Vau and Le Brun. The place was already splendid in 1677. The château stood on high ground facing the Seine and Paris. The façade to the courtyard was majestic, tall windows piercing carved stone. In the north wing was the Galerie d'Apollon, precursor of the Hall of Mirrors at Versailles; this magnificent gallery had thirteen windows, each facing a painting of one of the royal residences. Along the walls were tabourets of carved and gilded wood covered with crimson velvet. In the centre of the room, busts of Roman emperors stood on marble-topped tables. The entrance to the Galerie was flanked by the salons of Diane and of Mars; the latter led to the Salon des Rois, where the portraits of Monsieur's ancestors were hung.

In October 1678 Monsieur gave a party to show his brother the new Galerie and its decoration. The King, Queen and Dauphin arrived with all the court to see the elegant new appointments and the marvellous gardens. The Hall of Mirrors was just being started at Versailles and the King was very curious. It was important that Saint-Cloud be grand and royal, but it should not overshadow the rising glories of Versailles. The Salon de Mars, the Galerie d'Apollon, the Salon de Diane were shown, with their painted ceilings, gilded reliefs in stucco, marble columns. 'I very much hope, Madame,' remarked the King, 'that the paintings in my gallery at Versailles will be as beautiful as these.' For the sake of the architects at Versailles, everyone else hoped so too.

Monsieur had his private suite in the part of the building looking west over the Orangerie, running parallel to the state rooms which overlooked the courtyard. When the English visitor Martin Lister saw these rooms, he reported:

> The first you enter is furnished with a great variety of rock crystals, cups, agates upon small stands, and the sides of the room are lined with large panes of looking glass from top to bottom, with Japan varnish and paintings of equal breadth intermixt; which had a marvellous pretty effect. The other room had in it a great quantity of bijoux, and many of very great price; but the Siam pagodas, and other things from thence, were very ordinary.

Madame had a suite of four rooms overlooking the gardens to the south, all decorated with delicate frescoes and paintings by Nocret. In her antechamber hung his famous painting of members of the Royal family, living and dead, as the gods of Olympus, with Madame Henriette prominently displayed in *deshabillé* as Spring.

Madame's favourite room was her *cabinet* or study. It had three windows facing south and was furnished with a day bed covered in crimson damask, gilded chairs, tables of precious wood, a marquetry desk and, the most important possession of all, a writing table. Here she wrote her letters every day in her own hand, mostly to her Aunt Sophie in Hanover, but also to her half-brothers and sisters in Heidelberg.

Madame's windows looked out on to the Bassin des Cygnes and along tree-lined avenues. From every window of Saint-Cloud marvellous vistas stretched to the horizon, punctuated with pools and fountains. The parterres and statues, *bosquets* and allées, made Saint-Cloud the epitome of a formal French garden of the time. All through Philippe's childhood, wonders were unfolded there. Monsieur would give more than a thousand dinners, suppers and parties of all kinds at this 'palais des délices'.

Le Nôtre had worked such miracles with the difficult terrain and levels, so much so that many thought Saint-Cloud more agreeable than Versailles. Of course, none said so to the King. Monsieur had, perhaps, better taste than his brother, but that thought too had to go unexpressed. Madame, however, made no bones about it, telling Sophie that 'between ourselves, I find our gardens more pleasing than those of Versailles, even though they are not as magnificent, but they are more intimate and shadier'.

In August 1679 Sophie herself came to visit; she too was impressed by Saint-Cloud and preferred it to Versailles. But aunt and niece had many other matters to discuss, for they had not seen each other since that tearful day in Strasbourg over seven years before. And Madame was celebrating, if that was the word, the imminent marriage of her step-daughter, seventeen-year-old Marie-Louise, to the King of Spain, the imbecilic Charles II. Poor Marie-Louise was distraught; she had wanted to marry the Dauphin and stay in France, and she had heard the talk of her future husband's fragile hold on reality. His portrait could not disguise his ugly Hapsburg chin and feeble air. When Louis XIV informed her of the match and graciously said that he could not have done more for his own daughter, Marie-Louise had cried, 'But you could have done more for your niece!' Monsieur, impervious to his daughter's anguish, and thrilled at her new rank, busied himself with her trousseau. Sophie came upon him in his *bonnet de nuit* arranging the jewels for himself, his wife and daughters.

Marie-Louise left the Palais-Royal with the words of Louis XIV echoing in her ears: 'Madame, I hope to be saying farewell to you for ever; it would be the greatest misfortune to see you again in France.' Mme de Sévigné saw the new Queen weeping as she passed, her only consolation the two little dogs with her in the carriage. Madame sadly followed her as far as Orléans, leaving the maréchale de Clérambault to conduct her to the frontier. On the journey there were reports of a scandalous affair between the Princess and one of her entourage, the comte de Saint-Chamand. When Mme de Clérambault returned to Paris at the end of the year she was promptly dismissed by Monsieur and banished from the Palais-Royal.

Saint-Chamand was sent to his estates. If there had been a dalliance, it was Marie-Louise's last happy time. The next ten years would be tragic. Married to an imbecile, suffocated by the gloom and religiosity of the Spanish Court, she gave herself up to gluttony and despair.

Louis XIV did not concern himself with his niece's happiness; in the summer and fall of 1679 the King had a new mistress. She was one of the four filles d'honneur of Madame, a gorgeous redhead called Marie-Angélique de Fontanges. Mlle de Fontanges was very pretty, although not very clever.

The King made her both a duchess and pregnant. But her days of glory were short-lived; after a miscarriage she left the court for a convent and died in June 1681. By then the atmosphere at court was such that many people believed Mme de Montespan had had her poisoned.

How had Mme de Montespan, the dazzling beauty of the court, the radiant inspiration of all the splendid court fêtes, she for whom the Porcelain Trianon had been created, fallen so low? After 1674 she had given the King two more children, Françoise-Marie in 1677 and Louis-Alexandre in 1678. After that the King avoided her, although he did not dismiss her from court; she still lived in her spacious apartment at Versailles and at the nearby château of Clagny. But the appalling scandal known as the 'affair of the poisons' was the dark secret of the age. Since various unsavoury characters had been arrested in Paris in March 1679 – a collection of abortionists, black magicians, and swindlers – an official investigation had gradually been uncovering ghastly doings, including murders by poison. The names involved had become grander and moved disturbingly close to the throne. In 1680 warrants were issued for the arrest of the comtesse de Soissons, the duchesse de Bouillon, the marquise d'Alluye, the princesse de Tingry and the maréchal de Luxembourg. And then in 1682 the investigation was dropped; perhaps because, as was suspected, the name of Mme de Montespan was being mentioned with increasing frequency. Athénaïs stayed at Versailles for another ten years; her children by Louis were brought up as royalty by the pious and widowed Françoise de Maintenon. But Louis had irretrievably cooled towards her. And he was spending more and more time with the modest governess.

Philippe was too young to understand the ramifications of the affair of the poisons, but not too young to comprehend, however dimly, the peculiar, almost sadistic, relationship between the all-powerful King and his own father. It was clear that Monsieur was forbidden to compete with his brother on any level. Had not Louis said that the princes of the royal house must 'never have any other shelter than the court nor any other refuge than in the heart of the King'? The entire and crushing dependence of the younger brother was made manifest every day in public. When at court, Monsieur must humbly hand the King his shirt in the morning, his napkin at meal times and his nightshirt at bedtime. Only with the King's express permission might he sit at table with him, and then only on a stool. Monsieur seemed to revel in the abasement. At the Palais-Royal there were jealous scenes between Monsieur and his 'mignons', followed by abject apologies. As Philippe commenced his education, the formation of his mind, he had a great deal to observe.

# ❦ 2 ❦

# THE LITTLE PRINCE

In the households of the nobility an important rite of passage took place when boys were seven years old. They were taken out of petticoats and 'breeched', and their women attendants were replaced with tutors. In Philippe's case, protocol demanded that a nobly born governor replace his governess. This personage would nominally be in charge of the Prince's education, but, as the post was always offered to someone whose name and rank would reflect well upon the house of Orléans, rather than to someone with any discernible talent for developing the mind of a young boy, the best the pupil could hope for would be that he did not fall into the hands of a brute.

Philippe's governors were not brutes, but elderly gentlemen who limited themselves to their ceremonial duties of handing the young prince his shirt in the morning and his dressing gown in the evening, and presiding at his mealtimes. They tended to die in office. The marquis de Sillery, best known for his gambling debts, was replaced by the seventy-eight-year-old duc de Navailles, then the maréchal d'Estrades, who was even older, by the duc de La Vieuville, who was seventy-three when he died in 1689. The joke at court was that Monsieur was having a great deal of trouble bringing up his son's governors.

But luckily for Philippe, as these ancient noblemen tottered in and out of the schoolroom at the Palais-Royal, the home of the Orléans family in Paris, his education was proceeding in the hands of an excellent teacher and honourable man, Nicolas-François Parisot de Saint-Laurent. He was an exceptional choice; Boileau knew him well and wondered whether he should be called 'le saint Saint-Laurent'. And Saint-Simon, who had been brought up with the duc de Chartres and knew all the men around him very well, called Saint-Laurent the most suitable man of the century to bring up a prince and train a great king. He was in charge of the Prince's education until his death in 1687 when Philippe was thirteen.

And, busily looking up words in the dictionary, helping the little Prince prepare his lessons, was a young man with the quizzical expression of a squirrel, a man who was establishing such a strong bond with his pupil that it would last until the end of his life and make him the Regent's most trusted adviser. Guillaume Dubois entered the household of the duc de Chartres as under-preceptor in June 1683. He was not yet thirty, but was alive with energy and ambition, his eyes sparkling with wit. The son of an apothecary from Brive-la-Gaillarde, he had followed the route of all ambitious provincials to Paris, becoming the protégé of Antoine Faure, an influential philosopher and educator. He took religious orders and became an abbé, then worked as tutor for several good families, including that of the marquis de Pleuvault, Master of the Wardrobe to Monsieur. His intelligence drew the notice of Saint-Laurent, who offered him the relatively junior job of under-preceptor. That in itself was a coup for the apothecary's son: but when Saint-Laurent died, and Dubois was promoted to tutor, his ascent was assured.

Dubois clearly succeeded in interesting his pupil in his studies. Philippe enjoyed his lessons in history, geography, astronomy, geometry and languages. There exists in Dubois' hand a schedule for the Prince's day:

Rise at eight, attend the King's Lever,
At nine to the stables,
At ten to Mass,
See Monsieur and Madame,
Lunch,
Then German, Latin and History until the time for a walk,
Two hours outdoors,
What is left of the time until dinner in study.
To the King's Supper if he did not attend the Lever.

We see the essential elements: mandatory attendance upon the King, outdoor and indoor activities, Mass, and, rather unusual in those days, a daily audience with his parents.

Music, art and science were also part of the curriculum. Philippe would excel in all three. 'Monsieur le duc de Chartres is extremely sensible,' wrote the proud tutor at this time, 'he has wit and charm. He has nothing of the pedant in him, both by inclination and by character.' Being a good student was pleasing but, of course, one must not become a bore. A tract of 1705 asks the question, 'Is it necessary for persons of good quality to understand painting, music, and architecture?' The answer is, 'It is a good thing that they should be instructed in these matters ... but they must not let it appear that they are skilled in them.' The essential qualities of a prince were physical courage, courtesy, piety and generosity, but not necessarily intellect.

It was already clear, however, that the boy was highly intelligent. He had a good memory, a taste for work and a lively curiosity. The Ambassador from Brandenburg remarked on his 'beau et heureux génie'. He was seen to have 'beaucoup d'esprit' – a term which covered wit, cleverness, good humour and charm. Only in the other areas of princely education, riding, dancing and the study of arms, was Philippe less proficient. His short-sightedness made him clumsy.

Later it was alleged that Dubois had corrupted his pupil, introducing him to sex and teaching him to mock religion. But, as Dubois himself became more powerful, he made powerful enemies who did not hesitate to blacken his name. In their eyes he was a low-born adventurer who had the temerity to aspire to rise out of his class. The abbé was a man of few principles, bold, astute and unscrupulous; but he appears to have been a successful teacher, and he certainly had the confidence of Madame, who thought extremely highly of him and trusted him completely. She clearly blamed her son for his escapades, not his tutor. It is true that Philippe did not receive a conventional religious education. But in this regard, as in most others, it was his mother who set the tone for her son. Not pious, but practical, she thought for herself in matters of religion; she wanted no Jesuit indoctrinating her son. She herself chose some of her son's teachers and she always talked freely to him about adult matters. And his own curiosity ensured that he would venture into realms of ideas far removed from the orthodoxies of the Church.

This rather progressive education was very different from that received by Philippe's cousin, the Dauphin. From 1670 until 1680 he had been brought up by the majestic Bishop Bossuet of Meaux, the scourge of heretics, from Protestants to Jansenists. Bossuet believed, and taught his pupil to believe, that the Sovereign is all-powerful over his people, an instrument in the hands of God, to whom alone he is responsible. Bossuet discouraged thinking for oneself; he succeeded in deadening the (admittedly limited) curiosity of his pupil, and rendering him abject before his father – who, given Bossuet's precepts, the boy might be forgiven for confusing with God.

Philippe was luckier. Neither Saint-Laurent nor Dubois was a pedant. The under-governor, Claude de Nocé, seigneur de Fontenay, was a capable man; his *Letters on the Education of Princes* were published after his death. And M. de Fontenay had a son, Charles de Nocé, who came early into Philippe's life, complete with his Epicurean philosophy and a circle of literary friends. Nocé was ten years older than Philippe. He was handsome and charming, a brave soldier, a free thinker, amusing and attractive. His society included the philosopher Bernard de Fontanelle, who dedicated his book *Conversation on the Plurality of Worlds* to Nocé's wife. Through his long life, Fontanelle's passion was to try to awaken the *gens du monde* to the new worlds open before them. Through Nocé, Philippe came to know and respect Fontanelle, whose approach to life was much the same as his: curious, sceptical, amused.

The society at the Palais-Royal was by no means exclusively male. Philippe came into contact with his father's women friends, ladies too raffish for the court. One of the most prominent was Marie-Anne Mancini, duchesse de Bouillon. The Bouillon family were unpopular with Louis XIV: they were too grand and too independently minded. Philippe was on close terms with them all, particularly the chevalier de Bouillon, the duchesse de Bouillon's son, who had called the King 'an old country squire living in the provinces with his aged mistress', and who was in perpetual disgrace as a result. Mme de Bouillon's sister, Hortense, lived in London, where she had briefly been the mistress of Charles II. Her close friend was the amiable philosopher Saint-Evremond, who also lived in exile in London. Philippe would have agreed with his Epicurean view that 'fame, fortune, love, pleasure, well understood and well handled, are our great bulwark against the rigours of life, the miseries attached to our existence. Wisdom has been granted us principally to know how to handle our pleasures.'

With these influences it is hardly surprising that Philippe became a libertine, an *esprit fort*. The men who educated him were not so much the Don Juans of the later eighteenth century as men who questioned conventional religion and prided themselves on their free thinking, while paying little heed to moral restraints. When Philippe was growing up he was attracted to the worldly society of the *libertins*, to their intellectual probing and their refusal to accept dogma, but also to the licence of their opinions and behaviour. La Bruyère remarked, 'I would like to see a man who is sober, moderate, chaste and equitable say that there is no God; he at least would speak without self-interest; but there is no such man.' And in truth Philippe was neither sober, moderate nor chaste. But it was not only the pleasures of the flesh which fascinated him; he was also absorbed by those of the mind.

He was very much of his time; his views were volatile and often contradictory. While he struggled to comprehend the new discoveries in the sciences and to accommodate them to the notion of a God, he was also drawn to séances and the world of the supernatural. His was a world where the Devil stalked and Hell gaped, yet where man was claiming to understand and explain everything – from the circulation of the blood to the laws of gravity – by reason alone. It was the dawn of the Enlightenment; but it was still the Grand Siècle.

As Philippe was forming his mind and learning his pleasures, the world around him was changing dramatically. The year Philippe came out of skirts and into breeches, Louis XIV moved his court and government permanently to Versailles. It was a little premature; the palace was splendid, but unfinished, overcrowded and uncomfortable. The Hall of Mirrors had been completed but the North Wing was covered with scaffolding. The sounds of masons and carpenters were everywhere. Things were so chaotic that the Dauphine, who was pregnant, had to move to the nearby hôtel de Beauvillier, where in August 1682 she gave birth to her first son, the duc de Bourgogne. The poor Queen enjoyed her grandchild for only a year; in July 1683 she died. 'This is the only trouble she has ever caused me,' remarked the King, magnanimously.

Louis did not remain bereft for long. The general view is that he secretly married Mme de Maintenon, perhaps as early as the autumn of 1683. The evidence is largely from her own letters, in one of which she asks a priest to pray for her as 'I greatly need strength to make good use of my happiness.' From now on she lived next to the King, at the top of the Queen's staircase at Versailles, rarely seen but omnipresent. Mme de Montespan, a rather unnerving and increasingly plump presence, remained at court until March 1691, unable to tear herself away, forgotten but not gone.

From its earliest days as the official residence of the court, Versailles had as its Queen not Marie-Thérèse, not the marquise de Montespan, but Françoise d'Aubigné, 'la veuve Scarron', marquise de Maintenon. Her piety, sense of propriety and insistence on decorum would dominate the atmosphere at Versailles. No fairy story could be as remarkable as the life of this woman with whom Philippe would have to reckon. Born in 1635 in Niort, a little town between Angers and Nantes, she was the daughter of a Huguenot father who was, for reasons not entirely clear, incarcerated in the local prison. When her father was released the family were swept off to the island of Marie-Galante in the Antilles. Three years later they returned to France in even worse circumstances than when they had set out, and found themselves once more the poor relations. Françoise was put to work in the fields but, soon taken up by her godmother, Mme de Neuillan, she was sent to the Ursulines in Paris.

She was a beautiful girl with a fine figure and wonderful eyes. But she was so poor, and so anxious to escape her dependent position with Mme de Neuillan, that she did not hesitate to marry the witty, crippled play-wright Paul Scarron, who was twenty-five years her senior. They made an odd couple, but lived together in apparent harmony. At his death in 1660 Mme Scarron had made a place for herself in Parisian society by her charm, beauty and gentleness. But she was still desperately poor. With the help of well-placed friends, she received an offer to become governess to the children, born out of wedlock, of a noble lady. Mme Scarron accepted the offer and found her vocation, that of a teacher. She also found herself in the dizzying position of governess to the children of the King himself and of Mme de Montespan, his mistress. Mme Scarron became responsible for four-year-old Louis-Auguste, the duc du Maine, and the infant Louise-Françoise, Mlle de Nantes.

It seems that at first the King disliked Mme Scarron; 'he took me for a blue stocking', she said, 'and imagined that I was a difficult person who only liked lofty things'. But she quickly gained favour and was amply rewarded; in 1675 she became marquise de Maintenon. And she was treated with respect, and even deference, by the King. When other children came along after Mme de Montespan had sworn to give up the King in Holy Week of 1675, she refused to take them on. Françoise-Marie, Mlle de Blois, and Louis-Alexandre, comte de Toulouse, born in 1677 and 1678, were handed over to Mme de Louvois, wife of the powerful War Minister.

Mme de Maintenon remained devoted to Louis-Auguste, duc du Maine, all her life; the boy was lame and somewhat sickly, so she took him to the waters at Barèges in the Pyrenees, writing such tender letters about the little boy that Louis began to look more favourably upon her. He commented that she knew how to love and 'it would be delightful to be loved by her'. By the end of 1679 Mme de Maintenon was having four-hour conversations alone with the King and according to Mme de Sévigné was 'parfaitement bien avec le centre de toutes choses'. By the time the Queen died in July 1683 Louis XIV already depended on Françoise de Maintenon, or 'Her Solidity', as he affectionately called her.

From now on, as Philippe grew, so too did the influence of Mme de Maintenon, much to the despair of his mother and the disdain of his father. Philippe was brought up to be wary of the uncrowned Queen, although encouraged to make fun of her in the family circle.

Gradually, the duc de Chartres began to step on to the court stage. In May 1685 the Doge of Genoa came to Versailles to pay homage to Louis XIV. A painting records the scene in the Hall of Mirrors that day, and the first public appearance of the ten-year-old duc de Chartres, adorable in red velvet. The Doge bows low before the French King; the silver throne has been placed on a dais covered with a Persian carpet. Around the King stand his son the Dauphin (Monseigneur), his brother (Monsieur), his nephew (the duc de Chartres), his sons by Mme de Montespan (the duc du Maine and the comte de Toulouse), and a Prince of the Blood (the duc de Bourbon) of the Bourbon-Condé branch.

These were the men with whom Philippe would have to live and compete. Monseigneur, although the heir to the throne, was already regarded as somewhat irrelevant. He had sired three sons and, having done his duty, still in his twenties, was already retiring into a life of hunting and gambling, but mostly sleeping. Philippe's father was also past his glory days. The coming generation was represented by the duc de Bourbon, known simply as Monsieur le Duc, a violent, evil-tempered little man, and the brave and dashing prince de Conti (who was not on the dais that day as he was fighting the Turks in Hungary). These two junior branches of the royal family, the Condé and the Conti, were of lesser rank than Philippe; they were Princes of the Blood, he was a Grandson of France. The sons of Louis XIV and Mme de Montespan ranked lower again. The day would come when these distinctions of rank would almost cause a civil war. But, as far as Philippe was concerned, such matters were of no consequence that day compared to the magnificent spectacle of which he was part.

These years should have been joyful and serene. The country was at peace; the French were dominant in Europe. During the summer the King was entertained by Louvois, the War Minister, at Meudon and by Seignelay son of the late minister Colbert, at Sceaux. 'How original and entertaining is this century of ours!' breathed the amiable and well-born Mme de Sévigné, in one of her famous letters. 'How new everything is, how romantic, how varied!' But there was a darker side; Louis XIV revoked the Edict of Nantes, which had allowed the Protestants in France to practise their faith, setting the stage for brutal repression, forced exiles and civil strife. He seemed intent on regularising his own life and that of everyone else.

Perhaps his sour mood was due to the first indications that his magnificent constitution was weakening. In 1686 he had to submit to the 'grande opération' for an anal fistula. For many historians the 'year of the fistula' marked the peak, and therefore the beginning of the decline, of the glory of Louis XIV. With typically unfortunate timing, the duc de Chartres, along with his sister (known at court simply as Mademoiselle, the title given to the highest-ranked single princess) were allocated rooms at Versailles at that very moment. Philippe's suite was in the North Wing, close by the Chapel. In June that year he became a chevalier of the Order of the Holy Ghost. Wearing a black velvet cloak lined with orange silk, a mantle of silver dotted with doves and tongues of fire, and a gold collar with its cross of fleur-de-lys and the royal arms, he went in solemn procession to the Chapel, where he knelt before the King. When he was asked if he liked ceremonies and dressing up, he replied, 'I do not hate them as much as Madame does, but I do not like them as much as Monsieur.'

His parents were now physically and emotionally estranged. Monsieur had fallen more and more into the homosexual society of his 'mignons'. Madame had gradually lost her special favour with the King; the jokes and outspoken frankness, which had once appealed to Louis XIV, now irritated him. The chilling influence of Mme de Maintenon was beginning to make itself felt. Concerned about his immortal soul and obsessed with the need for repentance, Louis was no longer amused by Madame's indiscretions and started to lecture her on her behaviour. Specifically, he complained that she was too free in her speech (she had told Monseigneur that if she were to see him naked from head to toe she would not be tempted by him), that she acknowledged her maid of honour took lovers, that she joked with the Princesse de Conti about that lady's lovers. She was pointedly excluded from the King's presence.

Letter-writing became her main resource; with a certain defiance, knowing her letters might be opened, she relentlessly pilloried the hated Maintenon, the 'vieille ordure', the Old Drab, the Trollop, every single day for the next ten years. This passionate hatred became her chief distraction, after the hunt, carriage drives and long walks. 'Although I am no longer young, the old bitch is even older than I am; I can hope then that I will have the pleasure before I die of seeing the old witch kick the bucket.' But she had to wait a quarter of a century.

She also had to contend with the hostility of the chevalier de Lorraine, who lived publicly as the master at the Palais-Royal, and who became emboldened to defy her as he saw her favour wane. She suffered to see her servants dismissed and replaced by creatures of Lorraine. Her maître d'hôtel was the same man who prowled the parterre of the Opéra looking for pretty boys for his master and concluding the bargains. The chevalier de Lorraine spread vicious rumours about her.

Homosexuality itself did not shock Madame; she was much more concerned with the waste of money which should have been hers and her children's. She affected a blasé air about the milieu in which she found herself, explaining to her half-sister in Germany that homosexuality was common among the French nobility and that it took specific forms. 'Some hate all women and only love men. Others like both men and women. Others like only boys of ten or eleven, others again young men of seventeen to twenty-five, and they are the most numerous.'

Philippe could not have been unaware of the constant arguments and hostility of his father's humiliations and his mother's growing isolation. He certainly felt the effect of his mother's worsening temper. I get annoyed rarely,' she wrote, 'but when it is necessary I lay into my children, which makes more of an impression. If they follow my advice they cannot go wrong, despite all the bad examples which these poor children have constantly before their eyes.' The bad examples were in full view at the Palais-Royal, where Monsieur spent a part of every winter entertaining Paris. Those who were unwelcome at Versailles were perfectly at home there: high-stakes gamblers, gossips, homosexuals, a world of intrigue. For Philippe it was much more entertaining than the court. At the Palais-Royal and at Saint-Cloud, an undercurrent of viciousness surrounded Monsieur and his ever-changing boy favourites. Tempers frequently became inflamed in this hothouse atmosphere; the comte de Tonnerre was banished for declaring that Monsieur was the stupidest woman in the world, and Madame the stupidest man.

Philippe's world was a confusing one. 'I engaged a German teacher for my son,' wrote Madame,

> and after he had studied the language for four solid years I told him that in order to learn a language it was necessary to practise conversation, and asked him to speak to me in German every now and then. Once when we were in the gallery, where you never know what might be going on, my son, intending to quote the German proverb 'Art lasst nicht von Art' exclaimed 'Arsch lasst nicht von Arsch' [Arse is drawn to arse]. I was utterly shocked. Thinking that he had meant to say this dreadful thing, I cried, 'Boy, be silent!' I really thought he had noticed some beastliness, which wouldn't have been at all uncommon here. But when he explained in French what he had meant to say and I had explained the difference between Art and Arsch he laughed fit to die. But this showed, he said, that he would never learn German, and he has since given it up.

The question of who should become Philippe's governor in 1689 to replace the aged duc de La Vieuville provoked another explosion. The post's duties were purely ceremonial; but there was the pension attached to it and the favour it conferred on the recipient. Monsieur wished to appoint his old crony, the marquis d'Effiat, to the post. Madame was outraged. This was, after all, one of the men suspected of poisoning the first Madame and, worse, a notorious pederast. 'It doesn't seem compatible with my son's honour to be regarded as the mistress of d'Effiat,' she wailed to Sophie, 'for there is no greater sodomite in France. Monsieur assured me that d'Effiat had cured himself of his vices long ago ... but I don't consider it necessary to use my son to test this notion ...' Madame took the battle to the King, an extremely courageous thing to do, even for her, and succeeded in heading off the appointment of d'Effiat. The new governor, René Martel, marquis d'Arcy, a former ambassador to Turin, was a man of impeccable reputation and conduct, whom Philippe always admired and respected. But the whole incident raises questions about the effect of this homosexual milieu on the young boy.

He was certainly curious; he heard, from his mother, that count Zinzendorff used to go to the Tuileries gardens and whistle for young men. He decided to try this himself and was shocked when several boys approached him, including one of his own pages. Whatever he consciously or unconsciously felt about all this, he acted decisively. He had his first sexual relations at the age of thirteen, initiated into manhood by a noble lady of a certain age, as was the custom. He then promptly fathered a child on 'la petite Léonore', the daughter of the concierge at the Palais-Royal. (Madame took care of the child and later saw her married.) He was now a seductive young man whose dazzling skin, dark curls and 'a red so perfectly placed on his cheeks that one would have thought it artificial' made him irresistible to women. He did not fight the temptation. His mother, while not exactly encouraging him in these pursuits, was clearly relieved at his inclination.

Philippe was a man; but he was still too young to comprehend all the nuances of the outside world. When the King came to Saint-Cloud at the end of November 1688 to admire the new staircase and gallery, he understood that his mother was in distress. Several days earlier Louis had given the order to raze Mannheim to the ground, having invaded her native Palatinate on the pretext of establishing the rights of Madame herself to her unpaid dowry. She told the Dauphin, who was sent to the front and who said he hoped to take Mannheim, 'If you take my advice, do not go, as I avow that I can find only grief and no joy in seeing them make use of my name in order to destroy my poor country.'

Heidelberg fell to the French in October, Mannheim in November. Worse was to come. In January 1689 the destruction of Heidelberg was begun and continued through March. The whole of the Palatinate was brutally, barbarically and systematically ruined. Madame's sufferings were cruel; the destruction of her country was carried out in her name, the money extracted known as Orleansgeld. The courtiers laughed at her misery; the King regarded her coldly. The Dauphin, back from ravaging

Madame's beloved homeland, complimented her on the quality of the trout and hares he had eaten there. Philippe, trained to look upon war as a glorious enterprise, had food for thought.

At the same time his half-sister, Marie-Louise, the Queen of Spain, died suddenly in Madrid at the age of twenty-seven. She had been gone for ten years and Philippe barely remembered her; but Madame, convinced that her step-daughter had been poisoned, was once more distraught. Marie-Louise had arrived in Spain as a pretty and pleasure-loving princess, but had been isolated and abandoned to her cretinous husband and his hostile court. Her charm and grace, not valuable commodities in a Queen of Spain, soon faded. For ten years the couple struggled to bear a child, failing publicly and humiliatingly. Confiding to the French an important state secret, namely that her husband was impotent, she gave herself up to gluttony. Marie-Louise was the victim of plots and calumny. She wrote to Louis XIV begging for an antidote to poison, saying she knew her life to be in danger. The French Ambassador in Madrid agreed that she was in peril. Louis did nothing. On 8 February 1689 Marie-Louise fell from her horse, went to rest, took a light meal of Chinese oranges, milk iced with snow and a pastry. The next day she ate veal broth, oysters, olives and oranges. Then after two days of agony she died.

The French court was certain she had been poisoned, particularly given the presence in Madrid of the notorious Olympe Mancini, comtesse de Soissons, a woman deeply implicated in the poisoning scandals in Paris some years earlier. Louis XIV said nothing; it was important that Spanish opinion not be irritated. The dead woman's father, Monsieur, kept quiet; Madame, who remembered her step-daughter fondly, could only mourn her discreetly. A year later the pathetic King of Spain married a German princess; of course, as the French knew, there would be no children. The fate of the immense inheritance of Spain, from the New World to the Pacific, was now a matter of urgent debate.

And then in April 1690 came the death of the Dauphine. A princess of Bavaria, she was only thirty when she died, but had been ill for some time, languishing and melancholy. Madame thought she had been destroyed by the hostility of Mme de Maintenon. 'I am a tougher nut to crack,' she told her aunt Sophie. And she was. But her greatest trial awaited her. The destruction of her homeland, the deaths of her step-daughter and the Dauphine, paled besides the prospect of the threat to her beloved son.

In the shadows a plot was unfolding. At the end of 1688 the King announced a great promotion to the Order of the Holy Ghost. There had not been a promotion for over twenty years and the news caused a stir. Becoming a chevalier de l'Ordre was a great honour, one of the greatest the King could bestow, and carried enormous privileges, including the *cordon bleu*. Among the seventy-four men named were the chevalier de Lorraine and his brother the comte de Marsan. Monsieur, who was allowed to name two men, nominated the marquis d'Effiat and the marquis de Châtillon. Behind these announcements was an intrigue. The nomination of the chevalier de Lorraine together with d'Effiat, Châtillon and the comte de Marsan, all members of Monsieur's coterie, was the bribe with which the King won the support of his brother to the plot to marry the duc de Chartres to Mlle de Blois, younger daughter of the King and Mme de Montespan.

Madame had her eyes open. 'I have been told in confidence the real reasons why the King is treating the chevalier de Lorraine and the marquis d'Effiat so well: it is because they have promised to persuade Monsieur to beg the King most humbly to marry the Montespan's children with mine.' She was determined to prevent such a misalliance if she could, but Louis XIV was systematically winning over Monsieur. In addition to the honours to his favourites, Monsieur was promised the Palais-Royal in Paris, which he leased from the crown, as a gift outright. He immediately began expensive rebuilding work; heretofore he had been unwilling to spend his money there, as he was not the owner, but clearly he now knew that the expense would not be wasted.*

The plotters had to wait until the eleven-year-old Mlle de Blois reached puberty. Nothing was said, especially not to Madame. She nursed her suspicions, watched with alarm the marriage of Mlle de Nantes, the sister of Mlle de Blois and the duc de Bourbon, worried that not only her son, but also her daughter, would be sacrificed to the King's bastards. She tried to believe that the King would not so dishonour his only nephew. The storm did not take long to break.

---

* Monsieur was dependent financially on his brother, as in every other way. He received pensions and grants of more than a million livres a year as well as the income from his *apanage*, lands given to younger sons of the royal family as a kind of indemnity for the sovereignty of which they were deprived. But his *train de vie* was always more extravagant than his huge assets. By 1698 there were 1,226 servants and officers in the Orléans household.

# ❧ 3 ❧

# ROYAL WEDDING

The duc de Chartres' life at court was, like that of all the courtiers, one of gilded servitude. But the system imposed by Louis XIV meant that the higher one's rank, the more one was enslaved.

As a Grandson of France, Philippe was one of the first admitted to the King's Lever, witnessing His Majesty in his nightshirt and on his *chaise percée*, the upholstered version of the chamber-pot. Occasionally he might have the supreme privilege of handing Louis his shirt. After the long ceremonious robing was over, with more people admitted at various stages, he would hurry to the Chapel to await the King. After Mass, at which a respectful demeanour was required, he could repair to his rooms or to the grounds while the King held council. He must appear for the *petit couvert*, standing as the King ate. Then a hunt or a walk in the park. Attendance at the Débotté, when the King took off his boots. The public dinner. A play or music. The Coucher. A futile, wearisome, demeaning life and, for one with no taste for cards, riding or gossip, a leaden existence. 'They want only humble people at court,' noted the envoy from Brandenburg. 'On those of strong, independent spirits, mockers, the King has imposed the fear of exile.' Philippe was nothing if not a strong, independent spirit, certainly a mocker; the tedium, the forced assiduity, were profoundly unsympathetic to him.

He was not alone in his view. Versailles had been the official seat of the court for less than ten years, but the sad fact was that Louis XIV was already somewhat bored with it. The King, with his new-found pleasure in domestic life, found himself with an uncompromisingly grand and public home. Increasingly the court saw him disappearing in a cloud of dust to Marly or Trianon. Only very few favoured courtiers were granted the privilege of accompanying him. The Porcelain Trianon had been replaced by the Marble Trianon and Louis liked to dine there on summer evenings with a few selected ladies. But pretty Trianon, sparkling new and luxurious, also seemed out of tune with the mood of the King.

Marly was the place Louis XIV loved best and where he spent more and more time as the years progressed. The first recorded house party took place there in 1686, a little before the new Trianon was finished. But whereas Trianon became something of a pink and gold elephant, Marly became the King's lasting passion. Versailles remained the imposing main royal residence where Christmas and the winter seasons were spent; the court went every year to Fontainebleau in the late summer; but they were at Marly for weeks at a time all year round.

Marly was a secluded estate comprising a little château and twelve pavilions strung six on either side of an ornamental lake. The King and his family lived in the little château, his guests in the pavilions. A great cascade rose behind the château, a reflecting pool stretched in front of it, leading to a basin flanked by the celebrated Marly horses, statues of Fame and Mercury sculpted by Coysevox. The site, shut in by high wooded hills, has preserved a feeling of intimacy. Along the lake the guest pavilions were linked by tunnels of hornbeam. Each pavilion contained apartments for two couples, one on each floor, with a bedroom and an anteroom and a privy. Philippe lodged on the ground floor of the first pavilion on the side of the Chapel with the prince de Conti or Monsieur le Prince, then the duc de Beauvillier above him. In 1710 he moved into the château itself.

The grounds were a 'paroxysme du jardin à la française'. Eighteen million bulbs were taken to Marly in four years, and Louis XIV constantly added to the attractions. 'It is as though the fairies have been at work here,' wrote Madame in July 1702, 'for where I had left a pond I saw a wood, and where I had left a clearing there is now a great artificial lake. This evening it will be stocked with more than a hundred carp. These are extremely handsome, some gold, some silver, others are a beautiful deep blue, or yellow-spotted, or black and white, gold and white, or white-gold with red spots or black spots...'

The heart of Marly was the octagonal Salon in the château. Four apartments were situated at the corners of this room; that of the King overlooked the lake and gardens, and was hung with crimson damask, Monsieur's was decorated in green, Madame's in *aurore* (a soft peach colour), and Mme de Maintenon's in blue. In the lofty room, which ascended through two floors, decorated with Corinthian columns and caryatids, Louis spent more and more of his life. He took his meals in the *antichambre* of Mme de Maintenon's apartment, where three tables were laid and where the ladies had the privilege of being seated with him. There were constant theatrical performances, gambling parties and concerts here;

Louis insisted that 'no one be bored at Marly'. But even Marly was not perfect: the Salon was a very draughty place. Mme de Maintenon said the winds there reminded her of the hurricanes in America. She also said, as the numbers of guests increased, 'Marly will soon be a little Versailles.' She was right; at Marly's height sixty guests could stay, attended by more than a thousand servants.

The King's *voyages* to Marly grew longer; by the end of his reign he was spending months at a time there. His courtiers were expected to beg for the privilege of being invited. Invitations to Marly were so coveted that the grandest noblemen humbled themselves to whisper 'Sire, Marly,' as the King passed by. In later years the King got tired of this and had a footman stand in the Hall of Mirrors and take the names of those who wished to go. The fortunate guests, who had been waiting anxiously outside the door, were notified as the King left his *cabinet*. If a lady was invited, her husband could go of right.

This feeling of privileged exclusivity was the chief delight of Marly; that, and the relative informality. Men could, if Louis uttered the words 'Chapeaux, Messieurs,' wear their hats in the King's presence; women need not wear the *grand habit* (the court dress, décolleté and off the shoulder, the bodice laced at the back, with a paniered skirt and lace-flounced sleeves), although they had to wear a proper boned bodice with their *robe de chambre*. The sense of intimacy with the King, and superiority to the uninvited, quite apart from the delightful walks, the bowling green, the fountains and cascades, the lakes and fishponds, made Marly as close to heaven as a courtier could get.

In 1691 Philippe was preoccupied with his coming début at the war. He approached it with a mixture of bravado and anticipation. At seventeen he was still shy and timid in society, partly due to his bad eyesight, which made him self-conscious, and he already knew that the things he liked, reading, studying, learning, were unnecessary requirements for his future life as a royal personage. But he was eager to take the field.

The atmosphere between his parents was deteriorating and there were quarrels at every turn. Also, his mother had found one more reason to complain about Mme de Maintenon. Madame loved the theatre, which she attended as often as she could in Paris and at Versailles. But Mme de Maintenon disapproved of these spectacles. She commissioned Racine to write a play on a biblical theme which she could have performed at Saint-Cyr (the boarding school she had founded to educate the daughters of gentlefolk for a useful and pious life). There, in 1689, before a small audience, in an atmosphere of propriety, Racine's *Esther* had been performed by the girls. At the beginning of 1691, *Athalie* was to be put on. Madame would have loved to go; but 'as long as the old whore is alive, things will go badly with me at court. She detests me, and the more civilly I behave towards her the worse it gets; so I am never one of the chosen few who are permitted to watch the play at Saint-Cyr...'

No doubt relieved to get away from the interminable bickering, Philippe left for the front that spring. This was an important rite of passage at which a young man had to prove his manhood. France had been engaged since 1689 in the War of the League of Augsburg, in which all Europe, alarmed at French expansionism, was ranged against Louis XIV. But the French still had the best generals and the finest troops. In the ceremonious way of war of those days, the King took Monsieur, the Dauphin, the duc du Maine and the duc de Chartres along to witness the besieging of Mons. Maine had already campaigned twice before, without making a mark; but the King asked his commander-in-chief, the maréchal de Luxembourg, to give Maine every chance to shine. As for Chartres, by contrast, the King asked that he be treated as a simple soldier and be accompanied by his governor, the marquis d'Arcy, and by Dubois. The thirteen-year-old comte de Toulouse, Maine's younger brother, also made his début in the same campaign.

Maine and Chartres saw each other occasionally, and Maine dutifully reported their meetings to Mme de Maintenon:

> M. le duc de Chartres has joined us, and repeated to me all the advice you gave him when he was leaving, and the promise he made to correct his conduct in certain little matters. You should be contented with him, and believe that he is a man of his word. He is very friendly with me, and I respond, as is seemly, with respect, but without affection. I think I ought to tell you that since he has been here, he has not mentioned the name of Mlle – .* I have had him to dinner, and he has been to supper with M. de Luxembourg; he too has given us a meal. He was full of excitement [*gaillard*] when he saw the enemy; in short, he is doing marvels.

There is no evidence that Maine and Chartres became friends; they were very different personalities. Maine was and remained the obedient pupil of Mme de Maintenon, Chartres was already a rebel. And of course the question of rank pervaded their relationship, as it did that of everyone else. Maine with his 'intermediate' rank between the Princes of the Blood

---

* Mlle – was probably the actress Florence Pellerin, with whom Philippe had started an enthusiastic affair before he left Paris. It was rather shocking, as Florence was some years older than the Prince, and was a celebrated *grande horizontale*.

and the dukes was much less grand than Philippe. But he was also much closer to the King.

After some desultory manoeuvrings, the town of Mons fell to the French; Luxembourg wrote to the King: 'Never has a young man been so excited as the duc de Chartres when he thought we were going against the enemy; and to be frank, his joy was followed by a little *poltronnerie* which really was nothing more than dying of fear that we would not give battle when he saw the obstacles ahead.' The King was not impressed; he noted rather sourly that he had heard that Chartres was spending too much time studying with his tutors.

The first of the very few surviving letters from Madame to her son date from this campaign. 'I hope the beautiful weather cures your cold,' she writes solicitously, 'together with the great joy at being where you are. That is a good tonic and cures many pains ... if only God had given me even a part of your hard heartedness, that would do me a lot of good, but I would need a lot of it ... and you can rely on the fact that, whatever tears and pains you cost me, I shall not stop loving you most tenderly.' The tears and pain arose from Philippe's desire to be *à la mode*, to ride his Spanish horses too fast, to smoke tobacco ('ce vilain tabac') and drink too much, and to let his companions be too familiar with him. These complaints are heard again and again in Madame's letters; they clearly had little effect.

'I did not plan to write to you today, my dear child,' she wrote after the news of her son's first exposure to fire,

> but having learnt from Monsieur's letters how happy he is with you, of the good countenance with which you have withstood the blows of cannon and musket, and your reputation being as dear to me as your life, I cannot prevent myself rejoicing with you and telling you, my dear son, that despite the anxiety I have for you, I have felt a great joy at knowing that Monsieur has reason to be happy with you. He is a good connoisseur, and I am delighted that he recognises his blood in you. But remember, my dear child, that although having courage is an excellent virtue for a prince like you, it is not the only one which you should have, and it will never have merit except when accompanied by other virtues.

The exposure to danger and the society of much admired older men like the prince de Conti was intoxicating for a sixteen-year-old boy. Conti was a hero, ten years older than Philippe, and a polished, witty man of the world. He possessed great charm, seducing both men and women; 'he was gallant with all the ladies', noted Saint-Simon later, 'in love with several, well treated by all, and even more of a flirt with all the men'. Conti had earned the lasting dislike of the King for being too much of an independent spirit, and was merely tolerated at court, but on the field of battle he shone. Philippe admired him and the men around him, but Conti, although constrained to show the duc de Chartres all the marks of outward respect due to his rank, could not be bothered with him. These two talented men never became close.

When Philippe returned to court that autumn of 1691, he found a new friend had arrived – the sixteen-year-old duc de Saint-Simon. We do not know how the two men met. Saint-Simon merely says, 'I had been brought up with him and, if age permits the expression between two young men so unequal in rank, we were close friends.' They had probably shared lessons at the Palais-Royal; Saint-Simon lived with his mother just across the river in the rue des Saints-Pères and was of the age and rank to become a companion of the Prince.

Saint-Simon was brought up by his mother; his father, sixty-eight years old when his only son was born, was too old to play much of a part in the boy's upbringing, and all his father's friends, who might have been expected to help the boy, were infirm or dead. His mother never ceased to remind him that he was alone in the world and would have to rely on himself for advancement. She was no doubt discountenanced by her son's early passion for reading and the study of history, tastes little suited to move him ahead in the world. When all his friends, including Philippe, went off to war in 1691, the sixteen-year-old Saint-Simon implored his mother for permission to join them. His aged father came up from Blaye to petition Louis XIV personally; the King, having noted that the young man was small, and appeared delicate, nevertheless gave his assent to him joining the Grey Musketeers. (All young noblemen had to spend a year in one of the two companies of Musketeers, the Black and the Grey, named after the colour of their horses, before joining a regiment.) Elated at the thought that the next year he would be able to join his friends, Saint-Simon rushed to Versailles, anxious to hear all about campaigning from Philippe, who had already won his spurs. But the talk at court was all about the announcement of Philippe's marriage. Instead of telling war stories to his friend, Philippe found himself at the centre of the worst family feud of his life.

The trap which had been laid some years ago was now ready to be sprung. The girl chosen as the bride for the duc de Chartres, Françoise-Marie de Bourbon, had reached the age of fourteen in May and was ready to be married. Monsieur, paid off in advance but still uneasy, undertook to raise no objection. The King, in consultation with his brother, decided to talk to Philippe immediately, not giving Madame the opportunity to object until it was too late. Neither Louis nor his brother had any illusions about the nature of Madame's reaction to the news. They proceeded with caution.

Philippe, summoned to the presence of his intimidating uncle, must have had some idea of what was to be proposed. His mother, scenting trouble, tried to stiffen his resolve. But she knew that the terrifying majesty of Louis XIV reduced everyone, especially members of his own family, to a state of nervous trepidation; she could not have expected her son to stand up to the most formidable personage of the century. And he did not.

The account of the interview of January 1692 provided by Saint-Simon has the ring of truth; it was probably described to him by Philippe himself. The King was affable and charming; he expressed his fondness for his nephew and his desire to give him an establishment of his own. Unfortunately the war prevented him from finding a suitable princess abroad and there were no Princesses of the Blood of the right age. He could not therefore better express his tenderness than to give Philippe his own daughter in marriage. Philippe was silent. Monsieur, who was present, said not a word; the King persevered. He would not force the duc de Chartres into anything; he was free to make his own decision. So what did he think? Placed in an impossible position, Philippe stammered that the King was the master, but that he would have to consult his parents. 'Good for you!' replied the King heartily; 'but here is your father and he has already agreed. Let us ask your mother to join us now.' In the pause that followed the King chatted amiably with Monsieur, neither of them seeming to notice that Chartres was about to expire from apprehension at the prospect of his mother's wrath.

Madame arrived. 'Well, Madame,' said the King, 'I take it that you will not oppose a matter in which your husband and I are agreed? I mean, of course, the marriage of your son to Mademoiselle de Blois.' This was said as if Madame could not be other than delighted. There was utter silence. Shocked and speechless, unable to raise more courage than her son, looking daggers at her husband, Madame could only summon up the strength to curtsey and withdraw.

'My eyes are so thick and swollen', she told Sophie, 'that I can barely look out of them, since I confess that I was foolish enough to cry all night.' She hated bastardy and had a horror of misalliances; her own peculiar upbringing had confirmed her in the firm belief that no good came of unequal unions. She considered Mme de Montespan 'the wickedest woman on earth and the most desperate'. She had wanted Philippe to marry a proper, German princess. That the King's only nephew 'so far above the Princes of the Blood by reason of his rank as a Grandson of

France and the court which his father held' would be humiliated by this misalliance was more than she could bear. Not to mention the pleasure Mme de Maintenon would take in her discomfiture, nor the glee with which the courtiers would greet the news. At Versailles, the humbling of the mighty was always a source of great amusement. Madame was distraught.

Greatly diverted, the court looked forward to an exquisitely embarrassing evening. They assembled for what was known as Appartement, the gathering of all the court which lasted from seven in the evening to ten in the magnificent salons of Apollo, Mercury, Mars, Venus and Diana. There was music; the tables were set up for every sort of card game; billiards were played. One room was set aside for refreshments; everything was brilliantly lit. That evening in January, after the music, the King summoned Monsieur and Madame, who were playing cards, the duc de Chartres, who was playing chequers, and Mlle de Blois, who had only recently come into society and who that evening was extravagantly got up. She was so nervous that Mme de Maintenon had to hold her on her knee.

The fourteen-year-old girl about whose head all the fuss was raging seems to have remained composed. She was pretty with admirable skin, eyes and throat but had pendulous cheeks and no eyebrows. And while not exactly crippled, she had one shoulder higher than the other which gave her a slight limp. She had been born nine months after the reconciliation of the King and Mme de Montespan in 1677 and Mme de Caylus said she bore on her person the marks of the conflict between love and duty. She had her mother's wit; her only known utterance on the subject of her marriage was: 'I don't care about him loving me as long as he marries me.'

In the King's *cabinet* the discussion was confined to practical matters. The bride received a huge dowry of two million livres (but this was not to be paid until the war was over), an annual pension of 150,000 livres, and jewellery worth 600,000 livres, including *parures* of diamonds, sapphires, rubies and topaz. The duc de Chartres, in expectation of commands to follow, received the promise of a pension of 200,000 livres when his father died, in addition to the one of 150,000 livres he already enjoyed, and was further promised great promotions and a marvellous future as son-in-law of the King.

Outside the King's *cabinet*, discussion was freer. Like everything that happened at Versailles, the impending marriage was viewed by everyone through the prism of rank and precedence. Love never entered anyone's head. The questions were about the changes in the pecking order which would ensue.

Louis XIV had mastered the art of dividing his family and subduing his courtiers; by awarding distinctions and honours, however trivial they might seem, to some and not to others, he set up a desire for such things and an anxiety about losing ground. In the case of his own family he created fine distinctions between say, a granddaughter of a Son of France relative to a daughter of a Prince of the Blood. Among his courtiers he allowed the dukes to have important privileges; their wives could sit on a stool in the presence of the King while the wives of other members of the nobility had to stand. The only men who could sit in the King's presence (and then on stools) were the Children and Grandchildren of France; Princes of the Blood and dukes had to stand at all times. The overwhelming proof that Mme de Maintenon had secretly married the King was that she sat in an armchair in his presence. When Mlle de Blois became the duchesse de Chartres she would become the wife of a Grandson of France, outranking her elder sister, who had married the duc de Bourbon, a mere Prince of the Blood. She would have a longer train than her sister, could sit in an armchair whereas her sister had to perch on a chair with a back but no arms, and her sister had henceforth to address her as Madame. When these sisters had children the disputes over precedence would be ferocious.

When everyone emerged from the King's *cabinet* the marriage was formally announced. As the courtiers rushed to congratulate the bride and groom, Madame walked up and down the Hall of Mirrors, gesticulating and weeping, her handkerchief in her hand. No one dared approach her. Saint-Simon compared her to Ceres after the rape of Proserpine. Monsieur, somewhat disconcerted, took up his cards again. Philippe seemed miserable, his bride-to-be embarrassed. At the King's supper Madame's eyes were full of tears; neither she nor her son could eat anything. Finally, at the end of the dreary meal, when the King made her a particularly deep bow, she dropped the briefest possible curtsey, swung round, and left the King staring at her retreating back. Saint-Simon adds a description of Madame giving her hapless son a slap in the face in full view of the gaping crowd. There are no other witnesses to that; but the accounts of Madame's fury were repeated across Europe, making Sophie fear that she had gone too far. Madame denied that she had acted childishly: 'I put the best possible face on it and affected a satisfaction which, frankly, I am far from feeling.'

All that remained were the engagement ceremony and the wedding itself. The former took place at Versailles at six o'clock in the evening of 17 February. The duc de Chartres wore a suit of gold brocade trimmed with rose pink and gold ribbons and Spanish needlepoint. His shoes and coat were studded with diamonds and emeralds. His fiancée wore a dress

of gold, embroidered with little black flowers, the hem edged with gold
Spanish lace, and a garniture of diamonds and rubies. And in her light
brown hair were diamonds and a green and gold ribbon. Monsieur was
dazzling in golden brocade with silver Spanish lace. Proceeding to the
King's Salon they were blessed by the cardinal de Bouillon and the marriage
contract was read. There was a ball with two orchestras, hundreds of
servants in blue and silver livery serving preserved fruits and liqueurs. The
bride's sister, Madame la Duchesse, was so chagrined that she could not
bring herself to put in an appearance.

The wedding the next day was magnificent and rather depressing; these
were, as Saint-Simon put it, the 'tristes rejouissances de commande', that
is, sad celebrations, obligatory and hollow. Chartres wore a suit of black
velvet embroidered with gold and decorated with pearls and diamonds.
His shoes were also studded with fine pearls and little diamonds. The
bride was in a rich tissue of silver decorated with silver Spanish lace. The
married couple, as was the custom, were put to bed in the presence of the
court. The exiled king of England, James II, who had been at the French
court since 1688, handed Philippe his nightshirt, Madame handed the new
duchesse hers. The next day the duchesse de Chartres received congratulations from the court as she lay in bed. There followed another ball
at which Philippe wore a velvet suit with a pattern of diamonds and pearls
designed by Jean Bérain, the court interior decorator who was also called
upon for gala clothes. The new duchesse de Chartres was given a princely
household: a chevalier d'honneur, a dame d'honneur and so on. Never
before had anyone other than a Daughter of France been granted such a
grand establishment. Her sister merely had two ladies to accompany her.

Sodomy and double adultery had triumphed, said Saint-Simon, referring to the bribing of the chevalier de Lorraine and to the liaison between
Louis XIV and Madame de Montespan.

One wonders if Philippe himself felt as strongly as his mother did about
the horror of the match. He would never have expected to marry for love;
nor would he be expected to be faithful to his wife. Possibly he believed
the promises of high command and preferment, but he was probably
already aware that the King and Mme de Maintenon viewed him as
something of a threat rather than as a dutiful son-in-law. For the time
being, seventeen years old and bursting with enthusiasm, he did not plan
to alter his way of life in the slightest.

He had proved himself a brave soldier but he was still a young man
prone to the bad habits of youth, still exploring his world and his place in
it. Paradox abounded: he was of studious disposition, shy and short-
sighted, eager to please his parents and his tutors, interested in questions

of art and science and history; he was also a self-professed *bel esprit*, full of bravado, passionate about girls, wine, tobacco and fast horses. He wanted to impress the King with his military exploits, but he longed to join the men of *bel air*, the avant-garde, the *libertines*, who mocked the King and religion, albeit from the safety of their privileged redoubts.

This tension between the demands of his rank and the urge to rebel, between the pleasure he took in study and the need to gratify all his senses, profoundly marked his character. He was beset by contradictions and ambiguities: the son of a feminine father and a masculine woman; of high rank but limited in opportunity; immensely privileged yet tightly constrained. For the present it seemed easiest to plunge into the simple life of a soldier. In the spring of 1692 Philippe was eager to leave the hypocrisies of Versailles and go to war again. He waited impatiently for May and the start of the campaigning season.

# ❧ 4 ❧

# WAR AND PEACE

Newly married, hungry for action, the duc de Chartres set out in May 1692. The armies of the King, one under his personal command, the other under the maréchal de Luxembourg, marched to Flanders and the siege of Namur.

In this fourth year of fighting some of the spring had gone out of the step of the once all-conquering French King. Louis was suffering from gout and had to conduct his councils of war from his bed. When he visited the front Mme de Maintenon accompanied him, but added to the gloom by complaining constantly about the draughty rooms and the state of the roads. Madame, who had been excluded from the voyage as a mark of the disapproval felt over her conduct at Philippe's wedding, claimed she did not care: 'It's all the same to me whether I'm here or in Flanders. My desire to be with those who make up our court has completely disappeared.' But she followed events with interest. 'They say that the old Rumpumpel is very bad tempered in the town where her sweetheart has installed her. I hope it will make her ill.'

The duc de Chartres was with the army of the maréchal de Luxembourg, in command of the reserve. Even though he was a married man, he was still attended by Dubois and by the marquis d'Arcy, no longer officially the Prince's governor, but his First Gentleman of the Chamber. It amounted to the same thing; he was the 'directeur discret de sa conduite'. D'Arcy had a soldier's concept of his duty. He had forbidden Philippe from attending sessions of the Académie française, where the young man had gone to hear Boileau and Racine, La Fontaine and Fontanelle, discuss topics of literary and philosophical significance. The pleasure he took in these meetings marked him out from every other prince of the house of Bourbon. Louis XIV simply sneered: 'let him be the doctor in the family'. D'Arcy hastened to remove from his master the taint of bookishness.

Wanting to excel, watched over by his tutor and deluged with advice from his mother, Philippe performed creditably during the siege of Namur, at which Louis XIV personally led his troops, and for which Boileau wrote an ode. But he got his first real opportunity to fight when the French army was surprised by the forces of William of Orange at the village of Steinkerque.

The imagination fails at the bloody shambles these seventeenth-century battles must have been. The frightful carnage of Steinkerque was typical of the age; but mercifully, battles were relatively rare events. This was the time when the armies spent most of the summer campaigning season marching from place to place, conducting siege operations and *belles retraites*, skirmishing and sallying forth to impress the other side. A pitched battle was the ghastly culmination of these activities and not entered into lightly. Being brought to battle in the wrong place and at the wrong time was disastrous; and so each side feinted and manoeuvred for advantage in the choice of a site. During the long years of the War of the League of Augsburg, the armies would leave for the front in May and remain in the field until the autumn. The infantry, armed with swords and muskets and pistols, marched to the music of fife and drum. The elite French units were gorgeously attired, particularly the Musketeers, mounted on either grey or black horses, attired in red coats with blue revers and gold and silver embroidery. Such uniforms were a relatively new thing; the infantry were not so glamorously kitted out. Behind the troops came the artillery, an increasingly important weapon.

For young men of noble birth, warfare was a healthy, robust life, a day's march followed by a fine meal and much carousing. It was also an escape from court ceremonial, although, even at the battle front, etiquette was rigorously enforced. The duc de Chartres went to war with an entourage of servants and aides-de-camp, priests and tutors. Contact with the enemy was polite and ceremonious; prisoners were treated honourably, with rank and birth as usual counting for everything. For the footsoldiers, often Irish or German mercenaries, as well as English, Dutch, French and Danes, the military life was not so glamorous. In return for risking their lives they were fed and watered; when the campaigning season was over, they were put into winter quarters while their superiors went off to the balls and entertainments of Versailles, London or Vienna. From Blenheim to the Somme these rules of war hardly changed; only the wounds caused by the increasingly powerful weaponry deepened.

The battle of Steinkerque lasted from eight in the morning until noon of 3 August 1692, a bloody hand-to-hand conflict. It was typical of the age in its tactics and in its bloodshed. Line after line of men advanced towards each other, firing their weapons, falling and dying, until a commander deemed a cavalry charge appropriate. In the background, cannon would roar, but they were still too heavy to be mobile, and only very small ones could be brought to the front. The battle soon degenerated into a contest of attrition.

Philippe, sword in hand, charged at the head of the Gardes français. D'Arcy begged him to be careful, but he was possessed. Twice wounded in the arm, he was finally taken from the field, unable to participate in the eventual French victory. But he had made a name for himself, and news of his courage and spirit soon made its way to court. His mother wrote: 'You are at a high point of glory which has made everyone forget your past weaknesses. I am charmed that you have at last made the decision to show your good side ... Carry on like this, my dear child, I beg you, and make yourself a perfect prince ...'

Back at court for the winter, all the young men were wearing their cravats 'à la Steenkerque', loosely tied and carelessly tucked into the second button of their coats. It was the only remotely informal thing about the way they dressed there; huge periwigs, canes, swords, gloves, plumed hats, all had to be carried around. High-heeled shoes were *de rigueur*. Men carried muffs in the icy galleries of Versailles. Women were awash with beauty spots, elaborately constructed headdresses, frills and furbelows.

Philippe found his parents in magnificent new rooms at Versailles. They each had their own large suite, extending all the way from the centre of the Wing of the Princes to its southern extremity, commanding views of the Orangerie and the Hundred Steps. Here his father hung his paintings and 'all the gilt, the mirrors and the pictures look very well together. There are five crystal chandeliers. When the candles are lit in the evening, everything looks very brilliant and beautiful.' Madame was pleased even though Monsieur had, rather tactlessly, hung three masterpieces pillaged from Heidelberg in his room, 'the Virgin surrounded by the Apostles, the painting of Samson and the Philistines, and the picture of Prometheus with the vultures feeding off his liver'. Philippe and his wife had an almost equally splendid set of rooms next door.

Social life in these imposing surroundings was not always so decorous. One night in January 1693 Madame described an evening *chez* Orléans. She and her husband, Chartres and his wife, were together after supper. Monsieur, after a long silence, 'let off a great long fart (by your leave). He turned to me and said, "What was that, Madame?" I turned my behind in his direction, let one off in the same tone and said, "That, Monsieur." My son said, "If it comes to that, I can do as well as Monsieur and Madame," and let off a good one, too. Then we all laughed ...' According to Madame her son had 'so much wind that he can produce any kind of note, which is why he now plays the flute. I think that if he held it against his behind instead of his mouth, it would sound equally musical.'

In the spring of 1693 the French armies moved again into Flanders. This time Philippe commanded the cavalry in Luxembourg's army and on 29 July took a bold and daring part in the battle of Neerwinden. During the twelve-hour engagement, fought under a blazing sun, Philippe put himself at some risk, to the alarm of Luxembourg, but he was once more heaped with praise and acclamation. 'He has led five charges of the cavalry of which he is the general,' boasted his mother. 'He was in the thick of the fighting for two hours, it's a wonder he is still alive.' He saw d'Arcy fall wounded at his feet when his horse was hit, and two others of his entourage seriously injured close by. The battle was one of the bloodiest of the whole century, with nearly thirty thousand casualties.

At the end of the campaigning season, however, and despite kind words from the King ('I could not be more pleased with your application and energy'), he was given no further command, whereas the duc du Maine received that of the Artillery.

At the end of 1693 Philippe's first child was born – a girl, who was to live only a year. According to the custom of the day, she was given a title, Mlle de Valois, but no Christian name. In August 1695 the duchesse de Chartres gave birth to another daughter, Marie-Louise-Elisabeth. Philippe was pleased to have a healthy child, but this marriage was not a close one, nor were the young couple helped by Madame's insistence on finding fault with her daughter-in-law. The Duchess, she wrote, was preoccupied with her appearance and her beauty spots, even though she was decidedly no beauty; got drunk three or four times a week; talked as though she had her mouth full of soup; was lazy, arrogant and spoilt. Indeed, the pride of the duchesse de Chartres was legendary; she was 'Granddaughter of France even on her *chaise percée*'. Philippe seems to have enjoyed teasing her; he called her 'Madame Lucifer', to her face, and she had the grace to laugh. But, isolated in this difficult family, she turned in self-defence to a few trusted women friends, most of them related to her through her mother, Mme de Montespan. Her closest companions were her Montespan cousins, the marquise de Castries and the duchesse Sforze. She drew her support from them, submitted patiently to her husband's desires, and ignored her mother-in-law as best she could.

Philippe was an accomplished young man. He played the flute, guitar and clavichord. He adored Italian music and had his own ensemble to play it. He, the Dauphin and the princesse de Conti discussed music all the time; 'I often say to my son that he will go mad, when I hear him discussing B-sharp and B-flat and other things I know nothing about,' grumbled his mother, feeling left out. He was taught composition by Marc-Antoine Charpentier and had written an opera before he was twenty. Around this time he also wrote a motet which was performed before the King, with the princesse de Conti and the comte de Toulouse taking part.

He had also become a talented artist. Surrounded from birth with great masterpieces, he started to paint when still very young and continued to do so all his life, including portraits of his mistresses and murals for the boudoir of his wife.

> My son has such a great talent for all aspects of painting that he never uses any expedients for designing and sketches everything from nature and living models. Coypel, his former teacher, says that all the painters should be glad that my son is a great lord, because if he were an ordinary fellow he would surpass them all. He can draw anything that comes into his head, his conceptions are strong, and he knows how to make the most difficult postures look easy . . .

He particularly admired the Italian masters. When he bought Raphael's *St John in the Desert* it became the starting point for a collection of almost five hundred paintings.

We can see an image of him at this time, at the wedding of the duc de Bourgogne, eldest son of the Dauphin, to Marie-Adélaïde of Savoy, in December 1697. Marie-Adélaïde had arrived at the French court a year earlier. Although she was the granddaughter of Monsieur, the daughter of Philippe's half-sister, Anne-Marie, the King and Mme de Maintenon had no intention of exposing the eleven-year-old girl to the goings-on at the Palais-Royal. Mme de Maintenon personally selected the household of the Princess, intending to pursue her vocation of governess once again. Madame was hurt; 'the girl makes little fuss of her grandfather, hardly looks at my son or me, but as soon as she sees Mme de Maintenon she smiles and goes up to her with open arms. You see how clever she is already.'

When Marie-Adélaïde reached her twelfth birthday, she and the duc de Bourgogne were married, although not yet put together. The celebrations were stately, with a party at Trianon and a performance of *Issé*, a heroic pastoral with music by Destouches and words by La Motte. The painting of the ceremony shows the young couple and all the court; on the groom's side stand the King, rather portly, Monseigneur with his sons, the groom's younger brothers, the duc d'Anjou and the duc de Berry, and the duc du Maine and the comte de Toulouse; on the bride's side stand Monsieur, Madame and Philippe with his wife and sister.

Philippe cuts a handsome figure. He stands with his back to the artist, slightly turned to look over his shoulder, hat tucked under his arm, full-skirted coat, red-heeled shoes, magnificent perruque. The painting cannot do justice to the gold and silver embroidery nor to the jewels which studded his coat and even his shoes. But the splendour belied the fact that, at twenty-three, the duc de Chartres was somewhat at a loss. The Peace of Ryswyck had just been signed. There would be no more campaigning. He could, for the first time in years, spend the summer with his wife at Monsieur's perpetual parties at Saint-Cloud, or with his mistress Florence in Paris, with occasional appearances at Versailles and Marly. He could paint and make music. Only one serious matter occurred. His daughter fell dangerously ill at this time and seemed near to death. It was Philippe who nursed the child devotedly, and who rejoiced the most when her life was saved. The consequences were profound; the girl became and remained his most beloved child. He adored her until the end of her life.

As Philippe cast about for a role, his attention was drawn to the great question agitating Europe, that of the Spanish succession. The King of Spain, Charles II, was at death's door; he had reached the age of thirty-six in spite of multiple disabilities, both mental and physical, but he was incapable of begetting an heir. The Bourbons of France and the Hapsburgs of Austria had competing claims to Spain through the sisters of Charles II, Marie-Thérèse, the late Queen of France, and Marguerite, the late Empress, wife of Emperor Leopold. (The claims were redoubled through the half-sisters of Charles II, Anne of Austria, wife of Louis XIII, and her sister, Maria Anna, wife of the late Emperor Ferdinand.) Poor demented Charles II would have to decide to leave his throne either to a Bourbon or to a Hapsburg, to the Dauphin or his sons, or to the Archduke Charles, Emperor Leopold's second son.

The rest of Europe was terrified that either France or Austria would be made invincible by the gain of such wealth and territory. Philippe, who had a claim to the throne of Spain through his grandmother Anne of Austria, studied the situation with more than passing interest. Dubois, who was still attached to the prince as a kind of secretary and aide, studied with him. Was it not conceivable that the junior branch of the French royal family might be called to the throne of Spain if the powers could not agree? Louis XIV had already sent the comte de Tallard to England to discuss possible solutions to the Spanish question. At the behest of his master, Dubois also set off for London to see what he might glean.

Philippe and Dubois were curious about England, an unusual monarchy where a king could be put to death, a commonwealth declared and removed, a dynasty peacefully disposed of and a foreigner called to the throne, all in the last eighty years and still leaving the country calm and prosperous. Dubois noted the freedom of expression he found, the cultivated society. When he met the French philosopher, Saint-Evremond, to whom King William had given the post of looking after the ducks in St James's Park in order that he would have time and money enough to philosophise, he was enchanted. On his return to France in May 1698, he regaled Philippe with the wonders of liberty and the English constitution. The duc de Chartres started to develop an interest in these notions, particularly in the idea that a less than absolute monarchy might have benefits for its citizens. He later told Saint-Simon that he admired a country in which the people could not be sent into exile or arbitrarily arrested, in which the King was bound by certain limits. Profoundly ir-religious himself, he attached less importance to the Divine Right of Kings.

Philippe had recently suffered the insult of being passed over for the post of Governor of Brittany, despite the King's promise that he would be awarded the first vacant position after his marriage. The post was given to the comte de Toulouse. Monsieur complained bitterly to the King; Louis listened gravely, had the chevalier de Lorraine soothe his brother's feelings, and handed out some money for gambling and 'pour embellir Saint-Cloud'. No more was said.

Philippe felt the contrast between his own treatment and that of his cousins, all the more because he knew himself superior to them in courage and ability. The duc du Maine had married a princess of the Bourbon-Condé family two months after Philippe's own marriage, a woman so tiny that Madame la Duchesse referred to her and her even smaller sisters as 'les poupées du sang'. Maine himself was a timid, gentle, rather mild young man, brought up by Mme de Maintenon to be pious and obedient. He was no warrior. Lacking the confidence to command troops, he had recently revealed himself as embarrassingly inept on the field of battle, where, ordered to attack by the maréchal de Villeroi, he hesitated, dithered and allowed the enemy army to escape. Nevertheless Maine, the apple of Mme de Maintenon's eye, was heaped with honours and privileges. Philippe, who found him dull and a sneak, pretended not to care. He began his lifelong pattern of flaunting his vices.

Philippe had installed Florence near the Palais-Royal. Setting up a mistress so visibly, and making the choice of a much more experienced woman, suggests that there was a degree of bravado involved in the decision. Madame was chagrined; 'The thing that made me worry that my lecture had had no effect', she confided to Dubois, 'was that I found out that the day he left here, he went to Paris that very morning and stayed an hour with Florence, although he had promised me the day before that he would try and get rid of her.'

But Philippe was insouciant. While continuing his liaison with Florence, he began a new one with a young actress, Christine Desmares, whose sweet face gazes at us from many sketches by Watteau. Philippe was also moved to paint her, as Antigone, a work of which there is no trace.

'With my son and his mistresses, everything is going along merrily, without the slightest chivalry. This reminds me of those old patriarchs who had many women. My son has much of King David in him; he has courage and wit; he is musical, small, brave, and he willingly sleeps with every woman he can. He is not difficult in this regard; as long as they are good humoured, impertinent and have a hearty appetite for food and drink, he does not worry about their looks.' When Philippe defended himself, saying, 'It's true that I do not know how to act like the hero of a novel or a man in love like Celadon, yet I make love in my fashion,' Madame had the last word: 'Your fashion is to visit them as you do your *chaise percée.*'

Florence gave birth to Philippe's son in April 1698, his first male child. He was named Charles and was immediately destined for a career in the Church. Unfortunately, when his wife gave birth in August of that year, it was to another daughter, Louise-Adélaïde.

Madame was worried not only about Florence and the low company her son kept, but also about his growing interest in the supernatural. Philippe, already interested in the occult and in the sciences, was reported by Saint-Simon to be working with 'all sorts of obscure people' to try and see the Devil and speak to him. He had once vainly spent several nights making magic incantations with M. de Mirepoix of the Black Musketeers in Vaugirard and Vanves. He was not alone in his curiosity. Many members of the nobility regarded magic as a slightly dangerous social game, a particularly exciting one, being a little dangerous. Amongst the most notorious was the sinister marquis de Feuquières, a man with a bad reputation and an aura of sulphur.

Feuquières was interested in black magic, love philtres, astrology and perhaps worse. He, together with his cousin the maréchal de Luxembourg, had been deeply implicated in the affair of the poisons of the 1680s. Although his career had been ruined, he had continued to serve in the army and had met the duc de Chartres at Neerwinden. Philippe was taken by the menacing nature of the man who was called 'le Diable' by his friends, and who, remarked Voltaire, had a black soul, as bitter as it was enlightened. According to Saint-Simon, on the other hand, Feuquières had neither heart nor soul; 'one could write a book about his crimes'. Such a man was an unsettling companion for Philippe, but the world he represented had the glamour of forbidden things. Philippe and Feuquières took to dabbling in fortune-telling and the calling up of spirits.

The world in which Philippe lived was a world in which men were making extraordinary breakthroughs in the sciences, discovering every-thing from the circulation of the blood to the laws of gravity. The world was changing shape every day with new landfalls in the Far East and in the Americas. Microscopes, burning glasses and telescopes were transforming what men knew about themselves and things around them. Yet while science seemed to offer proof of the power of man's ability to reason, there was still belief in the proximity of Hell and the Devil, the power of magic and the efficacy of superstition. Philippe believed both in the laws of science and in fortune-telling, in looking at the heavens through a telescope and in making incantations to the Devil. He did not pursue his interest in the occult, as many did, in order to make mischief or do harm; he was possessed of a restless curiosity, a certain naivety, and too much leisure. In his quest for knowledge he stepped on to dangerous ground. His activities with Feuquières smacked of godlessness. Louis XIV, irritated, and beset by anthrax in his neck, frowned at his turbulent nephew. Mme de Maintenon piously prayed for his salvation.

King Charles II of Spain died on 1 November 1700. Speechless, stone deaf, suffering from attacks of dizziness and nausea, the wretched man was sub-jected to grotesque attempts at treatment. Freshly killed pigeons were placed on his head, the steaming entrails of slaughtered animals on his stomach, but it was hopeless. With him the Spanish Hapsburg dynasty came to an end. When the contents of his will were revealed, it set Europe by the ears.

Charles II left the immense empire of Spain to the seventeen-year-old duc d'Anjou, second son of the Dauphin, and grandson of Louis XIV. If the duc d'Anjou did not accept the crown it would go to France's deadly rival, the Archduke Charles of Austria. Louis XIV was faced with a crucial decision. If he accepted on behalf of his grandson, there would be war in Europe. Austria would not accept that France and Spain should be ruled by the Bourbons and would certainly go to war. But if Louis refused the throne of Spain, the Hapsburgs would rule the greatest empire the world had ever seen, and France would have to fight. In all probability, the English and the Dutch would be drawn in. It was the most important decision of Louis' reign.

On 9 November there was a tense meeting of the King's council at Fontainebleau which lasted for seven hours. There was another during the evening of the next day. Mme de Maintenon was present at both, with the

Dauphin, the Chancellor, Pontchartrain, the duc de Beauvillier and Torcy, the Secretary of State for Foreign Affairs. Opinions were divided. The Dauphin, who rarely spoke at all this time was adamant: his son must take the throne; it was his by right of birth. Others argued against. Louis XIV recognised the difficulty of his position, commenting, 'I am sure that, whatever decision I make, many people will condemn me.' Then, having weighed all the options, he decided: the duc d'Anjou would go to Spain as King Philip V, even though another war was now a certainty.

The explosive news was to be kept secret until the court returned from Fontainebleau to Versailles on 15 November. But Madame heard the rumour on the 12th; 'People went whispering to each other yesterday, "Don't tell anyone, but the King has accepted the crown of Spain for the duc d'Anjou." ' Monsieur, who saw the implications for himself and his son, immediately raised a protest against the omission of his and his son's name in the will of Charles II, and signed a declaration, with Louis' assent, affirming that this omission could not deny the rights of his family. This act served to put the Orléans family ahead of the Hapsburg Archduke Charles, and immediately after the duc de Berry, the duc d'Anjou's younger brother, in the line of succession to the Spanish throne. It would later prove a significant move.

At Versailles the King of France presented the King of Spain to the courtiers. For the next three weeks there were two kings at the court with all the attendant difficulties of ceremonial. The duc d'Anjou, King Philip V, who now outranked his own father and his elder brother, gravely accepted the turn of events, being a young man who rarely showed emotion. He seemed only dimly aware of the momentous change in his life. The rest of the family were more sensible of the drama.

Monseigneur, when he heard that his son had arrived at Meudon, came rushing in from the garden all out of breath. 'I see one must never swear to anything,' he exclaimed jovially. 'I could have sworn I would never make myself short of wind coming to meet my son, but here I am.' He seemed oblivious to the prophesy that he would be son of a king, father of a king, but never king himself. Monsieur, who was in Paris when the announcement was made at Versailles, had been instructed to break the news at a certain time, and was so excited that he stood under the clock in the salon of the Palais-Royal until the moment came for him to do so.

Two weeks later, on 4 December, Philip V left Versailles for Spain. Louis XIV waited for him to arrive in Madrid, six weeks later, all the time observing the Emperor's reactions. When he observed the Austrians preparing for war, he made some pre-emptive notes of his own. At the beginning of February 1701 he sent to *parlement* letters registering the right of Philip V or his male descendants to the throne of France in the event of the death of the duc de Bourgogne without male heir. This was a bold challenge to Europe, as the will of Charles II had specified that the two thrones would not be united. Then five days later he marched French troops into the Spanish Netherlands and took possession of the fortified places. Namur, to the resignation of its inhabitants, became French again. Perhaps Louis thought that the English and the Dutch would accept the fait accompli, and sit by as he and the Emperor settled their differences. After all, both countries had recently recognised Philip V as King of Spain. But if he thought so, he was wrong. During the summer of 1701 the English, Dutch and Austrians renewed their alliance – warlike manoeuvres began.

Louis XIV began to select his generals for the inevitable campaigns. Boufflers would go to Flanders, Villeroi to the Rhine. The duc de Bourgogne was told that he would command in Germany and it was announced that the duc de Chartres would also go. But the announcement concealed an elaborate plot. Louis did not want Philippe to go, either because he worried that he would outshine Bourgogne, or because he was angry about Philippe's behaviour. (Philippe had managed to annoy the King even further when Christine Desmares presented him with a daughter, who was born at almost the same moment as his wife gave birth to her fourth girl.) Louis counted on Monsieur refusing to allow his son to go the front unless he was named commander-in-chief. But Monsieur raised no objection. Louis was forced to reveal his true intention: that Chartres should not join the army in any capacity. Philippe stayed at home under a cloud.

Monsieur was beside himself. He asked the King what was he to do with his son, who was bored with walking the halls at Versailles, with being married as he was, and of living all unprotected while his brothers-in-law, the duc du Maine and the comte de Toulouse, were honoured with appointments, governorships, establishments and position, all, as Saint-Simon put it, 'without reason, without policy, and without precedent'. My son, said Monsieur, is in a worse condition than anyone of his age in France, held back while others serve and are given promotions. 'Idleness is the mother of vices,' Monsieur continued, with the voice of experience. 'I am most unhappy to see my only son abandon himself to *débauche*, to bad company, and to folly, but it is cruel to have him treated so.'

The King tried to mollify his brother; Monsieur asked that Philippe be made commander-in-chief. Louis refused. They both sulked. The King and Monsieur kept their distance from each other after this. For the first time that the courtiers could remember, Monsieur stayed away from court. Philippe witnessed the argument with chagrin. He decided he must explore the possibility of going to Spain to offer his services to the new King. He was desperate for a position, for an opportunity for *gloire*. To forestall him, Monsieur approached his brother once again, lunching with him at Marly on Wednesday 8 June 1701. When the King arrived, he immediately set about attacking the duc de Chartres; not content with fathering children on Florence and Christine Desmares, Philippe had now gone too far. He had begun an affair with Marie-Louise de Séry, a lady of his mother's household, and had made her pregnant. The King was out of patience with his son-in-law's behaviour. Actresses were bad enough, particularly when they gave birth to sons, and the duchesse de Chartres did not. But, by flaunting Marie-Louise, Philippe was insulting not only his wife, but also the King.

Monsieur, equally furious, reminded his brother acidly of his own behaviour. Had he not been flagrantly unfaithful to his wife for years? Had he not forced her to endure the presence of his mistresses in her carriage and at her table? The conversation approached the dangerous topic of Mme de Maintenon, whom Monsieur had never been able to abide. Monsieur quickly moved on to his son. Philippe had been promised marvels at his marriage, but nothing had materialised. 'I passionately desired that he serve in the army,' Monsieur complained, 'and I have tried to make him give up his *amourettes*. But I have no intention of preventing him from amusing himself.'

After this stormy lunch Monsieur returned to Saint-Cloud. He was very red in the face, seething with rage. That night after dinner, taking a liqueur with the duchesse de Bouillon and other company, he suddenly started to stutter and gesticulate. At first they thought he was speaking Spanish, as he sometimes did. But then he fell back unconscious into the arms of his son. They shook him, walked him, bled him, gave him emetics, but there was no sign of life. A messenger was dispatched to Marly at once. But the King, still upset with his brother, did not rush to Saint-Cloud; he consulted Mme de Maintenon and then merely ordered that his carriages should be ready if Monsieur worsened. An hour and a half later the duc de Chartres sent an aide to say things were indeed worse. The King left Marly at three in the morning.

At Saint-Cloud there was no hope. Monsieur was comatose. The ladies who had so recently been gossiping with the dying man, the duchesse de Bouillon, the duchesse de Ventadour and her sister the duchesse de La Ferté, the boyfriends, the members of the household, were all in disarray. Père du Trevou was at the bedside, causing some hilarity: 'Monsieur, do you not recognise your confessor? Do you not recognise good little Père du Trevou?' Madame, roused from her room somewhat tardily, was shrieking, 'No convent for me! No one speak to me of convents!'

The next morning, when it was clear that Monsieur would not recover, Louis heard Mass before preparing to return to Marly. As he was leaving, Philippe, overcome with grief, knelt at his feet and said, 'Ah! Sire, what shall become of me? I have lost Monsieur and I know that you do not love me.' The King, touched, gently gave the young man his assurance that he would be well treated.

Monsieur died two hours later and Louis' doctor, Fagon, took the news to the King. 'Eh bien! Monsieur Fagon, my brother is dead?' 'Yes, Sire, there was nothing we could do.' Louis wept, tried valiantly to eat with the ladies as usual, but had to retire with Mme de Maintenon until the evening, when he went for a walk in the gardens. Stoically he worked with Chamillart, the Minister for War, and with Pontchartrain, and then gave his orders for the ceremonial of the funeral. He went to bed early. The next day he seemed quite recovered; he was heard singing opera prologues, and later he ordered the duc de Bourgogne to start playing cards in the salon. 'Cards!' exclaimed the duc de Montfort. 'You cannot think of it yet! Monsieur is still warm.' 'Excuse me,' replied poor Bourgogne, 'I have thought a great deal; but the King wishes that no one be bored at Marly and, afraid that no one would dare start to play, has ordered me to set the example.' A short time later the salon was full of gaming tables.

Mme de Maintenon, meanwhile, was inflicting exquisite pain on the distraught Madame. She indicated to Philippe that it was time for his mother to be reconciled with the King, by which she meant with her. Graciously, Madame sent word that she would be delighted to receive Mme de Maintenon in her rooms at Versailles. When Mme de Maintenon arrived Madame offered her a chair, they exchanged compliments, and then Madame commenced to say that she had never given the King any reason to be displeased with her. In silence Mme de Maintenon pulled a letter from her pocket. It was one of Madame's to Aunt Sophie discussing the concubinage of Mme de Maintenon, the foreign policy of the King and the misery of the Kingdom. With this in hand, Mme de Maintenon proceeded to bring up all the insults directed at herself over the years – all taken directly from Madame's own letters which for years had been opened by the king's spies, at the Bureau des Postes. It was an appalling moment.

Mme de Maintenon savoured her triumph coldly and at length; 'it was a terrible humiliation for such a proud German princess', as Saint-Simon noted. Eventually Mme de Maintenon relented, as she had intended, having taken all her revenge. The two women embraced and promised to forget everything and begin a new friendship. This they never did, but a truce was declared. The two women could never like each other, but their relationship became more polite.

On the death of his father, Philippe had become duc d'Orléans and a wealthy man. The King, perhaps feeling a little guilty over his role in Monsieur's death, treated him with prodigious generosity. His pension amounted to three quarters of a million livres. He inherited all the privileges of his father; an escort of Swiss Guard and companies of Gardes du Corps and Household Cavalry, with their own guardroom in the château of Versailles. He had his own Chancellor and Procureur général and was granted the right to nominate his own candidates for church appointments on his own territories, except for bishops. He became the owner of the Palais-Royal, Saint-Cloud, Villers-Cotterets and other estates. (Despite all this wealth, part of Monsieur's huge collection of jewels had to be sold to pay his enormous debts.)

Madame was allowed to keep her pension from the King of 250,000 livres. And her son was generous, adding a further 200,000 livres a year from him. She was not ungrateful, telling her half-sister Ameliese, 'It is rare to find a son who loves his mother and does not scorn her after his father's death, so my son has more merit in this respect than you may think.' Although it was suggested she retire for a time to the abbey of Maubuisson, where her aunt was abbess, she went to Versailles and refused to budge. She brought her two old friends, the maréchale de Clérambault and the comtesse de Beuvron, back to court from the exile to which Monsieur had consigned them and resumed her letter-writing, with a little more circumspection.

From now on, in the new spirit of reconciliation, Madame was allowed to join the King in his *cabinet* after supper along with the other members of the royal family. She was given a tour of Marly: 'The King came to meet me and took me for a walk. He has made many improvements since I was last here; there is a new bowling alley, so shady that one can play at high noon without feeling the sun. We made a tour of the entire garden, and climbed a small hill to see the new waterfall ...' She settled into widowhood without too much regret.

# ❧ 5 ❧

# WAR AGAIN

'And so ended this year, 1701,' wrote Saint-Simon, 'and all the happiness of the King with it.' By installing his grandson on the throne of Spain, Louis XIV had ignited a fuse which would lead to war, and he knew that France would have to fight almost alone against most of Europe. At the end of the year, Louis also recognised James Edward Stuart as King of England on the death of his father, the exiled James II. This recognition went specifically against the Treaty of Ryswick, and was an insult to King William. England had already decided to ally herself with Austria, but Louis had now made her more enthusiastic for war.

With hostilities undeclared, the winter season at court seemed particularly dazzling. Balls, masquerades, ballets and concerts continued at Marly and Versailles. Chez Mme de Maintenon there were intimate theatricals, with members of the royal family, instructed by the famous actor Baron, taking the leading roles. As there was room for only forty spectators, invitations to these performances were much prized.

In January 1702 Racine's *Athalie* was performed there, with Philippe playing the part of Abner and the duchesse de Bourgogne Josabeth. Soon after, Mme de Maintenon graciously sent Madame a ticket for a performance of *Absalom* by Duché, in which her son played the part of King David. 'I should have thought my son's voice was too rough to sound well on the stage,' she reported, 'but it sounds splendid. I had already been told that he's not a bad actor, but I never dreamt he could be so good.' The play was followed by a little comedy by J. B. Rousseau in which Philippe played a swindler. Philippe had a good voice; he had already sung in Lully's *Alceste*, and in motets before the King.

And he continued to paint, even though he had to wear *petites lunettes* to do so. He studied with Antoine Coypel, who was at work decorating the ceiling of the gallery in the Palais-Royal. He took his easel out into the gardens of Versailles; later he decorated his wife's boudoir with scenes from *Daphnis and Chloë*. In 1705, when Charles de La Fosse was painting the cupola of Saint-Louis-des-Invalides, he climbed up the scaffolding to have the technique explained to him.

Painting and composing paled, however, beside passion. For the first time in his life Philippe was seriously in love, with Marie-Louise Madeleine Victoire Le Bel de La Boissière, Mlle de Séry. She was the twenty-year-old daughter of a diplomat, a dark, imperious beauty; 'pretty, *piquante*, with a lively, sulky, capricious and agreeable air.' Having been placed in Madame's household by her distant relative, the duchesse de Ventadour, she had soon come to the attention of the susceptible Philippe. Within a short time of their first encounter, Marie Louise was pregnant and installed in a pretty house near the Palais-Royal.

But even a grand passion could not make Philippe forget that France would soon be at war, and that he might have an opportunity for glory.

There had been some sporadic fighting in Northern Italy in the autumn of 1701 as Prince Eugène of Savoy took the offensive against the French. Prince Eugène was one of the most brilliant generals of the century, and should, by rights, have been fighting for the French, not against them. The younger son of the comte de Soissons and his wife, Olympe Mancini, he had been brought up at the French court. On his father's death (poisoned by his wife as the rumours insisted), Prince Eugène's position had become precarious. His mother fled the country, he and his brother were passed over for promotions and positions, so the disappointed Eugène left France and offered his services to the Emperor. After defeating the Turks at Zenta in 1697, he quickly became a hero. Bent on avenging himself for the insults he had suffered at the French court, he had moved into Italy, in alarming proximity to his cousin, and France's uncertain ally, the Duke of Savoy.

Even more ominously for France, on the death of the English King William III in March 1702, Queen Anne appointed the aggressive and capable John Churchill, Duke of Marlborough, as commander-in-chief of her armies. Marlborough could not wait for the opportunity to show his mettle. The Grand Alliance of England, Austria and the Netherlands declared war on France and Spain on 15 May 1702. Louis XIV chose his commanders, trying to balance the need to send a royal prince with that of providing a competent general. The duc de Bourgogne, who was now twenty years old, had to be sent on his first campaign. He was to 'command' in Flanders with the experienced Boufflers 'under' him. To protect the Spanish territory of Milan, and bar the way south, the duc de Vendôme was given the command in Italy. This was a blow to Philippe, as to the prince de Conti and Monsieur le Duc, the Princes of the Blood; they had felt for a long time the King's preference for his own bastards, and for Vendôme, who was descended from Henri IV and Gabrielle d'Estrées. The duc du Maine was sent to Flanders and the comte de Toulouse took up his position as Admiral of the Fleet. Philippe received no command. He was mortified.

Vendôme was twenty years older than Philippe, the son of Laure Mancini, and thus another cousin of Prince Eugène. He was a good general, popular with the troops, but filthy, lazy, debauched, vainglorious and arrogant; Vendôme was notorious for giving his orders while seated on his *chaise percée*. 'He was', wrote Saint-Simon, 'pride itself, a pride which wanted everything, devoured everything.' His homosexual adventures were legend; the result was the necessity to undergo the *grande opération* for syphilis twice. The first time he left the court with an aquiline nose, but returned pug-nosed; the second time he lost half the pug nose and all his teeth, his face so changed he looked like a simpleton. (The *grande opération* for syphilis used mercury salts and was very toxic; it stimulated saliva but inflamed the mucous membranes, loosened the teeth and corroded the gums.)

This disreputable Prince launched his campaign well in Italy, defeating Prince Eugène at Luzzara on the Po in August 1702. The King of Spain, who had sailed to Naples, and was making a stately progress through Italy to show his confidence in his allies there, participated in the battle of Luzzara, displaying a perfect imperviousness to fire. But away from the field of battle he was agitated and morose. He had married Marie-Louise of Savoy, sister of the duchesse de Bourgogne, at the end of 1701, and was suffering a great deal in his separation from his young wife. Refusing any commerce with other women on religious grounds, he was maddened by his ungratified desires. His entourage was alarmed at this first manifestation of Philip V's lifelong mania for sex.

Philippe, on the other hand, found himself at the side of his wife as she held her first court at Saint-Cloud since the death of Monsieur. He was trying to behave better and gain Louis XIV's approbation, but was finding it difficult to suppress his boredom and longing for Mlle de Séry. His habits were too firmly acquired; 'le pli de la débauche était pris' (the habit of dissipation was well established). One benefit of his attempt at reform was the re-establishment of his friendship with Saint-Simon, who had served in the army, married and started a family, just as Philippe had done. But the two men were less close than they had been. While Philippe preferred the delights of Paris, Saint-Simon was intoxicated with life at court, even though he was never favoured by Louis XIV. Frustrated with his career in the army, which was leading nowhere, he had left the service in April 1702, claiming ill-health. The King never forgave him. From then on Saint-Simon remained at court on sufferance, never invited to Marly, passed over for every ambassadorship or official post. He turned to his journal with increased appetite.

Invited to Saint-Cloud with his wife, Saint-Simon was transported by what he saw. 'The company was well chosen, the diversions and amusements continual, M. le duc d'Orléans and Mme la duchesse d'Orléans presided over this beautiful place with dignity, the opulence and the relaxed air made our stay most enjoyable and for the first time one could see Saint-Cloud without embarrassment.' The chevalier de Lorraine was gone, the pretty boys with him. Best of all, Saint-Simon and Philippe rediscovered their intimacy. 'Everything passed with such good grace on his part', exulted Saint-Simon, 'that I thought I was back at our old Palais-Royal.' Their friendship resumed, with the proviso, on Saint-Simon's part, that they would see each other at court, but never in Paris, where the raffish inhabitants of the Palais-Royal, and the ménage with Marie-Louise de Séry, offended the Duke's sense of propriety.

Philippe had become an armchair critic of this war in which he had no part; he claimed to foresee every calamity that occurred and did not spare the unlucky generals. If he had been in command he would never have chosen to fight in such a place, would have employed quite different tactics, would have been victorious. His friends were men out of favour in the army, such as Vendôme's own brother, the Grand prieur, and the ageing Feuquières. They were all too ready to criticise and ridicule. Men Philippe regarded as idiots were given important commands; men he respected were ignored. His frustration was extreme.

Philippe's first legitimate son was born at Versailles on 4 August 1703. When he went to the King at Marly to ask for permission to give the child the name of duc de Chartres, and the honour of being the King's godson, Louis asked if that was all he wanted. Philippe said that his staff had wanted him to ask for more, but that he felt it would be presumptuous. Well, said the King expansively, I give your son the pension of the First Prince of the Blood, that is 150,000 livres. Philippe was suitably grateful. The court chronicler, the marquis de Dangeau, reports that the King said he hoped the infant would bear the title as worthily as his father had done, a remark which led some to suspect irony. But Louis XIV rarely joked, especially about his family. Whatever indiscretions Philippe had committed, at this stage he was still *persona grata* with the King, although not to the extent of being trusted with command.

His eyes were most closely on Spain. Philip V had finally recognised his rights of succession to the Spanish throne. Philippe began to entertain notions of a future there. Perhaps Philip V would have no children, nor the duc de Berry; and thus perhaps he, Philippe d'Orléans, would found the dynasty of Orléans in Spain. These were dangerous thoughts. He shared them with very few.

The dominant influence in Madrid was not the King but a formidable, sixty-year-old Frenchwoman, Anne Marie de La Trémoïlle, princesse des Ursins. Mme des Ursins, widow of an Italian prince Orsini (thence Ursins), had been handpicked by Louis XIV and Mme de Maintenon to act as governess to the Queen, who was only thirteen when she married Philip V. She had become indispensable to the royal couple and, having surrounded herself with men who owed everything to her, had become the ruler of Spain. Philip V was born to be ruled. 'God has given His Majesty a subordinate spirit,' wrote the marquis de Louville, who had known him since he was a child, 'and, if I dare say so, a subjugated one.' The King's day was ordered by the Queen; if he wished to change the time of his hunt or his pall-mall, he was obliged to send his equerry to ask her permission. At the end of the day he was told what had been decided in his name. The French shook their heads over this royal abject.

In 1704 Philippe was sufficiently emboldened by the stories of Philip V's feeble character to demand a role in Spain. The Archduke Charles, the Austrian claimant to the Spanish throne, was preparing to land in Lisbon, courtesy of the British fleet, and an attack on Spain would surely follow. But Louis XIV was not ready to trust his nephew. The Duke of Berwick, son of James II of England and Arabella Churchill, nephew of the Duke of Marlborough, was sent instead. Saint-Simon described him as 'cold and taciturn, always very much in control of himself, with the talents of a great courtier.' He was also a competent general.

While the French were on the defensive in Spain, decisive action was being taken in Germany. The Duke of Marlborough was on the move, marching south from the Low Countries. To the astonishment of the French, he marched his army two hundred and fifty miles into the heart of Europe to rendezvous with Prince Eugene near him. The French went in pursuit.

As the armies approached each other in the heart of Europe, Madame was at Marly: 'the weather is perfectly beautiful ... the forest is full of cowslips and violets; together with the young foliage this gives a wonderful smell to the air. The woods are full of nightingales ...' The mood at court was optimistic. In June the duchesse de Bourgogne gave birth to a son. This was an occasion for rejoicing, as she had miscarried a year earlier.

The King gave a party at Marly for the newborn duc de Bretagne and the courtiers outdid themselves in celebrations. Bontemps, the King's valet de chambre, organised a fête at Versailles with the theme of Mars visiting the earth; the gilded façades of the château were so brilliantly illuminated that the *Mercure galant* said it looked like the palace of the sun. On 9 August there was a performance of Philippe's opera *Penthée*. And at Marly on 12 August an illuminated *arc de triomphe* appeared at the end of the gardens with the words 'Pour Adélaïde' written in the sky. As the festivities continued, the court did not yet know the dreadful news of the battle of Blenheim, which had been fought on 13 August.

The Duke of Marlborough had destroyed the French army, using his cavalry to deadly effect. When the battle was over there were almost forty thousand French killed, wounded or taken prisoner. The French Commander Tallard was among the captives. Marlborough, exhausted and proud, scribbled a note to his wife on the back of tavern bill: 'I have not time to say more, but to beg you will give my duty to the Queen, and let her know her army has had a glorious victory. Monsieur Tallard and two other generals are in my coach...'

As a sombre prelude to the news of the débâcle at Blenheim, Louis XIV learnt of the loss of Gibraltar to the English on 18 August. Then three days later, news of the catastrophe came to Versailles. Louis learnt that Tallard's entire army had been taken or lost, while the general himself was missing. The court went into mourning. 'One can judge the consternation,' noted Saint-Simon, 'where each great family, without mentioning the others, lost a loved one, dead, wounded or prisoner.'

After Blenheim, the King angrily disbanded some regiments and punished some officers. But, determined as usual to put on the bravest possible face, he ordered that the celebrations for the birth of the duc de Bretagne go ahead as planned. On 27 August there were fireworks at Meudon. The next day Monseigneur, the duc and duchesse de Bourgogne and the duc de Berry watched from the Louvre as a more costly fireworks display erupted over the Seine; the theme was the Seine victorious over the rivers of Europe. It was a profoundly depressing event, perhaps prefiguring the death of the child eight months later.

With the terrible French losses and the incompetent leadership, Philippe's frustration grew. Condemned to perform such vital duties as entertaining the Duke of Mantua at Versailles, he could perhaps forget, as he listened to Couperin's music, sung by the composer's cousin Mlle Couperin, that his talents and energy were being squandered. He must have read with pleasure the song which went the rounds after Blenheim:

Tout un peuple alarmé n'a plus qu'une espérance,
Prince; à mille plaisirs livre tes jeunes ans,
Reçois plus que jamais la Séry, la Florence;
Dans l'état ou l'Anglais vient de mettre la France,
On ne peut trop avoir de bâtards d'Orléans.

(A whole people in alarm have only one hope;
Prince, give over your young years to a thousand pleasures,
Take up with la Séry, la Florence;
In the state in which the English have put France,
We cannot have enough bastards of Orléans.)

Philippe judged the generals at Blenheim responsible for the disaster. Louis XIV was more forgiving. When the duc de Duras died in October 1704, his post of governor of the Franche-Comte was given to Tallard, known by then to be a prisoner in Nottingham. This huge favour to a man who had been so badly defeated caused a scandal at court. The duc d'Orléans commented impulsively that, after all, it was necessary to give something to a man who had lost everything. His words greatly displeased the King.

Philippe turned to other pursuits. He had a new interest, and was busy setting up a laboratory at the Palais-Royal fitted with a large 'burning glass', ovens, and all kinds of apparatus. Instructed by his doctor, Guillaume Homberg, a jovial German, he had become intrigued by chemistry and the wonders of empirical observation. But, being the contradictory man he was, he was also plunging into séances, fortune-telling and various mystical happenings with Marie-Louise de Séry and her friends. Disappointed and bored, he had given up hope of playing a part in the war. Then his luck changed.

# ✄ 6 ✄

# ITALY

As he prepared for the campaigns of 1706, Louis XIV was faced with the necessity of protecting all the frontiers of France. The Allied forces were in Flanders, the Archduke was in Barcelona, and Prince Eugène was in Northern Italy. While Flanders always remained the most crucial theatre, Louis considered the situation in Northern Italy almost as important. The formidable Prince Eugène was on the way there, intending to join up with the Duke of Savoy in Turin, and take the Spanish territories around Milan. (The Duke of Savoy had been a French ally, but in 1703 had defected to the other side, despite being the father-in-law of both the duchesse de Bourgogne and the Queen of Spain.)

Louis decided to order Vendôme back to Italy to stop Prince Eugène's advance; he also decided to lay siege to Turin to keep the Duke of Savoy at bay. To command the siege, he chose the duc de La Feuillade, son-in-law of the War Minister Chamillart. It was a poor choice; this 'well-beloved son-in-law of an all-powerful minister' was not proven in such a difficult enterprise. Saint-Simon thought little of any of the generals that year; he considered them all 'généraux de goût, de fantaisie, de faveur, de cabinet', and no doubt the duc d'Orléans, confined to the sidelines, thought the same.

The King must have felt as discouraged as his critics. His own family were particularly disappointing soldiers. Louis had long since recognised the utter futility of sending the Dauphin to war; the duc du Maine had revealed himself as unfit, and now it was becoming clear that his grandson, the duc de Bourgogne, was not a natural soldier. Bourgogne was kept at home after two undistinguished appearances in the field. The risk of his being involved in a major defeat was too great.

Vendôme was at Marly in February 1706, hugely fêted, promoted to maréchal général. When he attended a performance of Lully's *Roland* at the Opéra in Paris, put on expressly for him, the audience gave him an ovation at the beginning and end of the opera, clapping and shouting 'Vive Vendôme!' Vendôme's confidence was infectious; he convinced Louis XIV that he could easily hold off Prince Eugène while La Feuillade took Turin.

Louis watched Vendôme depart for Italy with some optimism. And on arrival at his headquarters near Mantua, the general did indeed justify the King's expectations, attacking and defeating a strong Imperial army at Calcinato on 6 April. Unfortunately, he did not have long to savour his victory. Prince Eugène arrived the next day and re-established matters so speedily that Saint-Simon lamented that 'we could not reap any reward for our success'.

Meanwhile the French army in Flanders was preparing to go on the offensive. The maréchal de Marcin went to the Moselle to join up with Villeroi. The orders were clear: nothing was to be done before this junction was made. But Villeroi was too hasty and chose to give battle. The duc d'Orléans, watching every detail with a jaundiced eye, told everyone who would listen that Villeroi would be defeated. He knew the terrain, it was near Neerwinden, and he said that Luxembourg would never have fought there. The battle of Ramillies proved him right. Villeroi's army of sixty thousand men fought bravely, but the Duke of Marlborough was the superior general. After a cannonade of two hours, Marlborough sent in his cavalry, wheeling them round almost to right angles from their original position, breaking the French line. 'I have five horses to two!' he exclaimed, himself in the thick of the battle. The French lost fifteen thousand men, as well as all their guns and baggage; the Allies lost five thousand.

The battle was fought on 23 May; Louis XIV heard the first news three days later in a long, confused letter from Villeroi. Then came six interminable days without another courier. The consternation at court was so great, and the delay in news so agonising, that Chamillart himself set off for Flanders to find out what had happened. When he returned to Versailles five days later, it was with terrible news. Marlborough had occupied Antwerp, Malines, Louvain and Brussels, and nearly all the barrier fortresses which Louis XIV had seized. Only Namur and Mons remained in French hands. Villars, fuming on the Moselle, had to abandon plans to penetrate Germany. When Villeroi returned to court, Louis XIV seemed sympathetic. 'Monsieur le maréchal,' he sighed, 'we are no longer lucky at our age.' But the King was so clearly uncomfortable with his old friend that Villeroi, 'an old burst balloon, from which all the air had been let out', as Saint-Simon put it, soon left court for his country estates.

The situation in Flanders was so perilous that Louis XIV turned to his best general, transferring Vendôme from Italy to the north. Vendôme was delighted. Now that Prince Eugène had arrived, the situation in Italy was deteriorating. Vendôme knew he would be regarded as a saviour in Flanders even if he won only modest victories.

As Vendôme prepared to depart, so did his entourage, including an Italian abbé named Alberoni, who had been in the suite of the Bishop of Parma, sent as envoy to Vendôme in 1702. Vendôme chose to receive the Bishop while sitting on his *chaise percée*. Midway through the exchange of compliments, he proceeded to rise and wipe his bottom. The Bishop, disgusted, left at once. Alberoni, when treated to the same spectacle, had the presence of mind to exclaim, 'O culo di angelo!' and hastened to kiss the said behind. He made himself useful to Vendôme, particularly for his introduction of cheese soups into the diet of the household. From his role of 'buffoon and chef of soups and strange stews', Alberoni rose to become Vendôme's principal secretary and confidant. But no one would have thought, on seeing the little abbé trotting after his master to Flanders that summer, that, ten years later, Cardinal Alberoni would be the *de facto* ruler of Spain.

Moving his generals round Europe, Louis XIV needed a replacement for Vendôme in Italy. The duc de La Feuillade was already before Turin preparing the siege; he had sixty battalions, powder, mortars, cannon, everything he needed. It seemed that the French would surely bring the city to its knees; Vendôme's replacement would be required only to keep watch on Prince Eugène. Louis XIV made his decision. The duc d'Orléans would go to Italy.

The news was astounding. Neither the duc d'Orléans nor the other princes dreamt that they would serve. They had lost all hope and no one even considered them possible candidates, for, as Saint-Simon remarked, the King had made clear his extreme repugnance at the idea of his relatives going into the field. So on 22 June at Marly when the King, having given the *bonsoir* to all those in his *cabinet* after dinner, called back the duc d'Orléans, who was leaving with the others, and kept him for a good quarter of an hour, there was great surprise. 'I was enjoying myself that evening in the salon,' says Saint-Simon, 'when the buzz started to sound. We were not in the dark for long; M. le duc d'Orléans, coming out with the King, passed through the salon to go to his mother, returned a moment later, and revealed that he was going to command the army in Italy, that M. de Vendôme would wait for him there and then leave for Flanders to replace the maréchal de Villeroi.' It seemed that the chance for glory was once again at hand.

The fact is that there were not many competent French generals from whom to choose; the duc d'Orléans had once been a fine soldier and was eager to serve. But selecting him to command against Prince Eugène was a risk. Secretly, Louis made sure that Philippe's freedom of action would be limited; he would also send Villars to Italy and it would be Villars who would have the real authority. As far as the court was concerned, however, after ten years away from the field of battle, Philippe d'Orléans, France's best general, was suddenly in high favour.

Full of congratulations, Saint-Simon followed his friend from the salon. When he heard more of the details, he realised that the command was not as glorious a thing as it might appear. Orléans was not to do anything without Villars' advice. Philippe, albeit reluctantly, had given the King his word, 'feeling less the insult than the joy of being at the front when he had given up all hope'. Saint-Simon advised close co-operation with Chamillart, to preserve his political base in such difficult circumstances. He also undertook to write regularly, and in code, to Philippe, giving him the benefit of his advice on strategy and tactics. Gravely the duc d'Orléans thanked him; he made no mention of Saint-Simon's startling lack of knowledge on such matters.

Philippe's rivals and enemies were chagrined. The prince de Conti, bitterly disappointed, was gracious, but Madame la Duchesse, who was playing cards in the salon on the evening of the announcement, did not bother to get up, merely calling to Philippe as he passed that she congratulated him. He made no reply. (Her husband, Monsieur le Duc, who was too unpredictable and impulsive to be considered for a command, was on his estates in Burgundy; in his absence his wife and the prince de Conti had begun a passionate affair.)

Philippe was beside himself with joy. He rushed to put his affairs in order before departing. There were some personal matters he had to attend to before he left, mostly concerning his mistress. Marie-Louise de Séry lived openly at the Palais-Royal, where she ruled the roost and presided over a little court. Advised by her distant relative, the duchesse de Ventadour, she now made her demands, seizing her lover's moment of good fortune to ask for the recognition and the legitimisation of their four-year-old son, Jean-Philippe. The day before Philippe left for Italy, on 1 July 1706, Mlle de Séry, whose address was given as the rue des Victoires, received an annual pension of 25,000 livres on a capital of 500,000 livres which would revert to her son. The boy was recognised as the chevalier d'Orléans. Fearing difficulties in registering the title with *parlement*, and even though he was preparing to leave and was burdened with many problems, the duc d'Orléans went himself to the magistrates and took care of matters*.

His head filled with dreams of glory, the duc d'Orléans prepared to depart. As he was about to do so, there was a startling development. With astonishing arrogance, Villars refused to leave the Rhine for Italy. Such a refusal would have ruined anyone else, and was probably due to the rich pickings available in Germany, for Villars was a noted pillager, but Louis XIV accepted it without demur. He simply ordered the maréchal de Marcin to go in Villars' place. Philippe was told to regard Marcin, not Villars, as his tutor and do nothing without his advice.

This change of plan was critical. Philippe might have trusted Villars, who was an experienced and skilful campaigner. Marcin was a different matter – a better courtier, or rather valet, than soldier. He had a trifling wit, but little judgement or learning, and all his energies were devoted to pleasing, according to Saint-Simon, who adds, succinctly, that the man was a featherbrain.

Marcin, who had played an undistinguished part in the battle of Blenheim, and who had been somewhat traumatised by the experience, no doubt had his own concerns about his task of tutoring an impetuous, high-spirited royal prince, and about the capability of La Feuillade. But he dutifully set off for Italy.

After a long interview with the King at Marly, Philippe left Paris on 1 July. His mother tried to be stoic. 'I admit that I have been made very happy by this,' she wrote to her son-in-law, the duc de Lorraine; 'but my joy was lessened when I saw him leave ... one does not know when one will see each other again, and it's sad to think about.' She also wrote to Dubois, who was accompanying Philippe, asking him to keep her informed of her son's progress. Other members of the party included the comte de Sassenage, his gentleman of the chamber, the marquis d'Étampes and the marquis de La Fare, his captains of the guards, and the marquis de Nancré, in command of the Swiss Guard. His confessor, Père du Trevou, his premier valet de chambre Saint-Léger and his surgeon Lardy were all with their master too.

Philippe set off south with twenty-eight horses and five chaises, making such good time that he arrived at Lyon three days later, and at headquarters outside Turin on 8 July. He was so anxious to get there that he abandoned his chaise for a horse and made his entrance to the French camp at the gallop, with a flourish.

---

* The boy was baptised at Chilly on 8 July and the letters patent registered on the 27th. Philippe was now the father of four legitimate children and at least two others, besides the new chevalier. Charles, the son of Florence, was being brought up by the Jesuits at La Flèche in Normandy, and his daughter by Christine Desmares was at the Palais-Royal.

La Feuillade received him with great pomp before showing him all the earthworks. Philippe was not pleased with what he saw. The siege was being conducted sloppily, the officers doing the minimum in order to show their contempt for La Feuillade, the artillery in poor shape, morale bad. The Duke of Savoy, a traitor to France and Spain, had sent his wife (Philippe's half-sister) and his mother (Vendôme's aunt) away from Turin in the middle of June, to the coast, and had himself left the city's defence to the comte de Thaun. Taking his whole court, his carriages and three thousand horses, leaving only five hundred hussars in the city, the Duke roamed the countryside, hoping to distract La Feuillade from the siege. La Feuillade had fallen into the trap, sending his men after the Duke, leaving the conduct of the siege to his subordinate Chamarande. There were only forty battalions remaining before Turin and they were exhausted and making little progress. Thus the siege works remained undone at Turin. La Feuillade himself was concerned, although he tried to sound confident: 'the length of the lines alarms us; it puts the enterprise in no doubt; but I know how precious time is . . .'

As for Vendôme, having assembled a large force at Castiglione delle Stivere, near Mantua, he had made no effort to bring it to battle. When Philippe joined Vendôme there on 17 July, he was hoping for help and advice. He received little of either. Vendôme was eager to leave. He had allowed Prince Eugène to cross the Po and was not anxious to become involved in a potential disaster. 'Eh bien!' he said, 'they have passed, I can do nothing about it; they have many other obstacles to overcome before reaching Piedmont.' And turning to Philippe: 'Your orders, monsieur, as I have nothing more to do here and I leave tomorrow morning.' Vendôme stayed another twenty-four hours, then hastened away, leaving Philippe in an unenviable situation, Prince Eugène advancing on the one side and La Feuillade precariously placed on the other.

Philippe encamped at Guastalla between Mantua and Parma. He asked the prince de Vaudémont, the governor of the Milanais, for advice on the terrain. Vaudémont, who could have helped him, did nothing. Having started the war as an ally of the Emperor, he had switched his allegiance to the French and proclaimed Philip V at Milan. But his loyalty was somewhat suspect. Philippe did what he could. He sent a company under the comte de Médavy to protect the lines between the two French armies. Seeing the danger of Prince Eugène about to cross the Tanaro, he wanted to position himself between Alessandria and Valenza to prevent such a crossing and, if necessary, to give battle. Marcin overruled him. Philippe returned to Turin, very aware that, with the enemy army approaching, the siege needed to be pressed.

Before Turin Philippe found no progress. The lines were badly drawn, 'very imperfect, very long, very poorly guarded'. Marcin and La Feuillade continued to throw obstacles in his path. Philippe wished to attack, Marcin wanted to await reinforcements from forty-six battalions he had in reserve under the command of the experienced comte Albergotti. Albergotti had been the favourite of the maréchal de Luxembourg and was intimate with Vendôme. A man of sombre mien, cold and disdainful, he was given to spending entire days without saying a word. At the siege of Turin he carried his uncommunicative behaviour to harmful extremes.

In the knowledge of Prince Eugène's approach, a council of war was held at which Philippe urged an attack on the oncoming enemy. 'If we remain in our lines', he said, 'we will lose the battle . . . when a Frenchman waits to be attacked, he loses his greatest advantage, that "impetuosité", those first moments of ardour. . . . Believe me we must march towards the enemy.' His officers repeated: 'We must march.' Voltaire reports that it was at this meeting that Marcin revealed that he had secret orders obliging the duc d'Orléans to defer to him; it was probably only a confirmation of something Philippe already knew, but it exacerbated his frustration. He realised that they had sent him to the army 'comme un prince de sang, et non comme un général'.

He precipitously removed himself from the decision making, declaring that, being master of nothing, it was unjust that he should try to avert the affront which the nation was about to receive. He asked for a chaise de poste and stated that he was leaving. Prevailed upon to remain, he declared he would have nothing to do with the command of the army, but would refer everything to Marcin and to whomever else wanted the responsibility. Such an outburst might seem childish, but it was a cry from the heart. Philippe had not yet learnt to be discreet. He was still naive, and vulnerable. He railed at his fate in the face of older, more cynical men, men who were tired of fighting.

Marcin and La Feuillade appeared to believe that Prince Eugène would not attack. They were wrong. On 1 September he succeeded in linking up with the forces of the Duke of Savoy at Superga, to the east of Turin, having crossed the Tanaro precisely where Philippe had wanted to attack before being overruled by Marcin. That this was not mere coincidence seemed clear when a courier of Prince Eugène's was intercepted with coded letters; these letters, decoded by Dubois, revealed that the enemy knew that the duc d'Orléans' opinion had been rejected. Philippe did not know whom to trust. Had the slippery Vaudémont betrayed him? Or was Marcin, as the French historian Jules Michelet thought, persuaded by the duchesse de Bourgogne to protect her father the Duke of Savoy? Whatever the truth, the atmosphere in French headquarters was sulphurous.

On 6 September Philippe wrote to Louis XIV that, given the opposition of more experienced officers, 'it is not fitting for me, a novice commander, to make such an important decision on my own. I therefore refer everything to them, even though there are difficulties whatever course we take.' That night Philippe received a letter from a partisan telling him that Prince Eugène was encamped at Venaria, to the north-west of the city. This was grave news; it meant that Eugène had swung round the south of Turin and was now in a position to attack.

Philippe himself went to Marcin's tent and tried to make him see the urgency of the situation. Marcin would not budge. After his experience at Blenheim, perhaps he was paralysed by the disaster he saw coming. Perhaps, but less credibly, he had orders to leave Turin alone. In any event he seemed to be in a kind of morbid trance. Wearily, he told Philippe to go back to bed. There would be no attack. Philippe resigned himself to the inevitable. But he was deeply discouraged. When reports started coming in of Prince Eugène's approach, he needed to be roused by one of his men to put on his sword and mount his horse. Philippe eventually responded, but Marcin seemed more dead than alive.

As the enemy drew closer, Philippe sent for the Albergotti's troops, but they did not come. He mixed the cavalry and the infantry and reinforced the first line, still counting on Albergotti. He met with resistance amongst his own officers; when he called up some troops, La Feuillade in person refused to allow them to advance. When an officer of the Anjou regiment refused an order to move, Philippe slashed at him in frustration. The French army was in disarray.

The battle began at ten in the morning. Prince Eugène broke through the French lines with ease. Almost immediately Marcin was taken prisoner. Seriously wounded in the stomach, he died shortly after the battle. (They found on his body a letter which Philippe had written to Louis XIV in which he strongly criticised Marcin's conduct; Marcin had been given it for comment before Philippe sent it on. After the battle it was returned to the duc d'Orléans, who then sent it sadly to the King.)

With Marcin a prisoner, La Feuillade became distraught, incapable of giving any orders. Philippe took charge; 'he performed miracles', noted Saint-Simon, 'always in the thick of the battle, with a cool courage', and was lightly wounded in the hip and more seriously on the left arm just above the wrist. When things became grave he called on his officers by name, shouted encouragement, and himself led the charge. Finally, weakened by loss of blood, he was forced to retire; but he soon returned to the place where the fighting was fiercest. A débâcle was in the making.

Some valiant officers charged at the head of their men, but most were discouraged and defeated. Saint-Simon said that the officers were more interested in taking away their plunder than in fighting.

At the end of the day Turin was open to the Duke of Savoy, who entered his capital in triumph. La Feuillade retired, leaving Philippe to make provision for the light artillery and munitions. Having restored the situation as best he could, Philippe gathered the officers around him and delivered his opinion that they should cut off the retreat of Prince Eugène's army, which was beginning to make its way back towards Milan, and make a junction with the French army under Médavy which was near Mantua. La Feuillade and the other generals, however, preferred not to go forward, but to move back to the fortress of Pignerol where, they asserted, the Duke of Savoy had left provisions and supplies.

Outnumbered, the duc d'Orléans nevertheless gave the order to move forward and told Albergotti to follow. The mood was tense. The officers were reluctant to follow the orders and hesitated. In utter frustration Philippe announced he was tired of arguing and that he commanded them to march forward. He himself marched a little way, but, exhausted and in pain, had to climb into a chaise de poste. The troops followed him so reluctantly that Philippe stuck his head out of the window and insulted the nearest soldier roundly. As Saint-Simon, who no doubt heard it from Philippe himself, noted: 'the duc d'Orléans reproached him with his mistress whom he called by name and telling him that for all the good he was doing on the field of battle, he should have stayed with her'.

When the bedraggled French army arrived at the bridge across the Po, a messenger from Albergotti arrived with the news that the passes ahead were occupied by the enemy and that it was impossible to go on. The officers agreed that it was madness to advance without provisions; in rage and despair Philippe collapsed back into his carriage. Instead of regrouping and moving towards the enemy, the French struggled back to Pignerol in the hope of finding food and supplies. But the warehouses at Pignerol were empty.

The decision had to be taken once again; to go forward towards the enemy or to retreat. Philippe remained convinced that the best course was to repass the Po and make for Alessandria or Casale. There they could link up with the other French army. Once again he was overruled. Utterly defeated, he allowed himself to be taken back to France. The retreat through the mountains at night was filled with confusion. Carriages were pillaged and lost, many men deserted. When Philippe arrived at the mountain village of Oulx on 14 September, he learnt that Médavy had won a great victory over the enemy at Castiglione. The victory came too late. Milan fell on 25 September, soon followed by Pavia, Lodi, Tortona, Cremona and Alessandria. Prince Eugène and his forces controlled Northern Italy.

Philippe heard the news with chagrin, but he had more immediate problems. 'I find here nothing to give the men, not even a quarter ration of bread,' he told Chamillart. In great pain from his wounded arm, he took to his bed, weeping with frustration. 'I found His Royal Highness in bed in despair at the course they had made him take,' noted Albergotti, 'with only sixty sacks of flour in the town, the troops living on boiled wheat, some vegetables and grapes . . .' Albergotti and La Feuillade quarrelled at his bedside and had to be thrown out by Sassenage. La Feuillade wrote piteously to Louis XIV asking permission to join Médavy in Italy to expiate his failure, but was recalled to Briançon.

In this awful situation Philippe mourned the loss of friends. The abbé de Grancey, his almoner, 'a mediocre priest, but a very brave and very good man', had been killed two steps away from him. The comte de Roucy remarked that, if the abbé had known he had been killed on the field of battle, he would have died of joy. Villiers and La Bretonnière, Bonnelles and Mursay, brother of Mme de Caylus, all dead. Poor Mursay, who had a horse called Isabelle and a valet called Marcassin, and a wife who wouldn't sleep with him on Sundays.

Philippe sent the marquis de Nancré to Versailles with news of the débâcle. In some suspense about his reception, Nancré was relieved to find Louis XIV disposed to be generous to his nephew, allowing the court to sense that the duc d'Orléans was not responsible for the catastrophe. 'I do not believe', said Saint-Simon, 'that there is another example of a man being so greatly praised after such a complete defeat.'

Madame had suffered a great deal through all this. Before the battle her worries seemed slight: 'If my son gains as much weight in Italy as M. de Vendôme did, he will soon approach my size.' With the lack of news and then alarming rumours, she had trembled for her son. When the battle was done, and it was clear he was not in danger, either from his wounds or from the court's censure, she gave expression to her joy. 'I would far rather die myself', she wrote, 'than live in fear for your life, my dear child!' Philippe was also consoled by a touching letter from his eleven-year-old daughter, Marie-Elisabeth: 'I have wept for my dear papa and I would still be weeping if they didn't tell me every day that your wounds are not dangerous . . .'

Madame said she had heard the King say that the loss of Turin was not Philippe's fault, but his own for putting Marcin in charge. Even Mme de

Maintenon remarked that heroes in novels did not take courage as far as the duc d'Orléans had done.

Despite the warmth at court, Philippe had been in the lowest of spirits following the disordered retreat into France over the Alps. Not only was he wounded and sick (he was being given opium for his wounded hand and Chirac, the French army doctor, had considered amputation), bitterly disappointed and humiliated, but Médavy's victory over the enemy near Mantua contrasted very markedly with his own defeat, the results of which were the complete loss of Italy to the Allies. How sweet then to discover that his adored Marie-Louise de Séry, chaperoned by Nancré, had arrived in Grenoble, having left Paris as secretly as possible in a chaise de poste.

Nancré, having delivered the bad news to the court, had wasted no time in setting off again with Marie-Louise. A chevalier de Quincy observed the party arriving near Grenoble and took the women for actresses as they were wearing so much rouge. Philippe himself had not yet arrived in Grenoble when he heard the news that Marie-Louise was there; we are invited to believe that he was displeased to hear this and sent word that she should leave. That was not her intention. And so, when he arrived, Marie-Louise and her party were let into his rooms by the back stairs. They stayed some five or six days. Unfortunately the King, Madame and of course Saint-Simon were unamused. 'This ridiculous journey caused a great scandal,' noted Saint-Simon, going on to assure us that the public were annoyed at this blemish on the Duke's glorious reputation.

Philippe stayed in Grenoble hoping to make another sortie into Italy and working hard at preparing an expedition. A thousand mules were assembled in Provence and Languedoc; money, horses, arms and eight thousand tents were readied. He wrote to Chamillart: 'I must beg and demand at the same time, for I am so occupied with this business, and the world turns its back on Italy. I shall bring shame to those who grow soft in the King's service.' But Louis had lost Italy and realised that the enemy had a force there superior to his. At the end of October the Prince was told to return. He bowed to this necessity, as he told Chamillart, 'only as one gives in to death', and added, 'I must look to the future for consolation.'

On 8 November at Versailles the duc d'Orléans was received by the King, who was in bed having taken medicine. His welcome was warm. Madame was full of maternal affection: 'his poor wounded hand has made everyone pity him, and his poor countenance has given me pain'. She worried that he would lose the use of three fingers on his left hand. But then, 'since he started to play tennis, his hand is much improved, to such a point that he can move all his fingers and play the flute'.

Saint-Simon visited him on the day he arrived. He wasted no time in criticising his friend for the 'miserable voyage' of Mlle de Séry. Philippe admitted his folly, but remarked with a perceptible shrug, 'It's true, but is there anyone who has never made a mistake?' He blamed La Feuillade for his rashness before Turin, but said he had tried to protect him from the full force of the King's wrath. However, when La Feuillade did eventually arrive at court, he no sooner appeared on the threshold of the King's room than he was greeted with the words, 'Monsieur, we are very unfortunate, the two of us!' and the door was shut in his face.

Philippe returned to Marie-Louise, his laboratory, tennis and playing the flute. He was in great good humour, introducing the court to the joys of Corelli and Scarlatti. 'The duchesse de Bourgogne does not like Italian music,' Mme de Maintenon told Mme des Ursins, 'but her husband and the duc d'Orléans find it very much to their taste, which is good; when one becomes used to it, other music sounds dull.' Despite the losses in Italy, Philippe was in a happy position; he was now at last a serious figure, both militarily and at court.

Louis XIV had given him every indication that he would receive a command in 1707. His eyes turned at once to Spain, where Philip V and the princesse des Ursins were in a better position than might have been expected. Although the Archduke Charles had advanced from Barcelona and forced the King of Spain to flee Madrid for a time earlier in the year, the Duke of Berwick had recovered the situation, and the Archduke had been compelled to return to Barcelona. The question for 1707 would be how to sustain the success and drive the Archduke out of Spain. Philippe thought he had the answers.

# ❧ 7 ❧

# SPAIN

A t Versailles, as the year 1707 opened with the usual winter balls and theatrical presentations, there was cause for rejoicing, despite the military reverses. On 8 January a son was born to the duchesse de Bourgogne; the birth of this prince, called the duc de Bretagne, third in line to the throne after Monseigneur and the duc de Bourgogne, was an occasion for celebration, even though the King forbade any extravagance. The festivities for the birth of the duchesse de Bourgogne's first son in 1704 had been costly; and that little boy had died before he was two years old. This time the fireworks were replaced by sober thanksgiving.

Soberly too, Louis XIV chose his commanders. Villars to Germany, Vendôme to Flanders. And the duc d'Orléans to Spain. Despite the unfortunate results of the campaign in Italy, Louis XIV clearly felt that his nephew deserved another chance at command. Philippe had shown qualities of leadership of which the King stood in dire need. He would now be given a chance to show what he could do in another critical situation, this time with full powers, with the Duke of Berwick under him.

The task of the duc d'Orléans would be to drive the Archduke Charles from Barcelona, to subdue the rebellious provinces of Aragon and Valencia, and to keep the hostile Portuguese at bay. This was difficult political terrain; Aragon, Valencia and Catalonia were privileged enclaves, where the King had to negotiate taxes and troops, and where the grandees had much power and influence. Philip V was bent on an unpopular policy of centralisation, reducing the power of the grandees. To do so in the midst of a war was a difficult enterprise, requiring political acumen as well as military might. Louis XIV must have known that it would be hard for Philippe to keep out of the political arena, but he decided to take the risk.

On the ground, there were reasons for cautious optimism: the inhabitants of Madrid had not supported the Archduke when he entered the city in 1706, and his mostly Protestant army was unpopular. But the challenge to the Bourbons in Spain remained formidable.

Philippe's appointment dismayed the other princes, in particular the prince de Conti, who was still languishing at court in perpetual disgrace. Conti had always thought of Philippe as a novice and had never bothered to get to know him. Now that the younger man was on the path to glory, glory he felt he deserved for himself, Conti despaired. His circle, in particular his mistress, Madame la Duchesse, would never forgive Philippe for his advancement. And as Madame la Duchesse was the wittiest, most malicious of women, she would use every opportunity to denigrate and blacken the name of her lover's rival and her own brother-in-law. Believing that in the next reign, that of Monseigneur, she would be able to dispose of affairs, this dangerous woman determined to destroy a potential competitor. Her weapons would be calumny, libel, malice and mischief.

Insouciant in the face of such hostility and the gravity of his new responsibility, Philippe did nothing to calm the feverish atmosphere at the Palais-Royal, where he and Marie-Louise de Séry had become fascinated by supernatural doings, holding séances and calling up the spirits. Under the influence of his mistress, Philippe indulged in the titillation of trying to predict the future, laying the foundation for later accusations of unbridled ambition and 'a thirst to rule'. His mother was irritated: 'I would be very relieved if my son took leave of his spirits.' Madame thought this foolish behaviour, ill befitting her son's rank and dignity, and blamed his mistress and her disreputable friends. Considering the good opinion of the King indispensable to Philippe's future success, she shuddered at the thought of Louis' reaction to these faintly sinister goings-on.

The King was not in a tolerant mood. In February he had banned a book by the maréchal de Vauban, in which the author proposed the 'dime royale', a revolutionary new kind of taxation, applicable to everyone, including the nobility. Vauban's book had been printed at Rouen 'without privilege' and without the name of the author. These precautions were necessary, as printers, bookbinders and gilders were all strictly controlled. Permission to publish a book had to be obtained from the police or someone chosen by them to issue a permit. The printer had to attach a seal to each book and pay a fee. If these permissions were not secured the book risked being banned and the author imprisoned. The result, predictably, was a rising tide of songs and poems passed from hand to hand in manuscript, and books printed abroad, usually in Holland, or 'without privilege'.

Philippe would have been interested in Vauban's book, as he was already curious about politics, and intrigued by new ideas. But he was more occupied with preparations for his next campaign. His departure from France was not without drama. The King and Mme de Maintenon were most concerned in the composition of his suite; they clearly felt that the events at Grenoble should not be repeated in Spain, and at first forbade Nancré, whom they blamed for the Grenoble imbroglio, to accompany his master to Spain. Nor did they want Dubois, whom they thought too likely to interfere in politics. The King interviewed Philippe on the subject, asking him whom he proposed to take. When Philippe mentioned the name of M. de Fontpertuis, the captain of his hunt, a good tennis player and a friend of Charles de Noce, the conversation took an odd turn. 'Comment, mon neveu!' exclaimed the King. 'Isn't he the son of that mad woman who followed M. Arnauld everywhere, that Jansenist? I wish nothing of that for you.' Philippe responded, 'Sire, I know nothing about his mother, but the son is no Jansenist. Actually, he doesn't even believe in God.' 'Really,' mused Louis XIV, 'and you're sure? If so, there's nothing wrong; you may take him with you.' Philippe found this hilarious and repeated the story to everyone at court. Fontpertuis joined the entourage.

Then Philippe was almost kidnapped by the enemy. Madame described the drama:

> Yesterday thirty enemy officers from Courtrai came to near the pont de Sèvres and kidnapped the marquis de Beringhen. If my son's journey had been for tomorrow, he would have been there, alone with an equerry in a chaise de poste, and he would have been taken like Monsieur de Beringhen ... This is an insolent strike. They had resolved to take a prince, and not to depart until they had at least a *cordon bleu*. It is mere chance that it was Monsieur de Beringhen who was taken, but they could not have struck a bolder blow. Monsieur le Dauphin had gone to Meudon without an escort and returned the same way. If these men had done as well as they did at Sèvres they could have taken him.

Surviving kidnap attempts, the seditious ghosts of the Palais-Royal, and the King's disapproval, Philippe took leave of Marie-Louise on 1 April, having installed her in a little house in the Neuve-des-Bons-Enfants, next door to the Palais-Royal. Marie-Louise was his wife in everything but name; his relationship with the duchesse d'Orléans was purely one of form – he no longer even shared her bed. After the birth of the duc de Chartres in 1703, there had been no more children.

\*

In Spain the news of the appointment of the duc d'Orléans was greeted with some alarm. The princesse des Ursins would be on her guard. The other Frenchman who ruled Spain, the Ambassador Amelot, an upright and competent diplomat, did not want a reckless Bourbon prince disrupting his carefully laid plans for a docile centralised Spain. The duc d'Orléans would be closely watched.

The Spanish King was an exceedingly strange man. Melancholy, grave and reserved, he was tormented by his need for sex and by his fear of sin. His wife, Marie-Louise of Savoy, was a girl of charm and intelligence like her sister the duchesse de Bourgogne, and she soon became the ruler of her husband. Mme des Ursins ruled them both. She was particularly occupied this spring with the health of the Queen, who was pregnant for the first time.

Whatever the princesse des Ursins thought about the duc d'Orléans, she showed nothing but pleasure at his coming. She offered to help him find suitable accommodation and to furnish it with 'chairs, desks, tables, mirrors, fire-irons', as well as ridding the tapestries and beds of fleas. She told him she hoped she could help with more important matters when he arrived. She fondly recalled the friendship the Duke's father had always shown her. No mention of the fact that the duc d'Orléans had reclaimed his rights to the Spanish throne or of the rumours swirling about that he would interfere in the internal affairs of Spain. She left that to Amelot; he wrote to Louis XIV, who warned Philippe to stay out of any matters other than purely military.

Finally Philippe was on his way. As befitted a royal prince, he was accompanied by a large entourage, including his First Gentleman of the Chamber, his Captain of the Guards, his Master of the Wardrobe, his Captain of the Swiss Guards, Nancré, to whom the King had withdrawn his objections, and the controversial Fontpertuis, as well as valets, servants and soldiers. But the King had frowned on Dubois; he considered the abbé too likely to encourage his master to take an interest in politics, and that would be particularly inappropriate in this campaign. They travelled south through the early spring full of enthusiasm and martial ardour. Philippe was in a hurry to get to a country where he hoped greatness awaited him. He was intensely curious, full of hopes and dreams. His good humour was apparent even when he received from his mother a song with insulting implications which was circulating among his enemies:

> Gendre et neveu de ce grand Roi,
> Vous allez donc paraître
> Encore une seconde fois;
> Vous vous ferez connaître...

(Son-in-law and nephew of this great King,
So you are going to appear
Yet a second time;
You are going to make yourself known...)

Philippe merely laughed, remarking that the song wasn't badly written and was pleasing enough. 'I forgive them.' His confidence was high, yet his journey was not without its problems. He was delayed a week because of civil unrest in Cahors, where troops meant for Spain were diverted. New taxes were the cause of riots, not only in Cahors, but in Quercy and Périgord. The peasants complained that they already paid the taille and the capitation, the dime to their priests, the dues to their seigneurs, they could pay no more.

In fact France was almost bankrupt. Chamillart, who was Finance Minister as well as War Minister, was resorting to desperate measures, including 'assignats', paper money. The resources for 1708 were devoured in advance. Exhausted and overworked, Chamillart handed the Finances to Desmarets, Colbert's nephew. But the essential reforms were not made; he did not, as Michelet put it, 'make those who possessed the land pay for the defence of the land'.

When Philippe and his party reached Bayonne they were obliged to halt and pay a courtesy call on the Dowager Queen of Spain, Mariana of Neubourg, who was living in exile there. This was one of those occasions, so common in the time of Louis XIV, fraught with problems of etiquette. What sort of chair should Philippe sit on, who should greet whom, at the door or on the steps? And so on. When he was given an armchair in the presence of the Dowager Queen, it meant that his rank as a Prince of Spain was being recognised. Philippe should have refused the armchair and sat in a chair without arms; once he accepted the armchair, however, the King of Spain dared not complain. The armchair meant that when he arrived in Spain he would receive all the honours of an Infant of Spain.

Philippe arrived in Madrid 'on a mule with very long ears' on 18 April, almost three weeks after leaving Paris. He was received with acclamation and lodged at the Alcazar with the King and Queen. Everything compared very unfavourably with the court of France. Madrid was still a medieval city, with narrow, stinking streets, teeming with monks and nuns, and religious of all kinds, sealed in a Castilian mist of empire, ruled by sloth and foreigners. As Philippe submitted to the endless visits of ceremony, he quickly perceived the dominant influence of the princesse des Ursins and her wary welcome to him. He found the nineteen-year-old Queen charming, the King vacuous and reclusive. But he was longing to leave the city and join the Duke of Berwick, who was preparing for battle at Almansa, north-west of Alicante, on the road from Madrid to the sea.

Even though Philippe stayed in Madrid for only three days, he was too late for the battle which followed. On 25 April the enemy attacked; Berwick had to engage. He recorded a victory over the Anglo-Portuguese forces in a matter of hours. It was a typically cosmopolitan affair, the French army being led by an Englishman, the Duke of Berwick, the English forces by a French Protestant, Henri de Massue, Lord Galway, who lost an eye in the battle. Berwick took eight thousand prisoners. It was a most significant victory; now Valencia lay open to the Bourbon cause.

Philippe once again cursed his ill-luck. He was crushed by his missed opportunity at Almansa but was gracious in his disappointment, writing to Louis XIV: 'I have had the misfortune to arrive here a day too late despite every effort I could make. I cannot prevent myself from telling Your Majesty that, if the glory of M. de Berwick is great, so too is his modesty, and his courtesy, in which he goes so far as to apologise for giving battle when the enemies attacked and for recording a victory as complete as he did.' This was handsomely put. Philippe does seem to have developed a regard for his 'big English mule', as he called Berwick, although they did not always agree. Berwick, labouring under the burden of being the Duke of Marlborough's nephew, was prudent and cautious to a degree, Philippe the opposite. Often Berwick would disagree with a course of action proposed by Philippe. But if that action were resolved upon, no one would be a more loyal and dedicated follower than he. This phlegmatic Englishman, not very entertaining perhaps, but sure, competent and trustworthy, was one of the men with whom the duc d'Orléans would most willingly go into battle.

The news of Almansa arrived at Marly on 5 May; Madame was sorely tried when she and the court heard of her son's absence from the battle. The courtiers took pleasure in whispering to each other as she passed, 'I wasn't there . . . I wasn't there.'

Philippe turned his attention to putting down the revolt of the provinces of Valencia, Aragon and Catalonia. These provinces had traditionally enjoyed certain freedoms with regard to the crown, such as needing the consent of the Cortes to make subsidies to the King or for new laws or military recruitment. In 1701 Philip V had gone to Barcelona, the capital of Catalonia, and confirmed those freedoms. But in 1705 the Catalans sought and received aid from England and proclaimed the Archduke Charles King of Spain. Supported by Valencia and Aragon, they started a civil war. Philippe concentrated on bringing the rebels to heel. It was not an arduous campaign. 'The city and the kingdom of Valencia, Madame, are at last subdued,' he told his mother in May. 'This is a pleasing country full of orange trees, jasmine, pomegranates, all kinds of fruit; in a word, very different from the awful country through which we passed to get here.'

He proceeded to move north against the rebellious inhabitants of Aragon; at the end of May he took Saragossa, the capital of Aragon, in a bold pre-emptive strike. But he moved too slowly for the court at Madrid, who wanted action. Mme des Ursins remarked sourly that he had done almost nothing in Aragon. The Princess and Amelot did not want Philippe as a warlord in their own country, gaining popularity and prestige. And they were suspicious that he had some sympathies with the rebels and with their wish to maintain their ancient liberties of constitutional courts. They disapproved when he used his own authority to pardon the inhabitants of Saragossa and appointed his own magistrates there. Amelot was particularly displeased when Philippe wrote to him regretting that the provincial nobility, which had tried to remain loyal to the crown, could not be treated with respect. He disagreed with Madrid's policy of rushing to impose the laws of Castile upon the conquered provinces, advising caution. This was not at all in accord with Amelot's policy of control from the centre (the Neuva Planta). At the end of June, in a move advised by Louis XIV, the regional *fueros* (charter rights) were abolished. Not for the first time, Philippe was out of step with the powers that be.

He remained an energetic commander, always careful of the well-being of his men. Lacking all kinds of supplies, he wrote frequently to Chamillart to complain that he had to act as chief provisioner and treasurer of his army as well as its general, but that he was determined to maintain the crown on the head of the King of Spain. He also wrote to Saint-Simon, who was giving him the benefit of tactical advice in coded letters; to his friend's idea of marching his army across Spain to Portugal to confront the Allies there, Philippe replied that it was an excellent one for an army of non-eaters and non-drinkers.

At thirty-three Philippe was at the height of his powers. There is a portrait of him dating from this period showing him on horseback in a blue costume trimmed with gold, proudly holding his baton. Under a towering dark wig he is the picture of confidence and pride. Philip V presented a sad contrast; superstitious and timid, he was an uninspiring leader. But there were reasons to think he could survive: his wife was pregnant and he might hope for an heir, and he was a zealous Catholic, as were his subjects. Gradually his base of support widened, greatly helped by the duc d'Orléans' energy and charisma.

After taking Saragossa, Philippe prepared in July to move on Lérida, the gateway to Barcelona. But, as preparations were made, Louis XIV ordered Berwick to hasten to Provence with half the army to ward off an attack on Toulon from Prince Eugène and the Duke of Savoy with an Anglo-Dutch fleet. The attack on Lérida had to be postponed. On 11 August Philippe recounted his difficulties to his mother:

> Yesterday I was ordered to release some twelve battalions for Provence. I had no gunpowder or cannon, a bagatelle I ignored in order to take Aragon. Now they have denied me pontoons and even bread; I have still managed to cross rivers and take Monzon. At Monzon I found some cannon and I have now managed to find pontoons and bread. But because everything comes from the hands of God and no glory is given to man, they have taken everything away again ... Alleluia! I am sorry for bothering you with these follies but I must find something to joke about in order not to give in.

As usual, he continued to find humour in moments of crisis. But in his more serious moods, he complained about the influence of the princesse des Ursins on military affairs. His mother clearly heard a great deal on this subject, for she in turn complained about women at the head of regiments: 'When the Devil can't come, he sends an old woman,' she remarked cryptically. No doubt the veiled reference would not have been lost on her son.

After weeks of torrential rain, Philippe managed to begin the siege of Lérida on 13 September. Berwick returned and, to Philippe's irritation, counselled patience before any attack. Philippe complained, although with good humour, about Berwick's slowness and obstinacy, 'a saint would lose patience and unfortunately I am not yet altogether a saint'. At the same time Mme de Maintenon and the princesse des Ursins were blaming the unfortunate Nancré for the apparent misunderstandings between the two generals.

Before Philippe turned all his energies to the capture of Lérida, he made a request of the princesse des Ursins which he must have known would be refused and which would indeed irritate both courts. He asked that Mlle de Séry be given a post of lady-in-waiting to the Queen of Spain. Perhaps he wanted her to have the title, so that she could call herself Madame instead of Mademoiselle; perhaps he was simply missing her a great deal and wanted her to have an official reason to join him. Perhaps the lady herself had suggested the idea. But after the incident at Grenoble he must have foreseen the reaction.

Mme des Ursins replied, somewhat disingenuously, that she would be only too delighted to offer the post to Mlle de Séry, but that of course she must ask Louis XIV. Mme de Maintenon reacted with horror. Acknow-ledging that she would seem like 'a pious old lady, frightened of sin', she deplored the idea; 'her journey to Grenoble and his weakness in shutting himself up with her, destroyed all the credit he had won at Turin ... she is ruining this Prince altogether by distancing him from the court and making him spend his life with the worst company in the world ... you, Madame, understand perfectly that, even in evil, there is some behaviour more honourable than another'. The King delivered a categorical no from Fontainebleau in October.

Philippe, suffering from a bad cold and a fever, dosing himself with quinine, took the news in his stride. He continued to besiege Lérida, helped by the maréchal d'Asfeld's skill in provisioning and supplying the army; the town fell on 11 October and the duc d'Orléans turned his attention to forcing the citadel to capitulate.

He was much admired for his tireless energy and leadership qualities. Saint-Simon was overjoyed for his friend: 'His natural manner, the kind-ness with which he responded to everything, the clearness of his orders, his attendance night and day at the labours of the men ... his insistence on inspecting everything himself, his skill in foreseeing difficulties, and the money of his own he had 'given to those officers who needed it, made him adored, and provided the will necessary to make this difficult enterprise successful.'

Whatever suspicions and complaints the court at Madrid might have, Philippe had won significant victories in the face of great difficulties, and the French court approved of his actions. Mme des Ursins kept her worries about his sympathies for the rebel provinces to herself. But she and Amelot resolved to keep the Duke under close surveillance.

Meanwhile Philippe heard gratifying news from home. The King had invited his twelve-year-old daughter, Mademoiselle as she was now known, to sup with him at Versailles and come to his *cabinet* afterwards. The girl probably did not have much fun; 'everyone just eats away as in a mon-astery', recorded Madame, 'without saying anything, except perhaps a whispered word to a neighbour', but the invitation was a great honour. Only Sons, Daughters, Grandsons and Granddaughters of France ate at the King's table. The *cabale* of Meudon, Madame la Duchesse and the Princes of the Blood were alarmed by this mark of favour, coming on top of Philippe's military successes.

After Lérida, Philippe was eager to press on to Tortosa, but Berwick's prudence prevailed and Louis XIV agreed. Philippe told Louis XIV, 'I always distrust half-measures and it seems to me they suit neither side'; but he submitted to the King and to Berwick. Dubois told him he must get along with the latter as he was now popular in France; he also advised him to be moderate in his eating and drinking: 'Princes must fast as well as beggars.' Dubois sounded curiously like his mother; neither of them had the slightest effect.

On 30 November the duc d'Orléans returned in triumph to Madrid, where he attended the long-delayed baptism of the heir to the throne. The Queen had given birth to a son in August, but all celebrations had been postponed until the return of the armies. Philippe played a leading role in the ceremonies and, as always on great occasions, was the epitome of elegance, wearing a grey velvet coat trimmed with gold and studded with diamonds, which had just arrived from Paris. The ceremony itself was of the utmost magnificence. The priceless old tapestries of the royal collection were brought out to decorate the palace; a wooden staircase with a silvered iron balustrade was built to connect the Prince's apartment to the chapel. Cardinal Portocarrero led off the procession in a sedan-chair covered in gold, preceded and followed by a cortège of churchmen, gentlemen and pages. Six grandees each carried an important object: a spittoon, an *aiguière*, a basin, napkins, a little coat and a tall candle. After them and surrounded by his household came the duc d'Orléans in his grey velvet and diamonds. Next followed a sedan-chair decorated with mirrored panels and golden brocade in which Mme des Ursins carried the Prince. The baby was solemnly baptised Luis after his great-grandfather the King of France.

Philippe assisted at various meetings of the council of war, demanding that the King of Spain take financial responsibility for the troops the following year, claiming that he had spent 800,000 livres of his own money. On 18 December he left for Paris, 'superbe et triomphant', arriving at Versailles on the 30th in time for the King's Lever. 'His reception by the King and society was worthy of his happy and agreeable campaign,' noted Saint-Simon. He spent a long time along with the King, and then the courtiers, observing his high favour, greeted him as a hero. He went immediately to work on the problems of supply with the King and Chamillart, managing to obtain a promise of three million livres to equip the Spanish army, and a million livres' worth of wheat and oats to be sent to Valencia next spring. The rich banker Samuel Bernard was persuaded to deliver 600,000 livres each month by his intermediaries in Spain.

With these practical matters taken care of, Philippe turned his attention to Marie-Louise de Séry. 'My son may as well be abroad as I see little of him,' grumbled Madame. 'This girlfriend is a nuisance and not even pretty. My son did better at war than he does in Paris. To put it poetically, the myrtles of Paris obscure the laurels of Lérida.' But Louis XIV was inclined to turn a blind eye to his nephew's indiscretions, and even Mme de Maintenon remarked that, no doubt to her own surprise, she felt for Philippe 'great esteem and great tenderness'.

# ℀ 8 ℀

# DANGER IN SPAIN

Philippe spent less than two months in France at the beginning of 1708 before returning to Spain. He was preoccupied with the organisation of supplies and grand strategy. While Monseigneur gave supper parties at Meudon, followed by trips to Paris for the Opéra, while Mme du Maine played in *La Mère coquette* by Quinault at Clagny, he closeted himself with Chamillart and the King at Marly. Mme de Maintenon told the princesse des Ursins that he was working actively to assure the subsistence of the French troops, and praised his application.

He did pause long enough to commission Antoine Coypel to decorate the house he had given Marie-Louise de Séry in the rue des Bons-Enfants, overlooking the gardens of the Palais-Royal. Here, on the ceiling of the grand salon, Coypel painted a delicious *Gods of Love Expel the Higher Gods from Olympus*, in which Diana, Pan and Venus supplant Jupiter, Apollo and Hercules. It was, by all accounts, the depiction of a joyous surrender to the power of love and, according to the marquise d'Huxelles, 'a rare thing to be seen'. The ceiling, in its subject matter, was a step in the direction of Boucher and the Rococo, and yet the very idea of a painted ceiling was regarded as rather antique. In his artistic tastes, as in so many ways, Philippe was a man of two centuries*.

Philippe set off once more on the road south. As he departed, the French court were looking towards England. A vast and secret enterprise was being launched against that country, which Louis XIV hoped would change the course of the war.

Since September 1707 Louis XIV and his ministers had been planning

---

* The King also appreciated Coypel's work; in 1708 he gave him the commission to paint the central part of the ceiling of the chapel being built at Versailles. Coypel painted *The Eternal Father in his Glory*, while La Fosse painted the Resurrection in the cupola of the apse. And so while his work for Philippe has vanished, one can still see Coypel's work in all its vivid energy and grandeur at Versailles.

an invasion of Scotland, led by James Edward Stuart and intended as a bold diversion from the war on the European mainland. At the end of February thirty vessels were armed and ready at Dunkirk and neighbouring ports. Four million livres were sent to Flanders to pay troops and six thousand men dispatched to the coast. The twenty-year-old Pretender was advised by experienced French generals; it was hoped that he would find support among the Catholic Scottish Highlanders, disaffected as they were with the recent Act of Union with England. Representatives from Scotland had been secretly in France for several months.

On 6 March James Edward left Saint-Germain. Almost at once there was bad news. The British fleet, which French planners had thought was somewhere off Portugal, turned up near Dunkirk. The invasion force had to be hastily disembarked, then re-embarked. Then Stuart developed measles. Finally, only half recovered, he set sail at six in the morning on 19 March. The news of his coming was by now hardly a secret. During the night a furious storm blew up, scattering the French fleet. One ship made its own way up the Firth of Forth to Edinburgh; she found no sign of the rest of the fleet, but many people waiting expectantly on the banks. When the French fleet finally hove into view, it was pursued by twenty-six huge British warships. There was no way of effecting a landing under such circumstances. The fleet was then chased back to France with the loss of a warship and several transports. One French commander was taken prisoner and sent to Nottingham to join Tallard, still imprisoned there since Blenheim.

One month after he set out, Stuart and his battered fleet were back at Dunkirk. When he came to Marly the mood was sad. 'I am delighted to see you here in good health,' Louis XIV said, but I must confess that I am not happy to see you here at all.' Three days later the duchesse de Bourgogne miscarried. The King's temper worsened. 'Has she not already a son? And if he dies is not the duc de Berry old enough to marry and have children? And what do I care who succeeds me! . . . I shall no longer be prevented from doing what I want by doctors and matrons. I shall come and go as I wish, and have some rest.' The courtiers, who never saw Louis XIV lose his composure, were dismayed. It was clear that the failure of the Scottish enterprise was a major blow. In fact the King had hoped that a rising in Scotland would be accompanied by a similar uprising in the Spanish Netherlands, thus enabling the French forces to sweep through the Low Countries. It was not to be.

Philippe had had difficulty travelling south in wintry weather. 'He has had a cruel journey, and tells me he thought he would be stuck in mud and snow,' wrote Madame. 'It would be cruel if after so much trouble he could do nothing for the King's *gloire* and service. My God, shall we never have peace? ... My son does not speak of his plans, but one of his people wrote and told me that he thought he would pursue the resolution of the siege of Tortosa ... it seems to me he has *bon courage* and has adopted the proverb "Be bold in adversity". The ministers must believe my son a little divinity, able to make something out of nothing.'

In Madrid, Orléans found no trace of the millions he had been promised, nor artillery, carriages or food. He set about finding supplies, but his prolonged stay in the capital caused malicious gossip at the French court that he was in love with the young Queen of Spain. The rumours were spread and embellished by Madame la Duchesse, eager to besmirch the reputation of this upstart rival to her husband and her lover.

Then at a rowdy dinner with his colleagues, Philippe, 'a little tipsy and still upset about the lack of supplies', took a glass to make a toast and, regarding the company, said 'Messieurs, I drink to the health of Captain Cunt and of Lieutenant Cunt.' Within half an hour the word had reached the princesse des Ursins and very shortly thereafter Mme de Maintenon. Saint-Simon dates the beginning of Mme de Maintenon's implacable hatred for the Prince to this 'fatal word', but that is an exaggeration. Mme de Maintenon did not suddenly become hostile to the duc d'Orléans, although she must have been deeply shocked. As for the princesse des Ursins, she was always suspicious of his political activities and their relationship had already deteriorated.

When he realised that the word of the insult had got back to Mme des Ursins, Philippe did try to make amends. He told her not to pay attention to 'fine speeches, very *mal à propos*', and he went further: 'I can say truthfully that in the course of my life I have paid scrupulous attention not to say things which would cause me to repent. This is sufficient to make you see, Madame, how you should take similar speeches another time.' The Princess was not appeased. The relationship between them was irretrievably poisoned.

Philippe began his campaign near Tarragona, planning to drive north to Barcelona; his forces, on the lookout for provisions, took as many cows and sheep captive as they did rebels. They were short of everything; their supplies of wheat had been intercepted at sea by the English fleet. Despite the difficulties, his mother remarked how popular her son seemed to be, although 'I cannot understand his good humour considering all the troubles he has.' Marching through Aragon, he was succeeding in driving the Archduke, and the Allied forces under the command of Lord Stanhope, back to Barcelona. Slowly, he approached the strategic city of Tortosa, which he would have to take in order to open the way to Catalonia.

Tortosa was besieged on 15 June. Despite the shortages of equipment and the rocky terrain, the city fell to the French after only light skirmishing on 11 July. There were few casualties, and it was a clear-cut victory followed by successful harrying of the forces of the Austrian general Starhemberg. Madame was delighted, 'truly touched with his glory'. Once again she could rebut the malice of the court: 'I wish you could have seen the faces of M. le Duc and the prince de Conti,' she wrote to Sophie, 'they couldn't have looked more morose if someone had told them they were going to die. This, I admit, has increased my own joy.' Even better: 'The King seemed to me very sensible of the glory of my son. He talked to me about it with a goodwill which charmed me and penetrated me with joy . . .'

It was noble of Louis XIV to remember Madame in this hour of crisis. For the news of Tortosa had arrived at Fontainebleau only four days after that of the cruel defeat at Oudenarde. Although the duc d'Orléans was at the height of his military glory, the French were at the low point of theirs.


Oudenarde was more than a disaster for French arms; it was a humiliating defeat for the royal house. Louis XIV had felt he must, for the prestige of the dynasty, send the duc de Bourgogne to the front. He might have suspected that the young man would not make a proficient soldier, but he announced that Bourgogne would go to Flanders and that Vendôme would be 'under his command'. The duc de Berry, who was already twenty-two, went along with his brother. The princes left on a Friday, considered an ill omen, and there was apprehension among those who knew the duc de Bourgogne. He was no warrior; a pious, timid young man, he clung to his wife and to his confessor, in need of sex and terrified of sin, like his brother the King of Spain.

Bourgogne had never displayed any talent for leadership, but he was at the head of a magnificent army which Saint-Simon described as the best supplied, equipped and provisioned that had ever gone forth. The King's grandson was leading the hopes of the nation into battle. When the battle came, however, the French were in the wrong place at the wrong time. In a surprise attack, Marlborough and Prince Eugène challenged the French army while still in line of march.

Within an hour ten French standards were captured. The duc de Bourgogne, on the sidelines with thirty thousand men, did not come to the aid of Vendôme who was in the thick of battle, but simply watched as the French troops were outmanoeuvred and surrounded. At the end of the day there were six thousand French dead and wounded, nine thousand prisoners. The Allies suffered three thousand casualties. That night the French retreated.

Oudenarde was, as Sir Winston Churchill remarked, 'a specimen of modern warfare which has no fellow in the rest of the eighteenth century'. From the initial decision to attack to the dramatic pincer movement which enveloped the French, Marlborough and Eugène had improvised a remarkable victory. Vendôme was beside himself with fury. He made no secret of the fact that he blamed Bourgogne for the defeat, all but accusing him of cowardice. 'I see, messieurs, that you all think we should retreat,' he said in the aftermath of the battle and then, looking directly at Bourgogne, 'You, monsieur, have wished to do so for some time already.' Writing to Louis XIV, Vendôme could not restrain his bitterness: 'I could never have believed that fifty battalions and nearly one hundred and twenty squadrons of our finest troops would have been content to spend six hours watching us do battle, for all the world as though they were seated in a box at an opera.'

The King was devastated at the thought that his grandson had failed in his duty, but he also knew that he could never publicly admit that a member of the royal family was a coward. Mme de Maintenon delivered the official view to the princesse des Ursins: 'M. de Vendôme, who believes according to his wishes, insisted on fighting a battle; he lost it, and we are in a far worse plight than before.'

She was right. As Vendôme and Bourgogne stood by, too involved in quarrelling with each other to pay attention to the ominous Allied troop movements, Marlborough turned his army towards the French fortress city of Lille, where Boufflers commanded a garrison of fifteen thousand men. Lille was in dire peril.

Despite the King's obvious desire to treat the question of his grandson's conduct with discretion, the court fell to the work of demolishing the young Prince's reputation. At Meudon the *cabale* of Monseigneur mounted a campaign of denigration against Monseigneur's own son. Bourgogne became the subject of a vicious whispering campaign, accused of extreme piety, timidity, and a lack of the 'furia francese'. A letter-writing campaign was orchestrated by Alberoni to defend the duc de Vendôme and excoriate Bourgogne. Bourgogne did little to salvage his reputation. When, at the end of October, Boufflers surrendered the city of Lille and retired to the citadel, the officer sent to inform the duc de Bourgogne of the grave news found him playing battledore and shuttlecock.

The situation of the army in Flanders was so embarrassing that the princes were ordered to return, so that they would not be implicated in the fall of Lille. 'Since the monarchy began,' wrote the maréchal de Tessé to the princesse des Ursins, 'one has never seen a Son of France conduct such an ignominious campaign.'

In Spain the duc d'Orléans heard with horror of the débâcles in Flanders. But he was facing the perils of calumny himself. The slight indications of unhappiness at the court in Madrid ('Why was the garrison of Tortosa not taken prisoner?') began to grow. As early as August Philip V was complaining about Philippe's criticisms of Spanish affairs and his refusal to obey orders. On the 17th of that month Mme des Ursins made mention to the duc de Noailles of 'worries which spoil everything and are ruining most of our affairs'. She had her suspicions that the duc d'Orléans might be indulging in seditious activities; but she had as yet no inkling of what was really going on. If she had known, she would have been incensed. For, five days after her letter to Noailles, Archduke Charles in Barcelona was mentioning that 'Stanhope talks in secret with the duc d'Orléans.'

It is clear that Philippe did have some dealings with the enemy. He and James Stanhope had met a decade earlier when the Englishman had been in Paris and they had attended the same parties. They got to know each other, as the phrase went, 'between the pear and the cheese'. During the summer of 1708 they found themselves commanding opposing forces. Messages were exchanged through intermediaries, in which the possibility was raised that, in the event of Philip V being forced to give up his throne, and as part of a peace treaty, a deal might be done between the Allies and France, which would see Philippe d'Orléans as a future king of a part of Spain. It seems that it was Philippe who broached the matter first; we know that Stanhope sent him a message saying he had received the packet of snuff and liked it. The conversations continued.

At the end of September Port-Mahon, chief city of Minorca, fell to the British. Following reports of the ill-treatment of French troops there, one of Philippe's aides-de-camp, a man called Joseph Flotte, met Stanhope halfway between Tortosa and Barcelona, ostensibly to discuss that matter. What they actually discussed was a possible arrangement between the Allies and the duc d'Orléans; it seems that Orléans was to be offered a kingdom in Navarre if Philip V abdicated. Stanhope said he might defend the interests of the duc d'Orléans at any peace negotiations in Holland. Flotte agreed to arrange a passport for Stanhope to Holland, and took a letter back to the duc d'Orléans.

Orléans was also meeting with dissident grandees. He told Mme des Ursins that he was actually doing her a service in talking to them as it prevented their ill-humour degenerating into something worse. But his disavowal was ambivalent. 'They wish that I act as the Prince of Orange did,' he wrote, 'but that will never happen, at least only if the King of Spain leaves his kingdom.' Flotte also met members of the Spanish nobility and found them impressed with the qualities of his employer. 'They knew Orléans as a man of war, hardworking, intelligent, capable of ruling, very far from following the maxims of the French government, capable of maintaining himself in the independence which alone can ensure the peace of Europe.'

Philippe departed from Madrid at the end of the campaigning season, leaving his private secretary, Regnault des Landes, in Spain to continue his conversations with the grandees and to keep his ear to the ground. He did not know that the princesse des Ursins and Amelot had sent Mme de Maintenon a list of all the things they disapproved of in his conduct, particularly his interest in local politics. Mme de Maintenon had asked for their views and they had hastened to inform her. 'I wish that this Prince had as much firmness with his staff as he does at the head of the armies,' Mme des Ursins wrote delicately. 'They do not hesitate to tell him things which it would be better that His Royal Highness did not hear, and they should not be so well informed as they are; they hear him say things in their presence and repeat them, often against the wishes of their master; for having so much intelligence and goodwill, I know that he regrets it when certain things escape him, things which he knows himself are not appropriate.'

Such criticism would not have concerned him. He was dealing in much graver matters. His contacts with Stanhope were, on the face of it, treason. If he was acting on his own behalf, without the knowledge of Louis XIV, he was in considerable danger. But there is reason to believe that Louis XIV did know some – if not all – of what was going on. The King was anxious to find a way to make peace without giving up on Spain and perhaps thought that the duc d'Orléans would come in useful if Philip V did indeed fall. He hinted to the King of Spain that he might not be able to help him much longer. 'I have always worked to maintain you in the rank in which it has pleased God to place you. You see that up to now I have made the utmost efforts to keep you there . . . and you can be assured that those feelings will lead me as long as the state of my affairs permits . . .' If Lille fell, it was possible that France would have to sue for peace. Louis XIV wanted all his options open, perhaps including that of a partitioned Spain ruled by his nephew.

Philippe returned to court on 7 December and was received 'as handsomely as his glorious and difficult campaign deserved'. He was the only French general to report a victory. His mother was delighted to see him, writing fervently, 'I cannot thank the Lord enough for the blessing of seeing my beloved son again in good health after all the dangers he has passed.' Fortune did indeed seem to be favouring the brave.

# ℀ 9 ℀

# THE END OF THE WORLD

Seventeen hundred and nine was the pivotal year in Philippe's life. He began it at a peak of good fortune, a man of influence and prestige; he ended it in total isolation. The events of 1709 changed everything.

On his return to court Philippe found the King as close to despair as he had ever seen him. The citadel of Lille had fallen. The court was divided into rancorous cliques, with deep hostility between the *cabale* of Monseigneur and the supporters of the duc de Bourgogne. Everyone was calculating their position in the event that Louis XIV, so clearly aged by his misfortunes, departed the scene. Fully expecting to return to Spain, Philippe steered clear of the *cabales* and directed his attention to the delights of Marie Louise, and the frisson of his own intrigues.

During the worst misfortunes, Louis XIV had insisted upon a brilliant winter season at court, but even his courage broke a little at the beginning of 1709. The worst winter for a hundred years paralysed the country. The Seine and other rivers were frozen; even the sea froze. A thaw, followed by a harder frost, destroyed all the fruit trees and many other crops. News of the crop failure sent bread prices soaring. Hunger raged. There were serious riots in Paris. And people died; in Paris alone twenty-four thousand people perished during that cruel January.

At court the problems were different. 'The news is very brief,' wrote the marquise d'Huxelles, 'as the ink has frozen at the end of my pen.' There was a grand ball at Versailles for the Prince of Denmark on Mardi Gras, but there were no other balls at court and only one voyage to Marly as the carriages could not make the journey. Many courtiers suffered broken legs from slipping on the freezing ground. Madame sat in front of her blazing fire, wrapped in sable, her feet in a bearskin sack, but shivering so much that she could not hold her pen. 'There has not been such a winter in living memory. During the last fortnight people have been found dead of cold every morning, and the partridges are picked up frozen in the fields. All the plays have been stopped and so have all the law-suits, for the judges and advocates can't sit in their chambers because of the cold.'

When the Comédie-Française did reopen on 14 February, it presented Lesage's masterpiece *Turcaret*. The play parades decadent nobles, crooked financiers, and knowing servants, embroiled in a plot dark with cynicism but cheerfully insouciant. Lesage had had a struggle to stage his play; it was delayed due to opposition from 'financiers and stockbrokers'. And it received only eight performances, despite a success justifying many more. The authorities were wary of satire at such a volatile time. Only the year before, Paris had been inundated with a pamphlet entitled *New School of Finances or How to Fly without Wings* in which the anonymous author named four hundred financiers guilty of robbing the people and advocated violence against them. 'Quoi! The millions of souls which fill Paris cannot destroy four hundred miserable jumped-up lackeys who continually steal their wallets?' In this atmosphere of hostility, sharpened by the winter famine, *Turcaret* was considered too dangerous. Lesage never wrote for the Comédie again, devoting his talents to the far more free and easy theatres of the Fairs. He announced his decision in the Epilogue to *Turcaret*: 'Let us go to the Fair to see new faces.' Wherever Lesage wrote, he was writing about a world already present, even if not acknowledged officially. On stage, in Paris, the spirit of the Regency had already arrived.

Philippe's year began auspiciously. On 27 January Mme de Maintenon wrote to Mme des Ursins that he had apologised for his 'vivacity and imprudence' of the year before, and had done so with so much charm that she was convinced he was sincere. Encouraged, Philippe took the opportunity to ask Mme des Ursins again to try to persuade Louis XIV to give Mlle de Séry the title of lady-in-waiting to the Queen of Spain. Again he had no success. But the King, in a concession to his son-in-law, did allow Philippe to purchase for Marie-Louise the barony of Argenton in Berry, and she became comtesse d'Argenton.

Philippe now turned all his energies to Spain, expecting to return there very soon. He wrote a detailed memo for Philip V with his plans for taking Catalonia. He wrote to Mme des Ursins of his efforts to raise morale at court and to resist defeatism:

The king's views are lofty, noble and right as usual ... Mme de Maintenon, entirely discouraged, no longer knows to what to have recourse, and the ministers of the same mind are entirely against us. I have spoken to them all in private and have made them recognise fully that they will lose one goal without saving the other, and yet they are in such lethargy that, despite what they know to be true, they cannot resolve themselves to do anything. And to tell you the truth, matters are in such a state that I dare not let you envisage them. That which alone can save us are the monstrous propositions of our enemies.

But at the same time, through those wickedly cold days, he was considering Stanhope's proposition that he put himself forward as a candidate for the throne of Spain, 'if Philip V fell on his own without hope of return'. How much did he and Louis XIV talk to each other about the possibilities for Spain? The British believed that Louis knew what was afoot. Marlborough's view was that 'the Duke of Orleans would not act this part, but that he had the King of France's permission'. And Stanhope himself was clear: 'The judgement I was able to form by all I could gather from what has passed is, that when things went ill for France, that court has indirectly led the Duke of Orleans to believe that it would be no disagreeable expedient to get a peace to let him be King of Spain.'

That February in Madrid Mme des Ursins, hearing the echoes, was distraught. She scented a plot to dispossess Philip V, and she attacked. She started to complain of the lies of those 'with evil intentions', of the ingratitude of those who were obliged to her, the hostility of others. Without yet mentioning his name, she began to look with greater alarm and suspicion at the dangerous duc d'Orléans. She was warned that Orléans had accused her of ill-will towards him, stating that she knew too much about 'many malversations and dangerous intrigues ... only able to ruin Their Catholic Majesties and their crown'. Wounded and threatened, Mme des Ursins began a campaign to prevent Philippe from returning to Spain.

Events began to move quickly. During the winter Philippe had left Pierre Regnault des Landes as his representative in Spain. Regnaut, according to Saint-Simon, was 'a character, full of ingenuity and enterprise, energetic, bold, and intelligent'. He put these qualities to work in his meetings with the Spanish provincial nobility, listening to their grievances against the regime of Mme des Ursins. Mme des Ursins was aware that something subversive might be going on, telling Mme de Maintenon that some nobles were plotting against the King and claiming to have at their head the duc d'Orléans. 'HRH would be very wrong, if I may say so, to show such little recognition for the sincere attachment I have always felt for him.'

This was a very dangerous game for the duc d'Orléans, even if Louis XIV were tacitly aware of his dealings with Stanhope and the Spanish grandees. He could be disavowed as soon as things became embarrassing, thrown to the wolves at any time. But, for Philippe, the chance to act, to have a role, to use his powers to the full, was irresistible.

The atmosphere at court remained grim, while in the country at large it was tragic. After the great cold there were shortages of everything. There were bread riots in Paris and in Burgundy. 'Here you hear of nothing but sadness,' wrote Madame, 'how bread is dearer every day, how people are dying of hunger.' Angry crowds took to the streets, seditious placards were everywhere, and there was a multitude of scurrilous songs and verse attacking the King and the court. The ducs de Bouillon, de La Rochefoucauld and de Beauvillier received anonymous letters reminding them that there were still Ravaillacs (the name of Henri IV's assassin) and praising Brutus. The relics of Sainte-Geneviève were taken through the streets of Paris in the hope of her intercession, but people continued to die.

In March Louis XIV secretly sent one of his most experienced diplomats to Holland to try and negotiate a peace. As the weeks passed, Philippe remained at court along with the other generals. There would be no fighting while the peace talks continued. Then, just before Philippe was due to leave for Spain, Philip V complained in more detail about Regnault's activities. He accused Regnault of plotting with dissident grandees and making promises of money and help from abroad. Philip V said he would gladly keep the matter quiet for reasons of state, but went on to blame the duc d'Orléans. 'The ill-will of this Prince', he wrote, 'has shown itself only too clearly in his words, in public and in private, against two Kings to whom he owes respect. I would like to attribute this behaviour to his frivolousness, but I cannot doubt that he has been involved in plans too serious to ignore.'

Louis XIV clearly found the complaints about Philippe tiresome. He was more concerned with trying to arrange a peace. But he could not ignore the charges, and on 29 April he wrote to Philip V expressing a desire for calm. Although he proclaimed the duc d'Orléans innocent of any wrongdoing, he agreed to keep him in France. Such matters were not uppermost in his mind. The day before he wrote to his grandson he had attended a meeting of the council at which he decided to consent to the withdrawal of his troops from Spain and the dispossession of Philip V. At this meeting he had wept, overwhelmed by the bitterness and humiliation of defeat.

Philippe took stock. Mme des Ursins had prevented his return to Spain, the country to which he had devoted so many resources. But Louis XIV was ready to give Philip V up for the sake of peace. Did this not mean that he himself should persevere in his plans to stake a claim in Spain? If Philip V had to go, and Louis XIV was willing to allow it, was not the duc d'Orléans the perfect candidate to step into the void? And the Allies had already intimated that they would make no trouble.

With or without the support of the King, Philippe took a bold step. He sent another aide to Spain, Joseph Flotte, described as a 'pigeon privé' of the Prince. Flotte's mission, ostensibly, was to repatriate the duc d'Orléans' carriages. His actual instructions were to create a party for the Duke in Spain. He bore a letter from the Prince, dated 5 May: 'Messieurs, I send Flotte to you. You can speak to him as you would to me and trust what he says as coming from me. I shall agree to everything he decides with you and shall ratify that which he has signed in my name.' If Louise XIV was in ignorance of this communication, Philippe was, at the very least, acting with enormous imprudence. If the King of France did know something, but preferred not to admit it, then Philippe was acting as an agent of French policy, however murkily.

At this critical moment Philippe left court 'for reasons of health'. Perhaps Louis XIV suggested he remove himself from the increasingly recriminatory atmosphere; perhaps he himself thought it more prudent to withdraw, in order to pursue his plans in privacy. He remained away from 19 May until 13 June, during which time Chamillart was replaced as Minister for War by Voysin, and Torcy returned from Holland bearing the news that the Allies' terms for peace were unacceptable. The Allies were demanding that France surrender her most important frontier for-tifications as a pledge of good faith for a two-month truce, during which time Philip V must leave Spain. If he refused, the French armies would be required to drive him out, or face reopening the war in Flanders. Louis, who had been ready to agree to give up Dunkirk, Lille, Ypres and Tournai, could not agree to drive out his own grandson from Spain with his own arms.

Philip V would stay in Spain; but he would have to look after himself. France would need all her soldiers to defend her northern frontier. 'I have asked M. Amelot to inform you of my enemies' excessive pretensions,' Louis wrote to his grandson on 2 June, 'and how they are supported by the confidence that they have in their strength . . . I am obliged to oppose them, and consequently to recall my troops currently in Spain . . .'

When Philippe left court, he understood French policy to be to give up on Philip V, and was preparing for his own initiative in Spain. When he returned to court Philip V was not to be dispossessed, merely abandoned. Philippe decided to maintain his own initiatives, but also to use all his influence to have some French troops left in Spain. The King was persuaded to leave twenty-six battalions there.

At this point, Philipp's activities caught up with him. On 2 July Flotte was arrested in Spain, under the nose of the French commander, Bezons. Bezons, a friend of Philippe, had the presence of mind to send an urgent message to Paris, with the result that Philippe knew of Flotte's arrest six days before Louis XIV did; the King received the news by the regular messenger only on 12 July. Madame, who also knew of the arrest before Louis XIV, complained bitterly that Flotte, this honest gentleman, who had simply been on his way to take the waters at Barèges, should be treated as 'criminel d'Etat'.

The King of Spain demanded explanations for what he said was damaging information linking the duc d'Orléans to Flotte and to Spanish dissidents. Louis XIV had to act; he summoned the duc d'Orléans. Philippe expressed his shock at the arrest, asked his uncle to establish why it had happened, and declared that he would wait for his justice and protection. More news arrived; Regnault had also been arrested; he and Flotte were both imprisoned at Segovia. Amelot detailed the accusations against Orléans: that he had negotiated with Stanhope during the previous campaign to establish himself in Spain with the approval of Britain and the Archduke, that he had sent Flotte and Regnault to conspire with the grandees against the King of Spain. Philippe stood accused of high treason.

At court, Monseigneur was enraged, demanding that Philippe be punished for these crimes against his son. The Meudon *cabale* lost no time in making public its version of events; namely, that Philippe d'Orleans was determined to rule in Spain and that, having plotted with the British and the Archduke and having achieved his goal, he would have divorced his wife, married the widow of Charles II and, when she died, made Mme d'Argenton Queen of Spain. Philippe was fortunate that his wife, who was pregnant and experiencing violent nausea, did not die. Otherwise, remarked Saint-Simon, accusations of poison would have certainly been levelled against him.

Philippe had few allies. The duc de Bourgogne was one. He wrote to his brother in Spain, 'I believe that the duc d'Orléans is incapable of doing anything directly against you.' But there was talk of Philippe being tried for treason. Saint-Simon was extremely disturbed: 'His idleness, his constant trips to Paris, where he amused himself in his laboratory doing chemistry, and researches into the future, his abandon to Mme d'Argenton, to *débauche* and bad company, with an air of licence, of little respect for the court and even less for his wife, had done him great wrong in the opinion of the world and in particular of the King.' He was in no position to fend off these distressing accusations.

Pressed by Saint-Simon, Philippe put forward his own version of events. He said that some grandees had asked him to help hasten the fall of

Philip V and put himself forward; that he had rejected that proposition with the contempt it deserved, but that if Philip V had fallen without any hope of a return, he had allowed himself to consider the idea, as doing no harm and indeed as being a good thing for the King and for France, of keeping Spain in the family; he felt he could pursue this idea without the participation of the King, and was convinced that peace might have been possible if he had renounced his rights to the throne of France in favour of Spain. For, he argued, the enemy would not be pained if he were to be called to the throne by the Spaniards themselves, because Spain would then be separate from France. The appearance of union and liaison which persisted while Philip V was king would fade away. This rationale sounded laboured and disingenuous to Saint-Simon: 'His explanation gave me no great opinion of the project, nor any desire to know any more about it, supposing there was more to know.' He defended his friend as best he could, remarking that there was never so terrible an outcry for something which was a folly, not a crime, for if it had been a crime in the end one would have known. But Saint-Simon's account, while loyal, conveys his discomfort.

At court there was an air of crisis. The King had spoken to the conseil d'Etat and asked if the duc d'Orléans should be questioned, had even ordered the Chancellor to examine the proof for legal action. But then the King let it be known that he had looked into the affair, was surprised at the fuss it was creating, and found it very strange that people held such erroneous views. Eventually, on 2 August, Philippe had a long audience with the King from which he emerged 'very reassured and very happy'. The King let it be known that there was no question of treason. The rumours that the duc d'Orléans had been imprisoned in the Bastille suddenly ceased.

We will never know how much Louis XIV knew about his nephew's activities. On the balance of the evidence it seems he was in *demi-complicité*. But Philippe had probably gone further than he should. After weeks of tension, Louis tried to calm the outraged rulers of Spain. 'Not only does my nephew completely deny these intrigues,' he wrote almost pleadingly to Philip V, 'but he leaves it up to you to take the actions you think fit. In my opinion the best thing to do now is to put this affair immediately to rest. Its reverberations have already done too much harm.' But Philip V persevered: 'What really concerns me is that Flotte has the gall to say that you knew all about this affair and that he has done nothing without your permission.' He threatened to put Flotte and Regnault to the question. Louis had to beg Amelot to prevent 'these enquiries whose results can only produce a bad effect'.

Mme des Ursins continued the attack. She claimed that Regnault had plotted to assassinate several people in Madrid, that Flotte had planned to rule Lérida and raise Aragon. She then turned to Mme d'Argenton. On 30 August she sent Mme de Maintenon a copy of an anonymous letter denouncing Mme d'Argenton as the soul of a conspiracy, the goal of which was to place her on the throne of Spain. Mme de Maintenon was deeply shaken; she felt sure that the duc d'Orléans must have been led astray by this intriguing woman. Mme de Maintenon, usually perceived as a sworn enemy of Orléans, was at this stage rather supportive. 'The respect I owe M. le duc d'Orléans ensures that I shall say nothing about this affair,' she wrote. 'I see with displeasure the wrong that it does him in the world.'

Gradually the storm subsided. But from now on the King was dry and constrained with Philippe. He clearly thought his nephew had been imprudent; and he particularly resented being put in such an embarrassing situation. On 30 November Torcy noted with tantalising discretion, 'the King gives me a secret order at his Lever on the subject of the duc d'Orléans. Some days earlier HM had spoken to the council very well informed of several items. At the same time he imposed secrecy.'

Shunned by the court, expertly calumnised without a means of defending himself, Philippe withdrew further into himself. His mother wept, his wife showed passive support, as did the comte de Toulouse. The duc du Maine, according to Saint-Simon, 'under pretext of helping his brother-in-law, stabbed him gallantly in the back'. Philippe went more and more to Paris; but, utterly cast down, he took little trouble to appear in society. For distraction he turned to his laboratory, which became his consolation and his passion. He closeted himself there with his friend Guillaume Homberg, a cheerful, congenial man who had stimulated Philippe's interest in scientific experimentation. 'He started to do experiments, not to make gold, he made fun of that, but to amuse himself with the curious workings of chemistry,' his mother noted.

Philippe was consumed by curiosity about the natural world. Fire was fascinating; why did things burn? (Oxygen was not discovered until much later.) What was matter made of? Boyle had advanced the notion of atoms. Men were making discoveries through their telescopes, microscopes, barometers, thermometers. A universe governed by scientific law was coming to life. This led to the question: where was God in this new world? The Church and the King were made uneasy by all this questioning. The more Philippe indulged himself in his laboratory, the more uncomfortable they became.

The duc d'Orléans tried to find comfort and reassurance in science. Buried in the Palais-Royal, he could escape the scorn of his enemies. But he could not escape the news of yet another savage engagement in Flanders. The battle of Malplaquet, which took place on 9 September, 'this glorious and unfortunate action', was the bloodiest battle fought in Europe before the Napoleonic Wars.

At Malplaquet Marlborough used all his customary weapons, including the climactic assault, with forty guns bombarding the French centre, and the cavalry, thirty thousand strong, charging with sabres drawn. But for once the French had managed to keep most of their own cavalry in reserve. The outcome of the battle wavered; rather than risk a complete defeat, Boufflers, who had taken over command in mid-battle from the wounded Villars, ordered a retreat. There was no pursuit. With twenty thousand casualties on each side, the armies had exhausted themselves.

When news of the battle came to court, Madame's assessment was: 'The French are defeated, it is true, but it was not a total débâcle; the maréchal de Boufflers retired with the army in good order.' But she, like everyone else, was overwhelmingly tired of the war. 'Never in my life have I seen such wretched, miserable times,' she told Luise. 'God grant that a good peace may change all that.'

As Madame wrote, a young man was painting the very wretchedness to which she referred. Antoine Watteau, a native of Valenciennes, had moved to the capital some years earlier and was earning a living painting scenes from the Italian comedies and decorating theatre sets. Malplaquet was fought near Valenciennes and Watteau returned home to record the retreating army. His paintings and drawings of the French soldiers at rest and in camp convey all the tedium and resignation of defeat. The men display an unmistakable air of lassitude, which boded ill for future campaigns.

At this sombre moment, both diarists on whom we rely for detail left court. The marquis de Dangeau, who had recorded daily life at Versailles for years, suspended his journal; his only son, the marquis de Courcillon, twenty-two years old, lost a leg at Malplaquet, amputated near the belly. His mother was reported to have said that 'his wooden leg will do him more honour than the baton of a Marshal of France', but his father was so overcome with grief that he could not bring himself to continue his journal. At the same time the normally assiduous Saint-Simon also left court. Thoroughly out of favour, with his lodging at Versailles lost after the fall of Chamillart, and his friend, the duc d'Orléans, in disgrace, Saint-Simon decided he would spend some time at his property of La Ferté in Normandy, and in Paris. For the last months of this terrible year neither of the great chroniclers was there to paint the gloomy picture.

For this reason, we have no account of the brutal eviction of twenty-five aged nuns from the abbey of Port-Royal des Champs, on the ground that they were Jansenists, members of a Catholic community which Louis considered subversive. The nuns were given fifteen minutes to gather their belongings and then expelled. Such was the first fruit of the King's new confessor, the Jesuit Père Le Tellier, a man determined to eliminate what he considered heresy from the French Catholic Church. He found Louis XIV more than ready to agree that Jansenism, in particular, was a dangerous, heretical theory, one which must be destroyed. The King, always prone to see the misfortunes of France as caused by God's unhappiness and not by mortal frailty, began to believe that, if the Jansenists were extirpated, then God would smile upon him, and France would know success. In the King's mind, Jansenists were seditious and unreliable, all the more so because many members of the Paris *parlement* were of that persuasion. He was determined, even as France was fighting for its life, to show his iron hand*.

Philippe took little interest in religious quarrels. He felt himself to be finished, abandoned as the prince de Conti had been. His mother agonised over his predicament. 'All are opposed to my son; they are afraid that the King look upon him with a favourable eye ... The King has a good deal of affection for him; if he were willing to force himself to stay with the King he would enjoy more favour than any of the King's children. But he will not force himself to spend as much as a week here and haunts nothing but bad company.' Perhaps Madame was right and if Philippe had stayed at court he would have been favoured again. Even though Louis XIV now regarded his nephew with suspicion, he was still willing to listen to him. And Mme de Maintenon was sympathetic, preferring to blame the influence of Mme d'Argenton. But Philippe fled to Paris, to his laboratory, to Marie-Louise, trying to forget his dashed hopes and broken dreams.

His enemies at court took full advantage of their opportunity. No lie was too outrageous for them: high treason, an affair with the Queen of Spain, a burning thirst to rule, spells and incantations at the Palais-Royal, even incest with his fourteen-year-old daughter. One historian, Jules Michelet, believed that at this moment of crisis the duc d'Orléans did succumb to the charms of his daughter. Philippe did indeed find his daughter good company and a welcome solace, but this is much less than what was being imputed. The poison no doubt started with Madame la

---

* Jansenism started with the publication of the *Augustinus*, a book by Bishop Jansen of Ypres, first seen in Paris in 1641. Jansen's followers believed that sinful man is powerless to gain salvation without the miracle of grace. They were optimistic, predestined by God. But to the Jesuits they were heretics. Pascal, a Jansenist, said the Jesuits 'placed cushions under the sinners' elbows'. The Jansenists thought the Jesuits worldly and corrupt, the Jesuits thought the Jansenists dangerously independent. The conflict would divide French society for the next fifty years.

Duchesse, who was occupying herself with writing a novel set in the time of the Emperor Augustus, with all the characters based on her contemporaries at Versailles. Incest was rife at the court of Augustus. Madame la Duchesse had a vivid imagination and evil intent. She whispered that Philippe was painting his mistress in the nude and had invited his daughter to join the two of them. Philippe's reputation as a general and a leader was all but forgotten in the swirl of innuendo.

In this impossible position Philippe despaired, although he could not stop his provocative behaviour. He entertained the Elector of Bavaria at Saint-Cloud, in itself not a shocking thing to do. The Elector was a valued, if incompetent, ally, a bon vivant who was frequently wined and dined at court. But at this gathering Mme d'Argenton appeared as *maîtresse de la maison*. Not only that, but Philippe's wife, humiliated in her own house, was pregnant after an interval of six years, and about to give birth to her seventh child. Philippe, who had been at court all year, had revisited her bed; the couple were not close, but he was not a man to neglect his marital duties for ever. He was perhaps rather less besotted with Marie-Louise than he had been, rather less 'amoureux ailleurs avec éclat'. Mme d'Orléans did not possess the qualities to amuse him for long. She was too lazy, too stiff, too timid and too proud to keep him at her side. But they shared common aims, and needed to preserve a united front against their common enemies at Meudon. And so they stayed together, even when Philippe's behaviour sorely threatened their union. Unfortunately when Mme d'Orléans gave birth, on 11 December, it was to another girl. The King was scandalised by his nephew's want of propriety, Mme de Maintenon bitterly disappointed in him. Philippe, they complained, was nothing but a 'fanfaron des vices', a man who flaunted his vices.

# ✕ IO ✕

# DISGRACE

Philippe seemed to have been cast into outer darkness. The King, preoccupied with finding a way to peace, sending plenipotentiaries to Holland, and warning Philip V that he must be prepared to abdicate, ignored him. Let the duc d'Orléans kill himself with his dissipations.

But Philippe was not bereft of supporters. The duc de Saint-Simon, back at court after his short, self-imposed exile, finding Orléans isolated and marginalised, decided to throw himself into battle to save his friend's career and reputation. Saint-Simon believed that the most important thing Philippe could do would be to discharge Mme d'Argenton from her position as *maîtresse declarée* thus showing the King that he would no longer publicly insult his daughter and would lead a more regular life. He also enlisted the help of the rough but straightforward maréchal de Bezons, whom Philippe liked and trusted. Bezon was 'a peasant', remarked Saint-Simon, 'naturally brutal, with the head of a Rembrandt or a Van Dyck, with bushy eyebrows and a huge wig'. Philippe had greatly helped him advance in the army and for the last month he had been the only person other than servants to come to Philippe's apartment. Everyone else seemed afraid to be seen with the duc d'Orléans, and regarded it almost as a duty to ignore him.

On New Year's Day 1710 Philippe was at Versailles for the annual ceremonies; Saint-Simon sought him out in his apartment after Vespers. The two men had not seen each other for four months and their conversation was rapid and tumultuous. Saint-Simon asked Philippe how he stood at court. 'Ni bien ni mal' was the answer. Saint-Simon promptly produced all the evidence to the contrary, finally eliciting the fact that Philippe's 'affaire d'Espagne' had indeed estranged him from the King. Then Saint-Simon, by his own account, declared his plan. 'There is only one thing to do! Mme d'Argenton must go!' At first glance this seemed a somewhat irrelevant answer to the problem. But Saint-Simon pitilessly reminded Philippe of all the reasons for his disgrace, and of Mme d'Argenton's role in it.

> You are regarded as a man tormented by a thirst to rule, encouraged by your seances and fortune-telling; you are suspected of acting in concert with the court of Vienna to marry the Dowager Queen of Spain, whose great wealth would enable you to force your way to the throne of Spain; then you would repudiate her; the Emperor would force the Pope to annul your marriage; and at the death of the Dowager Queen you would marry Mme d'Argenton, to whom the spirits you had called up had promised a crown. Of course you would have poisoned your wife. People said you were not the son of Monsieur for nothing . . .

On listening to this preposterous litany of accusations, Philippe was seized with horror and grief. Whatever imprudences he had committed in Spain, he knew that this tissue of lies was much more damaging than the facts. Saint-Simon pressed on: if he cast aside his mistress, he would prove that there was no plot. He should go at once to the King, ask for protection against himself, and beg him to send Marie-Louise away from Paris. After all the King had always liked him, had got along with him better than with his own son. Louis would be gracious. Philippe initially resisted: 'You wish that I charge her with all the wickedness they have imputed to me, and that I get out of trouble at her expense? Is it not enough to break with her, if I decide to do so, without connecting her with matters in Spain with which she had nothing to do?' Nevertheless he succumbed. He would let his mistress go, he would beg the King to banish her, he would never see her again.

Thus, according to Saint-Simon, were ten years of devotion cast aside; the overpowering eloquence of the duc de Saint-Simon, according to himself, had changed the course of history. The fact is that Philippe did now take steps to have his mistress banished; and he did recover a modicum of favour. But there were many other reasons for his actions other than the rhetoric of his friend. He himself knew that Mme de Maintenon was inclined to blame Marie-Louise for his troubles and would be gratified by the lady's departure. He also knew that his eldest daughter, now noticeably nubile, was a prime candidate for an important marriage, namely to the duc de Berry, brother of the duc de Bourgogne, and that her prospects would be greatly improved if her father were not such an obvious sinner. Perhaps he was already tiring of poor Marie-Louise. There were reports that she had irritated him by having an affair with a certain chevalier de

Sade while he was away in Spain. And of course she was no longer as young as she had been. The decision was made; Marie-Louise would have to be sacrificed.

On the real reason for Philippe's disgrace, the suspicion of treason, Saint-Simon preferred not to dwell. That was altogether too serious a matter for him. If, on the other hand, he could restore the duc d'Orléans to respectability in his family life, that would surely redound to his credit with Louis XIV. Saint-Simon had his eyes on a return to grace. He relentlessly pursued his friend with arguments, monologues, hectoring and supplications. A stronger man than Philippe would have cracked.

Philippe went first to inform Mme de Maintenon of his intention. The lady was cool, but gracious. Then he rushed to tell the King before his courage failed him. He was received very badly; the King did not like being surprised and was worried that the duke might be asking for something else. He coldly agreed to the banishment of Mme d'Argenton, but appeared shocked and out of countenance. Finally Philippe went to see his mother, where he hoped for consolation and sympathy. He received neither; Madame spoke very ill of Marie-Louise. And at the thought of witnessing his wife's pleasure at the news, Philippe let himself fall into an orgy of weeping, humiliated, chagrined, helpless before the injustice of the world.

Mme d'Argenton was in Paris. It was decided that the awful news would be delivered to her by the mysterious Mlle de Chausserais, a woman involved in all kinds of intrigue, friendly with all the ministers and with Mme de Maintenon. Madame describes her as looking like a ghost in her habitual costume of a cotton *robe de chambre* and white bonnet. She was, said Madame, 'toujours gaie et toujours malade'. From her little house in the Bois de Boulogne, the château de Madrid, she embroiled herself in many plots, particularly Jacobite ones, earning the sobriquet 'La Sibylle'.

This useful woman was asked to tell Mme d'Argenton, on behalf of her lover, that it was time for her to go. Protesting, she did so, summoning the doomed woman from a card party at the princesse de Rohan's. After a tearful scene, she handed over a letter from the abbé de Thésut, Philippe's secretary, with the practical details. Philippe would pay her a pension of 45,000 livres of which 15,000 would be for the education of their son. Terrat, the chancellor of the duc d'Orléans, was ordered to pay her very considerable debts, and she was allowed to keep her jewels, rumoured to be worth 400,000 livres and to include the pearl necklace of Anne of Austria. She also kept the proceeds of the sale of her house in the rue des Bons-Enfants, its silver and furniture.

She was told that she could go anywhere she liked, except Paris and the territories of the duc d'Orléans. But her first choice, the abbey of Gommefontaine in Picardy, where she had been brought up and where her sister was a nun, was promptly vetoed by Mme de Maintenon. That lady sent some of the girls from St Cyr to this convent and did not think it suitable for them to mingle with such a creature. Mme d'Argenton, she wrote to the Abbess, would have arrived at the convent 'desperate, hysterical, rouged, in splendour, in a word totally of the world, and even criminal'. It was clear that Marie-Louise was to be held responsible for Philippe's failings.

After four days in Paris, Mme d'Argenton went to her father's château at Brenoville near Chantilly. There is no record of her ever seeing Philippe again. Her eight-year-old son, Jean-Philippe, recognised as the chevalier d'Orléans, remained at the Palais-Royal and would soon be sent to the Jesuit college in the rue Saint-Jacques.*

Swallowing his humiliation, Philippe now tried to become a model courtier and son-in-law. He gave stately parties at Saint-Cloud with his wife, receiving chilly approval from the King and Mme de Maintenon. His wife and mother, on the other hand, could not conceal their delight. 'My son has at last broken with his petite brunette,' exulted Madame. 'He will see her no longer. It costs him because he still loves her but he has the most powerful motives in the world to do this as she was terribly greedy; he could never give her enough. In fact she treated him like a slave and called him names one wouldn't call a dog. She even kicked him ... she had him mix with the worst company in the world, mainly prostitutes, both men and women ... All Paris was scandalised ...' And she added, 'I find that my son deserves more praise for this victory over her than for any battle he has won.'

The affair of Mme d'Argenton was soon overshadowed by a more joyful event. In February 1710 the duchesse de Bourgogne gave birth to another son. Given the title of duc d'Anjou, he was a fine, healthy baby, and the whole court came to admire him, a fact which his three-year-old brother, the duc de Bretagne, did not appreciate. The royal family now comprised in the direct male line Monseigneur, the duc de Bourgogne and his two young sons, and the duc de Berry. Philippe was very far from the throne.

After the birth came a death. Monsieur le Duc, who had been suffering from constant headaches and seizures, was taken ill in his carriage while on his way across Paris to his house near the Luxembourg. By the time he arrived he was able to do no more than grimace and he died soon after.

---

* Mme d'Argenton took up with the chevalier d'Oppède, a younger man who treated her with some brutality, and then settled down with a chevalier des Alleurs. She lived until 1748.

He was only forty-one years old, but few regretted his passing. So short of stature that he was almost a gnome, his face a livid yellow colour, he had an air of perpetual fury. He was clever and well educated, but malign and perverse, jealous of everyone, constantly in a rage. There was no one who did not regard his death as a personal deliverance. Madame la Duchesse, still mourning the death of her lover, the prince de Conti, the year before, was left with nine children, most of them daughters, not well off, and her sixteen-year-old son, who became known as Monsieur le Duc in his turn. The boy was almost as deranged as his father.

Disappointed in life, Madame la Duchesse entered into battle with her old foe, her sister the duchesse d'Orléans, and with Philippe. The stakes were high. The duc de Berry, youngest son of Monseigneur, was twenty-four years old and in need of a bride. He was the most brilliant match in France; his wife would be second lady in the land. Madame la Duchesse had a fifteen-year-old daughter, so too did the duchesse d'Orléans. Let battle commence.

Madame la Duchesse might have thought that Philippe's disgrace would help her attain the prize. But Louis XIV was always loath to break the iron rules of precedence; the daughter of the duc d'Orléans, Grandson of France, was of indisputably higher rank than the daughter of the duc de Bourbon, Prince of the Blood. Given that the girls seemed equally attractive, there was really no choice for the old King. Perhaps he thought that the duc d'Orléans had been punished enough. He certainly did not consider the wishes of the parties themselves. At Versailles it was said that the duchesse de Bourgogne had made the match, fearful of the influence of Madame la Duchesse if the Dauphin became king and her daughter was duchesse de Berry. In June it was announced that the duc de Berry would marry Philippe's eldest daughter, Marie-Louise-Elisabeth.

Apart from the mark of favour, Philippe found some pleasure in the wedding. His mother wrote that he was busy with his daughter's finery, taking after his father:

> The splendid diamond earrings, a mass of diamond drops, that Monsieur used to own ... since his death Mme d'Orléans has worn them all the time, but my son intended to give them to his daughter. When he handed them over and the mother realised he was in earnest, she began to weep bitterly. The daughter, seeing her mother cry, brought them back at once. The mother was all smiles, but when the daughter saw that the mother meant to keep them she burst into tears. My son and I laughed so much that we nearly split our sides.

The wedding of the duc de Berry took place on 6 July 1710 in the brand new Chapel at Versailles. There was a supper for twenty-eight people in the salon of the Oeil de Boeuf, but there were no public rejoicings, due to the war and the condition of the country. The newlyweds were not given their own household but would take their meals with the duc and duchesse de Bourgogne. The duc de Berry was blond, cheerful and not very bright. He loved shooting, playing cards and eating well. He was no match for his wife in spirit or energy. She had plenty of both, in addition to being arrogant and impulsive. Her father doted on her; she made him laugh with her outrageous remarks and provocative behaviour. But she was not as popular in the sober centre of the royal family, where decorum was expected and where solemn evenings in the presence of Mme de Maintenon were obligatory. Very soon her excessive eating and drinking became public knowledge. Only six weeks after her wedding she was carried out of a party at Saint-Cloud too drunk to know what she was saying. 'The effect of the wine both below and above ...' Saint-Simon prudently said no more. (His prudence was all the more necessary as his wife had most unwillingly been forced to accept the post of Lady-in-Waiting to the new Duchess.)

In Spain the news of the marriage brought shock and surprise. Mme des Ursins was chagrined, mortified. That her mortal foe should be so favoured seemed to her a slap in the face.

Mme des Ursins was fighting France's desire to rid herself of Spain. Her cause was greatly assisted by the Allies themselves, who at the peace negotiations in Geertruydenberg were insisting that Louis XIV use his own troops to expel his grandson from the throne of Spain. The old King refused their ultimatum on 16 July, the French envoys returned from Holland, the French gritted their teeth and chose to fight on.

The war in Spain was not going well for the French side. In desperation Philip requested once more that the duc de Vendôme, languishing in disgrace, be sent to command. Mme des Ursins and the Spanish King believed that Vendôme alone could save them. In a sign that Louis XIV was inclining to forgive the turbulent Prince for his attacks on the duc de Bourgogne after Oudenarde, Vendôme was allowed to marry Mlle d'Enghien, sister of the late Monsieur le Duc. She was thirty-three and extremely ugly. 'If it took ambition to resort to Mlle d'Enghien,' observed Saint-Simon, 'it took great courage to marry the duc de Vendôme, almost without a nose ...' She would inherit all Vendôme's wealth and pass it on to the duc and duchesse du Maine (the duchesse was her sister), as the Maines, who made the match, may have expected. Then in August it was announced that Vendôme would be sent to Spain.

Préparons, dessus nos musettes,
Pour Vendôme nos chansonettes
Il donne dans le sacrament.
L'épouse sera bien baisée
S'il est sur elle aussi souvent
Qu'il est sur la chaise percée!

(Let us prepare, as well as our dances,
For Vendôme our little songs
He is getting married.
The bride will be well blessed
If he is on top of her as often
As he is on top of his *chaise percée*.)

The supple abbé Alberoni, still clinging to Vendôme's coattails, was overjoyed. 'You will have heard that His Highness is to take command in Spain,' he wrote to the Duke of Parma, 'and I am to have the honour of accompanying him. You can therefore suspend the presents of sausages and cheese. You can redouble them on our return if God be pleased to bring us back safe and sound.' (But he changed his mind and asked for the presents to continue: 'In France they say that gifts foster friendship.')

As Vendôme made his way south, the Spanish cause fell to its lowest ebb. Philip V, having fled to Madrid in disarray, then abandoned the city with his court at the beginning of September. At Valladolid, where Vendôme and the duc de Noailles joined the disconsolate King of Spain, Noailles brought more bad news: the French had decided that, with things going so badly, they had to make peace before the ultimate débâcle in Spain. Philip V must be persuaded to abdicate. Then, just as matters seemed desperate, the war turned decisively in favour of Spain. The Archduke Charles had entered a deserted Madrid on 28 September. He found there only hostility and a lack of provisions. His generals, Starhemberg and Stanhope, were quarrelling bitterly. After two hungry weeks in the city, the Archduke withdrew to Toledo, making for Barcelona.

While the wind was shifting, Mme de Maintenon, always ready to give up her friends, did not write to Mme des Ursins for over a month. Finally, when the Archduke's retreat was known, she told the princesse that Noailles had succeeded in pleading Spain's cause and defending Mme des Ursins herself. France would help defend Spain; twenty-seven battalions and six thousand horse were sent with Noailles to Roussillon. Vendôme, however, decided to take the initiative himself. Having surprised Stanhope at Brihuega on 9 December, and taken him prisoner, he routed Starhemberg the next day at Villaviciosa, saving the throne for the Bourbons*. The news of Villaviciosa arrived at Versailles ten days later. Vendôme, although still unpopular at court, had clearly preserved a king whose abdication was being discussed earlier in the year.

'Villaviciosa changes the whole face of the affairs of Spain without argument at the same time as those of Europe' – Torcy's judgement on this unexpected turn of events was correct. The victories of the Franco-Spanish army adjusted the balance of power. In London there was a new, Tory government, led by Harley and Bolingbroke, men dedicated more to the pursuit of trade than to that of war. This new regime soon showed its colours; just before Christmas Torcy, the Secretary for Foreign Affairs, was told the English would no longer insist upon the restoration of the Hapsburgs in Spain 'provided France and Spain give us good security for our commerce'. Torcy's agent in London, the abbé Gaultier, was given the green light for more serious negotiations.

As for Philippe, he felt himself more and more of an irrelevance. Events in Spain had conspired to hand his enemies there a victory; Mme des Ursins was more entrenched than ever. In France, the likely demise of Louise XIV, and the ascension to power of the men and women around Monseigneur, darkened his future. Even the one piece of good news of the year, his daughter's marriage, had become an embarrassment.

On 13 December Madame described a frightening scene at Versailles:

all of a sudden the duchesse de Berry fainted dead away; we thought it was a stroke, but after Mme la duchesse de Bourgogne poured vinegar into her face she came to again. Then she had a horrendous fit of vomiting; nor is this surprising, for in the theatre she had continually stuffed herself for two hours with all kinds of filth, caramel peaches, chestnuts, a paste of gooseberries and currants, dried cherries, and lots of lemonade with it, then at supper she ate fish and drank on top of that. So she felt sick, and when she wanted to hold it in, she fainted. Today she is hale and hearty again, but one of these days she will make herself really ill with gluttony, for she will not listen to any admonitions.

Madame tried to overlook the public drunkenness, but others at court had much worse to say about Philippe's daughter. Madame was compelled to address those calumnies too. 'My son has such a passion (in all honour) for his daughter that she rules him as surely as the Maintenon rules the King.' Further than that, she could not go.

---

* Starhemberg got back to Catalonia; Stanhope was held captive at Saragossa, then Pamplona, returning home to England only in August 1712.

When he fell from his horse out hunting and dislocated his shoulder, Philippe might have been excused for thinking that his luck would never change. With his arm in a sling, slandered, ridiculed, ostentatiously cold-shouldered, the duc d'Orléans was nevertheless graciously granted the lofty privilege of an apartment in the main château at Marly, above the salon, next to his wife. This was a great honour; only Sons of France and the Captain of the Guards *en quartier* lodged in the château. Philippe was also allowed to ride in a little chariot in the grounds, a privilege shared only with the King himself and the Dauphin.

But as he trundled around the stately parks and gardens in his chariot, or descended from his apartment, he found himself alone, scorned. He fled to his daughter's rooms and caused more tongues to wag; he left for Paris whenever he could; and he watched Vendôme succeed in Spain, the country he thought to rule, the place where he thought his destiny lay, where he was now passionately hated. Around him the country was devastated, the people laid low, the armies destitute, the generals discouraged. The King and Mme de Maintenon wept and prayed. The King ordered plays and soirées at Versailles, trying to divert attention, says Saint-Simon, from the extremity of the country. But 'Paris did not remain less sad, nor the provinces less desolate.'

# ❧ II ❧

## DEATHS

Just when it seemed that war would never end, that nothing could change, the French court was thrown into turmoil by a death which changed everything.

On Wednesday, 8 April 1711 Monseigneur, the Dauphin, went directly from the council meeting at Versailles to Meudon for a week's house party, taking with him the duchesse de Bourgogne, Madame la Duchesse and her daughters, and a few others. On his way to Meudon the Prince met a priest carrying the Host and, as was customary, got out of his carriage to kneel as it passed. When he learnt that the priest was coming from a person who had smallpox, Monseigneur, who had had only a light, fleeting case of the disease when he was a child, became somewhat nervous. The next day, as he prepared to go and hunt the wolf, he fainted. Three days later smallpox was declared.

Louis XIV came from Marly to visit his son and stayed by his side until it appeared that he was improving. But then, six days after the disease was declared, Monseigneur fell into a coma and died. Louis grieved for his son, still not yet fifty, but in his heart he knew that Monseigneur had been a disappointment, and would have made an incompetent king.

The Dauphin had been a tall, ruddy, fairhaired man with 'the most beautiful legs in the world': Saint-Simon thought that his legs were perhaps his best feature. 'He had no vices and no virtues, no intelligence, no knowledge of anything and was incapable of acquiring any, very lazy, without imagination, without taste, without discernment, born to be bored, and to be a ball pushed around by others, stubborn and opinionated, drowning in his own fat . . .' The Dauphin did have taste; he used the best artists at Meudon, and his apartments at Versailles were the most elegantly decorated. But he had been erased as a personality by his powerful father, poorly educated and reduced to a nullity. 'He would sit in a corner of the salon at Marly, tapping his fingers on his snuff box, fixing his big eyes on everyone without looking at them, no conversation, no amusement, no sentiment, no thoughts.'

The death of this man, so insignificant but for his birth, brought real change. With brutal finality, the plans and hopes of the *cabale* who had surrounded him were ended. The new Dauphin, the former duc de Bourgogne, was a very different proposition, with his own coterie. As Monseigneur lay dying, the court spotlight turned its relentless glare on Bourgogne and his wife, who were at Versailles.

Philippe was surprisingly affected by the death. Saint-Simon was amazed to find him in tears. You are right to be surprised, said Philippe, but 'le spectacle touche', and after all Monseigneur was a good man, a man with whom he had passed his life, who had treated him kindly and with as much friendship as he could. 'I know my sorrow won't last long; but for the moment blood, proximity, humanity, everything touches me, and my heart is stirred.' At this, Philippe rose, turned his head to the wall, and sobbed bitterly, 'a thing which I would never have believed if I had not seen it'. He was roused from his emotion only when his friend reminded him that, if he appeared in public with his eyes full of tears, people would think he was acting a comedy and would make fun of him. At this Philippe dried his eyes.

Once over his emotion, the duc d'Orléans reviewed his position. On the face of it, his future under a prince of such devout stripe as the new Dauphin seemed uncertain. But Bourgogne had supported Philippe when he was accused of treason by his brother the King of Spain, and the duchesse de Bourgogne and the duchesse d'Orléans were friends, albeit more from reasons of self-preservation than genuine regard, united against their common enemies at Meudon. Certainly Philippe would not be persecuted and vilified by this young couple as he had been and would have been by the circle of Monseigneur. His most bitter enemies had been intimates of Meudon. Now their influence was gone, even if their hostility remained.

Madame la Duchesse had lost a great deal, and looked for solace in the pleasures of life, that is new houses, eating and drinking, and intriguing more viciously than ever. 'She sought to drown her sorrows and succeeded' was Saint-Simon's comment. About this time her gaze fell upon the fascinating marquis de Lassay – 'with the face of a monkey, he was perfectly made' (Saint-Simon again) – and took up a public liaison with him which lasted until her death. While the King lived they remained fairly discreet, although Saint-Simon thought that Louis let many things pass 'out of fear of annoying himself and giving himself trouble'.

As Madame la Duchesse distracted herself, the duc de Maine, prodded by his wife, emerged to try to build a friendship with the new Dauphine. Unfortunately she could not abide him, remembering only too well how he had supported the duc de Vendôme in his attacks on her husband after Oudenarde. Failing to charm her, he turned his attentions to the duchesse de Berry, who was always on the lookout for a chance to provoke her popular sister-in-law. In the aftermath of Monseigneur's death, new *cabales* were initiated.

While the court was preoccupied with these manoeuvres, there came another death, this one even more significant for Europe. Two days after the death of Monseigneur, the Emperor Joseph died, also of smallpox, aged thirty-two. A violent man, with intelligence below the mediocre, his death, like that of Monseigneur, was much more meaningful than his life had been, for, as Joseph left only daughters, his younger brother, the Archduke Charles, became Emperor. Madame, like many others, saw the point at once: 'What a miracle it would be if this should bring us peace; but time will tell.'

With the Emperor Joseph's death, many of the reasons for continuing the war vanished. Everyone hoped that Archduke Charles would go back to Vienna and give up his claims in Spain. Philip V wrote to him in Barcelona proposing a fair settlement. But there was no reply; the Arch-duke, it appeared, wanted to fight on. He wanted to be King of Spain as well as Holy Roman Emperor. The Tory government in London, eager for peace, were exasperated. In April Great Britain seceded from the Alliance, signalling her intention of making peace.

The hope that peace might be at hand went along with a new feeling of optimism at Versailles. The Dauphine animated everything, made the court seem more fun, more glamorous. Marie-Adélaïde was twenty-six, a young woman of overwhelming charm, cheerful, good-humoured, lively and spirited. The King, Mme de Maintenon, her husband, and almost all the Royal family (with the conspicuous exception of Madame, who found her impertinent) adored her. Louis XIV was immensely proud of her. He gave her complete control over her household, a thing no other Dauphine had had, saying, 'I trust her enough to wish that she need not give me an explanation of anything, and I leave her absolute mistress of her household. She would be capable of more difficult and more important things.' She exhausted herself taking the leading role in every ceremony, every entertainment. As a warning that she was now too grand to be flirted with, the young duc de Fronsac (later to become notorious as the womanising duc de Richelieu) was sent to the Bastille for a year, accused of being too familiar with her. She even persuaded Philippe to spend a little more time at court, assuring him that his days of disgrace would soon be over. But not even she could ameliorate the harsh treatment meted out to her sister-in-law, the duchesse de Berry.

In July Mme de Berry was almost three months pregnant; even so she was obliged to make the annual journey to Fontainebleau. Louis XIV insisted on her presence, made more as a token of her obedience than for the pleasure it gave him, and ordered her to make the journey against the advice of her doctor, and despite Madame and Mme de Maintenon intervening on her behalf. The most the King would allow was that she could travel by boat and not in his carriage. Her voyage was tightly circumscribed; she would be permitted to spend one night en route at the Palais-Royal, on condition that she not set foot outside its doors, even to the Opéra, which was actually in the same building. She must then re-embark for Fontainebleau the next day. Mme de Berry followed her orders to the letter, spending a cloistered night in Paris, and embarking again for Fontainebleau. On the last leg of the journey disaster struck. Her boat almost hit the bridge at Melun and her party barely escaped drowning. When she arrived at Fontainebleau, at two in the morning, she was dishevelled and exhausted. Four days later she miscarried. Taking their cue from the King, no one was sympathetic, least of all her grandmother, who wrote, 'The misfortune of Mme de Berry has not upset me, after all she is all right ... and the child was only a girl.'

The duchesse de Berry was definitely the black sheep of the family. Things came to such a point that Mme de Maintenon, not without a certain malicious pleasure, asked Madame to lecture her granddaughter on her bad behaviour. Madame did so with enthusiasm, causing the young woman to weep bitter tears and faithfully promise to change. 'I hope to God it will last,' she sighed. 'Neither father nor mother says a word; they were quite moved by my lecture. I didn't use a single harsh word; on the contrary, I heartily sympathised with her because she has been so badly brought up, a sensible girl like her, that she had not learnt where her duty lay, nor what her duties demanded. My son often spoils the good I do.' 'One must expect some improvement in a person of sixteen years of age,' wrote Mme de Maintenon, somewhat wearily.

Philippe took himself off to Paris. His laboratory remained his chief distraction, but he was also reading voraciously. Madame asked Sophie to send her Leibniz's new book, the *Théodicée*, assuring her that 'my son is very keen on reading new books'. This is the book which, almost fifty years later, Voltaire was to caricature so effectively in *Candide*. Leibniz's argument, greatly simplified, was that this world is the best that God could have created, given that men are free to choose good or evil; Voltaire created Dr Pangloss to demolish the argument. When Philippe read Leibniz in 1711, Voltaire was still François-Marie Arouet, a seventeen-year-old, precocious student of the Jesuits in Paris. He had not thought of *Candide*, Philippe had never heard of Arouet. But it is easy to imagine Philippe reacting with ironic laughter to Leibniz's Christian optimism, the same ironic laughter which would infuse *Candide*.

Cautious optimism seemed justifiable at the beginning of 1712, for the pace of peace negotiations had quickened. Secret meetings had begun in London between French diplomats and representatives of the Tory government. The propositions under discussion included France's recognition of Queen Anne and the Protestant succession, guarantees that the thrones of France and Spain would never be united, demolition of the French fortifications at Dunkirk. On behalf of Philip V, who was not consulted, Louis XIV was prepared to accept British sovereignty over Gibraltar and Minorca, even to grant London the lucrative *asiento*. (The *asiento* was a contract between the King of Spain and a foreign company which engaged itself to pay an annual fee in return for the monopoly of the supply of slaves to the Spanish Indies.) A great peace conference was planned at Utrecht. As a gauge of their sincerity, the British released the maréchal de Tallard, the vanquished general at Blenheim, from his seven-year captivity.

French hopes also rose when the Duke of Marlborough was called home to answer charges of accepting bribes from an army supplier. In December 1711 the House of Commons condemned him, and he was dismissed from all his offices, going into voluntary exile for the rest of Queen Anne's reign.

The great general's disgrace was indeed good news for the French. The court went to Marly in January 1712 in high spirits. The Dauphine was as usual the centre of attention, playing cards in the salon, as gracious as ever. But suddenly she was taken ill with a severe headache and retired to bed, getting up later that day to preside over the card tables, '*en déshabillé*, all wrapped up in a shawl'. It seemed a minor ailment; but ten days later, when the King returned to Versailles, she was still unwell.

Seized by fever and shivering, the Dauphine took to her bed. She had such a searing headache that she asked the King not to come and see her, she was in too much pain. Mme de Maintenon, greatly worried, sat with the suffering young woman, writing to the princesse des Ursins, 'She has convulsions, she cries like a woman in labour and at the same intervals.' For three days the Dauphine, in her feverish state, underwent bleedings, purgings and doses of tobacco. The Dauphin, distraught, would not leave her room. Mme de Maintenon sat with her at night and, alarmed by her worsening state, talked to her of the Sacraments. Marie-Adélaïde seemed surprised that they thought her state so desperate, but agreed to confess. However, when her confessor, the Jesuit Père La Rue, arrived, she seemed uncomfortable and asked instead for M. Bailly, a priest of the Mission of the parish of Versailles; this caused great astonishment as Bailly was not far removed from Jansenism. When Bailly turned out to be in Paris she asked for a Franciscan friar, Père Noël, to be called. By now the Dauphin was himself unwell and was sent to bed. After a long confession, the Dauphine was brought Extreme Unction and the Holy Viaticum, which the King received at the foot of the stairs. She then asked for the prayers for the dying, but was told it was not yet time. The night was cruel. The next day she was heard to whisper, 'Princess today, tomorrow nothing, and in two days forgotten.' She died that evening, 12 February, at the age of twenty-seven.

The King, overcome with grief, left immediately for Marly with Mme de Maintenon. They were both so shocked and stunned that neither had the strength to visit the Dauphin, himself now very ill in his room at Versailles. The court was devastated. Saint-Simon summed up the mood: 'With her disappeared joy, pleasures, amusements, every kind of grace. Shadows covered the surface of the court. She had animated everything; she filled all the places at once; she was busy everywhere; she penetrated all the interior. If the court existed after her, it was only to languish. Never was a princess so regretted, never was one so worthy to be so.'

At Marly all was silence and anguish. 'Everything has gone, everything seems pointless,' Mme de Maintenon was writing with a broken heart, 'there is no more joy, no more occupation.' And it was not over. Ill as he was the Dauphin was brought to Marly the day after his wife's death. Her body was being embalmed in the room above his and he could not bear to listen. At Marly he grew worse, remaining in his room, visited by his brother and a very few others. Then, a week after his wife, he too died. His coffin was taken to Versailles to be placed next to hers. 'A spectacle so unlooked for, so tragic,' noted the diarist the marquis de Sourches, 'that none of those who had the pain of witnessing it could afterwards recall the scene without shuddering.'

With everyone else, Philippe had been a helpless witness of events. Now that the worst had happened, he had to play his part in the obligatory funeral ceremonies. At nightfall on 22 February a procession left Versailles with the two coffins. The duc d'Orléans led the mourners through the night; they did not reach Saint-Denis until half-past seven the next morning. To add to the horror, murmurs were heard accusing Philippe of poisoning the Dauphin and Dauphine. When the five-year-old Petit Dauphin, the elder son of the dead couple, himself died on 8 March, these murmurs grew louder. The authors of the insults were clearly aware that the duc d'Orléans had suddenly become much closer to the throne. The only surviving direct descendants of Louis XIV, except for the King of Spain, were the two-year-old son of the late Dauphin, and after him the duc de Berry and then the duc d'Orléans. This seemed so threatening a prospect that Philippe's old enemies wasted no time in spreading the vicious rumours and covering him with calumny.

Poisoning was the great fear of the age. Every disease was so mysterious, and so hard to cure, that it was easy to see evidence of foul play wherever one wanted. The Dauphine and her family probably died of scarlet fever; there was an epidemic in Paris which reached the court, along with smallpox, a few weeks later. But Philippe was an easy target for troublemakers who did not want to consider the unlikeliness of him disposing of a couple known to be well meaning towards him. Already unpopular with the King and Mme de Maintenon, he rapidly became a pariah. Deeply shocked at the hatred directed against him, Philippe went into seclusion at the Palais-Royal.

This was fuel for more rumours; why did he have a laboratory if not to learn alchemy and make potions? Was not this the source of whatever had killed the Dauphin, Dauphine and their son? He was a monster. Did he not sleep with his daughter? Outside the Palais-Royal were hung signs proclaiming, 'Here they play Lot's game and make fine poisons.' Accusations of murder became so frequent that Philippe's old tutor, the marquis d'Effiat, advised him to go to the King and demand to be admitted to the Bastille and questioned, and that Homberg be arrested as well in order to clarify everything. In desperation Philippe did go to the King. Saint-Simon relates that Louis XIV actually wished to put his nephew on trial, but that his doctor and confidant, Mareschal, had said, 'What do you mean, Sire? To proclaim everywhere the alleged shame of your nearest family? And what will be the result? To find nothing and to be ashamed yourself!' Louis hesitated.

The Prince, said Saint-Simon sadly, was 'profoundly outraged and defeated'. The duc d'Orléans, already suspected of treason, now stood accused of triple murder. And yet the only time he allowed himself to be provoked was when the pitiful duc de La Feuillade, the incompetent general at Turin, saw fit to join the slanderers. Philippe was enraged; but this was the only time Saint-Simon saw him lose control.

His mother was in agony. Almost immediately after the deaths, she had written to Sophie:

When my heart is as fearful and sorely troubled as it is now, I have no other comfort but to pour out my grief to Your Grace . . . People with black hearts have put it about that my son has poisoned the Dauphin and Dauphine. I, who would place my hand in the fire for his innocence, at first thought that this was only foolish talk and that no one could possibly say such a thing in all seriousness . . . Some say that this wicked rumour was brought in from Spain. If this were true the princesse des Ursins would be a true devil and carry her revenge against my poor son very far indeed; he is paying a high price for having made fun of this lady.

She herself believed that the doctors had killed the Dauphin, Dauphine and their son. Her old friend the duchesse de Ventadour, governess to the Dauphine's children, had refused to hand over the younger boy to the doctors, had kept him warm, and given him a little wine and biscuits. The boy was the only one of his family to survive.

After the shock and grief subsided a little, the political star of the duc du Maine began to rise. Mme de Maintenon, who always before had given Philippe the benefit of the doubt, was now deeply suspicious of him. Maine encouraged her in her doubts, presenting himself as the only person she could trust. Her grief tormented her and made her look for someone to blame. Madame told Sophie that 'when the doctors went and reported to the King that they had examined everything minutely and that it was absolutely certain that the two had not been given poison, the King turned to Mme de Maintenon and said, "Well, Madame, have I not told you that what you said about my nephew was wrong?"'

Life went on more drearily. The duc and duchesse de Berry were given the Dauphin's apartment and expected to hold a court. Madame was allowed to join the King's intimate circle, despite her son's deep disgrace. The old King and Mme de Maintenon needed all the comfort they could find.

Then there came another storm of intrigue against the duc d'Orléans. In April in Madrid a French merchant revealed to the authorities the existence of a plot against the life of the King of Spain, involving a monk by the name of Le Marchand. The princesse des Ursins placed such credence in the story, or saw an opportunity to blacken Philippe's name further, that she sent her nephew the prince de Chalais to France under a false name in search of the monk. Chalais found the man near Bressuire in Poitou, had him arrested and sent to the Bastille. Chalais then hastened to Marly, saw Torcy and had a private audience with the King. The rumour began that the man had been hired by Philippe to murder the King of Spain; another wave of outrage crested.

Beside himself, Philippe demanded not only that the monk be interrogated, but that he himself submit to questioning at the Bastille. The wise and wily Prefect of Police, d'Argenson, was firm: 'Monseigneur, behold the speech of a young prince; but know that, for whatever reason, a prince is worth nothing in the Bastille.' The monk, however, remained there for almost three months. In the end d'Argenson told Torcy, 'I do not know, after reading the interrogation record, whether the witness will not seem more suspect than the accused.' Eventually Chalais took the mysterious monk back to Spain; he was imprisoned at Segovia, where he died more than ten years later.

The truth about this murky tale is impossible to state with any confidence. Le Marchand seems to have been a defrocked priest who had a knowledge of poisons and had deserted several times from both the French and English armies. He might well have been involved in nefarious doings. But of Philippe's involvement there is no evidence at all. He was convinced that Mme des Ursins had orchestrated the whole affair to tarnish his reputation further and cause him to be hated by Louis XIV. He never forgave her for her part in this. The only consolation he could draw was that he had found an honest and courageous friend in d'Argenson, whose common sense and probity came to mean much to him in later years.

It was only in May that Madame felt able to say, 'Thanks be to God! All is over here!' It was not really over, because the rumours were sedulously kept alive. But the King indicated that the duc d'Orléans would not be accused of any crime.

While the death of the Dauphin caused Philippe to suffer the torments of unjust accusations, it had thoroughly alarmed the British. If the new little Dauphin died, it was possible that Philip V would claim the French throne. By right of birth, his claim would be unassailable. The British urgently demanded that Philip V renounce his and his children's rights to France. There could be no peace in Europe if the thrones of France and Spain were united.

Louis XIV seems to have wanted his grandson to give up Spain and take a minor throne, perhaps Savoy, while waiting for fate to bring him the crown of France. 'I have been very touched by the idea that you could continue to rule,' he wrote, 'and that I could still see in you my successor and that you could visit me from to time ... If the Dauphin lives, he would have a regent accustomed to command and able to extinguish *cabales* ... If the child dies, as his feeble complexion seems to indicate, you would follow me in the succession ...' These were touching words; they also revealed how much Louis XIV hoped for an alternative to the duc d'Orléans as regent. The King of France was at this point convinced that his nephew was a troublemaker who should be kept at arm's length.

Despite Louis' words, however, Philip V preferred to remain in Spain and renounce France, albeit reluctantly. 'The King of Spain will cede France to his brother, the duc de Berry,' wrote the French Ambassador, 'but, if the duc de Berry dies without issue, he does not wish to make a cession which benefits the duc d'Orléans.' The seeds of future discord were sown.

While Philip V prepared to make his decision public, the British lost no time in instructing their army in Flanders to stop fighting. A Franco-British Armistice was declared in July 1712, and Queen Anne henceforth considered her country at peace with France. Her commander in Flanders, the Duke of Ormonde, withdrew his twelve thousand men on orders from the Cabinet, leaving Prince Eugène, who was preparing to lay siege to the town of Landrecies near Cambrai, shocked and vulnerable. The maréchal de Villars took full advantage of the situation, marching to Denain. On 24 July the Dutch defenders were routed; Prince Eugène arrived too late to save the day. Denain was a great French victory. After the news of the battle came to court, Louis XIV, for the first time anyone could remember, thanked his courtiers for their congratulations, a sign of the huge relief he felt and the importance of victory.

As the threat of war receded in Flanders, the celebrated duc de Vendôme died while engaged in a desultory campaign in Valencia. In a dusty village, with no entourage around him, only the faithful Alberoni, the great general came to the end of his days. As he lay dying his servants fled, stealing as they went. This most superb of men, so proud of his ancestry and so glorious in his state, died without a mattress to lie on. Only a few months earlier Vendôme had watched with satisfaction the death of the Dauphin de Bourgogne, feeling he was on the verge of power in both France and Spain. 'The Prince may well become the chief personage of Europe,' Alberoni had gloated. 'May God keep him for the good of our two monarchies, of which he is nowadays regarded as the sole support.' Now he was gone and Alberoni left to look after his own future.

That summer of 1712, while Versailles was still enveloped in gloom over the deaths of February, Paris was experiencing a renewal of energy. Peace might not be official, but there was a feeling of anticipation, heightened when Lord Bolingbroke himself came to Paris and was received at Fontainebleau, where the courtiers were astonished to see the staid old duc de Beauvillier drinking many toasts and breaking many glasses with his British guests. Bolingbroke and his colleague, the Tory diplomat and poet Matthew Prior, were fêted in Paris; they were taken to the Opéra, where, rather embarrassingly, the Pretender was found sitting in the next box, although, as Dangeau remarked, 'it was purely the effect of chance'; they saw *Le Cid* at the Comédie-Française; and were invited to the salons of

Mme de Ferriol and his fascinating sister, Mme de Tencin. This lady had just arrived from Grenoble, where she had managed to flee from a convent, and hungry for life, ambitious and enterprising, was beginning to attract notice.

Bolingbroke warmed to Mme de Tencin and to Paris society, and left reluctantly. As he was departing, he met James Stanhope, who had just been released from captivity in Spain and was on his way home. The Tory Bolingbroke was on top of the world, the Whig Stanhope out of favour. Stanhope attended a party at the duc de Noailles' at which he no doubt saw his old enemy and collaborator, the duc d'Orléans. What a great deal they had to talk about. Both had had such heady dreams, both had suffered stunning reverses. (And both would rise once more to power.)

In artistic circles, the young painter Antoine Watteau was causing great excitement with some paintings presented at the Académie in July. The Académie, which he was seeking to join, did not know what to make of this mysterious artist and his work; he seemed to fit into no genre, with these haunting, teasing pictures of characters from the Commedia dell'Arte. He was elected provisionally, subject to the usual condition of submitting a 'morceau de réception'. Unusually, however, instead of the subject being specified, Watteau was to be allowed to paint what he liked. Shy and sombre, fragile in health and uneasy in society, Watteau brought out the protective instincts of others. He was taken up by the collector and connoisseur Pierre Crozat (brother of Antoine Crozat, the richest man in France, and known jokingly as Crozat le Pauvre to distinguish him from his brother, Crozat le Riche) and lodged in his splendid house on the rue de Richelieu. Here he continued to refine his art, paying for his keep by painting wall panels in Crozat's dining room, but absorbing the potent influences of the day, from Harlequin and Colombine at the theatre, to the Rubens masterpieces at the Luxembourg palace, to the Italian paintings and drawings in Crozat's own collection. He took five years to present his *morceau de réception*, frequently prodded by the Académie. When he did so in 1717 he produced the *Embarkation for Cythera*, one of the sublime works of the Regency. But as early as 1712 the educated Parisian public was intrigued by the young artist and his work.

As if to punctuate the growing irrelevance of Versailles, two men close to the King now purchased houses in the capital; the comte de Toulouse bought the magnificent hôtel de La Vrillière and the duc d'Antin, the son of Mme de Montespan, the nearby hôtel de Travers. There was great surprise that these men, particularly d'Antin, 'courtisan au suprême', should acquire property in the capital. The life was going out of Versailles.

Philippe was often in Paris. For him the court had become a place of torture. 'In a word, I was the only one,' said Saint-Simon, 'I mean precisely the only one, who continued to see M. le duc d'Orléans as usual, to approach him, to sit down the two of us in a corner of the salon, where we certainly had no third party to fear, to walk with him in the gardens and in front of the windows of the King and Mme de Maintenon.' Despite the fact that the death of the Dauphin had placed Philippe in the position of a man who would count in any future reign, Louis XIV gave no sign that he recognised the shift; Philippe was not invited to participate in the administration of the state. Perhaps some of his calumniators truly believed that he had had a hand in the deaths of the duc and duchesse de Bourgogne; but most tried to smear him to such an extent that he would be impossible to accept as a man of influence in any future reign. 'They already fear', wrote his mother, 'that he will be part of the government. That is why they try and make him hateful to Paris and to the court.'

Mme de Maintenon was particularly alarmed; she seems to have come to believe that the duc d'Orléans might have done harm to her beloved Dauphine. He also represented a part of society she despised, the free thinkers, the men of *bel air*. She turned her attention to the duc du Maine, who she hoped might take up the standard of the values of Louis XIV; she must have known the unsuitability of her candidate, his retiring nature and political naivety, but he was the only available high-born counterbalance to the duc d'Orléans. For the rest of Louis XIV's life the duc du Maine and his ambitious little wife would position themselves as the champions of the people and representatives of Louis' legacy. The remnants of the *cabale* of Monseigneur joined forces with him.

Madame deplored her son's isolation, but she deplored his reaction to it still more. She compared his birth to the fairy tale in which all the fairies bring gifts to the cradle, but that one fairy, who had not been invited, ensured that all the gifts would not profit him:

> I will give him such an ugly gait that he will look like a limping hunchback; I will cause him to have a heavy black beard and with that I will give him grimaces that will distort his features; I will give him a dislike of exercise and will fill him with such boredom that he will abandon all his arts, music, painting and drawing and will give him a love of solitude and a loathing for honourable people. I will often give him bad luck in war; I will make him believe that debauchery is becoming to him and I will give him a loathing of his best friends' advice.

This brutally frank assessment was crafted with love. The mother and son were very close. The baron de Pollnitz described Philippe's exemplary behaviour: 'He does not miss a single day in paying his respects. Every evening he comes to her *cabinet* at eight-thirty; he plays at draughts with her until the time for the King's supper. Only during the game does he sit down. On entering and leaving he always kisses her hand.'

These were Philippe's moments of consolation. His mother tried to convince him that the King still favoured him. 'The King treats my son well, which gives me hope that the lies have not made any impression upon His Majesty,' she told Sophie. Both mother and son needed all their courage in such a hostile world.

# ✄ 12 ✄

# ENDS AND BEGINNINGS

Louis XIV was seventy-five years old in 1713. He had lost most of those he held dear, his mood was melancholy. He spent more and more of his time in the rooms of Mme de Maintenon with a small group of ladies, listening to music or acts from plays. The maréchal de Villeroi was his constant cavalier, reminding him of his glory days long ago, the comte de Toulouse, who loved music, would sometimes join them, the duc du Maine hardly ever, and no other men at all. The King could not do without the presence of Mme de Maintenon; she was the only person absolutely necessary to him. The loss of the Dauphine would never be assuaged. As he listened to Lully's familiar melodies, Louis XIV braced himself for his final battle, not against the Allies this time, but against his own mortality. The question of the succession came to haunt him; as he approached his Maker, he thought more and more of how to plan for the day of his death and beyond.

Even though a peace treaty was not officially signed, the British and French were exchanging ambassadors. The Duke and Duchess of Shrewsbury arrived in Paris on 12 January and took up residence at the hôtel de Soissons. Five days later the Duke had an audience with the King at Marly and the Duchess was presented at Versailles. In order to avoid embarrassment the Pretender, Stuart, under the name of the chevalier de Saint-Georges, was sent off to Bar-le-Duc, where the duc de Lorraine provided him with a magnificently furnished château.

The Duchess of Shrewsbury caused a sensation; an ageing beauty, still décolletée, covered with rouge and beauty spots, she became very fashionable, her opinions sought after. She was astonished to find all the French ladies wearing their hair very high 'in veritable towers of ribbons and lace and hair, more than two feet high, which made women look as if their face was in the middle of their body'. She opined that these coiffures were ridiculous. In a moment all the princesses and ladies of fashion dismantled their towering creations and began to do their hair more naturally. The King was piqued; he grumbled that he had been complaining about these hair-dos for years and no one had taken any notice. One word from the Duchess of Shrewsbury, and all the ladies had gone from one extreme to another. (Twenty years earlier Mme de Sévigné had written, 'there is something which has caused His Majesty more worry and cost him more time than all his conquests: this is the defeat of the coiffure).'

The French Ambassador, the duc d'Aumont, was also creating a memorable impression in London. The house in which he was staying, the Hotel de Powis in Great Ormond Street, burnt down. He claimed the fire was the work of terrorists, but it was generally thought that he had had it done himself in order to obtain reimbursements from the crown and to hide his smuggling activities. He was a great connoisseur of furniture, ornaments, jewels and carriages, extravagant to a degree. Before his father died he had taken a rented house and, according to Saint-Simon, gilded everything in it, even panelling the stables 'like a fine set of rooms with a very elaborate cornice all around, and decorated them throughout with pieces of porcelain'.

With the ambassadors in place, it was time for the next step in the peace process, for the duc de Berry and the duc d'Orléans to register their renunciations of the Spanish throne at the *parlement* of Paris. This was to be an imposing ceremony, giving legal substance to the preliminaries for peace. Leaving Versailles at six-thirty in the morning of 15 March, the two princes travelled together from Versailles. Saint-Simon was in the carriage with them. Berry was extremely nervous; he had rehearsed his very short speech with Mme de Saint-Simon the night before, but was completely unused to public speaking and was naturally timid. He remained silent and apprehensive in the carriage as Philippe, who was in great good humour, regaled the company with stories of his youthful life in Paris and his nightly wanderings.

On arrival at the Porte de la Conférence they were greeted by trumpets and cymbals which accompanied them all the way past the Tuileries to the Sainte-Chapelle. After hearing Mass they went in procession to the Grand Chambre, crowded with dukes and magistrates, as well as the British Ambassador. The Premier président delivered his compliments to the duc de Berry and waited for a reply. There was an excruciating silence. The duc de Berry was rendered completely speechless, petrified with nerves. Philippe could only look at the floor. They were both undone. With great presence of mind, the Premier président bowed low as if he had received the reply he had expected, and the affair was hastily brought to a conclusion.

The royal party drove soberly the short distance to the Palais-Royal where a banquet of prodigious grandeur was served in the Grand Appartement. The duc de Berry sat in an armchair and received his napkin from the duc d'Orléans, who did the honours with perfect grace and naturalness. But poor Berry remained preoccupied and silent throughout the meal.

On their return to Versailles the princes had to pay their respects to the newly wed duchesse de Tallard, who was awaiting them. (She was Marie-Isabelle de Rohan, a granddaughter of the duchesse de Ventadour.) Berry wished only to go and hide, but unfortunately ran into the garrulous and somewhat senile princesse de Montauban, who gushingly told him how charmed she had been by accounts of the grace and dignity of his speech. Blushing furiously, Berry said nothing, did his duty to the bride and fled into his *cabinet*, taking Mme de Saint-Simon with him. Throwing himself into a chair, he sobbed that he was dishonoured, that he had behaved like a sot and an imbecile. It was a heartrending scene. 'I have been taught nothing but to hunt and play cards,' he said, 'they have made me stupid. I will never be fit for anything. I will be the laughing stock of the whole world.'

In a further blow to the unfortunate young man, his wife gave birth prematurely to a son who lived for only three weeks. The succession still hung by a thread on the life of the three-year-old Dauphin.

Then finally peace. On Good Friday, 14 April 1713, at eight in the evening, Torcy took the chevalier de Beringhen to the King. Beringhen had arrived with news that at last the Peace of Utrecht had been signed on 10 April. There was rejoicing in Paris where the duc and duchesse du Maine, 'who from then on dreamed of making themselves popular with the people', threw money to the crowd from the balcony of the duc de Rohan's house in the place Royale. At Marly an idyll on the subject of the Peace was performed before the King, produced by the duc de Noailles with music by Delalande.

Under the terms of the treaty, Philip V kept his throne on condition that it would never be united with that of France. France lost her maritime empire and her commercial advantages to Great Britain; she gave up part of Flanders to the Dutch; and she promised to destroy her fortifications at Dunkirk. Even so, France did not do as badly as seemed likely in 1709. But the country was in parlous state domestically; taxes, levies, famine, devaluation of the currency, epidemics, had sent hungry bands of men around the countryside; uprisings in the Cevennes and Guyenne compromised the central authority; the provinces were desolate.

There were other spoils for the victors. The Elector of Brandenburg became King of Prussia and the Duke of Savoy became the King of Sicily. Madame found some reason to rejoice: 'I shall neither gain nor lose by the peace, but one thing I shall enjoy is to see our Duchesse of Savoy become a queen, because I love her as though she were my own child. For another thing, there will be fewer lamentations, which were tedious, and for a third I hope that the posts will be faster.'

Louis XIV, having made his peace with Great Britain, now turned to making war on the French Catholic Church. The Papal Bull called *Unigenitus* was published in Rome on 8 September 1713. The Nuncio brought it to Fontainebleau on 2 October and the King cancelled a promenade around the canal to study it. The Bull actually judged a book called *Moral Reflections* by Père Quesnel and found 101 propositions in it to be Jansenist and heretical. To Louis XIV it was the weapon he needed to bring the French Church into line. He promised Pope Clement XI that the Assembly of the Clergy would accept the Bull and the condemnation of Quesnel's book unanimously.

This meant war. Cardinal de Noailles, the Archbishop of Paris, refused to accept the Bull in his diocese and preparations began for an Assembly General of the Clergy in early 1714. On 24 November Madame wrote cautiously about the controversy to her aunt: 'because of the Pope's decision there is a great gathering of bishops in Paris; what they will do about it will not rob me of any sleep.'

Ironically, all this religious furore profited the irreligious duc d'Orléans. Those known to be close to him were already seen as coming men, because even if the little Dauphin died and the duc de Berry succeeded, Berry was considered merely a tool of his father-in-law. All those who talked of English ideas, the independence of the French Church, the hypocrisy of Louis XIV and his ministers, the arrogance of the Jesuits, came together; Philippe would be their standard-bearer, albeit an unlikely one. The duc de Noailles appointed himself leader of an Orléans party, and geared up his efforts in Paris to co-ordinate support for the duc d'Orléans. Philippe gave him his blessing. The old fires still burned.

Noailles was a considerable personage at court. He was a brave soldier, a gifted courtier and, married to Mme de Maintenon's niece, intimate with the King. He had run into trouble three years earlier when he was accused of suggesting to Philip V that he take a mistress rather than suffer the agonies of ungratified desire when he could not sleep with his wife. Mme de Maintenon and the Dauphine, the Queen of Spain's sister, had been outraged. Noailles was summoned back to France and entered a state of mild disgrace. To the astonishment of his fellow nobles, he began to study the financial affairs of France, helped by the Controller of the Finances, Desmarets. He had also assembled around him a group of talented men who were as ambitious as he. Foreseeing that the duc d'Orléans would have considerable influence in the coming years, he decided to try and renew their relationship. The two men had been friends, but there had been a falling out when Regnault (whom Noailles had introduced to the duc d'Orléans) was arrested in Spain, because Noailles thought Philippe had put Regnault in danger through his own recklessness. In 1713, however, Noailles wanted to put himself at Philippe's disposal. They thought the same way about the failings of Mme des Ursins, about the need for a new economic policy in France, about the general need for reform. Noailles turned to two of Philippe's intimates to effect a rapprochement. It took courage for him to approach the marquis de Canillac, Philippe's bosom friend, for Canillac despised Noailles and made fun of him in private.

Canillac was a sarcastic, cynical, mordantly witty homosexual. Tall, well made, with chestnut hair and an expression promising much intelligence, he had a cultivated mind and had read a great deal. He talked 'beaucoup trop' according to Saint-Simon, but so pleasantly that one let it pass. He hated the King and all the ministers, complaining about them with great liberty in the presence of his friends. Although he liked neither wine nor women, he became a fixture at the Palais-Royal, so much so that, whenever Philippe went to Paris, he always sent word ahead to Canillac to come and join him. Canillac's worldly morality impressed Philippe. Awaiting the Regency, from which he expected so much, Canillac did not fail to make himself useful.

One of Canillac's friends was the président de Maisons, a rich and powerful leader of the Paris *parlement*. Maisons was a personage. His grandfather had built the superb château of Maisons close to Paris, and was famous for his remark, on being dismissed from his post of Controller of the Finances, 'They are wrong; for I have made my pile and was about to make theirs.' The grandson was anxious to play a part in the unfolding drama of the succession, and told Canillac how useful Noailles could be. In a regency of the duc d'Orléans, a triumvirate of Canillac, Noailles and Maisons would be all-powerful.

Noailles approached Canillac with feigned humility. He listened to everything Canillac said, admired him, begged him to teach him. For his part Canillac discovered that 'ce garçon-là avait bien du bon et bien de l'esprit'. These three men were the central figures in Philippe's party, along with the ever-present and indispensable Dubois. The abbé retained his influence despite hostility from Madame, who considered that 'Dubois is the greatest scoundrel and impostor in Paris. My son knows this very well; he sees him as ever and believes everything he tells him.'

On the other side, efforts were being made to circumvent the duc d'Orléans. Torcy recommended that any regent be designated by a meeting of the Estates General (when the three 'estates' – the nobility, clergy and third estate came together in matters of national importance). He also suggested the alternative of a regency council composed of delegates from each *parlement* in France. The Spanish envoy thought a 'junta' of generals was being considered. And of course Philip V hovered in the background, letting it be known that he was available, despite his renunciations. The duc du Maine, pushed by his wife and with the support of Mme de Maintenon, glided into the role of chief representative of the opposition to the duc d'Orléans.

Philippe stirred. His mother noted that he began to distance himself from his disreputable daughter: 'My son and his daughter who, as Your Grace knows', she wrote to Sophie, 'used to love each other so much that unfortunate rumours were spread about them, are now beginning to hate each other like the Devil, quarrel every day, and, worst of all, the daughter creates trouble between the father and her husband; the father left for Paris in a huff. The father keeps all of this secret from me, but I find out about it just the same; his wife tells me everything.' The duchesse de Berry was becoming impossible; Mme de Maintenon described her as extraordinarily fat and slovenly that winter. Even her father was starting to realise that her charms were not infinite.

On New Year's Day 1714 Louis XIV wrote to Philip V urging him to make peace with the Emperor. But poor Philip V was in no state to listen. His wife was dying of consumption; confined to her bed, with no appetite, a fever and a cough, she was too weak to be moved. On 15 January she managed to rise to receive the marquis de Brancas, the new French Ambassador. It was her last effort. When they told her the end was near and that, there being no hope, she must confess, she wept. But from then on she was heroic. Helvetius, the young doctor of the duc d'Orléans, was sent urgently from Paris, but he knew the minute he saw her that there was no hope. Having given her blessing to her three sons, the Queen of Spain expired, reproaching her husband for his tears; 'I am reaching the moment of my death without fearing it, yet you are showing so much weakness ...' She died two years almost to the day after her sister the Dauphine, at eight-thirty in the morning of 14 February. Philip V, who had shared her bed until a few days before her death, was extremely moved, but *à la royale*: meeting her funeral procession when he was out hunting, he continued to hunt, prompting Saint-Simon to wonder whether princes were made like other men.

Soon, however, Philip V installed himself at the palace of Medina-Celi, seeing no one but the princesse des Ursins and his children. Mme des Ursins appointed herself governess of the King's sons and erected a secret passageway between her rooms and his. She kept Philip so isolated that rumours started that the twenty-nine-year-old King would marry the seventy-two-year-old princesse, rumours which reached Mme de Maintenon and shocked her deeply. 'They are already starting to say that you wish to keep the King in the country so that he does not see anyone.'

In fact the Princess had decided that the King, who could not live without a woman and stay sane, must have a new wife soon, preferably one who would be docile and recognise Mme des Ursins' supreme position. Miraculously, Alberoni reappeared; he had stayed in Madrid after the death of Vendôme in 1712 as chargé d'affaires for the Duke of Parma. He had Mme des Ursins' ear and, better still, a wife ready and waiting for the King, none other than Duke of Parma's step-daughter, Elisabeth Farnese. Alberoni went to work.

He found the princesse des Ursins in a bitter mood. Her beloved Queen Marie-Louise was dead; and she felt deeply betrayed by the King of France. In March 1714 Louis XIV had signed the Treaty of Rastadt with the Emperor; handing over the Spanish Netherlands and almost all Italy. Furious, she took steps to declare her independence from France, refusing to deal with the French Ambassador, the marquis de Brancas, calling him a creature of the duc d'Orléans. She was still obsessed with the notion that Philippe was plotting against her, and had the King of Spain write to Mme de Maintenon asking for the recall of Brancas, claiming that he was in close liaison with the duc d'Orléans and had the same 'esprit de cabale'.

Brancas had his own complaints. 'I have very strong suspicions that my last letters ... have been opened,' he wrote to Torcy in March. Ten days later he abruptly left Madrid for Paris, one day before the departure of an official Spanish delegation consisting of the cardinal del Giudice and his nephew the prince de Cellamare. Each party was eager to tell Louis XIV its version of affairs in Spain. Saint-Simon and Philippe thought that the Cardinal's mission was linked to a modification of Philip V's renunciation of the throne of France. Philip V himself told Louis XIV that del Giudice was coming to warn of the far-reaching consequences 'if the King my grandfather does not severely punish the temerity of those involved in such an important *cabale*'.

What did he mean? What *cabale* was the duc d'Orléans leading in March 1714? Did Philip V think Brancas was somehow in league with

Spanish dissidents and that Orléans still thought of Spain, or was working against Mme des Ursins? Was the duc d'Orléans maintaining his intelligence network, even though he had renounced all rights there? He was certainly attempting to have Mme des Ursins removed. On 4 April he wrote to Louis XIV asking that she be recalled. One can see the indistinct outlines of the plots and counter-plots. Philippe believed that Mme des Ursins was stirring up more trouble for him by insinuating that he was plotting against her and the King of Spain; and that Philip V had been convinced to re-assert his right to the French throne in order to prevent Orléans seizing power.

Brancas reached France ahead of the rival deputation, and was received at Marly on 16 April. Louis XIV listened attentively to his account of the goings-on at the court of Spain. Del Giudice and Cellamare did not arrive in Paris for another four days.

As Louis XIV weighed the accusations, another tragedy overwhelmed the court. The duc de Berry fell ill at Marly with a violent fever. He was bled and given an emetic, and the King came to visit him. His wife, who was pregnant, was told to stay in Versailles. The next day he had difficulty breathing, but told Madame that he was feeling better and hoped he would not die. He quickly worsened, however, and later that evening was given the last rites with Louis XIV in attendance. The end was near; he died at four in the morning of 4 May, in his twenty-eighth year, holding a crucifix to his heart. It was thought that he had probably ruptured his stomach muscles on the pommel of his saddle, falling from a horse.

The cheerful, blond young man, who had never thought he would amount to anything, passed from the scene. He had loved the outdoor life and parties and having fun; when his brother became King of Spain he said cheerfully, 'I will have less trouble and more fun than you; I will be able to hunt in France and in Spain; I will go after the wolf all the way from Versailles to Madrid.' He was not very intelligent, but towards the end of his life had been made miserable by the knowledge of his limitations and by the cruelty of his wife, who flaunted her affair with her equerry La Haye. Of all the dull or troubling direct descendants of Louis XIV, he had at least a little charm.

His body was taken in state to the Tuileries, where it remained until the heart was taken to Val-de-Grâce and the body to Saint-Denis. The King's mood, said Madame, was very dark; but she did not think he was deeply grieved and contented himself with keeping up appearances. There had been so many deaths; wearily he went to the little Dauphin and said simply, 'Now you are all I have.'

The widowed duchesse de Berry miscarried in June. If she had had a son, she would have been a personage at court. Now she was a useless commodity. 'If my son's portrait could talk,' wrote Madame to Aunt Sophie, 'it would speak sadly now, because he grieves over his daughter's unhappiness.' Shortly after this letter she heard of the death of Sophie herself, in her gardens at Herrenhausen. 'Our loss is immense,' she told her half-sister Luise, now her chief correspondent, 'perhaps my tears will never cease to flow, my sadness never end.'

Two months later, in August 1714, Queen Anne died in London and Sophie's son became King George I of the United Kingdom. He was Queen Anne's closest Protestant relative, by virtue of his descent from Elizabeth Stuart, the only daughter of James I of England, Sophie's mother. The probability of his succession had been clear for years, but many in London were not eager to see him leave Hanover. Even as Anne lay dying, there were violent political quarrels over the succession. The Tories had hoped to persuade her to forgive the Pretender, but she died before she could do so, and the Hanoverian succession was safe. The Tory leader, Bolingbroke, had compromised himself by calling for support of the Stuarts and was obliged to flee to the Continent, uttering a few bitter words: 'What is then this world? And how does fortune play with us!'

Philippe himself could only wonder at the ways of destiny. At the end of 1714 he was heir to the throne of France, next in line after a three-year-old boy. When Louis XIV died, Philippe would be Regent for the boy. If the boy were to die, which most observers thought probable, Philippe would be King of France. This was such an unnerving prospect for so many Frenchmen, not to mention the King of Spain, that Versailles became the scene of feverish plans to render the duc d'Orléans null and void.

# ❧ 13 ❧

# THE END OF A REIGN

Louis XIV was an old man surrounded by the wreckage of his plans, alone in the splendour which he had created, and which even he now found oppressive. He was given no peace; Mme de Maintenon and Père Le Tellier began to press him to make a will which would limit the authority of the duc d'Orléans, balancing it with that of the duc du Maine. Maine was a reluctant leader; but he allowed himself to be pushed to the head of a party while Philippe, to all appearances, did nothing.

In Spain, Philip V was deeply agitated at the death of his brother the duc de Berry. Already at loggerheads with his grandfather over Mme des Ursins, he now had to come to grips with the fact of the duc d'Orléans' proximity to the throne of France. He recalled that he had never actually promised to stand idly by if the duc d'Orléans tried to ascend the throne. Maddened by celibacy, suspicious and fretful, prodded by Mme des Ursins, Philip V mulled over his options. Forced to sign the peace treaty under threat of being abandoned by his grandfather, he sulked.

As Philippe observed the shifting scene, the fragile alliances, the changing loyalties, he awoke to the responsibilities and opportunities of his position. His ambition had been quenched by disappointment, calumny and disgust; he had turned to private pleasures and secret dissidence. Performing his duties at a court where he was ignored and insulted, he had fled to Paris, summoning Canillac, Brancas and Broglie, the girls from the Opéra, seeking oblivion in evenings of dissipation. Gradually he roused himself. And others approached him. Slowly and in the deepest secret, meetings were held at the houses of the duc de Noailles and the président de Maisons. There were many questions; how would a regency of the duc d'Orléans act towards the *parlement*, on *Unigenitus*, on taxes and foreign policy? The discussions were so discreet that Saint-Simon, who thought himself Philippe's only friend, knew nothing of them.

Louis XIV was concentrating on two vital matters of state. He wished to impose peace on the French Catholic Church and he wished to make a will with precise dispositions for the governance of the country when he had gone. He turned first to the Church and the simmering controversy over Jansenism.

The Assembly of the Clergy had met at the beginning of 1714 and, instead of unanimously approving *Unigenitus* as Louis XIV had promised the Pope they would, nine bishops had refused to do so, including the Cardinal Archbishop de Noailles of Paris. Although their number was small, the *refusants* were influential, supported by the Sorbonne, the majority of the lower clergy, the *parlements* and a large number of the faithful. These people saw themselves more as defenders of the independence of the French Church from the Vatican than Jansenists. But to Louis XIV they were rebels. He furiously forced the *parlement* to register the Bull.

The dispute was too much for the Chancellor, Pontchartrain, who resigned on 1 July. The King turned, at Mme de Maintenon's recommendation, to Daniel Voysin. Voysin was fully prepared to carry out the King's wishes, not only on the matter of *Unigenitus*, but on Louis' other great notion, that of proclaiming his sons by Mme de Montespan, the duc du Maine and the comte de Toulouse, able to ascend the throne in the absence of all other Princes of the Blood. Pontchartrain's resignation did not deter Louis at all. On 29 July the leaders of the Paris *parlement*, Mesmes and Daguesseau, were summoned to Marly and asked to have *parlement* register an edict placing the bastards in the line of succession.

This move strongly proclaimed the King's intention to protect the two men as far as he could when he was gone, but, more importantly, to create a political counterbalance to the duc d'Orléans. In 1714 the only male members of the royal family other than the little Dauphin and the duc d'Orléans were the two Princes of the Blood, Monsieur le Duc and the prince de Conti. They were both still very young and would be unable to provide what Louis conceived of as 'balance' to Orléans. Therefore, he reasoned, Maine and Toulouse would have to be raised from their 'intermediate' rank, between the Princes of the Blood and the dukes, to proper royal rank. Louis XIV well knew what an outcry his action would provoke, and had serious reservations. He told his son the duc du Maine, 'You have wanted this, but know that, however great I might make you in my lifetime, you are nothing when I am gone, and it is up to you afterwards to maintain what I have done for you if you can.'

The King had no illusions about his son's character. Maine had wit and talent but did not know what to do with them. Every day when his attendance was not required he spent his time alone in his study praying and reading, he was 'un idiot avec tout son esprit' who never knew what was going on in the world, and never cared to know, and although very charming and amusing was 'sauvage' as he did not wish to see people and take an interest in things which interested the court. He could not even keep order in his own house. Despite all this, he was the only chance Louis thought he had to mitigate the influence of the duc d'Orléans. *Parlement* dutifully registered the edict on the bastards on 2 August 1714, in the presence of Maine and Toulouse.

'Everyone became alarmed,' wrote Mme de Maintenon disingenuously, 'but have finally agreed that what the King has done for them does no harm to anyone. They say however that the dukes are upset and they claim in Paris, where they speak with more freedom, that the King has elevated the two princes in order to give them more of a role in a Regency, and to balance the credit of Monsieur le duc d'Orléans.' That could not be clearer.

Philippe, who had been kept completely in the dark, was deeply disturbed, but took great pains not to show his feelings. He realised that the edict was a direct hit against him, but preferred to keep silent and show as much dignity as he could while continuing to see friendly members of *parlement* in secret.

At the same time as Mesmes and Daguesseau were being told about Louis' decision on the bastards, they were probably also given advance word of the contents of the King's will, which they were shown at Marly three weeks later. Louis was blunt. 'Messieurs, here is my will; I am the only one who knows what it contains ... they wished it, they tormented me; they gave me no rest, whatever I said. So be it! I have bought my rest thus ...' He said much the same thing to Mary of Modena, James II's widow, and to Berwick, James II's son. But everyone knew that the will would somehow be disadvantageous to Orléans and helpful to Maine. A public edict stated that the King had made provision by his will for the organisation of the future Regency during the minority of his great-grandson, selecting the composition of the Regency Council. The choice was not made public.

In fact it would consist of Orléans, Maine, Toulouse, the Chancellor, the Controller of Finances, the Secretaries of State, the maréchaux de Villeroi, Villars, Harcourt, Huxelles, Tallard. The duc d'Orléans would have a preponderant vote only when the Council was evenly divided. Maine was given the responsibility for the King's education and Villeroi named as governor. Thus, as the contemporary historian François Bluche stated, 'everything was set up to limit and control the room for manoeuvre of the duc d'Orléans'. But, in the absence of specifics, a respectful and profound silence still seemed the only course open to the duc d'Orléans; he responded *en courtisan* to the King, retained an open and cheerful air, and unburdened himself only to a few trusted allies.

Meanwhile Louis XIV had been informed by Mme des Ursins that a bride had been found for Philip V. She was Elisabeth Farnese, Princess of Parma. The girl came from a relatively insignificant family and was poor, but her mother was a Bavarian princess whose sisters had made good marriages and the girl was well connected. One of her aunts was in fact the Dowager Queen of Spain, widow of Charles II, who lived in exile in Bayonne. She was also said to be intelligent and attractive. Louis XIV was too weary to enquire further; although irritated at being taken by surprise, he approved the match without further ado. Alberoni had done his work well. He told Mme des Ursins how docile and pliant 'la bonne Lombarde' would be, interested only in lace-making and sewing. Lulled into a false sense of security, Mme des Ursins had agreed to the Farnese marriage.

Elisabeth Farnese was twenty-two, seven years younger than her husband to be. She had a fine figure, fiery blue eyes, a large mouth and pretty teeth. In her love of music and painting she showed a Florentine spirit. She understood French well, but was totally ignorant of Spanish. She was, claimed Alberoni, naturally gay and charming; but docile she was not. She was reputed to have a strong character and to be extremely ambitious. It appears that Mme des Ursins, having received such accounts, was already having second thoughts about the girl's suitability even before her couriers reached Paris.

Alberoni was jubilant, writing to the Duke of Parma, 'I have told you that I have always considered that this tremendous stroke would be of the very greatest advantage if we knew how to play our cards ... If the Heroine has confidence she will not be badly served, I can assure you; but it will be necessary to conduct the whole matter with the greatest dexterity.'

Despite attempts by Mme des Ursins to delay it, the proxy marriage went ahead in Parma in mid-September. After the ceremony, the new Queen of Spain left immediately for Genoa to take ship for Alicante. Her journey was not without risks. There was a great storm as they set sail, and the party quickly returned to land. Elisabeth Farnese had lost her taste for the sea. Complaining about the conditions on board ship, the fleas and the lice, she decided to proceed by land to Menton, thence to Antibes, Marseille and Pau, where she met her aunt, the Dowager Queen of Spain. The two queens spent several days together, then went to the foot of the Pyrenees and parted with a great demonstration of affection. No doubt the Dowager Queen had reminded her niece that she should make sure to establish herself securely as soon as she arrived in Spain. Certainly Elisabeth Farnese listened.

At the end of October Louis XIV left Fontainebleau for the last time; he would never see it again. Madame had her own premonitions: 'This, alas, will be the last letter I shall write to you from dear Fontainebleau. Monday will be the last time we shall hunt in this beautiful forest. There is nothing in Versailles or Marly to compare with it.' Having spent only a week in Versailles, the King went to Marly, where he stayed for the month of November. The English were now placing bets on how long Louis would live; but Mme de Maintenon wrote, 'I never get used to the King's good health; it's a miracle which renews itself every day. Yesterday he fired thirty-four shots and brought down thirty-two pheasants. His strength, his sight, his dexterity do not diminish at all.'

The good health of the King contrasted with that of his nephew. At the end of November Philippe was taken ill in his rooms at Marly, red in the face, unsteady, his eyes fixed. He was bled and soon recovered; his mother blamed his illness on his 'guzzling like a wolf' and drinking too much with his daughter. The King did not visit him, and when his doctor, Mareschal, tried to tell him of Philippe's many talents, he made the famous remark, 'Savez-vous ce qu'est mon neveu? Il a tout ce que vous venez de dire; c'est un fanfaron de crimes' ('Do you know what my nephew is? He has all the qualities you talk of; but he boasts of himself as a criminal'). It was a perceptive and not wholly hostile comment. The old man knew he could not change Philippe. Perhaps he wished he had tried to know him better. It was too late.

Louis was just as jaded about his son, the duc du Maine, whom he considered too subservient to his wife. The duchesse du Maine was busy playing in Racine's *Athalie* at Sceaux with her ten-year-old son the comte d'Eu. Sceaux was more than ever 'le théâtre des folies de la duchesse du Maine', a place, sneered Saint-Simon, of 'shame and embarrassment, the ruin of her husband by the huge sums of money expended there, the spectacle of the court and the city, who thronged there and mocked ... She was revelling in the joy of her new grandeur.' But her husband had no stomach for a fight for his rights; he compared himself morosely to a flea caught between two fingernails, the Princes of the Blood and the dukes, both of which groups wished to crush him. Philippe was fortunate in his opponent.

As the Queen of Spain wound her way to Madrid the princesse des Ursins became impatient. Torcy was made aware that Mme des Ursins was developing a dislike for the Queen she had never met, and noted, 'the Queens seems to wish to fly on her own wings . . . but as one prepares here to clip them, I doubt that there will be as much harmony in the royal household as one might desire'. Mme des Ursins was playing into Alberoni's hands; she redesigned the royal apartments at the Retiro so that she had a finer set of rooms than the Queen, and the rooms were so arranged that the Queen could not go to the King without Mme des Ursins knowing. More crucially, she made the fatal mistake of allowing Alberoni to go ahead to meet the Queen.

Alberoni approached the meeting with 'two bottles of quinine and complete resignation as regards everything that may happen'. He knelt before the Queen and told her that the only way in which she could succeed in Spain would be to take the dangerous action of arresting Mme des Ursins; he asked her to take the night to decide if she was bold enough to do it. In the morning Elisabeth Farnese signified that she was ready to act. Alberoni was jubilant: 'She has a pious husband, full of honour and integrity, she is already mistress of his heart; imagine what that means if she spends two nights with him between the sheets.'

The plotters rode towards Jadraques, seven leagues from Madrid, where they were to meet Mme des Ursins. When the Queen's carriage drew up outside the palace the cold was so intense that Mme des Ursins did not go to the door, but remained on the staircase, from where she made a profound curtsey. The Queen raised her up with a few kind words and then they walked side by side into a private room.

Saint-Simon, who heard the story from the princesse des Ursins herself, recounted that she was very surprised by the Queen's lack of warmth. But surprise turned to shock when Elisabeth immediately accused Mme des Ursins of appearing before her improperly dressed, proceeding to call the guards. In a matter of minutes, the old lady was arrested, put in a carriage with her maid and two officers of the guard and, surrounded by an armed escort, driven north through the freezing night, wearing only her court dress and with no provisions of any kind. The wretched party did not reach Saint-Jean-de-Luz until 13 January, after three weeks on the road. Mme des Ursins was in a state of shock.

'Our great Queen has been a very Judith,' gloated Alberoni, 'and has effected a revolution that has already raised her to a pinnacle . . . As far as I am concerned she tells me roundly that she is well pleased with my humble services . . .' Alberoni had sent a hasty message to Versailles, relating the fall of the princesse des Ursins. Torcy was astonished. 'Behold a Queen who is indeed energetic!' he exclaimed, adding sarcastically, 'They have made the King of Spain play the part of a pleasing personage.' Torcy was a courteous man; while not completely regretting her fall, he deplored the brutality of Mme des Ursins' treatment. He went at once to tell Louis XIV, who no doubt felt rather the same way, and who immediately sent word of his esteem for Elisabeth Farnese and his affection for his grandson. He also wrote to the Princess herself, but with some reserve. As for Mme de Maintenon, she was characteristically oblique: 'I avow that I would never have thought that you would leave Spain as a criminal; one must keep silent, Madame, when one's misfortunes come at the hands of those whom God has made our masters.' Mme des Ursins had become something of an irritant at the French court. Alberoni expressed himself a friend of France. Louis XIV would wait and see.

As a distraction from the drama in Spain, Louis received an envoy from Persia at a grand audience in the Hall of Mirrors, where the whole court was assembled, the silver throne set on a dais, the ladies in their finest gowns. It was as though he wished to bring back the glorious days of 1685 when the Doge of Genoa had bowed before the same throne. On this day the little Dauphin stood with his governess. The duc du Maine and the comte de Toulouse were also present, but it was the duc d'Orléans who was the centre of attention. He wore blue velvet embroidered in a mosaic pattern and scattered with pearls and diamonds and 'took the prize for elegance and good taste'. He seemed newly confident. The King was magnificent in black and gold; but he walked unsteadily, and seemed broken and bent, with a 'très méchant visage'. It was a brave attempt to resist the inevitable.

Philippe was naturally delighted at the fall of the princesse des Ursins, but incensed at the thought of her coming to court, even as a victim. In his eyes she was the woman who had slandered him, accused him of treason, tried to embroil him in every sort of intrigue, and would still be plotting against him if she could. He dared to make a scene. 'M. le duc d'Orléans wishes to go to Paris,' Mme de Maintenon wrote to the Bishop of Soissons, 'as he fears that, if he finds himself in her presence, he would not be able to stop himself from insulting her.' He demanded that she not be allowed anywhere that he, his wife or his mother might be. And he forbade any member of his household or friend to meet her. From Madrid the word was also clear: any honours paid to the princesse des Ursins would be regarded as an affront to the new Queen.

The controversial lady arrived in Paris at the end of February 1715 and stayed with her brother in the rue Saint-Dominique, claiming that an eye infection prevented her from rushing to Versailles. In fact the King allowed her to cool her heels for some weeks. The abbé Mascara, a spy of Philip V's at the French court, reported with undisguised glee:

she is virtually abandoned, which causes her great pain, as the good lady was used to adoration. She has been with Mme de Maintenon to Saint-Cry, but, little by little, the ardent friendship, the protection are going up in smoke. The duc d'Orléans is upset, and so everyone realises that friendship with a diseased person can cause a contagious disease. She is as dead as Caesar; Mme de Maintenon herself is embarrassed at her presence.

As it was clear that the duc d'Orléans would be a man to reckon with in the future, Torcy wrote to the French Ambassador in Spain, Saint-Aignan, asking him to begin to interest himself in the release of Flotte and Regnault, imprisoned since 1709. Philip V, no doubt propelled by his wife, told his grandfather that he would set them free and that, despite his complaints against them, he felt himself obliged by religion, the ties of blood and the desire to please Louis XIV to seek a reconciliation with the duc d'Orléans. Philippe was emboldened to write to Philip and also to the Queen, for he well knew that it was she, and Alberoni, who were behind the effort at reconciliation.

Mme des Ursins finally saw the King at Versailles a month after her arrival, but her welcome was not warm. Mme de Maintenon herself was making her position perfectly clear: 'M. le duc d'Orléans is very ill advised: he regards me as his mortal enemy and believes it is I who persuaded Mme des Ursins to come here. In fact I try and stop her from sleeping at Versailles and am trying to get her to leave France as soon as possible.' So much for all those years of friendship. Mme des Ursins, a Frenchwoman who had given fifteen years of her life to serving French interests in Spain, saw that she would have no future in France. After a farewell audience with Louis XIV at Marly on 6 August 1715, and seeing his frailty, Mme des Ursins left France in a hurry, hastening to Lyon and thence to Genoa.*

On 13 April the King gave Voysin a codicil to his will. The contents were not revealed, but they were significant. The maréchal de Villeroi was given command of the household troops from the day of the King's death until the opening of the will; and the young King should go to Vincennes before going to Paris for the reading of that document. Villeroi was also named governor of the new King, with the duchesse de Ventadour in charge of the boy until he reached the age of seven. All the other provisions of the will were confirmed. (There was a second codicil on 25 August which named the abbé de Fleury as tutor to the King, and Père Le Tellier confessor.) The contents of this codicil indicated that Louis had some

---

* She died in Rome in 1722 at the age of eighty, having witnessed the fall of Alberoni and outlived Mme de Maintenon.

nervousness about the possibility of a *coup d'état*; the maréchal de Villeroi was the man he trusted the most to protect the little Dauphin in an emergency, and Vincennes was clearly seen as a place which could be defended if necessary.

The mood in Paris was more cheerful. Peace had brought an influx of foreigners, ready to taste the delights of French culture. Dufresny's *La Coquette de village* opened at the Comédie, featuring avaricious rustics, *arrivistes* and the lottery. *Zephyr and Flora*, with music by the younger Lully, was playing at the Opéra. At the rumbustious theatre of the Saint-Germain fair, Lesage was putting on *Les Eaux de Merlin*, starring Arlequin and Colombine at the court of Merlin, in the forests of the Ardennes and in contemporary Paris. Watteau was present at these performances, sketching, absorbing. And twenty-one-year-old François-Marie Arouet, who had not yet taken the name Voltaire, was working on his play *Oedipus*, and writing gossipy letters to the noble ladies whose salons he was beginning to frequent. 'I can tell you that la Duclos hardly performs at all ... every morning she takes several doses of senna and cascara, and in the evening several doses of the comte d'Uzès.'

There were many Englishmen and women in Paris, relishing the pleasures of French civilisation after years of war. The new Ambassador, John Dalrymple, Lord Stair, had quickly established himself in the salons of the city, and with those who counted. Dubois, still a fervent Anglophile, introduced him to the duc d'Orléans. Stair and Philippe immediately took to each other.

Stair was an interesting man, resourceful and shrewd, like Philippe himself. His father, an under-secretary of state, was held responsible for issuing the order for the massacre at Glencoe in 1692 at which the members of the clan MacDonald had been slaughtered on the excuse that they had arrived too late to tender their allegiance to William III. The elder Dalrymple spent the rest of his life in disgrace. His son, at the age of eight, is reported to have accidentally killed his elder brother with a gun; he became a man of mystery, bold and versatile, expert in cunning. Saint-Simon regarded him with suspicion: 'under the pretext of liking society, parties, and the good life, he never lost an opportunity to make acquaintances and procure contacts of which he could make use to better serve his master'. Winston Churchill thought him the most competent envoy Great Britain ever sent to Paris.

Stair had arrived in Paris in January and had immediately met the large British community there. He found himself in odd company; for many Jacobite Tories, having fled England at the death of Queen Anne, were also in Paris, prominent among them Bolingbroke and the former Com-

mander-in-Chief, the Duke of Ormonde, Jacobites both and busy conspiring with the Stuart Pretender against King George. The lively British
society in Paris also included Hanoverians, Catholics and Protestants,
Whig and Tories, spies and counterspies. Those who had fled the regime
of William of Orange mingled with those who had supported him and
then fled George I. English connoisseurs, who wished to adopt French
taste in houses and fashions, rubbed shoulders with bloodthirsty renegades.
Beautiful women were found on every side, among them the charming
Barbara Chaffinch, widow of Lord Jersey, who married the comte de
Clermont, Philippe's Gentleman of the Chamber. There were also Eleanor
Oglethorp, 'dangereuse créature, elle excellait en intrigues', and Elizabeth
Wilmot, Lady Sandwich, who entertained many English expatriates at her
salon. And, living in the place Vendôme, was a mysterious Scot, a reputed
genius with financial matters, by the name of John Law. He was the very
first person Stair saw on his arrival; they were of an age and both from
Edinburgh. What else they had in common was not known.

Stair's most important task was to survey the Jacobites and their allies.
There were rumours that the Pretender was preparing for an invasion.
Everyone was spying on everyone else. Philippe's views were eagerly sought
by both sides. The Jacobites used the most imagination; in August the
Duke of Ormonde approached Olive Trant, a beautiful young Irishwoman
known for her 'supple wit, enterprising, seductive, bold, a woman who
above all wished to make her fortune'. Mlle Trant was entrusted with the
task of putting Philippe to bed with another beautiful Jacobite spy at the
château de Madrid in the Bois de Boulogne, the home of Mlle de Chausserais, an ardent Jacobite and old friend of Philippe. Philippe gallantly
shared his bed, but not his secrets. When that encounter did not have the
desired result, there were suggestions of a marriage between the Pretender
and one of the duc d'Orléans' daughters; there were stories that Philippe,
disguised as an abbé, had gone to Saint-Germain to discuss the matter
with the Pretender's mother, Mary of Modena.

Philippe himself was fascinated by English ideas of tolerance, freedom
of speech and parliamentary democracy. And he liked the carousing blunt-
spoken Englishmen he had met. His connections with England were
strong and went back a long way. But the official policy of France, and the
view of the French people, was friendship with Spain and distrust of the
United Kingdom. The new regime in Spain professed itself friendly to
Philippe. He was prepared to follow the traditional course.

On 3 May there was an eclipse of the sun; the King walked out into the
gardens at Marly early in the morning to observe it, and the astronomer
Cassini came from Paris with a pair of glasses to explain what was hap-

pening. One wonders what the Roi Soleil felt about such a strikingly symbolic event. If he did not feel more strongly his own approaching end, others did. All that summer his health declined. When he left for Marly on 12 June many thought he would die there. In London bets were laid that he would die before 1 September. One day at Marly, Torcy was reading the Dutch newspapers to the King, after a meeting of the conseil d'Etat, when, seeing suddenly a reference to these bets, he came to a halt, stammered something and pressed on to another article. Louis XIV asked what was the matter. He insisted on knowing. Torcy, 'dans le dernier embarras', read the story. The King said nothing, but that night at dinner said to the company, 'If I continue to eat with such a good appetite, I will ruin many Englishmen who have made large bets that I am going to die before the first day of September.'

The new Ambassador from Spain, the prince de Cellamare, arrived in Paris on 18 June and four days later had an audience with the King at Marly. He gave Philippe a letter from Philip V which Saint-Simon described as 'fort obligeante', but was actually 'assez laconique'. Philippe, who would have been prepared to undertake a better relationship with Spain, treated Cellamare with courtesy and kindness; but the Ambassador had secret instructions from Alberoni to form a party in France for the King of Spain. Alberoni's professions of friendship meant nothing; he faithfully followed his master's implacable hatred of the duc d'Orléans. Spurning Philippe, Cellamare began to approach ministers, generals, the Princes of the Blood, anyone who could be useful in paving the way for Philip V to assume power in France.

In August the président de Maisons was surprised by a slight stomach upset; he took rhubarb two or three times, but then had to listen to cardinal de Bissy, which impeded the results of the rhubarb. 'Fire took his entrails even before he had decided he was ill.' He died within forty-eight hours, in a crowd of friends and clients, all enjoying themselves as at a party, not willing or not reflective enough to think of his approaching end. Maisons was only forty-six, and on the brink of a great role in the Regency.

Almost the last act of the reign was an acrimonious meeting at Marly on 9 August at which the King demanded that Mesmes and Daguesseau have *parlement* register *Unigenitus* immediately; when they balked, he threatened to come to Paris and demand registration in person. Daguesseau, who had been told by his wife to stand firm and forget he had a family, was deeply shaken by the sight of the King so frail and yet so impassioned.

After the confrontation, Louis went stag-hunting in his calèche but returned very fatigued. The next day, after a last walk in the Marly gardens he loved so much, he returned to Versailles. He visited Trianon once more, and he received the Persian envoy in a brief farewell audience on 13 August, his last public appearance. Then on the 16th he took to his bed. On the 25th, in great pain from sciatica in his leg which had turned gangrenous, he knew that he would not recover. He spent the next days making his farewells, in a fashion most noble and majestic. He told his servants, 'Serve the Dauphin with the same affection you have given me ... And follow the orders my nephew gives you. He is going to govern the Kingdom. I hope he will do it well ...' The end came on the morning of Sunday, 1 September. 'He gave up his soul without a struggle, like a candle going out,' wrote Dangeau. 'It was the grandest, most touching and most heroic spectacle that a man could ever see.' It was a most edifying, tranquil death. What followed was a rather less edifying, and definitely not tranquil, struggle for power.

# ❧ 14 ❧

# TAKING POWER

'The death of the King woke the duc d'Orléans from his idleness, as if it could not have been foreseen.' Thus wrote Saint-Simon, who was deceived. Philippe had been far from idle; plans had been made for the convening of *parlement* and for outwitting the opposition. But Saint-Simon, who was not privy to these secrets, saw only chaos at Versailles. While the late King's corpse was being embalmed, the courtiers rushed to pay their respects to the little boy of five who was now King Louis XV. Then they rushed to the rooms of the duc d'Orléans, where the crush was intense. Saint-Simon, who complained that Philippe was drowning in trivia, nevertheless detained him, expatiating at length on the details of the funeral.

At Versailles there was frantic preparation for the trip to Paris the next day. Until Louis XIV's will was read, few knew how the country was to be governed. There was apprehension at court; in the capital, an outburst of rejoicing. The death of Louis XIV was the signal for a world which had lain silent to take up its voice. Voltaire remembered seeing little tents set up along the road to Saint-Denis, along which the funeral cortège would pass. 'People were drinking, singing and laughing.' The old King had begun to seem immortal, doggedly presiding over an increasingly weary people. Paris, where opinion was formed and from where it spread, the Paris, that is, of the magistrates and lawyers, financiers and businessmen, poets and dramatists, pamphleteers and scribblers of all stripes, had grown bored and exasperated with the regime. There was no glamour or gossip at Versailles any more; there was only so much fun to be had at the expense of Mme de Maintenon, Père Le Tellier and Doctor Fagon. The salons of the city looked forward to a new government and new faces. They had been living in a Regency world for some time. Now they were ready to adore the five-year-old

King, but eager to observe the struggle for power which would assuredly erupt around him.

Many expected trouble; apart from the Regent's ability to hold power, there was the question of what would happen if the boy King died. Would the King of Spain, who had renounced his rights to the French throne, renounce his renunciation? Memoirs of the Fronde were dusted off, as if to prepare readers for a new civil war. Along with the relief at the end of an era which had lasted too long, there was apprehension as well as excitement. And the personality and reputation of the new Regent increased the tension.

At Versailles, as soon as Louis XIV had breathed his last, Philippe led a procession of the nobility to the little King, knelt before him and, 'as the first of your subjects', swore allegiance to Louis XV. For the rest of the day he closeted himself with his advisers. The plans they had made for the session of *parlement* and the overturning of the will were honed and polished. Carriages left regularly for Paris, where Mesmes, the chief magistrate, and his men were kept up to date, and where Canillac was co-ordinating the arrival of troops. The late King's long agony had given the party of the duc d'Orléans ample time to finish its preparations. When the Chancellor Voysin came to Philippe on 25 August 1715, five days before the death of Louis XIV, and offered to reveal the codicil added to the will that day, the duc d'Orléans already had matters in hand. On the 26th the British Ambassador, Lord Stair, was writing: 'The Duke of Orleans told me that the King had observed the treaties, that there was no question of the King of Spain, that he was going to have the Regency but that he believed there were some conditions planned to embarrass him with a Regency council and a guardianship for the command of the troops, but he told me that he was hardly troubled by this, being sure of *parlement* and the troops.'

That same day, 26 August, there was another defector from the old court. None other than the maréchal de Villeroi made his approach to Philippe, revealing the exact terms of the will in exchange for guarantees that he and Voysin would retain their positions; he confided the naming of the duc du Maine as guardian of the King and his own responsibility for the household troops under Maine. Philip V's agent at Versailles, the abbé Mascara, reported that Villeroi found Philippe 'bantering, playful and smiling'; the old maréchal was unable to drawn any commitments from him. At about the same time, five days before the death of Louis XIV, the duc d'Orléans, acting on his own authority, ordered his ally d'Argenson, the chief of the Paris police, to stop all couriers to Spain and to forbid the *bureaux de poste* to let a horse or carriage pass without a note from him. Philippe wished to be in control of events from the moment of Louis XIV's death, and was particularly concerned about what the King of Spain might have in mind. Philip V did not receive the news of his grandfather's death until 9 September, well after the new Regent was in place.

Between 29 August and 1 September Philippe met several times with the Chancellor Voysin and with the leaders of *parlement*.* The sudden death of Maisons had threatened to disrupt the lines of communication between the duc d'Orléans and the magistrates, but Philippe pursued his negotiations with M. de Mesmes, the Premier président, a majestic man with a sound political instinct. He had thus far supported the duc du Maine, but was prepared to abandon Maine in return for some concessions. With his colleagues, Daguesseau, the procureur général, and Joly de Fleury, the avocat général, he drove a hard bargain, demanding that Philippe agree to restore to *parlement* its ancient right of 'remonstrance', which had been withdrawn by Louis XIV. Philippe decided to restore it. He calculated that the political advantages to be gained from a good relationship with *parlement* outweighed any risk to the royal authority. The significance of remonstrances rose and fell according to the relative strengths of King and *parlement*; as Regent, the duc d'Orléans was confident that he would be able to restrain any egregious misuse of the remonstrance. And by presenting himself as the defender of public liberties he was assured of a peaceful reception in Paris during the crucial next days.

On 30 August, as Louis XIV lay close to death, Philippe sent a note to Mesmes, confirming that *parlement* would recover the right of remonstrance. Mesmes immediately sent a courier to all the other leading magistrates, asking them to come to the Palais de Justice early in the morning of the following day. When they arrived, he called them into his private office and showed them a *mémoire* outlining what the duc d'Orléans proposed. From this point on the *parlement* was securely behind Philippe. The duc du Maine, completely unaware of these machinations, was at the same time negotiating with Mesmes to rent his house in the Marais until such time as he could establish his own residence in Paris.

While Mesmes and the magistrates were meeting, a group of Philippe's

---

* This *parlement* was not a democratically elected body of the people's representatives; it was a sovereign court of appeal immediately subordinate to the King. One of its roles was to register royal enactments. 'It also acquired the right to remonstrate, that is to point out the inconsistencies or inequalities in any law sent to it for registration; the King might take account of the objections and modify the law, or he might order that the *parlement* register it in its original form' (J. H. Shennan).

friends met at the house of Mlle de Chausserais in the Bois de Boulogne to finalise their plans, in particular to prevent the slightest *coup de force* at the time of the session of *parlement*. One can assume the presence of Canillac and Dubois. The marquis de Contades, a professional soldier and man about town, was also there, a close friend of Maisons and even closer friend of Mme de Maisons. Contades had great influence over the duc de Guiche, the commanding officer of the Gardes françaises, and was responsible for Guiche having his men in place at the disposal of the duc d'Orléans for guard duty around the Palais de Justice and throughout the city the next day.

Philippe had also cemented an arrangement with another important player, Monsieur le Duc. This young man, would, by the terms of the late King's will, not be eligible to join the Regency Council for another year. He had made it clear that, unless he was given consideration in the new regime, he might gravitate towards the duc du Maine. Philippe, in secret discussions, had not only offered to invite him on to the Council immediately, but also encouraged him to demand his right, as first Prince of the Blood, to the post of Grand Master of the King's household, in order to dissipate some of the duc du Maine's authority. Monsieur le Duc had accepted the offer and in return had given his support to Philippe. But he was an unreliable ally. Impatient and ambitious, pushed by his mother, Philippe's old adversary, Madame la Duchesse, he had no loyalty to anyone but himself. He was well aware that, after the duc d'Orléans, he was next in line to become Regent and he intended to place himself in as strong a position as he could.

One other crucial person had also been approached: the British Ambassador, Lord Stair, who had been in Philippe's confidence since the summer when the King's health had started to fail. It was vital to both countries that the uneasy peace just reached in Europe after decades of war should be preserved; Philippe wanted to assure Stair and George I that they could count on him supporting the alliance. Stair was invited to attend the session of *parlement*, not only to witness the drama, but to act as a visible symbol of the friendship between the two nations. The British did not trust the duc du Maine and his Spanish sympathisers; Stair accepted the role he was assigned.

The duc du Maine seems not to have undertaken any pre-emptive moves of his own; while the duc d'Orléans was making sure of the troops and the magistrates, Maine seems to have persuaded himself to trust in the protection of the late King, protection which had never failed him before. He did prepare a paper to read at the session of *parlement*, in which he defended his position, so he had clearly expected the need to do so, but, while he was assuming that the will would be respected, his allies Villeroi, Voysin and Mesmes had already betrayed him. Perhaps he deferred to his wife, as usual, when she told him of the glorious future ahead.

Thus, when news of Louis XIV's death came to Paris in the morning of Sunday, 1 September, everything was ready.

The Great Hall of the Palais de Justice on the Ile de la Cité was full of activity from early Monday, 2 September. As officials took up their places inside, they could not have been unaware of the overwhelming military presence outside. In the place Dauphine, along the quais, stood companies of French and Swiss Guards, more than two thousand men. The duc d'Orléans' own guards were posted on the staircases. Lord Stair arrived and took up a conspicuous position. Spectators anxiously milled about, trying to find out what was going on.

Across the river, at the house of the Archbishop of Reims, Saint-Simon had convened a group of his fellow dukes. They had an agenda of their own. Determined to restore their influence in affairs of state, and pleased with what they heard about the duc d'Orléans' plans to bring back councils of nobles, they were also determined to intervene in the historic session to reassert their right to force the president of *parlement* to take off his hat when addressing them. This question, known as the 'affair of the bonnet', was one of those essentially seventeenth-century controversies over which passions raged. Philippe had no intention of allowing it to disrupt his day.

At nine-thirty the duc d'Orléans arrived from Versailles with Monsieur le Duc, the prince de Conti, the duc du Maine and the comte de Toulouse. Philippe appeared clam, Maine pale and nervous. Everyone settled down for the reading of the will. But, before the will was brought in, the duc d'Orléans seized the initiative, rising to his feet to demand that the Regency be conferred upon him in accordance with his birth, and immediately mentioning the rights and remonstrances of the *parlement* which he planned to restore. He read from a prepared text, leaning on a desk, speaking 'with all his accustomed presence of mind, wisdom, courtesy and nobility', as Saint-Simon testified.

His speech was a manifesto, surprisingly modern in tone:

Messieurs, after all the ill-fortune which has overwhelmed France and the loss we have suffered of a great king, our only hope is in him whom God has given us. It is to him, Messieurs, to whom we owe homage and faithful obedience. It is I, the first of his subjects, who must set the example of unbreakable fidelity to his person and of an attachment more dedicated than others to the interests of his state. It was these sentiments of mine which led the late King to speak kindly to me in the last moments of his life, a speech which I believe I should repeat to you. After having received the Viaticum, he called me and said, 'My nephew, I have made a will where I have conserved all the rights due to your birth; I commend the Dauphin to you, serve him as faithfully as you have served me, and work to conserve his Kingdom for him. In the event of misfortune, you will be the master and the crown will belong to you.' To these words he added others which are too kind to me to repeat: he finished by saying, 'I have made the dispositions which I have thought the wisest, but as one cannot foresee everything, if there is anything which must be changed, one will change it.' These are his very words.

I am therefore persuaded that, following the laws of the Kingdom and the examples of that which has been done in similar circumstances, and the intention of the late King, the Regency belongs to me. But I should not be satisfied if you do not join your votes to my other claims, and your approbation with which I shall not be less flattered than that of the Regency itself.

Having staked his claim, Orléans outlined his proposals:

But by whatever right I have to aspire to the Regency, I can assure, you, Messieurs, that I will deserve it by my zeal in the service of the King and by my love for the public good, being helped above all by your advice and wise remonstrances. I ask for your help in advance, declaring in this assembly that I will have no other plan than to ease the lot of the people, re-establish good order in the finances, cut back on unnecessary expenditures, maintain the peace in and outside the Kingdom, re-establish peace and union in the Church, and work with all the application possible in order to make the state happy.

What I ask now, Messieurs, is that you give your conclusions on the proposition I have just made, and that you deliberate, as soon as the will is read, on the claims which I have to the Regency, commencing by the first, that is the one I claim from my birth and the laws of the Kingdom.

This speech, at once noble and self-serving, was warmly received. But the will had not yet been read, and the *parlement* had already gone against the late King's wishes in hearing the duc d'Orléans speak before doing so. Mesmes and Daguesseau solemnly brought out the sealed document, and an envelope with the two codicils. The marquis de Dreux, who was known for his loud voice, began to declaim the contents.

The King's wishes were heard in silence; that a Regency Council be appointed; that the duc d'Orléans should have a casting vote in the

Council's deliberations only in the case of an even split; that everything should be decided by a majority of votes 'without the duc d'Orléans being able alone and by his own authority to determine, enact or expedite any order in the name of the King, without following the advice of the Regency Council'. The education of the King would be entrusted to the duc du Maine, who would also have control of the household troops. Without hesitation the duc d'Orléans expressed his surprise at the conditions set upon his Regency, so contrary to the rights of his birth and the sentiments expressed by the dying King. He insisted that the court opine immediately on his right by birth to the Regency, after which he would take the opportunity to discuss the particular clauses of the will.

With no intervention or complaint from the duc du Maine, the *parlement* solemnly and with dispatch voted to grant the Regency to the duc d'Orléans by right of birth; another special session of *parlement,* a *lit de justice,* would confirm it. This accomplished, Philippe started to dismantle the will. First Monsieur le Duc was granted immediate entry to the Regency Council instead of waiting a year. Then Philippe asked that the command of the household troops be given to him as Regent, not to the duc du Maine, adding that Maine could continue to be responsible for the guardianship of the King. He then took the opportunity to say that he wished to establish several different councils for different issues, finances, war and others about which he would reveal the details later.

Maine rose to his feet. He was holding three large pages from which he read in a wavering voice. He declared by way of preamble that he would willingly sacrifice his interests for the good of the kingdom, for he had always felt that the kindnesses of the late King had exceeded his merits; he was ready to submit with pleasure to the decisions of the parlement on the questions of the guardianship and education of the King, on condition that they left him the symbolic functions of Superintendent of the King's Education. He spoke hesitantly and seemed already to have conceded. A silence followed his remarks.

The chief magistrates decided in favour of Monsieur le Duc entering the Regency Council immediately, but asked for a little time to consider the claims of the Regent and the duc du Maine over the household troops and guardianship of the King. Everyone retired for lunch. Philippe was halfway to his objective. He had been declared Regent with no restrictions; now he needed to emasculate the duc du Maine. He made the short trip to his home, the Palais-Royal, where he met a few close friends as well as Daguesseau and Joly de Fleury. After a break of two hours everyone returned to the Palais de Justice. The Regent spoke forcefully; he could not accede to being simply the titular head of a Regency Council as the will indicated. He wished to be free to do good and agreed to be restrained from doing ill. (This statement was greeted with prolonged cheers.) He would govern with councils, and he would listen to them. But he had to have freedom of movement.

As for the command of the troops, the authority should not be shared in this unprecedented way. As Regent, he alone must command; he could not answer for the tranquillity of the Kingdom if the dispositions of the late King's will stood. Maine found the force to declare that all this was contrary to the wishes of the late King, that he could not charge himself with the safety of the King if he had not effective authority over the household troops. 'The guardianship and education of the King is one thing, command of the troops another,' said Philippe. The magistrates nodded yes.

Too late, the duc du Maine protested; he repeated that he could not answer for the King's safety without troops, and so he asked to be discharged as superintendent of the King's Education. The Regent, in a clear and biting reference to the rumours spread by Maine, asked what it was exactly that the Duke was afraid of. Why did he have so many scruples about the safety of the King? Stumbling, Maine replied that one could not predict what might happen. The Regent said he would not leave the King's side and could answer with his person; at this tense juncture the magistrates intervened. Their decision was to discharge the duc du Maine from the responsibility for the King's safety and to give it to the Regent.

Victory was his. He had the name and the powers of the Regent. With the help of the chief magistrates and Monsieur le Duc he had marginalised the duc du Maine, leaving him with the title of Superintendent of the King's Education and no power. At six o'clock in the evening the session ended. The Regent could return to Versailles, and to the other tasks at hand, well satisfied with the day. Arriving there two hours later, he was greeted with forced politeness by the maréchal de Villeroi, who had hoped for a different outcome, and as a conquering hero by his mother, 'ravie de joie'.

'The duc d'Orléans came into his Regency like a fox,' noted Pierre Narbonne, the Commissioner of Police at Versailles and an observer of the day's tumultuous events. Montesquieu (a member of the *parlement* in later years) wrote approvingly, 'this astute Prince went to *parlement*, and, laying out all the rights of his birth, overturned the will of Louis XIV, who, wishing to survive himself, seemed to have wanted to reign even after his death'. Philippe might be Regent in name, but he remained most anxious to have the final legal seal of approval affixed by the *lit de justice* schedule for 7 September. And he wanted to be in Paris, not at Versailles, which had an air of irrelevancy about it. In addition, although everything seemed calm, it was important that the King be taken to Vincennes.

While the complex logistics of the King's move, and that of the entire court, were being worked out, even as the body of Louis XIV still lay in state, Philippe took the initiative and returned to the Palais-Royal. He had much work awaiting him and was eager to start. After being excluded from affairs of state, he had now to take a crash course in governing. He peered diligently at the hundreds of documents put in front of him, interrogated the ministers of the former regime, took stock of these men and their possible usefulness to him. In order to establish a mood of tolerance and goodwill, he freed prisoners from the Bastille, 'earning countless benedictions for this act of justice and humanity', as Saint-Simon put it. One poor fellow, released after thirty-five years, with nowhere to go and no one to see, timidly asked if he could just stay in prison. He was permitted to do so.

Then, as *parlement* was assembling for the *lit de justice*, the Regent heard that the royal doctors, comfortably ensconced at Versailles, had forbidden the little King to travel, on the ground that he had a bad cold. Philippe, impatient to conclude the business at hand, summoned the doctors and told them to have the King ready to go to Vincennes the next day. And so, on 9 September, at two in the afternoon, the King left Versailles for Vincennes, sitting between the Regent and Mme de Ventadour, with the duc du Maine and the maréchal de Villeroi in front and the comte de Toulouse at the side. (Carriages in those days had their seats arranged with everyone facing the same way.) Large crowds stood along the ramparts to watch them pass; they saw the King, dressed in violet, cheerfully calling 'Vive le Roi!' to the bystanders. One of these, the lawyer Mathieu Marais, noted that the boy 'appeared handsome, well made, carrying his hat with a fine air, a little pale'. Earlier the same day, the body of Louis XIV had been taken to Saint-Denis. And Philip V of Spain finally heard the news of his grandfather's death.

The *lit de justice* was held on 12 September at the Palais de Justice. On his arrival, Louis XV was ceremoniously carried to the door of the Great Hall by his First Equerry, and then carried to the throne by the duc de Tresmes. The boy monarch spoke his part perfectly: 'I have come here, Messieurs, most happy to give you the marks of my goodwill; my Chancellor will tell you my intentions.' Voysin, in a robe of violet velvet lined with crimson satin, delivered a eulogy of Louis XIV. Then it was over. Philippe d'Orléans was the undisputed Regent of France.

# PART TWO
*Regent*

# ❧ 15 ❧

## PHILIPPE D'ORLÉANS

In September 1715 Philippe d'Orléans was forty-one years old. Although he had lost much of his youthful allure, he was still of pleasant countenance and attractive, even if rather stout and red in the face. Of medium height at most, his bearing was easy and extremely noble. He bore the scars of military campaigns and roisterous evenings; his left arm had been smashed by a cannonball and broken in a fall from a horse; his eyesight had deteriorated to the point that he had to peer closely at documents, often entangling his quill pen with his wig. His mode of dress was considerably more sober than it had been in his prime, and his wig was no longer the leonine glory of yesterday but a shorter, greyer version, tied back in the more informal military manner. In his private apartments he worked without wig, only putting it on when visitors arrived. He no longer robed himself in gorgeous silks, velvets and brocades, studded with diamonds and pearls; now he simply threw the obligatory blue ribbon of the Order of the Holy Ghost over his coat and went to work. Saint-Simon commented drily that no one had less work than His Royal Highness's Master of the Wardrobe, except his Confessor.

Like much else about him, however, even his appearance remains some-what mysterious. At Versailles there is a painting of a seated man gesturing to a boy who seems to be Louis XV. It is supposed to be the Regent. Doubts have been raised about the identification because of details of dress and surroundings; if it is Philippe, he seems smaller and older than his years. A portrait in Toledo, Ohio, once described as Philippe holding a painting of his mistress, is no longer thought to be him; a bust in Washington DC is impossible to identify with accuracy. So we cannot reconstruct his image exactly.

He was certainly a little less than at his physical peak. He had spent too many evenings drunk, and wasted too much time in gossip and gaiety with his daughter and his friends. The years of ostracism had taken a more insidious toll. To many observers he seemed tired, blurred. But in 1715 Philippe summoned up all his forces. And they were considerable. He still had an easy and dignified way of talking and a marvellous memory. Saint-Simon wrote that:

> he talked eloquently on the abstract sciences, affairs of state, finance, the law, military matters, and the doings of the court, as he did in polite conversation, or in the discussion of everything from engineering to the arts. He had read the histories and memoirs of great men, and put them to excellent use. To hear him talk, you would have thought him vastly learned. Not so, indeed, for he was a skimmer; but his memory was so uniformly good that he forgot nothing...'

He had charm. Most of the remarks attributed to him, and all the conversations recalled by his friends, show wit and a reluctance to take himself seriously. He appreciated wit and brevity, bons mots and jokes; he couldn't abide pomposity or prolixity. He had a devouring intellectual curiosity, admired Fénelon, read Rabelais, Cervantes, Leibniz, Malebranche. His mind was sceptical, probing, restless, unsatisfied. He would have agreed wholeheartedly with Fontanelle's statement, 'I am terrified by the certainty which reigns around me.' He himself did leave some writings, but they are fragmentary. Some letters to his mother and notes to Dubois, and, charmingly, verses to his mistress, as well as an opera, some engravings and drawings. His correspondence with Saint-Simon has disappeared. In his work, he prided himself on not writing anything down, believing that the least paper trail possible was best. His prodigious memory assisted him. And so his only real legacy is the official documents, a monument to industry and application.

Apart from his qualities of mind and intellect, he was more compassionate and tolerant than most men of his time. 'I never saw a man more violently opposed to murder or even to causing pain,' testified Saint-Simon. 'You might say that he carried kindness and tolerance too far ...' He would promise all kinds of things to people, partly out of calculation, but also because he liked to please. And yet he never forgot who he was; very proud of his lineage, he piqued himself on his resemblance to his great-grandfather Henri IV and for that reason, pride in birth, always treated the little King Louis XV with enormous respect. He was sensitive to any encroachment on his or his family's position. But he hated pomp and ceremonial, and the endless quarrels over precedence and prerogative bored and irritated him.

Proud in birth and full of bonhomie, passionate for work and pleasure, a scholar, a rake, a thinker, a buffoon. A subtle mind and a crude tongue. Loyal to all his friends, except to his women. Constant in nothing but inconstancy. As contradictory a personality as any in history. Such was the man who took power in France.

The King and his court would be established at the Tuileries, but France would be governed from the Palais-Royal. This rambling, unpretentious building was rather taken for granted by Parisians. In the centre of the city, with the Opéra in one wing, and a large garden, much frequented by the neighbours, extending to the rue des Petits-Champs, it was part of the fabric of the city. In 1715 the Palais-Royal stepped somewhat hesitantly into the place of Versailles.

Since inheriting the palace in 1701, on the death of his father, Philippe had done little to improve or modernise it. The grand rooms with their painted ceilings were still decorated with marble, hung with tapestries, filled with laquer cabinets and all the bibelots Monsieur had loved; but everything was rather haphazard and uncared for. Philippe, busy at war and with Mme d'Argenton, had devoted little time to its upkeep. He had commissioned Antoine Coypel, First Painter to the Orléans family, to paint the ceiling of the Gallery of Aeneas. The rest of the palace was like Sleeping Beauty, about to be woken from its trance. Now he summoned Coypel back to the Gallery of Aeneas to complete seven large canvases for the walls, and in one of the first acts of the Regency he named him to the long-vacant post of First Painter to the King. Coypel was grateful, dedicating an address he gave at the Académie to the Regent: 'for who better than I can attest to his knowledge of art, as well known as that of his knowledge of all the other sciences?'

Philippe had lived long enough at the court of Louis XIV to understand the importance of imagery in defining a ruler and impressing the population at home and the powers abroad. He decided to have plans drawn up for a thorough transformation of the Palais-Royal and turned to his First Architect, a young man called Gilles-Marie Oppenord. Oppenord had only recently been appointed to this post, and was a bold choice. Having studied in Rome, and been profoundly influenced by what he saw there, he had moved to Paris, to a house in the rue Saint-Thomas-du-Louvre, across the road from the Palais-Royal. He soon became highly regarded by the influential art connoisseurs of the city, in particular Pierre Crozat, Crozat le Pauvre, who often entertained the Regent at his soirées in the rue de Richelieu.

Oppenord's vitality and originality attracted Philippe. Although all of his work at the Palais-Royal has vanished, we can imagine what his rooms would have looked like from his amazing notebooks, published after his death in three volumes known as the *Petit, Moyen* and *Grand Oppenord*, which illustrated his designs for everything from clock-cases, chandeliers and chimneypieces to decorative panelling.

He treated all the elements of the traditional French room, wall panelling, marble chimneypiece, tall, arched mirrors, windows rising from floor to ceiling, with daring imagination and innovative detail. He loved to curve the edges of panels, the frames of mirrors, sculpting palm fronds, foliage, flowers, dragons, birds, shells in exuberant abundance. His rooms at the Palais-Royal, all white and gold, sparkling with reflections from large mirrors and crystal candelabra, hung with white brocade, crimson damask and blue velvet, crammed with precious objects, terracotta statuettes, bronzes, commodes, canapés, a Veronese or a Titian on an easel, must have been astonishing in their sumptuousness, a perfect synthesis of the *grand goût* and the modern taste of the day.

Philippe's rooms were on the *piano nobile*, to the left of the main entrance. Oppenord first redecorated his bedchamber with simple panelling, painted and gilded, and hangings of crimson damask, against which his favourite paintings were hung: Titian's *Philip II*, Van Dyck's *Marie de Medici* (she was his great-grandmother) and two other Van Dycks of the Snyders family. The bed, covered in crimson silk fringed with gold, canopied and plumed, stood in an alcove behind a balustrade as was customary for royal personages. A night table of violetwood, marble topped, two carved and gilded tables, eight armchairs, several stools, and a large pink plush armchair for the toilette were in this room along with a commode 'en forme de tombeau', a red satin screen in a corner. Arched mirrors faced each other across the room, another hung between the windows, which were draped in crimson damask. A crystal chandelier hung from the ceiling.

In his Cabinet de Travail stood a magnificent desk, six feet long, fitted in bronze, next to it a *chaise longue* in carved and gilded wood and a cabinet of Chinese laquer. Four screens protected against draughts. Oppenord's designs for the panelling show gilded trophies, palms, cherubs and pyramids. From here a door led down to the Petits Appartements, where there was a modern kitchen and where nightly supper parties took place.

Oppenord worked at the Palais-Royal throughout the Regency, producing two masterpieces. One was a magnificent chimneypiece for the Gallery of Aeneas which took up the entire wall, a riot of gilt, cherubs supporting candelabra and winged Victories bearing aloft a cartouche inscribed with the arms of the family of Orléans, from which a curtain with heavy folds was draped. Contemporary observers were much impressed by the original shapes, the curves and undulations, the fecundity of invention. The other masterpiece, the salon known as the 'Lanternon' came towards the end of the Regency. Oppenord also designed the Regent's new stables at the corner of the rue Neuve des Petits-Champs and rue Vivienne. Philippe had magnificent conveyances, one with an interior of crimson and gold Venetian velvet with seven mirrors bordered with gilded braid, another with an interior of silver and blue velvet fringed with gold. The interior of his calèche de ville was of green velvet fringed with gold, the windows draped with heavy curtains of green Tours brocade embroidered with gold. Splendid carriages were as desirable then as luxurious cars today.

As for the garden of the Palais-Royal, it was not surrounded by the arcades of today. These did not arrive until 1780 when Philippe's great-grandson, Philippe-Egalité, built them as a venture for profit. The houses of the rue de Richelieu and the rue des Bons-Enfants backed directly on to the palace grounds, separated by allées of elm and chestnut, yew and spruce. The garden was for many years one of the most popular promenades in the city. The English visitor Martin Lister wrote in 1698: 'the garden of the Palais-Royal ... is very large, has two or three great bassins with their jets d'eaux, but not well kept; nor hath anything elegant in it, but the good order and disposition of its shady walks and parterres. It is ever full of good company.' Compared to the much grander gardens of the aristocracy near by, particularly those of the duc d'Antin, Philippe's gardens were a real place for Parisians to stroll and talk and meet, as they still are today.

At the beginning of the eighteenth century Paris was a noisy, vibrant, smelly city, the largest in Europe, still medieval in its plan and its narrow streets. Even the widest streets, those radiating out from the centre, the rues Saint-Antoine, Saint-Martin, Saint-Denis, Saint-Honoré, du Temple, Saint-Jacques, were only five to eight metres wide. The roads were paved, but covered in filth; refuse, garbage, urine, excrement, slops, ran down them, turned to mud winter, baked to dust in summer. It was the smell which visitors noticed first; then the noise. Michel de Marolles, a writer and translator, gave a vivid word picture of a street scene in the city: 'A carriage overturned, a rogue arrested, some fishwives who quarrel, a thief they are taking away to hang, a crowd which gathers and disperses, the cry of those selling foodstuffs, the bills for theatres and bookshops, the songs of strollers, the display of merchandise, the meeting with a continual crowd of different faces.'

The day began with the bells of hundreds of churches sounding the Angelus. A throng of market people arrived at the city gates with bread, butter, cheeses, fruits, eggs and fowl. They crowded towards the main market at Saint-Eustache or the many lesser ones elsewhere. Shops opened and the crowd of workers increased. The streets resounded to the cries of the street vendors: 'Pears baked in the oven', 'Voilà, little rye breads!', 'Fresh eggs!', 'Wriggling ells!', 'Fresh salmon!', 'Romaine lettuce à la salade!', 'The milkman, come quick!', 'Whitings to fry!', 'Excellent vin de Bourgogne!', 'Berries to make into jam!', 'Mushrooms, mushrooms!', 'Turf to burn!', 'Matches and tinder!', 'Lantern, lantern!', 'Hats to sell, old hats!', 'Sweep your chimneys from top to bottom!'

The stagecoaches arrived from Calais, Rouen, Lyon, Bordeaux, Sedan, and Metz. Cabs waited for hire, at a fare of five sols. Wagons, carts and pedestrians fought for elbow room in the narrow streets. And then suddenly, at nightfall, the city emptied. The bourgeoisie closed their doors. Although the streets were safer and better lit than London – for Louis XIV, who cared little for Paris, had instituted one valuable improvement, the installation of five thousand new street lanterns – after dark the streets harboured only those on the lookout for trouble, deserters, lackeys, prostitutes, pimps, watched by patrols of city police. Most visitors newly arrived from the provinces felt as the playwright Marivaux did: 'I would not know how to tell you what I felt when I saw this great city, and its deafening noise, its people, its streets. For me it was like the moon.'

Paris, with its class of extraordinarily wealthy businessmen, had a vital social life, in the form of theatres and salons. Since the turn of the century it had offered much more fun and diversion than the court, where the King rarely ventured outside the apartments of Mme de Maintenon for his amusement. Not that the court became depopulated; it was still the only source of most jobs and favours. And it retained its magnetism for the nobility as long as the King was alive. But attendance there, particularly after the deaths of the Dauphin and his wife in 1712, increasingly became a duty rather than a pleasure, particularly for the young.

In 1715, therefore, the chance to leave Versailles and live in Paris was welcomed by most courtiers. But there would be problems, not for Philippe, who was elated, but for the thousands of people who had lived at Versailles, courtiers and servants alike. For thirty years the nobility had submitted to forced attendance at Versailles, dutifully following the King's every move and clinging as close to his person, the fount of all favours, as possible. They had regarded it as a great honour to be allowed a tiny lodging at Versailles, and had willingly abandoned their country estates; if they had gone to Paris at all it was almost surreptitiously. Paris was where the bourgeoisie and the tiresome magistrates lived, all those potential Frondeurs. Louis XIV had disapproved of his capital and was always jealous of its rival attractions. He refused to allow his family to go there without permission and his courtiers had followed suit.

But in the best years of Louis XIV's reign, with the comte de Toulouse, the duc d'Antin and the princesse de Conti leading the way, the attractions of Paris had become more apparent. The city was growing apace. In the first quarter of the century, Paris developed a whole new suburb, the faubourg Saint-Germain. The bustling area around the Palais-Royal had replaced the Marais as the smartest residential quarter. The brand new place Vendôme was a magnet for the richest men in town including Antoine Crozet, who had a splendid house at the north-west corner of the place. During the Regency, the place Vendôme became home to several of Philippe's closest friends, among them Charles de Nocé, and to one of his mistresses, Mme de Parabère. Louis XIV had hardly ever come to his capital; between 1673 and 1693 he attended only twenty ceremonies in Paris, and then did not return until 1701. After that he came to the city only four more times in his life.

While royal influence faded, the city developed into an intellectual centre quite separate from the crown. The theatre thrived, the Comédie-Française and the Opéra, as well as the more roisterous theatres of the great annual fairs. The Comédie-Française was based on the Left Bank in the rue Fossés-Saint-Germain-des-Prés in a fine theatre holding fifteen hundred spectators. There they put on the traditional repertory of Molière, Corneille, Racine, but also new plays by Crébillon, Dancourt, Baron and La Motte. Adrienne Lecouvreur, the greatest actress of her day, made her début there in 1717.

The Opéra, officially the theatre of the Royal Académie de Musique, was an integral part of the Palais-Royal; the repertory featured the old stand-bys of Lully as well as light-hearted, tuneful works such as Campra's *Europe galante*, composed in the year of the Peace of Ryswick 1697, and his *Fêtes Vénétiennes* of 1710. The Opéra staged two or three new productions a year, and performances three nights a week. As for the Italian players, banished in 1697 for presenting a play called the *False Prude*, thought to be a satire on Mme de Maintenon, they were brought back to Paris in 1716 at the Regent's personal initiative, and established in the hôtel de Bourgogne near Saint-Eustache. Unfortunately for them, tastes had changed in their absence and they found themselves less successful than they had been, their audience having gravitated to the theatres of the fairs.

The Saint-Germain fair was held in February and March; a large area of the faubourg Saint-Germain was covered over and turned into a twenty-four-hour spectacle for the public. Acrobats and jugglers, performing animals and strolling players animated the streets, but the main attractions were the four or five ramshackle theatres. Before 1715 the fair players were not allowed to speak, as the Comédie-Française insisted on the monopoly for that, so they used placards and signs, encouraging the audience to sing along. The solemnity of the classical theatre and the language barrier at the Comédie-Italienne made these performances true popular entertainment. The Saint-Laurent fair, which opened in August and lasted for six weeks, was a lower-class affair, as the wealthy were at their country homes at this time of year.

Philippe attended as many of these spectacles as he could, and was on good terms with many writers. When the playwright Dufresny wrote to the Regent, 'Monseigneur, Dufresny begs Your Royal Highness to leave him in poverty, so that he remains as a monument to the state of France before Your Regency,' Philippe replied, 'Je refus absolument,' and gave him a pension.

Art exhibitions were held regularly for an educated public. Disputes such as those which pitted Poussin against Rubens, draughtsmanship against colour, animated the salons. Art dealers proliferated, disseminating prints and genre paintings for a growing audience. This was how Watteau began. Private patrons had replaced the court; their taste was different, they preferred pastorals and *fête galante* to heroic landscapes and devotional pictures, although the taste for the gods and goddesses of Greek mythology persevered. Portraits became very popular; in the Salon of 1699 there were fifty, in that of 1704 two hundred. The artists associated with the famous portraits of Louis XIV, Rigaud and Largillière, had gravitated to portraits of the rich bourgeoisie, and introduced a graduated price list, depending on whether the sitter was shown only to the knees or full length.

The Académie française was in uproar over the dispute of the Ancients versus the Moderns, with all the educated elite of Paris taking sides. Did art progress, or were the classics the standard to which all artists aspired? The literary lions of the day, the philosopher Fontanelle and the dramatist La Motte, appeared at the salons of Mme de Tencin and her sister Mme de Ferriol, reading their work and discussing their ideas. Fontanelle, in particular, fascinated his listeners with his elegant explanations of the latest scientific discoveries, and his passionate defence of progress in the arts and sciences. He was comfortably ensconced as Perpetual Secretary of the Académie des Sciences, but still au courant with the latest discoveries, still extolling the virtues of scientific enquiry. His whole life was dedicated to making the mysteries of science comprehensible to more and more of the public.

The reading public pounced on the first volumes of *Gil Blas*, the picaresque novel by Lesage which had just appeared. Montesquieu's *Persian*

*Letters*, which satirised Paris and the Parisians, delighted those it mocked.

Adding to the tumult, there were hundreds of cafés in Paris in the last years of Louis XIV, nearly four hundred by 1723. The widow Laurent owned one on the rue Dauphine where the *beaux esprits* met, the headquarters of the La Motte faction at the corner of the rue Dauphine and the rue Christine; the Café Poincelet stood at the northern end of the Pont-Neuf; in the rue Rouillé was a café where only literary subjects were discussed; and at the Café Savant the periodicals of the day, the *Mercure galant* and the *Journal des savants*, were available. The most famous of all were the Café Procope on the Left Bank near the Comédie-Française, and the Café de la Régence, which was founded in 1685 opposite the Palais-Royal. Mme de Maintenon was right when she remarked that, in Paris, 'everyone wants to judge and decide for themselves about books, the government, religion'. But whereas she saw it as a threat, it was in fact a mark of intense intellectual vitality.

However, the vast majority of the inhabitants of Paris were uneducated and poor. They lived in the eastern quarters of the city, around the Bastille, on the rue Saint-Antoine, in another world. Here were the homes of the working men and women, the *petit peuple*, who lived in almost medieval conditions. The working-class quarters had been pushed eastwards by the expansion of the middle and upper classes into the centre of the city. 'Since His Majesty has settled in Paris,' reads a document of 1720, 'many government officers and seigneurs have taken up residence around the Louvre, Saint-Honoré and the Butte Saint-Roch districts, where several mansions have been built, which has forced artisans of various professions who lived in and around this district to leave and settle elsewhere...'

In their overcrowded houses the 'people' remained eerily unseen and unheard by the privileged. 'The *petit peuple* are inaccessible to reason,' pronounced Fontanelle. There was a fault line between the classes which widened calamitously through the century. But although they might be poor, overcrowded and dourly dressed, although their daily life was overshadowed by the fragility of the grain supply and the threat of crop failure, the existence of the 'people' was enlivened by a vibrant street life. There seems to have been a surprisingly high literacy rate in Paris, far above the national average. (From the end of the seventeenth century, 85 per cent of men and 60 per cent of women in the city were capable of signing their wills; there is, according to Daniel Roche, author of *The People of Paris*, a high degree of correlation between the ability to sign one's name and complete literacy.) Hawkers sold a host of publications, some clandestinely printed, or imported, others perfectly legal. Religious tracts, uplifting guides, and all kinds of almanacs were popular. Political pamphlets had a wide circulation. Travelling *chansonniers* stood at street corners playing their songs and selling the songsheets. And there was always the tavern and its promise of escape.

Into this bewildering milieu came the apparatus of court and government. For the first time in almost a century, Paris was the true centre and soul of France, home to the richest and poorest, all bound together and yet completely divided.

## ⚛ 16 ⚛

# POWER

The Regent quickly set about the task confronting him. In order to familiarise himself with all the details of government, he established an arduous daily routine. Even before his Lever, which was very brief, he was at work reading documents in his bedroom. He would then grant audiences, before starting his morning of meetings. Among those he saw the most often were Torcy, who was responsible for the bureau de Postes, and who had the secrets of the mail in his keeping; the maréchal de Villeroi, who kept him informed of the King's health and well-being; La Vrillière, the indispensable Secretary to the Councils; and the heads of the councils. Dubois was always in evidence, but discreetly.

At half-past two Philippe took a cup of chocolate in public and would chat with those who attended. This was the best time to ask for a favour. He would then go downstairs to visit his wife, or to a meeting of the Regency Council if it was sitting that day, and then always to the Tuileries, where he would wait upon the King. He treated the little boy with the same air of profound respect with which he had approached Louis XIV, and that pleased the King and set a good example.

In the autumn of 1715, immersed in his papers, the Regent hardly noticed his surroundings. His mother was deeply concerned. 'I see my son no more than once a day, and that for barely a half-hour. He works hard from six in the morning until midnight, and I fear he will make himself ill if he carries on like this.' But Philippe continued his debilitating routine: 'I am dying of fear that my son is working so hard that he will make himself ill. Yesterday he was so exhausted he went to bed at nine o'clock; he started to work again at five in the morning, and is still at work as I write. Eleven o'clock has just sounded; I have not seen him yet today.'

For Madame, all the stability of the old order had vanished overnight. 'Many reasons make me miss the King, the least of which is not seeing dear Fontainebleau again and not living in dear and agreeable Versailles and Marly . . .' Even Saint-Cloud was impossible. 'I must stay in Paris this winter. I have not thought of going to Saint-Cloud since the duchesse de Berry is there, with whom – between us – I wish to have nothing to do. We have no time for each other.'

Harried as he was, Philippe did ask Madame to start a correspondence with the Princess of Wales, in order that relations between the two royal families might stay on a cordial footing. In return for her help on this front Madame dared to ask a favour. 'I have kept my word and solicited in secret for the poor people in the galleys. I have obtained a promise but say nothing, dear Luise! let's hope that the Council of Conscience doesn't spoil it.' (It seems that some seventy Protestant prisoners were released from this initiative.) 'One thing is for certain; if my son followed his own inclination, no man would be persecuted on account of his faith.'

In addition to throwing open the prisons and freeing galley slaves, Philippe performed another meritorious action. He went to visit Mme de Maintenon at Saint-Cyr, a visit she described in detail:

> He told me that he had taken measures that I be given exactly what was mentioned in the King's will. I replied that I had found this out the night before and that I thanked him very humbly, but that it was too much given the state of the finances. He replied that it was a bagatelle, but that it was true that the finances were in a bad way. I said that what he gave me would be used in prayers for him to obtain God's grace, which he needed. He replied that he already felt the weight of the burden he was bearing. I told him that he would feel it even more.

There was little warmth between these two old adversaries, but mutual respect and a sort of peace.

On most evenings he entertained his friends at supper in his *petits appartements*. The stories surrounding the nightly supper parties of the Regent grew more lurid the more they were repeated. According to the gossip, women posed naked, sexual acts were committed at the dinner tables, gross indecency abounded. Tiberius and Messalina would have been jealous of these revels. Unfortunately, those who reported the supposed goings-on were not actually present. Saint-Simon himself never went, nor would he have been invited. His disapproval was caused by the mixed bag of guests, with no thought being given to rank or precedence, and by the free and easy conversation. Drinking eating, swearing and embracing to excess amid general hilarity seem to be what occurred. The truly horrible scenes of the times, scenes which gave the Regency a reputation for 'stupre, lucre et cruauté', went on at the houses of Monsieur le Duc, the prince de Conti and the prince de Rohan rather than at the Palais-Royal.

This was the time when fine French cuisine, sauces in particular, became established. Philippe himself liked to transfer his interest in laboratory experiments to those of the kitchen, creating elaborate sauces with wine, herbs and spices. The passion for new ingredients grew with their discovery. Vegetables were a novelty, and people became excited about peas and artichokes and asparagus. Philippe tried all the new foods and drinks, particularly chocolate, which he took every day and made fashionable. Chocolate had come to Europe from Mexico, thence to Spain, where it was always more popular than in France. Perhaps Philippe developed a taste for it there. The French generally preferred coffee, which had been widely available for thirty years. Tobacco was recommended by doctors to be taken by nose, or in smoke or by chewing, to ease pain and hunger, and to provide energy. Snuff and pipes were the commonest ways of using this new drug, cigars and cigarettes came later. Cigarettes perhaps made their first appearance in America; there exists a French document in Canada, dated 1708, which refers to 'the infinite quantity of paper' imported from Europe for 'the little rolls in which they wrap chopped tobacco to smoke it'.

Guests at the Palais-Royal included the duchesse de Berry, mistresses current and concurrent, girls from the Opéra, society ladies, interesting foreigners, men and women invited for their wit rather than their birth. The most regular visitors were the coterie of Philippe's old friends, Canillac, the duc de Brancas, the marquis de Broglio, Charles de Nocé; these were the *roués*, men who prided themselves on an Epicurean philosophy, on wit and impiety. They were cultivated and polished; many of them wrote poetry or music. The closest friends were men older than Philippe, many of whom he had known for years. To them he was as loyal as he was disloyal to his women. Many were homosexual, all were unconventional. These were men whom Philippe loved but who, with the exception of Canillac, played little part in his government. They were the best of company at table, but Philippe knew that they would have been ill suited to office.

The duc de Brancas was a good-natured, amusing man, a witty raconteur. He endeared himself to Philippe by telling him that he hated politics, and that if they ever discussed them they would bore themselves to tears. He teased the sombre Canillac, who talked incessantly, that he suffered from a loss of words like women suffered from losses of blood and dubbed him the 'caillette triste' (the sad flirt), whereas he, Brancas, was the 'caillette gaie'. He was from a distinguished family and his cousin the marquis de

Brancas, a very different character, was a diplomat and envoy whom Louis XIV had entrusted with important missions. But he was not at all rich and had a troubled family life, being separated from his wife and tormented by a taste for boys, a taste which increased as he grew older. Brancas always made Philippe laugh; he used to say that when he was approached by supplicants for favours on account of his closeness to the Regent, he always responded, 'monsieur le duc d'Orléans overwhelms me with kindness it's true, but the sad fact is that the duc d'Orléans has so little credit with the Regent, so little, so very little, that you would be amazed.'

The marquis de Broglio was also from a distinguished family; his father and his brother both became maréchal de France. But he was not destined for success, although well read and intelligent. He was of questionable character, priding himself on his complete impiety and 'débauche raffinée'. His nickname in the Regent's group was Brouillon, or Muddlehead. He was appointed director of the infantry in 1718 and persuaded the Regent to increase the amount of money available for the ordinary soldiers' pay; he also had the good idea of building barracks in military towns to avoid the scandalous overcharging of the middlemen who supplied the camps. But the vested interests were against him and the scheme came to naught.

Charles de Nocé had known Philippe longer than any of the others. He could take liberties with Philippe, who called him Bracquemardus de Nocendo and in 1719 he took the post of First Gentleman of the Chamber, rather to everyone's surprise:

> Veille-je, ou si je fais un somme?
> Et Nocé devient gentilhomme!
>
> (Am I awake or do I nap?
> Nocé has become a gentleman!)

Madame deplored the influence of such men, but her son told her that if he couldn't relax after his arduous work he would not be able to endure it. In his mind his friends were his reward for hours spent poring over documents.

But these long, noisy evenings tired the Regent, who seemed to regard this pursuit of 'pleasure' as no less of a duty than his other work. He lost a great deal of time this way, and was often indisposed in the mornings. But Mathieu Marais remarked how extraordinary it was that not the Regent's mistresses, nor the duchesse de Berry, nor his roués, ever discovered anything important about affairs of state, even when they were all drunk. Instead, the talk was of past and present court gossip, old stories,

Philippe, duc de Chartres, as a boy.

*right:* View of the chateau and gardens of Saint-Cloud in about 1677, showing the extensive work done there by Le Nôtre.

*below right:* Philippe d'Orléans on horseback. Here shown at the height of his powers, prepared, in all his military splendour, for glorious campaigns in Spain.

*above:* Monsieur, Philippe's father. Having fathered a son, Monsieur, younger brother of Louis XIV, could return to his preferred homosexual way of life.

*right:* Mme de Maintenon. Louis XIV called her 'Your Solidity' and made her his secret wife. Her piety and sense of decorum greatly influenced the atmosphere at court.

The Doge of Genoa at Versailles in 1685. The ten-year-old duc de Chartres stands near his father, adorable in a red velvet coat.

The marriage of the duc de Bourgogne at Versailles in 1697. Philippe is standing to the right of the painting, by his wife and mother, looking very elegant but somewhat detached from the scene.

Françoise-Marie de Bourbon, duchesse d'Orléans, Philippe's wife. Proud and lazy, she was known as 'Madame Lucifer' to her husband.

Portrait of Madame. Philippe's mother was a stern critic of her son but she loved him dearly and he reciprocated her affection.

*above: The Sacrament of Ordination* (1647) by Nicolas Poussin. One of the set of the *Seven Sacraments* bought by the abbé Dubois in The Hague in 1716 while disguised as an art dealer and secretly negotiating with the British.

*left: Jupiter and Io* by Correggio. Painting in Philippe's collection at the Palais-Royal.

Philippe in armour.

*Retour du bal* (1712-14) by Antoine Watteau. By 1712 Watteau was becoming known in Paris for such idealised and haunting depictions of the aristocratic society of the day.

The Council of Regency meeting in September 1715. The noblemen who made up the council initially found the problems of etiquette more absorbing than the affairs of state. Only when it was decided who should sit and who should stand and who might wear a hat could they move on to discuss the questions of the day.

Philippe with Mme de Parabère. He made Marie-Thérèse de Parabère,
his 'little black crow', his official mistress in 1715 and their stormy relationship
set the tone for the bawdy, fun-loving society of Regency Paris.

*above:* Fêtes vénitiennes (1718-19) by
Antoine Watteau. It is possible that
the woman in the painting is Christine
Desmares, a celebrated actress and
mistress of Philippe.

*left:* Embarkation for Cythera, detail (1717)
by Antoine Watteau. This painting was
the 'morceau de reception' with which
Watteau gained admittance to the
Académie. Critics have argued as to
whether it depicts an embarkation for
Cythera or a return from it. The
Academie recognised it as a 'feste galante',
an entirely new category of painting.

*above:* Versailles in 1722, the year when the court moved back there from Paris.

*right:* Marly in 1723. The young Louis xv loved the grandeur and magnificent forests of Versailles and Marly, but the Regent took no pleasure there and missed Paris very much.

*L'Enseigne de Gersaint* (1721) by Antoine Watteau. Watteau painted this masterpiece as a sign for the shop of his friend, the art dealer Gersaint. A street in Paris in 1721 is vividly brought to life. Significantly, a portrait of Louis XIV is being packed into a crate while the customers show more interest in the pastorals, nudes and society portraits of the new régime.

The Lit de Justice held for the majority of Louis xv on 22 February 1723 at the Palais de Justice on the Ile de la Cité in Paris.

The family of Philip v of Spain and his Queen, Elizabeth Farnese.

*left:* The young Voltaire. François-Marie Arouet took the name Voltaire in 1718 when he was in his early twenties, already a successful playwright and thorn in the side of the authorities.

*right:* Antoine Watteau by Rosalba Carriera. This pastel drawing was done from life by Rosalba, a Venetian painter who lived in Paris during the Regency and kept a diary of her meetings with Watteau and other contemporary artists.

GUILLAUME DUBOIS.
CARDINAL, ARCHEVÊQUE DE CAMBRAY
NÉ À BRIVES LA GAILLARDE LE 6 SEPTEMBRE 1656
DÉCÉDÉ À PARIS LE 10 AOÛT 1723.

The funerary monument of Cardinal Dubois in the church of Saint-Roch, Paris. Dubois died in August 1723 at the age of sixty-seven, having achieved the highest honours of Church and State. But his countenance expresses fully the still avid energy which he maintained until the moment of his death.

jokes, with no one spared. 'They drank, they became excited, they said unrepeatable things with the greatest enjoyment,' reported Saint-Simon, 'and, having made plenty of noise, they all went home and started again the next day.'

Philippe faced severe challenges. The country, although at peace, was in debt and exhausted; the Church was divided into warring factions; and there were enemies at home and abroad. To meet these tests, Philippe could not rely on the traditional loyalty accorded a king. Indeed many of his countrymen regarded him as an interloper who, in the event of the death of the boy Louis XV, should be replaced by the King of Spain. He had no mandate, either by right of birth or from Louis XIV, and was therefore forced to rely on a coalition. He was placed in the position of a modern politician, obliged to find his allies where he could. He had built a party in order to acquire power, composed of *parlement*, Jansenists, reformers, opportunists. But between these component parts there were major fault lines, which could crack open with the slightest shock.

The Regent had promised *parlement* to introduce a system of government by councils, and he began to establish these councils immediately: Finance, Foreign Affairs, the Church, the Navy, War, Commerce and the Interior. By thus involving the magistrates and the nobility in the process of governing, he made sure of their support, at least initially. But, in his heart, this man who had so often been accused of a 'thirst to rule', believed that he could better make decisions alone, or with a very few trusted intimates. He used the process of selecting men for the councils to reward his friends and conciliate his enemies. But from the very beginning of the vaunted council system Philippe relied on outside contacts for advice and help.

As far as the Regent was concerned, the two most important councils were those of Finance and Foreign Affairs. These were the only two whose meetings he regularly attended, in addition to the Regency Council itself. The duc de Noailles was the natural candidate for the presidency of the Finance Council; to the astonishment of his fellow nobles, he had studied with the Controller General Desmarets for two years, and wanted the job. The maréchal de Villeroi was made titular head, in deference to his rank, but he almost never attended. When he had something to say, which was seldom, he would bring a little piece of paper with him, put on his glasses and read it out. No one paid much attention. The old marquis d'Effiat, who had a reputation for managing his own affairs very efficiently, was also named to the Council, as was the capable son of Louis XIV's doctor, Fagon, and Noailles' friend and mentor Rouille de Coudray.

Noailles was more interesting than any of them. He was a scholar, with the tastes of an intellectual, possessed a restless curiosity and an ambition to get things done, and was particularly eager to modernise and reform the financial administration of France. Noailles was four years younger than Philippe, tall with a heavy gait, thickset. As well as being clever and industrious, he had charm. Even Saint-Simon, who loathed him, admitted that he could be 'gracious, affable, cheerful, amusing, pleasing, fertile in charming sallies, a congenial fellow, a good musician, with the language of a courtier, the jargon of women'. He was 'toujours à la mode'. Saint-Simon meant to leave a portrait of a 'false and smiling hypocrite'; but he has left a much more endearing impression than he intended. Noailles was an impressive man.

As for Foreign Affairs, Philippe took the gamble of naming the maréchal d'Huxelles to be head of the Council. Huxelles was a firm believer in the foreign policy of Louis XIV, that is, the Spanish alliance and caution towards Great Britain; Philippe was already considering a change in attitude. In addition, Philippe distrusted Huxelles, who had been a close friend of Mme de Maintenon and the duc du Maine, and part of the group most opposed to the duc d'Orléans. His appointment was probably a measure of the fact that, at the beginning of the Regency, Philippe needed his enemies where he could see them, and also that he himself was not fully committed to one course of action. Huxelles was a strange man. Tall and ruddy, he wore a huge wig and a hat pulled down over his eyes, his orders and decorations all hidden beneath a plain, tightly buttoned coat. He was a notable homosexual, fond of young officers whom he 'domesticated' and 'jeunes valets très bien faits'.

The maréchal de Villars was to be head of the War Council. As the most famous soldier in France, responsible for saving the country from Marlborough's armies, he was the obvious choice. Madame spoke for France when she said, 'Cet homme, c'est un romain vivant.' ('This man, he is a living legend!') Villars had been given the superb château of Vaux-le-Vicomte in token of his services to his country and, having renamed it Vaux-Villars, lived there with his beautiful wife, thirty years younger than himself, whom he had great difficulty controlling. His contributions to the Council were mainly blustering and posturing, and he was a supporter of the Jacobites and the King of Spain. Again, it was a case of having one's enemy in plain sight.

The comte de Toulouse headed the Council of the Navy. There was general agreement that Toulouse was a decent man and that, whatever trouble his brother Maine might cause, he would remain loyal. He was reserved, rather cold, difficult to decipher, secretive; he managed to survive all the pitfalls of the Regency, doing his duty in a somewhat pedestrian way, and keeping out of controversy. He was a man of taste, living very grandly at his huge house next to the Palais-Royal, at Rambouillet where he loved to hunt, and at the pretty little château of La Rivière, near Fontainebleau, where he discreetly entertained his mistresses (including the maréchale de Villars). He avoided the fraught question of whom he should marry by remaining single*.

Philippe wanted the maréchal d'Harcourt to head the Council of the Interior, but, since suffering a stroke a few years earlier, Harcourt had had great difficulty speaking, and so he declined. The duc d'Antin was then proposed for the post. But d'Antin was the only one of all his old foes whom Philippe could not forgive. All the bitter feelings about the calumnies and slanders he had endured for so many years, the lies and insinuations of incest and murder, centred on d'Antin, whom he called a man without honour. But, regarding him with repugnance and disdain, Philippe could not ignore his obvious talents. D'Antin was a very intelligent and capable man. After resisting for two weeks, Philippe finally agreed to his inclusion of the Council, but he never trusted him.

The composition of the Council of Conscience was particularly delicate. This body would have to handle the issue of the Pope's Bull *Unigenitus*. Jesuits and Jansenists watched with interest. Philippe's choice of the Cardinal de Noailles, Archbishop of Paris, was applauded by *parlement*. Noailles was respected by both sides, but leant slightly to the Jansenists. His appointment, and those of other pro-Jansenist members, was part of the bargain struck in the weeks before the old King's death. (Père Le Tellier, Louis XIV's confessor, who was responsible for so much bitterness, was unceremoniously exiled to Amiens.)

Finally Philippe had to decide upon the composition of the Regency Council itself. For the time being, he decided to work with the people whom the late King had nominated, none of them his admirers. They were joined by men of Philippe's own choosing, the duc de Noailles, Saint-Simon, d'Effiat and his old friend the maréchal de Bezons. Canillac was rewarded with a place, as was Cheverny, the governor of Philippe's son, the duc de Chartres. The only men of the late King's choosing whom Philippe refused to accommodate were Desmarets, the Controller of the Finances, and the maréchal de Tallard. Tallard was devastated and buried himself at his little house at La Planchette near Courbevoie. Having been

---

* Everyone was stunned when, a few days after the Regent's death, he declared his secret marriage to the widowed marquise de Gondrin, sister of the duc de Noailles. But it was very much in character with his secretive nature.

captured at Blenheim, and taken as a prisoner to England, his nerves were gone. Already weary and haggard, 'tormented by the devil of ambition', as Saint-Simon put it, he made himself ill with misery until he was recalled in 1717.

The Regency Council had its inaugural meeting out at Vincennes on 28 September with the heads of the other councils in attendance. (Everyone had to travel out to Vincennes until the King returned to live at the Tuileries at the end of the year.) There would be four meetings a week; Saturday after dinner, Sunday morning, Tuesday after dinner and Wednesday morning. The first meetings got under way with the usual disputes about precedence, who should sit on what type of chair and who could keep their hat on. When these weighty matters were resolved, they could get down to business.

On the financial front, Philippe and Noailles began their great task with enthusiasm, but the situation they found was daunting. The national debt stood at seventy-seven million livres; the revenues of the next two years were consumed in advance; there were only eight hundred thousand livres in the Treasury. Noailles put the case succinctly:

> There are no funds available to meet our most urgent expenses; neither in our royal Treasury nor in our receipts. We found the estate of our crown given up, the revenues of the state practically annihilated by an infinity of charges and settlements, ordinary taxation eaten up in advance, arrears of all kinds accumulated through the years, a multitude of notes, ordinances, and allocations anticipated of so many different kinds which mount up to such considerable sums that one can hardly calculate them.

Noailles acted quickly; he turned to Antoine Crozat, one of the richest men in France, for an immediate loan to the state of a million livres in silver bars and an engagement for a further two millions. He attempted to bring some order into the chaos by liquidating a certain number of offices and cutting down military expenses. He let go a thousand bodyguards at Versailles and Marly, four hundred gardeners, all the sailors of the Canal, a hundred porters, a hundred Swiss Guards. The budget of the maison du Roi fell from fifteen million livres to four million. The royal stables were reduced in size; the musique du Roi reduced; pensions were suppressed. Pursuing the popular path of blaming the tax-farmers and the administrators, Noailles established a Chambre de Justice to try those who had stolen money from the state. Noailles made a fast start; his actions were laudable and refreshing; unfortunately they went nowhere near the root of the problem which was the inability of the central government to extract its revenues from the inefficient and corrupt system of tax-collecting and accounting.

Internationally, there was one matter facing Philippe in the autumn of 1715 which was now of the utmost urgency. He had to decide whether France would support an invasion of Scotland by the Pretender, James Edward Stuart. Through the summer, the Pretender, in Lorraine, had been preparing for an invasion, with the tacit complicity of Louis XIV, and subsidies from the King of Spain and the Pope. Philippe must have known something of what was going on. On assuming power, he became responsible for either pressing ahead or drawing back.

This was the Regent's first test of statesmanship. The issue was complex. Despite the Peace of Utrecht, Louis XIV and the Catholic powers thought it their duty to restore the Catholic Stuarts to the throne in Great Britain. In London the Jacobites were regarded as a real danger by King George and his ministers; after all George was an unpopular new arrival, speaking only German, and clearly more interested in the affairs of Hanover than in those of his new country. Even his German mistresses, known as the Elephant and the Beanpole, were ridiculed. Many in the British government thought that the future of the Hanoverian dynasty depended on the ending of the Jacobite threat.

There was another difficulty. Philippe's own position was hardly more secure than that of his cousin King George. The majority of Frenchmen were in favour of the Pretender's claims. To be seen to abandon him would be to play into the hands of his enemies at home and of the King of Spain abroad. And running through every conversation was the unspoken thought that, if Louis XV died, the King of Spain would undoubtedly claim the French crown, in which case Philippe would need the help of the British to defend his own position.

Philippe weighted his options: to allow plans for the invasion to proceed, or to draw back? Characteristically, he did both. He assured Lord Stair that there was nothing to the rumours; and he told the Duke of Ormonde, who was in Paris on behalf of the Pretender, that the invasion would proceed. If it succeeded, he would benefit; if it failed he could claim ignorance. It seemed to him that the dangers of stopping it, and giving ammunition to his enemies at home, were greater than those of letting it proceed. He moved with caution.

Somewhat ironically, Philippe found the British side the more congenial. He knew and liked Stair, and the regard was mutual. Stair thought the Regent 'the most courteous man I ever met, the best educated, knowledgeable about so many mattes, but impenetrable'. Philippe was also familiar with the new Foreign Secretary in London, none other than James Stanhope, his collaborator in those heady days in Spain seven years earlier. Philippe was well aware that Stanhope, who 'never lost his sang-froid, rarely his courtesy', was a resourceful and imaginative man, and would be a dangerous opponent. Neither could he forget that King George was, after all, his mother's cousin, the son of her beloved Aunt Sophie. Stair pointed out to the Regent how much it was in his personal interests to ally himself with King George, in recognition of their mutual rights. Philippe listened. No doubt he had considerable sympathy for that point of view. But it was too soon to break so completely with the policies of Louis XIV; France was not ready for him, the Regent, to support the Protestants against the Catholics. And so before the goal of a treaty with Great Britain could be reached, there was the matter of the Pretender and his invasion plans. Philippe decided to let them proceed.

In September the Earl of Mar (known as Bobbin' John, for the number of times he had changed his allegiance) raised the Stuart standard at Braemar after sounding out the Highland chiefs.

On 7 October Stair had a long audience with the Regent. He wanted to know if France would support the Scottish rebels. Philippe equivocated. But he did declare that he had given orders for the Pretender to be prevented from leaving Lorraine. Stair was not satisfied with the Regent's answers, felt that Philippe was playing for time, and finally said that if the French regarded the troubles caused by the Pretender with indifference, the British would do the same with those that befell France. Despite the threats, Philippe saw the Duke of Ormonde at the Palais-Royal later in October, and assured him that Dunkirk would not be guarded if the Pretender passed that way.

Philippe walked a tightrope; he had promised the Pretender that he would close his eyes to his movements and favour his cause as long as everything was kept secret, but he also assured Stair that he would keep an eye on the Pretender. On 1 November Stair called upon the Regent again; he was given more assurances. Then, during the night of the 3rd, James Stuart left Bar-le-Duc with three or four men. Stair, who had very good intelligence, protested. To placate him, Philippe sent his trusted ally Contades to Château-Thierry to await the Pretender at the place where Stair's spies said he would be. Naturally, Contades had orders not to try very hard to find Stuart; 'he was well resolved and instructed to miss the man he was looking for', as Saint-Simon put it.

Relentlessly, Stair sent his own men in pursuit. A certain Colonel Douglas was in charge of the operation; he had been taken prisoner at Almansa, married a young lady of Metz and remained in France. No doubt he was a secret agent, but for whom? He was apparently 'on a footing of consideration and familiarity with the Regent', as well as Stair's *homme de main*. In this case it seems clear that Douglas' job was to make an attempt on the life of the Pretender.

Together with two colleagues, all of them heavily armed, Douglas stopped to dine at Nonancourt, a village nineteen leagues from Paris, near Dreux. At the post office he made enquiries about the post-chaise. The postmaster was away, but his wife, Mme L'Hôpital, was a woman of sense. She realised that these English were up to no good and decided to dupe them. When Douglas left to continue the search, Mme L'Hôpital promptly got the other two men drunk. When the Pretender arrived, she hid him. The Englishmen were arrested; James Edward remained at Nonancourt for three days, then, disguised as an abbé, escaped to the coast. He arrived at Dunkirk in the greatest secrecy, remained there for several weeks preparing his expedition, and sailed for Scotland on 27 December. In Paris Stair and Douglas complained of the arrests; then Douglas prudently disappeared.

Madame heard the echoes of the British complaints from Luise, who was in London as *dame de compagnie* to the Princess of Wales, and became somewhat defensive. 'I must tell you again that it is unjust of Lord Stair to accuse my son of having a part in the flight of the King of England. How could he know what happened in Lorraine, and how could my son guess where the chevalier was when he was passing through Brittany incognito? No one told him anything for eight days, and by then it was too late.'

When the Pretender finally disembarked at Peterhead on 2 January 1716 (22 December British calendar) his expedition was already a failure. His supporters had been defeated at the battle of Sheriffmuir, and all he found was misery and cold, wild weather. James Stuart made the rough and miserable crossing back to France, taking Mar with him. He had been in Scotland less than a month, and was back in Paris at the end of February.

As Philippe was awaiting the outcome of the Scottish expedition, he received bad news from Spain; on 15 December Philip V signed a treaty under the terms of which the British were accorded extensive commercial privileges. At the very moment when he had risked his relationship with the British over the Pretender, Philippe now found himself slapped in the face by Spain.

The duc de Saint-Aignan, the French Ambassador to Madrid, reported that Alberoni had isolated the King to such a point that no one saw him except his wife, his chief huntsman, his confessor, Père d'Aubenton, and the Grand Inquisitor. He and the Queen spent every minute of each day together, including that spent at their *chaises percées*, which were placed next to each other. They always shared the same bed, breakfasted together, went to Mass together, hunted together, saw the ministers together as the Queen worked at her tapestries, then retired together.

Philip V had become melancholy, vindictive and lethargic. He was already showing signs of the sloth and vacancy which marked his later years, when he listened to the castrato Farinelli sing the same four songs every night for nine years. He suffered from periodic mental crises in which he believed that rays of sunshine were piercing his brain. When he wasn't almost comatose, he was demented.

Philippe tried not to be provoked by Spain. In January 1716 he went so far as to sign a declaration forbidding French sailors to trade in the Caribbean, a great sacrifice on behalf of Spain. He told Saint-Aignan to cultivate Alberoni and make a measured response to any threats or bluster. But despite the conciliatory noises, the Regent remained very angry that the British had made a pact with Philip V, who had done much more for the Pretender than he had, and had done so at the expense of France. 'So then, you are friends with Spain,' he remarked to Stair; 'however, I can tell you that Spain has done things for the Pretender which I would not do, and I could give you proof of it.' Madame in her turn passed the same news to her half-sister Luise in London, more forcefully: 'I must say one more thing before it chokes me; it was the Pope and the King of Spain who gave the money to the Pretender. The Pope gave three million livres, the King of Spain three times a hundred thousand. He didn't get a penny from my son.'

Back in Paris and abandoned by the French government, the Pretender met the Spanish Ambassador Cellamare secretly in a corner of the Bois de Boulogne, complaining of Lord Bolingbroke, his 'Secretary of State', whom he suspected of treason, and of his half-brother, the Duke of Berwick, who had been supposed to help him. He asked Cellamare for money, and announced that his official representative was now a Monsieur Magny, a known eccentric and brawler. Magny did not have much to do. The Pretender trailed back to Lorraine in early March. His friends in Paris continued to work on his behalf, but without much hope. The Jacobite adventuress Olive Trant wrote to him in April, 'Monsieur Your Cousin has continually told me that he wished to do wonders for you and asked me yesterday to trust him, but I think one must arm oneself with patience.'

Philippe had recognised that he could not play the Stuart card again. In order to put a stop to Philip V's machinations, and in order to prevent France's isolation in Europe, for reasons both personal and national, he would have to make an alliance with the British. All he could manage for poor James Edward was to pay his debts. At the end of March 1716 the Pretender left Lorraine for the Papal enclave of Avignon. France had turned her back.

Thus Philippe's first foray into the troubled waters of European diplomacy had ended in failure. Both Great Britain and Spain were hostile. In 1716 it was essential that France end this diplomatic isolation. Philippe had to act.

# 17
# UNE ANNÉE FOLLE

Philippe's decision to seek an alliance with Great Britain, in the hope of securing peace for his country and stability for himself, would require the most delicate development, as most of his advisers, especially those on the Council for Foreign Affairs, did not relish such a change. He turned once again to Dubois, the one man in the world on whom he could rely for complete loyalty and discretion.

Dubois had been keeping very much in the background. He had somehow incurred the enmity of his former admirer, Madame, who seemed to have come to believe that he had played a dishonourable part in arranging Philippe's marriage, and was furious at being deceived all these years. She had asked her son for only one favour when he became Regent, namely to keep the abbé out of the government, and Philippe had promised to do so. Dubois had received no official post, and was not in the public eye. But he was never far from his master. At the beginning of 1716 he began to emerge from the shadows.

Dubois was appointed 'conseiller d'Etat' in January and instructed to increase his contacts with Lord Stair. This was not a difficult task, as Stair was very much part of the Regent's circle, and already knew Dubois, as well as Canillac, Noailles and Nancré. He was particularly friendly with Nicolas Rémond, a member of the duc d'Orléans' private council, a *bel esprit*, a poet, a philosopher, and an admirer of the English savants like John Locke. These men, brought together by Elizabeth Wilmot, Lady Sandwich, who chose to live in Paris rather than London, and was reputed to be *en galanterie* with Dubois, were pro-British, and wished to keep the King of Spain off the throne of France. Saint-Simon called them the 'cabale de Stair', and they began to play an important part in the Regent's change of policy.

While Dubois was making discreet soundings of Stair, Philippe was allowing himself plenty of diversion. At the suggestion of the raffish old chevalier de Bouillon, he opened the Opéra three times a week for balls. These balls became a feature of the Regency, held in the huge auditorium, a floor raised over the parterre to provide a space for dancing. The public flocked in, some masked, others not, paying an entrance fee of four livres, and the Regent himself sometimes put in an appearance after supper and danced a gavotte or a minuet. Before the second ball, the Palais-Royal nearly went up in flames when the braziers used to heat the hall ignited some drapery. Madame had to flee her room at three in the morning, complaining bitterly about these unnecessary novelties.

Philippe suffered his own accidents. Still a keen tennis player, he managed to hit himself in the eye with his racket; after this his right eye, which had been the weaker, became his good eye and his vision was compromised. From now on he would have to peer closely at documents, and would find it difficult to write, preferring to dictate. Hardly any writings in his own hand survive, except for notes in the margins of other documents.

Despite his workload and physical ailments, he continued to pursue his nightly quest for 'pleasure'. It is one of the greatest paradoxes of this paradoxical man that, while he evidently enjoyed the intellectual demands of his job and relished the chance to put his stamp on world affairs, he also felt obliged, by habit and temperament, to throw himself into parties and carousings detrimental to his years and rank. His mother had begun a correspondence with the German philosopher Leibniz, who had sent the Regent his latest work, *De Origine Francorum*. 'If my son, instead of going to the Opéra ball, had read your treatise on the origin of the Franks, his eye would not have caused him so much pain,' Madame remarked. 'I said to him jokingly that he was afraid that, if he started to behave like an adult, then I would start to grow old. Frankly, M. de Leibniz, I believe things would be better if he preferred to entangle himself with the robes of scholars than with the nightgowns of ladies.'

There were other family problems that spring. The duchesse de Berry, drunk on her own magnificence, was insisting on travelling through Paris with drums and trumpets sounding, even under the windows of the King at the Tuileries. The maréchal de Villeroi protested to the Regent and the music stopped. Then, on arrival at the Comédie to see Racine's *Athalie*, which was being presented publicly for the first time, she ordered the auditorium to be more brightly lit than usual, placed a dais in her box, and had the actors salute her before the performance. There was such an outcry that she stopped going to the Comédie, preferring the Opéra, where she had a little box in which she could be incognito. When she had the gardens of the Luxembourg walled up, there was more complaint, for the residents of the neighbourhood were accustomed to use the gardens as a promenade. In a pointed response, Monsieur le Duc opened his gardens nearby at the hôtel de Condé. Imperturbable, she had her former lover La Haye (known as Ready for Anything) named a *gentilhomme de la manche* to the King.

More disturbing than any of her follies was her preoccupation with a new lover, Armand de Rions, described by Saint-Simon as 'a short chubby young man covered in pimples who, with his green and yellow complexion, looked rather like a walking abscess'. But Armand was droll and vigorous; he soon had the haughty young woman enslaved. Each morning she would send messages to him asking what he would like her to wear; when she had obediently dressed according to his orders, he would make her change everything. He would make her go out when she did not wish to, and stay in when she wished to go out. There were constant tears. Every so often, to try and escape, she rushed to the Carmelites in the rue de Grenelle to repent. One of the nuns there said, wonderingly, 'I think you a saint when I hear you speak: but I no longer think so when I hear you spoken of.' Even there she could not resist sweeping in with her two ladies-in-waiting, Mme de La Rochefoucauld (née Prondre) and Mme d'Arpajon (née Le Bas), announcing, 'I have brought my two *bourgeoises*.'

The Parisians had great fun at her expense:

> La Messaline de Berry,
> L'oeil en feu, l'air plein d'arrogance,
> Dit, en faisant charivari,
> Qu'elle est la première de France.
> Elle prend, ma foi, tout le train
> D'être la première putain.

> (La Berry, that Messalina,
> With haughty look, full of arrogance,
> Said, as she made a hullabaloo,
> That she was First Lady of France.
> She does indeed make every show
> Of being the First Whore.)

When in June she bought the pretty country house of La Muette in the Bois de Boulogne, the Parisians were delighted to see her go.

Her brother, Philippe's only son, the duc de Chartres, was proving a disappointment. The boy, who was in delicate health, spent most of his time secluded with his mother. In March the comte de Cheverny was named governor of the twelve-year-old boy. Cheverny was a sound and experienced man, but was not expected to perform any serious duties; Philippe did not think highly of his son's potential and did not trouble himself too much about the details of his education. But he liked Cheverny and thought he deserved an honourable post and a pension. Later that year Mme de Cheverny was appointed governess to the daughters of the Regent.

(M. de Cheverny was famous for an incident which befell him years earlier in Vienna where he was posted as ambassador. One winter night he had his first audience with the Emperor Leopold. A chamberlain received him, led him through two or three rooms, and left. In this room, rather badly furnished, illuminated only by two candles, a man simply clothed in black was leaning against a table. Cheverny assumed he was in an antechamber and looked around, wandering from one end of the room to the other. This went on for half an hour. Finally the man in black, whom Cheverny had taken as a valet de chambre, asked politely what he wanted. When Cheverny said he was awaiting an audience with the Emperor, the man in black said, 'C'est moi qui suis l'Empéreur.' Cheverny dined out on the story for years).

Philippe distracted himself further with a new mistress, Marie-Madeleine Coskaer de La Vieuville, comtesse de Paràbere, a twenty-three-year-old brunette, gay, heady, with no malice. Her lover called her 'mon gigot' or 'mon petit corbeau noir'; the rhymesters called her 'Sainte-Nitouche', or goody-goody. Philippe probably met her at the Luxembourg, where her mother had been a lady-in-waiting to the duchesse de Berry. Her family was a distinguished one, her grandfather had been Philippe's gouverneur, and she was the kind of lively, good-humoured, charming woman he had always liked. On becoming Regent, Philippe no doubt felt that he should have an official mistress. It was a sort of perquisite of the office. Marie-Madeleine accepted with glee.

Madame naturally disapproved of Mme de Paràbere and considered her a gold-digger. 'My son is getting too fat for his height because he is small. He may no longer be handsome, but women still run after him out of pure self-interest because he pays them well.' But, by the standards of the times, Philippe was not unduly extravagant with his mistresses. He did give Mme de Paràbere, as a welcoming gift, a diamond worth two thousand louis and a golden snuffbox worth two hundred. Mme de Paràbere, the prototype of a character from *Les Liaisons Dangereuses*, showed her husband the diamond and the snuffbox, telling him that she could buy these things very cheaply from people who were in need of money; her husband was naive enough to believe her and gave her the money to buy them. Shortly afterwards, when the couple arrived at a party and Mme de Parabère's diamond was greatly admired, she told everyone how generous her husband was; and he replied that one could hardly be otherwise if one had a wife of quality who loved no one but her husband. 'There was hearty laughter, for everyone was not as simple minded as he and knew how the land lay.' Mme de Parabère enjoyed her diamond, her snuffbox and her ill-gotten gains; poor deluded M. de Parabère died shortly afterwards, saving himself more embarrassment.

While Mme de Parabère displayed her new jewellery, the duchesse d'Orléans was enduring another pregnancy. In June 1716, at the age of thirty-nine, she gave birth to her eighth child, another girl. After this Mme d'Orléans retired to her rooms at the Palais-Royal. There would be no more pregnancies. The Duchess spent her time reclining on her gold-embroidered canapé in her white and gold salon, admiring her collection of Chinoiserie, porcelain and lacquered boxes. She closeted herself with her son and her coterie of women friends, showing absolutely no interest in presiding over a court. Madame was unsparing: 'It is pure laziness which keeps Mme d'Orléans from dining with us; if she eats with me she must content herself with a stool, whereas when she eats in her rooms with her son and her favourites, she lies on a canapé or sits in an armchair.' Madame very much disliked being in Paris, which she hated, except for the theatre; every May she departed for Saint-Cloud, where she stayed until November.

Amid all this brouhaha, there were serious matters to attend to. Monsieur le Duc, supported by the dukes, had begun an attack on the Légitimes, presenting the Regent with a petition demanding the annulment of the decrees of 1714 and 1715 which made Maine and Toulouse Princes of the Blood and able to ascend the throne. The Regent handed the petition to the duc du Maine a week later. 'You observe', he remarked, 'that I am performing the duty of the sergeant-at-arms; I give you a month in which to respond.' Each side immediately hired lawyers to search for precedents, marshal arguments and come up with indictments of the other. The duchesse du Maine worked furiously at her documents at the Arsenal and at Sceaux. Philippe kept above the fray.

The most serious problems were financial. In March a *chambre de justice* was set up to examine the financial dealings of many leading businessmen and magistrates, and a tribunal established at the convent of the Grands-Augustins under the chairmanship of the respected magistrate Lamoignon. The policy of the Regent and of Noailles was to threaten the financiers, and thence make possible an important reduction of the state's debts; but at the same time it was too risky to punish the most important members of the financial community, as they were the only ones who could help the state in the event of emergency. Some lesser fry were punished. Le Normand was made to walk through the streets in his shirt holding a placard which read 'Voleur du peuple'; Paulin Prondre was fined and his château of Guermantes seized; the hôtel de Nevers, next door to the Palais-Royal, which had been sold in 1715 to the financier Châtelain, was also seized*.

The attack on the financiers was designed to recover money for the King's coffers; the end was desirable, but the means fell far short of solving the problem. The state never had enough money; war, the court, the myriad pensions, devoured the resources of the taxes. The taille, the oldest tax, was not paid by the nobility or by the clergy or by the inhabitants of the great cities; the capitation, a proportional tax on everyone, was suggested by Vauban in 1694 and tried out, but it was inefficiently administered; the dixième was imposed in 1710 but could not be enforced. The indirect taxes were collected by 'farms' who forecast the revenue and kept the difference if they collected more; if they collected less the government had to borrow. The system was hopelessly flawed.

Philippe, while approving Noailles' methods of chasing the financiers, searched for a more lasting solution. He was having long conversations with John Law. Law, pronounced Las by the French, was a Scot from Edinburgh; he was the same age as the Regent and had something of the same temperament. At some point in his youth he had been suspected of killing a man in a duel; a description of him as a wanted man in the *London Gazette* from 1695 speaks of 'a very tall black lean Man, well shaped, about six feet high, large Pockholes in his Face, big high-Nosed, speaks broad and low'. He fled to Amsterdam before eventually returning to England, but he was often on the Continent, leading the life of a professional gambler, a man with wild schemes of how to make money, anxious to speak of them with men of influence. He had already suggested his ideas on banking and commerce to the ruler of Savoy before coming to France towards the end of the reign of Louis XIV. Somehow he was introduced to Philippe; Saint-Simon recalled that:

> they mentioned him to M. le duc d'Orléans as a man of profound knowledge
> of banks, finance, the movement of money ... he saw him several times
> and was so impressed that he told Desmarets about him ... I also remember
> that the prince talked to me about him at the same time. Desmarets sent
> for Law and spent a good deal of time with him at several meetings; I have

---

* In November the abbé Louvois received permission from the Regent to have the royal library moved there from cramped quarters in the rue Vivienne, and there, as the Bibliothèque Nationale, it remains.

never known what went on between them ... except that Desmarets was impressed ... M. le duc d'Orléans after that only saw him from time to time at a distance ... Law ... who had some connection with Dubois, introduced himself once more to the Regent after the death of Louis XIV.

In December 1715 Law had sent Philippe a remarkable letter, stressing the importance of establishing credit and the prior need to create confidence; to meet both requirements a bank should be established. 'The bank is not the only nor the greatest of my ideas; I will produce a work which will surprise Europe by the changes it will bring in favour of France, the changes greater than those which have been introduced by the discovery of the Indies or by the introduction of credit.' Law believed that the more money in circulation, the more flourishing the economy would become. The money would be in the form of credit (banknotes), which would be accepted as true currency. The availability of credit would provide such a stimulus to commerce that gold and silver would flow into the coffers of the Treasury. His bank would be the catalyst.

This was not a new idea. The Bank of England was there for all to see. Samuel Bernard had produced a scheme in 1709 for a public bank in France to manage the nation's debt. Now Law, with the support of the Regent, tried to persuade Noailles and his colleagues that a national bank could do wonders for France. A proposal for a bank was discussed by the Finance Council as early as November 1715, when most of the members were against the idea, unable to comprehend how it could function in an absolute monarchy.

The French experience with paper money in the later years of Louis XIV had been traumatic; the country had been flooded with 'billets de monnaie', causing inflation and rapid decline in the value of the paper currency. To counter that, Louis XIV's Controller of Finances, Desmarets, had reduced the availability of cash, which in turn caused a reduction of commercial activity. The businessmen of France did not look kindly on any further attempt to introduce paper money.

Autocracy and credit did not mix. Law knew that; he realised that the introduction of his system would lead to radical changes. There would need to be more supervision of the finances by the state, and an end to financial privileges. Law did not shy away from the political implications of his ideas, but in 1716 he was more concerned with simply obtaining support for his bank.

Philippe was strongly attracted to Law's ideas. At a meeting of the Finance Council in May 1716 he pushed the members to propose the notion of a bank to the Regency Council itself. Before the crucial meeting Philippe took everyone aside to set out his views, carefully explaining the implications of this novelty. The Regency Council duly decided to let Law go ahead.

Law first installed his bank in the rue Sainte-Avoye in the Marais, in a house rented from Mesmes. It would have a modest capital of six million livres, underwritten by shareholders. Its notes, labelled in 'écus de banque', would be payable on sight in coin of a fixed weight and would not be subject to the fluctuations of the coinage. The notes of the bank were proclaimed as a safe and convenient currency, the value of which could not be modified by royal decree. The bank was a great success. Its customers were impressed with the efficiency of the operation. By October all the royal tax collectors in the provinces were told to send their funds to Paris in banknotes and to reimburse the notes as soon as they had the funds to do so. Paper money was catching on.

Saint-Simon was baffled by these new notions. But he began a relationship with Law – they met every Tuesday morning at ten to discuss money matters – and liked him. 'I have said here and elsewhere, and I repeat, that he had no avarice nor friponnerie; he was gentle, good, respectful, not spoiled by his excessive fortune . . . he was a man with a system, calculating, always comparing, very knowledgeable and learned in this kind of thing.' Saint-Simon, whose own knowledge of mathematics was lacking, greatly admired the skill of this seductive Scot who explained the mysteries of multiplication and division in his mangled French-Scots. As for the Regent, he was dazzled; he showed the same enthusiasm for Law's financial theories as he had done for alchemy and chemistry. In a way of course Law's theories were alchemy, and his belief in the marvels of credit the same as that in the philosopher's stone. Both he and Philippe were having a wonderful time letting their imaginations run riot.

Philippe took a respite from his financial headaches when the Italian players, newly arrived from Parma, made their debut at the Opéra. He was delighted to welcome Harlequin and Colombine back to Paris and he was not alone. Watteau was also in the audience, sketching the characters he would use to such haunting effect, as was the young Voltaire, François-Marie Arouet, stagestruck and eager to make his name. That summer Arouet succeeded, but not in the way he expected; he was exiled to the town of Tulle for writing satirical verses, on the subject of the Regent and the duchesse de Berry. At the request of his father, he was sent only as far as Sully-sur-Loire, where he became a guest at the elegant château of the duc de Sully. Saint-Simon deigned to take note of the event:

> Arouet, son of a notary who was employed by my father and me until his death, was exiled . . . to Tulle for some verses very satirical and impudent.

I should not amuse myself by writing down such a trifle if this same Arouet, having become a great poet and academician under the name of Voltaire, had not also become ... a manner of personage in the republic of letters and even achieved a sort of importance among certain people.

Arouet-Voltaire was lectured by his old friend the abbé de Chaulieu on the subject of his imprudence. Chaulieu advised him to soften his expressions concerning the Regent, and indeed his opinions, writing, 'His Royal Highness's devotion to the well-being of the Kingdom, his tireless work, the equity of his administration, and the rightness of his intentions, must put him beyond censure and beyond the frondeurs of whom you speak; it seems to me too hard to point out to this well-meaning Prince the little recognition his deeds have in France, as his actions place him above satire.'

The young rebel replied in ironic verse:

> Malgré le penchant de mon coeur
> A vos conseils je m'abandonne.
> Quoi, je vais devenir flatteur?
> Et c'est Chaulieu qui m'ordonne!
>
> (Despite the leaning of my heart
> To your advice I shall submit.
> But shall I become a flatterer?
> And shall it be Chaulieu suggesting it!)

Voltaire was restless in his gilded exile. He told Mme de Mimeure, whose salon in the rue des Saints-Pères he had often attended, 'it would be delicious for me to stay at Sully if only I were allowed to leave', and then went on to describe a scene straight out of Watteau:

You would perhaps be astonished if I told you that in the beautiful wood here we have *nuits blanches* just like at Sceaux! Mme de La Vrillière, who came here overnight to chatter with her sister Mme de Listenay, was extremely surprised to find herself in a large room of elm trees lit up by hundreds of Chinese lanterns, and to see there a magnificent collation served to the sound of music and followed by a ball at which more than a hundred masks appeared all dressed in superb garments. The two sisters found verses on their plates, which they were assured were those of the abbé C. Later in the summer he was musing this.

> Sous les ombrages toujours cois,
> De Sully, ce séjour tranquille,
> Je suis plus heureux mille fois

Que le grand prince qui m'exile
Ne l'est près du trône des rois.

(In the always silent shades
Of Sully, this peaceful place,
I am happier a thousand times
Than the great prince who exiled me
Tho near the throne of kings.)

Voltaire was quite correct in assuming that he was having more fun than the Regent that summer. Philippe was involved in a complicated diplomatic manoeuvre, attempting to ally himself with Great Britain in order to preserve France from another war; in the process he was being asked to do things of which the majority of his compatriots strongly disapproved. The British demanded that he expel the Pretender and all his followers, and that he destroy the port being built at Mardyck to replace Dunkirk. The Regent refused. He needed some concessions for himself.

When George I decided to make a journey to Hanover that summer, bringing Stanhope with him, Philippe saw a chance to begin a conversation. The British party would stop at The Hague; Dubois, to whom Philippe had entrusted the negotiation, was instructed to find the right disguise and go there too. What followed has caused one French historian to remark, 'the year 1716 was, from the point of view of diplomacy, *une année folle*'.

Dubois arrived in The Hague in early July, masquerading as M. Saint-Albin, antiquarian and collector. Characteristically, he entered into the affair with enthusiasm, actually purchasing for his master the *Seven Sacraments* of Poussin. Madame, glad to see the back of him, indiscreetly told Leibniz that God would have made her and many other decent people very happy if Dubois spent his whole life incognito and far from the court.

Two weeks later King George and Stanhope arrived at The Hague, and the next morning Stanhope and Dubois met at the residence of the British Ambassador. The old acquaintances talked in the greatest conviviality for three days; but their differences remained. Stanhope told Dubois how irritated King George was with the French; Dubois responded with the difficulty of the Regent's position. Eventually Dubois came away believing that he could have a treaty at the price of Mardyck. After all, the Pretender was already in Avignon and had already almost ceased to count. Stanhope set off to join King George at the spa of Pyrmont, and Dubois left for Paris, sending ahead a report on his meetings of 177 pages.

At the Palais-Royal the Regent was delighted with Dubois' acumen, and with his new Poussins. The two men decided to put to the Council of Foreign Affairs the option of making a treaty with Great Britain at the price of dismantling Mardyck. Predictably, Huxelles and the majority opposed the plan, and encouraged the Regent to seek a rapprochement with Spain. Philippe had already foreseen this difficulty, and had his riposte ready. He had tried to approach Philip V; he had sent the marquis de Louville to Madrid. And look what had happened.

Louville had been tutor to Philip V when he was the duc d'Anjou, and hoped for a warm reception from his former pupil. But the very respectable fifty-year-old diplomat was somewhat disconcerted to be handed a secret code, replete with sexual and amorous references, written in the Regent's own hand. He was told to use this code in his correspondence with Paris, employing such terms as 'I have found a pretty mistress' for 'I had an audience with the Queen', and so on. Burdened with this unwelcome requirement, Louville journeyed through the heat and dust of sweltering Spain, eventually falling ill on the road. Forced to halt for days at a time, he finally arrived in Madrid sick and exhausted, suffering from an acute attack of nephritis. As soon as he arrived at his lodging, he plunged into a bath for relief. But at that very moment Alberoni himself arrived at the house and insisted on being received. Louville, clutching his towel, had to listen to an order to leave Spain immediately. In his undignified position it was hard to argue. Alberoni was on the point of signing an agreement with the British and wanted no interference from the French. He closed down all means of communication between the King and his old tutor. Even though Louville managed to prolong his stay for three weeks, he never spoke to the King. He even went out into the street as the King passed, waving and smiling, but his former pupil ignored him. Acknowledging defeat, Louville came home.

With Spain recalcitrant, the Regent could turn more openly to Great Britain. In August Dubois, in the same disguise as before, left again for Hanover. His instructions were to consent to the expulsion of the Pretender from France, although that was not to happen until after the exchange of ratifications of a treaty, and to give assurances that the fortifications at Mardyck would be destroyed, leaving only a little port and a canal. In exchange, Dubois was to demand that the British guarantee the terms of the Treaty of Utrecht, including the rights of the duc d'Orléans to succeed to the throne of France in the event of the death of Louis XV without issue. (But this clause would figure only as an annexe, in order not to provoke opinion.) The Regent was attempting to secure peace for France, without giving away too much, as well as securing his own position in the succession. It was a delicate operation; the British were at once his opponents and his putative protectors.

When Dubois arrived in Hanover, he was accommodated in Stanhope's own house. The two men started work at once. 'We negotiated in our dressing-gowns and our nightcaps,' reported Dubois. He found Stanhope not prepared to give way on Mardyck, and somewhat condescending. 'At a time when your Regent needs us, suffice it to say that he is making too much fuss over a little canal.' After almost two weeks of hard bargaining, Dubois was in despair. The British made it clear that they were really not in any hurry to ally themselves with France; they were allied already with Austria.

Suddenly Stanhope changed his tone. Having left the strong impression that King George had little interest in a treaty, he started to soften his position. The British about-face occurred after King George became convinced that Peter the Great would make a deal with the Regent and the Russians would invade his beloved homeland, Hanover. Having had this thought, he saw the alliance with France in a different light. 'The King now wishes,' wrote Stanhope to London, 'and so doth your humble servant very heartily, that we had secured France . . . I was, you know, very averse to this treaty, but I think truly as things now stand we ought not to lose a minute in finishing it.'

On 24 August a preliminary convention was signed: the Pretender would be expelled from France; there would be a defensive alliance between France and Great Britain, and mutual guarantees of the succession. The question of Mardyck would be discussed in London between Iberville, the French Ambassador, and the Cabinet. King George protected himself against the Jacobites, and the Regent gained British protection for his own rights to the throne of France. More importantly, he secured peace for France.

Saint-Simon came to believe that Dubois was bribed in order to agree to the British terms, but there is no evidence for this. Dubois, on the other hand, did try and bribe Stanhope; 'when our negotiations at Hanover were undecided, I found so natural an opportunity to make to M. de Stanhope the offer which you directed', wrote Dubois to Philippe, 'that I hazarded the compliment . . . even to naming the price, which I fixed at 600,000 livres, to which he listened graciously, and without flying into a passion. My satisfaction was increased when he replied that Your Royal Highness was so great a prince that none need blush to be the object of your generosity.' Stanhope did not take the money.

When Iberville left Paris for London to finish the negotiations over Mardyck, he had instructions from the Regent to hasten towards a conclusion; he also had orders from Huxelles to do absolutely the opposite. It was Huxelles he obeyed, and matters dragged on, while at Hanover Dubois fretted, bombarding Philippe with missives. 'Remember, Monseigneur, that the candle is burning and my feet are getting scorched.' Eventually, on 18 September, the British Prime Minister Townshend delivered an ultimatum to Iberville: either accept the views of the British Admiralty or go home. Three days later Iberville gave in; Mardyck would be destroyed.

When King George heard this gratifying news in Hanover, he received Dubois and presented him to his daughter, Sophia Dorothea, who was married to King Frederick William I of Prussia. 'This alliance will assure the rights of His Royal Highness so strongly', wrote Dubois jubilantly, 'that it will not be possible to attack them ... it will determine the system of Europe for a long time and will give France a superiority which we could not otherwise achieve ... that said, it is not without a price: but if I were master of France, I would prefer to spend thirty million livres rather than miss it.' And Philippe wrote on the margin, 'I think as you do on all of this: no expense can counterbalance the importance of the alliance.'

There were indeed expenses. Apart from presents of wine and champagne, Philippe engaged himself to buy from Thomas Pitt, Stanhope's father-in-law, a marvellous diamond which Pitt had acquired in the Far East. The diamond, having cost France more than two million livres, arrived in Paris in the summer of 1717*.

When the Dutch signed the Triple Alliance in January 1717 at The Hague, Dubois was exultant. 'I signed at midnight. Behold Your Royal Highness free from anxiety.' Dubois had indeed helped bolster Philippe's personal position. Now, if the little King died, the duc d'Orléans would be guaranteed the throne of France by the British. But there were greater benefits. Peace in Europe was preserved for twenty-five years. The Regent believed that he was serving the cause of peace as well as his own.

Dubois was rewarded with the rich abbey of Saint-Riquier in the diocese of Amiens and with a seat on the Council of Foreign Affairs. Others were not so gratified by the treaty. Huxelles, Villars, Torcy and many others protested. In London Townshend resigned as Prime Minister and was replaced by none other than Stanhope. Stanhope himself was ecstatic; 'Your journey has saved human lives,' he told Dubois, 'and there are many peoples who will have an obligation to you for their tranquillity.' As for Philippe, in the face of prevalent scepticism, he laid out his position very clearly. 'I am Regent of France, and I ought to behave in such a manner that I can't be accused of having thought only of myself.'

* It is today at the Louvre, known to all as the Regent.

When the courier bearing the Treaty of the Triple Alliance arrived at the Palais-Royal in January 1717, Madame was with her son. Philippe could not hide his delight. He embraced his mother and, according to one account, 'Their Royal Highnesses kissed the treaty and made the maréchal d'Huxelles do the same.' Huxelles would not have been best pleased; Madame, who disliked Huxelles and called him 'the old dotard maréchal du Sel', rejoiced at his discomfort.

The 'année folle' had produced a solid result. The Triple Alliance was a step towards peace, and a personal victory for Philippe. It was also the making of the abbé Dubois.

# ❧ 18 ❧

## THE CZAR IN PARIS

At the beginning of 1717 the Chancellor, Daniel Voysin, reaching for an apple compôte at dinner at his house in the rue Saint-Louis-au-Marais, dropped dead. Typically for the times, there was an immediate rumour that he had been poisoned. The suspect this time was the duc de Noailles. (Many years later Louis XV remarked to Noailles, 'As for Voysin, he was got rid of pretty quickly, is that not so, monsieur le Maréchal?'

Noailles was no poisoner, but he did have his own candidate for Voysin's job. As soon as he heard of the death, he rushed to the Palais-Royal, arriving as the Regent rose from his bed and was approaching his *chaise percée*; 'his stomach very upset, his head thick from supper the night before, as it was every morning', as Saint-Simon attested. Noailles took the opportunity of recommending his friend Daguesseau, the procureur général, for Chancellor. Daguesseau had the job that very day. Philippe was convinced by Noailles that Daguesseau would be an ally for him against *parlement*. Unfortunately, Daguesseau did not really have the temperament for the job. He was a slow, deliberate man who could never come to a decision about anything and finally drove everyone mad with impatience. He and Philippe were to have a tempestuous relationship.

In February there was another transition. Louis XV reached his seventh birthday, and had to be taken from his governess, Mme de Ventadour, and delivered to his governor, the maréchal de Villeroi. The boy could not hide his grief when the moment came to part from the woman who had been the only mother he had ever known. As Mme de Ventadour handed him over to the Regent, with the words, 'Monseigneur, here is the charge with which the late King entrusted me and which you have continued; I have taken every possible care of him and give him to you in perfect health,' the sobs of little Louis XV rent the air. The boy would be in the

Regent's charge until his thirteenth birthday, in February 1723, at which time he would, according to French law, have reached his majority and be able to govern alone.

The most important relationship Philippe had to cultivate was that with this seven-year-old boy. Bluntly put, everything depended on whether Louis XV would live or die. No one even dared mention directly the possibility of his dying; the diplomatic phrase employed was 'en cas de malheur'. The stakes were enormous; if the King died, the King of Spain would seize the opportunity to reassert his rights in France, and there would be civil war between his partisans and those of Philippe d'Orléans. If, on the other hand, the boy lived and reached his majority, it would be important that he felt goodwill towards his uncle. Philippe realised the importance of being seen to be impeccable in his relations with the boy; but, imbued as he was with pride in ancestry, he found it natural to treat the boy King with the same profound respect with which he had treated Louis XIV. And he seems to have sincerely liked the timid child who stood between him and the throne.

Poor little King. Surrounded by adulation, the cynosure of all eyes, the focus of every quarrel of precedence, lonely, shy, no wonder he soon hated to be made to dance or dress up or appear before crowds, no wonder he soon showed signs of surliness. He became a silent, reserved, secretive child who grew into a silent, reserved, secretive man. But he was a very pretty boy. Madame said he had 'eyes as black as jet and what one could call a *beau regard*. His eyes are a great deal gentler than he is, in fact, for he has a violent temper ... He has beautiful brown hair in abundance and a perfect figure ... It would be nice if he spoke more often, as one has trouble extracting a word from him; he only talks to people whom he sees every day.'

The maréchal de Villeroi and the duc du Maine were nominally responsible for his education. But it was his tutor, the seventy-year-old abbé de Fleury, supple, unctuous, discreet, who was closest to him. A court in miniature was established at the Tuileries, similar in every way to that of Louis XIV except that the huge household served a child. A panoply of nobles attended him, gentlemen of the chamber, equerries, pages and Gentlemen of the Sleeve (so called because they were not permitted to touch a royal prince by the hand). All these were jealous of their positions and frequently quarrelled with each other. Everyone wanted to catch a glimpse of the human icon; he ate alone, watched in a worshipful silence by an audience of those privileged to enter his presence. Marais saw him eating heartily but sad and serious, saying nothing. The atmosphere at the Tuileries was taut; Villeroi, who slept in the King's room, took it upon himself to inculcate the boy with notions of his own superiority and ostentatiously to protect him against poison. His food and drink were tasted, his biscuits locked away. It was clear that Villeroi's suspicion was directed in the Regent's direction. Louis XV grew more silent every day, not knowing whom he could trust and preferring to trust no one.

All this attention caused the boy some confusion. When Madame, on her way to Mass, called on him to wish him happy birthday, she told him she was going to visit a greater seigneur than he. Louis XV seemed rather surprised, but after a moment of reflection, replied, 'No doubt, Madame, you are going to pray to God.'

About this time Philippe decided that he had to try to quell the uproar over *Unigenitus*. This Papal Bull labelled as heresy most of the propositions in a rather obscure book called *Moral Reflections* by Père Quesnel, and, by so doing, had polarised the Church: there was a serious schism between those who supported the Pope and the Bull, primarily the Jesuits and some bishops, and those who did not, the Jansenists, the Sorbonne, the minor clergy and the bourgeoisie. *Parlement* was Jansenist, and hostile to the Bull, and Philippe had been unwilling to go against it. But he had become concerned that the dissension would lead to civil strife and, with no religious leanings of his own, was coming to the conclusion that it would be the prudent course to let the Pope have his way.

As always he kept his intentions secret. He started to try out his ideas on some of those close to him and whose opinion he valued. One afternoon at the Palais-Royal he announced to Saint-Simon that he was going to the Opéra and wanted Saint-Simon to come along and hear him out about something important. 'To the Opéra, monsieur!; Eh! that is no place to talk of affairs of state! Let us talk here for as long as you wish, or if you prefer to go to the Opéra, let us talk tomorrow.' Philippe insisted; they would shut themselves up in his box and they would be as private as in his study. Saint-Simon protested that they would be distracted by the spectacle, that people would observe them, that everyone would spread rumours, that the Opéra was designed for relaxation and amusement, for seeing and being seen, and not for talking shop 'and making a spectacle of oneself at the spectacle'. Philippe laughed; he took his hat and cane from the sofa, and swept his friend from the room.

Sitting in his private box, Philippe laid out his options. He claimed there was little support for the anti-Bull position, despite all the noise from the Sorbonne, that it was supported by the Pope, most of the bishops, the Jesuits, all the seminaries, an infinity of confessors and curés all over the Kingdom, and that they would all support the King of Spain and cause endless trouble if the Bull was not approved. Saint-Simon, who took the side of the Jansenists and was anti-Bull, expressed his outrage at this cynical position. 'With your spirit, your erudition, your discernment, your enlightened understanding, the disorder of your life, your free access to all kinds of people, your extraordinary researches, so unusual for your rank, your distrust of religion and this libertinage which you affect at all times so publicly ... you of all men could never become the man of Rome and the Jesuits!'

The flourish at the end of the opera took the two men by surprise. The Regent was so concentrated on his theme, and so struck by Saint-Simon's observations, that he left his box 'assez sombrement'. He remained convinced that the only way towards peace in the Church was to pacify the Pope and get *Unigenitus* accepted as quickly as possible, but Saint-Simon had, as usual, reminded him of the difficulties ahead.

Perhaps he was feeling rather more pious than usual. That spring his nineteen-year-old daughter, Louise-Adélaïde, took the veil at the abbey of Chelles. The girl had clung to her determination to be a nun against fierce opposition from her mother and grandmother. Her mother wanted her to marry: her grandmother did not, she simply thought she was too pretty. Her father, who was fond of her, for she was amusing, simply said: 'Well, my dear, become the bride of Christ if you must, but don't expect me to be on very good terms with my son-in-law.' Nevertheless, he and his wife attended the ceremony, which passed with dignity and simplicity.

Philippe stood in need of the virtues of forgiveness and charity. In Paris atrocious pamphlets were raining down on his head, accusing him of every horror. Those opposed to his alliance with Great Britain, to his policies on the Church, to his very existence, loosely organised by the duchesse du Maine and the *vieille cour*, hurled abuse. One night at dinner a note was found under the Regent's plate threatening to set fire to the Palais-Royal and to burn him and his mother. 'My heart beats fast all the time,' sighed Madame, 'but my son worries about nothing. I beg him for the love of God not to go out at night in his carriage. He makes me fine promises, but will not keep them ...'

Two publications, however, did arouse the Regent's wrath. A pamphlet entitled *Puero Regnante* was circulating, the text of which included the following:

> A boy reigning;
> A Man Notorious for poisonings
> And incests, Administering;
> Councils Ignorant and Unstable;

The Treasury Empty;
Public faith violated;
Infuriate Wrong Triumphant;
Danger of General Sedition Imminent;
The country sacrificed
To the Hope of a Crown
All Inheritance basely Anticipated;
France about to Perish!

The *Puero Regnante* was the boldest attack on the Regent so far; but another pamphlet, the *J'ai vu . . .* or 'I have seen . . .', was equally inflammatory. 'I have seen', it read, 'the Bastille filled with brave citizens, faithful subjects! . . . I have seen the people wretched under a rigorous servitude! . . . I have seen the soldiery perishing of hunger, thirst, indignation, and rage!'

In connection with these pamphlets, the Regent's attention was drawn to the troublesome young writer Arouet, recently returned to Paris from exile at Sully. Arouet was placed under surveillance by spies from the War Office. One May afternoon Philippe himself came across the young rebel in the gardens of the Palais-Royal. Philippe touched delicately on the matter of the *J'ai vu*: 'Monsieur Arouet, you have doubtless seen a great many things, but I think I can show you something you have never seen.' 'Indeed, Monseigneur, and might I ask what that is?' 'The inside of the Bastille.' 'Ah, Monseigneur, allow me to consider it already seen!'

Philippe's warning had been serious. On 17 May Arouet was arrested and sent to the Bastille, where he remained for eleven months. A pathetic note from the new prisoner was delivered to Bernaville, the prison governor, requesting, 'Two copies of Homer, Latin and Greek, two cotton handkerchiefs, a little bonnet, two cravats, a nightcap, and a little bottle of essence of *geroufle*'.

His imprisonment for poems he was only rumoured to have written woke François-Marie Arouet to the horrors of injustice and absolute power. (A Jansenist called Le Brun later confessed to writing the *J'ai vu*.) In response, he began work on an epic poem, the *Henriade*, a plea for liberal and humane principles of government. It was also a shrewd choice of subject, in that the Regent was known to like to be compared to his dashing great-grandfather, Henri IV. Arouet-Voltaire was always a practical man. Fully aware of the arbitrary nature of the act which had imprisoned him, he never actually blamed the Regent personally. The two men retained a certain respect for each other despite the vicissitudes of their relationship.

Arouet was incarcerated at a time of high excitement in Paris. The Czar of Russia, Peter the Great, was making his first visit to France, and, as far as Philippe was concerned, the anxieties surrounding the visit far out-weighed any caused by the young radical. The Regent and Dubois regarded the Czar's visit as politically delicate. The Regent above all things did not want to compromise the Anglo-French rapprochement which he was busily nurturing; King George, as we have seen, suspected Peter the Great of having designs on his beloved Hanover. It was therefore vital that King George should not think that the French were going to ally themselves with Russia. The somewhat embarrassing guest would be treated mag-nificently and finessed, not rewarded.

Peter the Great was the same age as Philippe and had already brought about great change in Russia. He was intensely curious about the rest of Europe, and by the time he came to France had journeyed widely. Ignoring hints from the French that his visit was unwelcome, he arrived at Dunkirk on 21 April, accompanied by a suite of sixty, only two of whom spoke French. The party was met by the fashionable young marquis de Nesle, who was sent to do the honours. The marquis astonished the Czar by appearing in a different suit of clothes every day, causing Peter to wonder whether he had such a bad tailor that he could not find a suit to fit him. It was the first encounter with that French love of luxury which would startle the Czar and leave a strong impression on him.

The procession arrived in Paris in the evening of 7 May. The Czar immediately surprised his hosts by refusing the accommodation offered, a splendid apartment at the Louvre overlooking the Seine, explaining that he found it much too grand for him. He and his entourage were hastily moved to the hôtel des Lesdiguières in the rue de la Cerisaie near the Bastille. This was conveniently empty because the duc de Villeroi, son of the maréchal, who was not homme de grand train, thought it too far away from the centre of things and did not live there. The house was extremely grand, full of precious objects, chandeliers of rock crystal, antique bronzes and marble, gold plate and so on, but tapestries were quickly sent over from the Louvre to make it comfortable and officers of the household descended on the rue de la Cerisaie, marking with chalk the houses they would commandeer. The whole quarter was in an uproar.

When the Regent visited the next day, the two men talked for an hour seated in two armchairs and everything seemed amicable. But the ceremonious French noticed with disapproval that the Czar responded only casually to the Regent's deep bow, and Philippe himself was surprised that the Czar refused to budge from the house until the King himself came to call. Everyone commented on the Czar's 'majestic and grave regard', although he also appeared 'severe and rude, with a facial tic ... which is rather frightening'.

The little King visited him the day after the Regent, accompanied by the maréchal de Villeroi (visiting his own house and already alarmed at the destructive habits of his guests; they ruined every house and garden they visited, their standards of hygiene and cleanliness shocking even in those tolerant times). The Czar was delighted with the pretty boy King, astonishing the courtiers by lifting him up and hugging him. The sang-froid of the King was greatly admired.

With the demands of etiquette satisfied, the Czar could become a tourist. His curiosity was voracious, his pace frenetic. He first rushed out to see the three great squares of the city, the place Royale, the place des Victoires and the place Vendôme. The next day he went to the Obser-vatoire, then to the royal furniture and carpet factory at the Gobelins. There he was given a beautiful set of tapestries depicting the adventures of Don Quixote and Sancho Panza, but did not make friends, forgetting to give the customary tip to the workers to drink a toast to his health. Then he was off to the jardin du Roi des simples (medicinal plants) where Louis XIV's old doctor Fagon resided as administrator. The royal mirror-manufacturer in the rue de Reuilly in the faubourg Saint-Antoine also received a visit.

The next day Peter was in the Grande galerie of the Louvre to see the famous series of models of Vauban's fortifications, spending a long time examining them. He then toured the Louvre, went into the garden of the Tuileries, and examined the work going on at the Pont-Tournant, which was being built to facilitate the passage from the garden of the Tuileries to the Cours-la-Reine and the Champs-Elysées.

When the Czar called on Madame at the Palais-Royal, she was in a state of high excitement. For a long time she had admired him from afar and would not miss his visit, even though she was recovering from various minor ailments. She was not disappointed:

> Yesterday I had a visit from someone important, actually my hero, the Czar. I find him honest, that is without affectation. He is very intelligent; in truth he speaks German very badly but he can make himself understood. He is polite with everyone and very popular. I received him in a singular get-up; I cannot yet wear a corset and so wore what I wear when I get up, a nightdress, a camisole and a dressing gown with a belt.

As for the Czar, who did not seem to have noticed the odd costume, he remarked that Madame was extremely curious; that she wanted to know everything and asked too many questions; but that after all he had only told her what he wished her to know.

The Regent took him to the Opéra. The Czar asked for beer, and they brought a large glass set on a saucer. The Regent rose, took the glass and presented it to the Czar, who, with a smile and a polite inclination took it, drank, and put the glass back on the saucer which the Regent was still standing and holding. Philippe, no doubt rather amused to find himself treated as a servant in his own box, then presented a napkin and finally permitted himself to sit down. Unfortunately the Czar seemed bored with the performance and left during the fourth act. The duc d'Estrées told the comte de Toulouse:

> The Czar did not really enjoy himself at the Opéra because he does not under-stand the language and does not like music. He was however content enough with the girls, and the little Prévost [a première danseuse] appealed to him so much that I think he might have made her a proposition; but he wanted a condition difficult to meet among the girls of the Opéra, and he wished the duc d'Orléans to assure him that the girl in question was actually a virgin.

The Czar careened on to Saint-Cloud with the Regent and admired the house and gardens greatly. But Madame was very put out that he did not ask to see her there and did not even bid her adieu. From now on her tone changed with regard to her former hero. At Versailles the behaviour of the Czar and his entourage deteriorated. It was whispered that Peter slept with low-class girls in the very rooms of Mme de Maintenon, the 'temple de la pruderie'. Mme de Maintenon herself, peacefully enjoying her retirement at Saint-Cyr, had to submit to a visit from the barbarian who had defiled her rooms. Striding into her room, the Czar lifted the bed curtain to see her better and then left without saying a word.

Saint-Simon met the great man at the hôtel de Travers, the home of the duc d'Antin. D'Antin, 'toujours le même', had found a portrait which resembled the Czarina and had placed it in a prominent position over the fireplace. Gratified, the Czar presented the 'courtier suprême' with his portrait enriched with diamonds, and medals depicting the principal actions of his life, five in gold, eleven in silver.

After six hectic weeks, the Czar left Paris on 20 June, proceeding to the town of Spa to meet his wife. His views on what he had seen were, according to Louville, trenchant. 'He said a thousand times when he was here that he wept when he looked at France, and that he saw that our little King would lose his Kingdom because of the luxury and the excesses he found here.'

The Regent had handled the potentially troublesome visit with aplomb. He had promised to discuss a future treaty of commerce between France and Russia, but that was all. There was no formal alliance; Madame was correct when she wrote, 'they say that the Czar left not too happy with my son'. The success of Philippe's policy was further confirmed when France and Russia established diplomatic relations later in the year without the French making any concessions.

When Peter the Great left, Philippe had to face his more chronic problems once again. His opponents were stepping up their intrigues. There was civil unrest in Brittany, where the independently minded local authorities were protesting the need to obey the government in Paris. In the capital itself there was an atmosphere of cloak and dagger. Saint-Simon received a visit, in the greatest secrecy, from the maréchale d'Alègre, who warned him obliquely about plots against the Regent. 'These troubles in Brittany are only the beginning, Monsieur, let the Regent know this; you will see many others; but . . . ah! ah! . . . but . . .' Mme d'Alègre fell silent, then left, with dramatic parting words: 'It is not yet time, but I shall see you again; do not let down your guard, neither you nor M. le duc d'Orléans.' When Saint-Simon related this to Philippe he found him more concerned than he expected, and was urged to keep his door open for Mme d'Alègre and his ear to the ground.

Philippe took Mme d'Alègre's hints seriously because he had reason to believe that certain forces within and without France were conspiring to undermine his authority. The party of the *vieille cour* and the King of Spain were actively seeking to destabilise the Kingdom. The quarrel between the Princes of the Blood and the Légitimés provided further fuel for dissension and division. While the party of the Princes of the Blood and the dukes attacked Louis XIV for putting royal authority above 'the nation and the fundamental law of the Kingdom', when he decreed that his sons could ascend to the throne, the party of the duc du Maine and his supporters in the nobility called upon the Regent to summon the Estates General to decide the matter. In the meantime duelling documents flew from either side; it was a very good time for lawyers, pamphleteers and scribblers of all stripes.

Philippe decided to appoint six commissioners to examine the voluminous literature and to make a judgement at a special meeting of the Regency Council. In the meantime he issued an edict forbidding any members of the nobility from signing the petition of the duchesse du Maine demanding a meeting of the Estates General. When six members of the dissident nobility defied him by sending to *parlement* a request opposing the procedure of the commissioners, he had them arrested.

Finally, at a meeting of the Regency Council on 1 July, the Légitimés lost not only their case, but their right to succeed to the throne and their rank as Princes of the Blood. The Regent, however, decided to allow Maine and Toulouse, although stripped of their royal pretensions, to keep their precedence over the dukes. Such generosity did not appease the furious duchesse du Maine, who exclaimed, 'When one has had the ability to succeed to the throne, one would set fire to the four corners of the Kingdom rather than give it up.' Philippe tried not to listen to such provocation; he released the six men he had had arrested for supporting the claims of the Légitimés, saying, 'You know me well enough, Messieurs, to realise that when I punish someone, I believe myself obliged to do so.' Philippe still hoped to steer a path through all these competing claims and reach peace.

He was not greatly helped by the antics of the Princes of the Blood whose cause he was defending. In July there was an unsavoury occurrence involving the young and well-born Mme de Gacé, otherwise known as la Vigoureuse. At a dinner party attended by Monsieur le Duc, the intoxicated Mme de Gacé was encouraged to dance almost nude, and then delivered to the valets de chambre for their pleasure. The poor woman was denounced by her husband and sent off to a convent.

At the same time the prince de Conti was scandalising Paris with his public brawling with his wife, the daughter of Madame la Duchesse. When the princesse de Conti gave birth to a son that summer, the Prince remarked that he did not care for the baby, as he was sure that he was not the father; to which his wife replied, 'I don't care for him either, as I am sure that you are the father.'

While the feuding elements in French society openly skirmished, the King of Spain and Alberoni were opting for war. The King of Spain was looking for a reason to declare war on the Emperor and recover the territories in Italy lost to him under the terms of the Treaty of Utrecht. Elisabeth Farnese wanted war so that her sons might inherit these Italian lands; Alberoni was for caution, expecting as he was his cardinal's hat, and not wishing to do anything which might upset his plans. On 12 July he duly became a cardinal; five days later a Spanish fleet set sail from Barcelona, destined for Sardinia. Nine thousand Spanish troops were landed there on 20 August; there was no resistance from the tiny Austrian garrison.

Philippe was deeply concerned. If the Emperor marched into Italy to recover his lost territory, the British would be obliged by their treaty obligations to help him. Could France stand apart from the conflict, or would she be compelled to fight, and if so, on which side? With her new allies, the British, against her old ally, Spain? Or would the Anglo-French entente be destroyed and France fight with Spain? The Regent hesitated. The Council for Foreign Affairs strongly supported Spain, Dubois just as strongly supported the British.

In September Dubois was summoned to London by Stanhope. Philippe, racked with indecision, started to consider a plan put forward by the British exile Lord Peterborough which would link France, Spain and the Italian princes against the Emperor. Such a plan would obviously undermine everything Dubois was trying to achieve in England. Nonetheless, as Dubois was being fêted in London and taken horse-racing at Newmarket, his master was in touch with Alberoni about Peterborough's plan. 'I feel real joy', wrote Alberoni to Philippe, 'on learning ... that Your Royal Highness has taken the right road to secure your present and future interests.'

Then Peterborough was arrested at Bologna. The Jacobites around the Pretender at Urbino thought he was planning to murder their master and asked the Pope to arrest him as soon as he arrived in Papal territories. Peterborough was duly captured as he travelled from Parma in a chaise de poste. In the spirit of the age, he was disguised as a woman and was discovered when the guards noticed the ribbon and medal of the Order of St George at an opening in his petticoat. 'There must be something strange about my star,' Peterborough wrote to the Regent from prison, 'for here I am, deprived of my liberty at the very moment when I am working to free from slavery those who threw me into prison ...' Probably owing to the Regent's intervention, Peterborough was soon set free.

From London Dubois found himself unable to wield his customary influence over his master while his enemies had the Regent's ear. He dispatched hundreds of pages to Paris, supplicating, exhorting, beseeching that Philippe remain true to the alliance. The abbé was in a lather of indignation. He wrote from Hampton Court, referring to Spain: 'The lion who has a thorn in its foot lets it be removed with great gentleness, but when he has gathered his strength, it is only in the fable that he remembers the good deed.' Why would Philippe support the King of Spain, who made no secret of his willingness to sit on the throne of France? As always, Dubois sought to appeal to Philippe's personal interests as well as those of France, which Dubois believed were best served by making peace with the Emperor. But Philippe was proving obstinate: 'After all, it would be more to my advantage not to make an alliance with the Emperor than to ruin myself in the eyes of the great mass of the French nation, without whom I shan't have the Kingdom, despite all the treaties concluded with foreign powers.'

Philippe's hesitations were also occasioned by news of the grave illness of Philip V. If Philip V died, what an opportunity for the Regent of France to step into the affairs of Spain! Philippe began to have feverish thoughts of a second regency for himself; he went so far as to order French troops to the Spanish frontier. Spain always brought out his gambler's instincts.

At the end of November Philip V recovered, although he remained melancholy and could not be without his confessor even for a moment. Philippe set aside his Spanish dreams again and gave his attention back to Dubois, who, alarmed at his master's fluctuations, had rushed back to Paris at the beginning of December. 'A hundred letters would not do as much good as half an hour of conversation,' he told Nancré. He stayed in Paris for almost three weeks and, when he left again for London on Christmas Day, French policy was, definitely and officially, to go ahead and negotiate for an alliance with the Emperor, hoping to secure some concessions for Spain. The King of Spain and Alberoni had proved themselves their own worst enemies.

In this whirlwind of activity Philippe was suffering again with his eyes; he was either hit with a tennis racquet again, or with the fan of the marquise d'Arpajon, or with the elbow of Mme de La Rochefoucauld. 'He had been unable to distinguish colours,' wrote Madame,

> but now he can recognise red, because while I was there cardinal de Polignac arrived in his red robes, and he saw that at once, so there is an improvement. But what worries me is that my son, who practised great restraint while he was taking his medicines, will now resume his usual entertainments, and the debauched ladies will run after him and invite him to their suppers and make him lead his disorderly life, and ruin his eyesight or lose it altogether.

The debauched ladies were the target of Madame's wrath.

> It is quite true that if my son's mistresses really cared for him they would care for his health and well-being, but I can see, dearest Luise, that you don't know Frenchwomen. Nothing counts except their *débauches* and their greed, and money comes above everything; they don't care an iota for anyone. There is another thing too which I cannot understand; my son is never jealous, and doesn't mind if his servants sleep with his mistresses. That seems quite revolting, and clearly shows that he doesn't really love them.

Madame was probably referring to the fact that Mme de Parabère was now sharing her favours with Charles de Nocé, and that her son was rather untroubled by it. He was amusing himself with the pretty and spirited Mme de Sabran.

'He was not one to content himself with one mistress,' remarked Saint-Simon. 'He needed variety to pique his appetite.' Madeleine Louise Charlotte de Foix-Rabat, comtesse de Sabran ('mon Aloyau', or sirloin steak, to her lover) was 'charming, particularly at table'. Saint-Simon himself, notoriously faithful to his own wife, found her enchanting. 'No one was as handsome as she ... she had the grandest and most noble air, but without affectation. Her simple and natural manners made one think that she was ignorant of her own beauty ... She was a pleasing morsel, with few morals, but she had a good heart.' She it was who joked that princes and lackeys were made from the same cloth, which God, in the Creation, had separated from that which he gave other men. One of her letters to Philippe survives, breathtaking in its bluntness: 'Race de chien, I have been several times to your kennel to see you, but you have closed the door on me ... You do not know how to love, or to give, or to write. But can you read? Read then, monster. I will see you tomorrow morning, I wish you to make my husband your chamberlain; as for his salary, arrange it with your Chancellor. Adieu, chien.'

The comte de Sabran duly became chamberlain, a post worth six thousand livres, and Mme de Sabran was installed at Sèvres, at a reasonable distance from Mme de Parabère at Asnières. Madeleine de Sabran amused Philippe, but occasionally she went too far. One evening, when she insisted on interrogating the Prince on political events, he took her to a mirror and said: 'Regarde-toi, vois si c'est à un si joli visage qu'on doit parler d'affaires' ('Look at yourself, and tell me whether I must talk politics to such a pretty face'). Philippe could never rid himself of a fear of being ruled by women; his experiences with Mme de Maintenon and with the princesse des Ursins had marked him indelibly.

One envisages Mme de Sabran and Mme de Parabère as sketched by Watteau, wearing their hair low and necks exposed, powdered and rouged, dressed in delicate colours, shell pink, sage green, dove grey, ice blue, in flowing skirts, of silk and taffeta and mousseline, mules on their feet, their ankles revealing coloured stockings. Perhaps they were not as ethereally beautiful as Watteau presented them; but, like Alfred de Musset, one likes to think so.

> Beau marbre, as-tu vu La Vallière?
> De Parabère, ou de Sabran
> Laquelle savait mieux te plaire?
> Entre Sabran et Parabère
> Le Régent, même après souper,
> Chavirait jusqu'a s'y tromper.
>
> (Fine marble, did you see La Vallière?
> Did Parabère or de Sabran
> Know better how to please you?

Between Sabran and Parabère
The Regent, tipsy after supper,
Could not tell one from the other.)

At the end of August 1717 Watteau himself had finally presented to the
Académie the *Embarkation to Cythera,* his *morceau de réception.* He had
been given four reminders before he delivered the painting, and, although
he had been told, unprecedentedly, that he could paint what he wished,
the result was startling. His work fitted into no category; indeed there was
some confusion over whether it depicted a pilgrimage to Cythera, or the
return from Cythera. In the end the Académie simply called it a 'fête
galante', the first recorded. A calm sense of happiness suffuses the painting,
as does a sense of the fragility of life and love. It is a moment of perfect
equilibrium, pervaded with the memory of happiness just past and the
prospect of happiness to come. Watteau's enchanted world is not that of
the Regency, it transcends time; but his images remain those in which the
age would have liked to believe.

## ✖ 19 ✖

## COUP D'ETAT

The most pressing matter for the Regent at the beginning of 1718 was how to sustain and continue the nation's economic revival. Law's bank had proven itself a great success; the shareholders had been awarded a dividend of 8 per cent at the end of 1716, and all through 1717 steps were taken to make banknotes the official medium of exchange throughout the country. In August 1717 Law scored another coup.

The financier Antoine Crozat had been fined a considerable sum by the Chambre de Justice for misuse of public money; he decided to make a deal with the authorities, namely to give up his monopoly on trade with Louisiana in exchange for the alleviation of part of the fine. Since 1712 Crozat had had the monopoly in this vast territory, stretching from the Gulf of Mexico up the Mississippi to Canada, but had done little with it. Despite his lack of success, it was generally believed that Louisiana (today's Mississippi, Arkansas, Missouri, Illinois, Iowa, Wisconsin and Minnesota) had the potential to be another Mexico, filled with mines of gold and silver.

Law jumped at the idea of taking over the trade monopoly. He suggested founding a company, to be called the Compagnie d'Occident, which would assume the management not only of the Louisiana territory, but also of the beaver trade in Canada, and persuaded Noailles that he could eliminate the national debt by having the public purchase shares in the company, partly in cash, partly in government notes. Noailles thought this a brilliant idea. He conceived the Compagnie d'Occident primarily as a scheme to retire the debt; but Law, on the other hand, was already thinking more in terms of establishing a single banking and trading enterprise, its tentacles extending into every aspect of state finance.

By the beginning of 1718 the two schools of thought, Noailles' conservatism and Law's radical ideas, were in increasing conflict. Philippe was ready to make fundamental changes in his administration of the finances. He had come to the conclusion that the measures adopted by the duc de Noailles were not working quickly enough. The Kingdom needed more drastic measures. He was sure that John Law, already successful with his bank, was the man to take the lead. On 6 January Philippe met with Law, Noailles and Daguesseau at La Raquette, a little house in the faubourg Saint-Antoine rented by Noailles. Noailles set forth his achievements: more efficient tax-collecting, the cutting of expenses, some debts paid off. There had been some success with the experimental new tax, the graduated taille, based proportionately on income. But all of these paled besides John Law's dazzling proposals for a national financial and economic enterprise. Philippe thought Noailles tired and defensive, Daguesseau tedious, Law full of energy and ideas. Law was his man.

Before making any changes, Philippe had to consider the reaction of *parlement*, which was in a cantankerous mood. Deputations were constantly arriving at the Palais-Royal to demand that the Regent give an account of the finances; the magistrates were complaining about Law's growing influence, and about the councils, which they accused, with some justice, of ineptitude and tardiness. They were making full use of their restored power to remonstrate, reading their grievances before the King at the end of January. Philippe was unbending: 'As long as I am the depositary of the royal authority, I shall not suffer it to be abased . . .'

In this recriminatory atmosphere, it was clear that *parlement* would never accept Law, a foreigner, a Protestant and a man determined to upset the status quo, as Controller of Finances. Philippe therefore decided to replace both Noailles and Daguesseau with one man, his old ally, the marquis d'Argenson, the chief of police in Paris, who became both Chancellor and President of the Council of Finances. The move immediately increased Law's power, as d'Argenson knew little about finance, and, being no friend to *parlement*, would support Law against their opposition. Law would have more leeway to proceed with his system.

On 28 January Daguesseau was relieved of the seals; he received the news calmly and, having sent a note of warning to Noailles, left for his country house at Fresnes-sur-Marne and his pregnant wife. The next day Noailles, duly alerted, resigned as President of the Finance Council; his conversation with the Regent was brief. 'Do you ask for nothing?' enquired Philippe. 'Nothing at all.' replied Noailles. 'I grant you a place on the Regency Council.' 'I shall make little use of it.' But Noailles went to the next meeting and after that never missed one.

Marc René de Voyer de Paulmy, marquis d'Argenson, was already in his sixties, and had been lieutenant de police for twenty years. He was a resourceful man, a shrewd operator, who knew everyone's secrets and the value of discretion. He was of a dark and sombre mien, called Rhad-amanthus for his resemblance to the judge of the underworld, but his looks deceived. He was an amusing companion, liked to tell jokes and loved the company of women. 'He was of cheerful disposition,' wrote his son, 'with a good constitution, and liked to enjoy himself without grossness or indecency; the best company sought him out; he drank a great deal, without it interfering with his life, had as much to do with women as he could, whether secular or religious did not matter, but he had a little more taste for the religious ones, snub-nosed or with large noses, thin and fat; with a fund of good stories at table, he was the best company conceivable.' He had a particularly intimate friendship with Mme de Veyney, perpetual Prioress of the Benedictines of the Madeleine de Trainel in the faubourg Saint-Antoine, and kept an apartment at her priory.

Philippe liked d'Argenson because he possessed both integrity and dynamism. Like the Regent himself, he worked all day and all night; those who had business with him had to accommodate themselves to his strange hours. Even the duc de La Rochefoucauld, who was seigneur of his province, had to call on him at two in the morning at his house in the rue Vielle-du-Temple, near the Grands-Jésuites. He was wont to take his meals in his carriage as he went to and fro, reading by the light of a candle. In this iconoclast, Philippe felt he had a strong ally in the inevitable confrontations to come.

At about this time Philippe introduced his fourteen-year-old son, the duc de Chartres, on to the Regency Council. Recalling his own lack of instruction in affairs of state, Philippe thought it right to expose his son to the decision-making process, however ill-suited for such deliberations he might be. Saint-Simon was unimpressed. 'I have never understood who gave the Regent this premature advice, which has borne no great fruit.' The duc de Chartres showed little sign of distinction. His grandmother thought him 'a nice boy and has intelligence, yet he is a bit too serious for his age and so dreadfully delicate that I cannot look at him without worrying. He must not drink a drop of iced beverage, or else he immediately gets a fever, nor must he eat fruit or anything but the things to which he is accustomed. I keep fretting that he will not last very long, and that would be a dreadful calamity for all of us.' Almost as an afterthought she added, 'It would also be a pity for the child, who is so clever and kind-hearted and who learns everything he is taught. He is not beautiful but more on the pretty than on the ugly side and resembles his mother more than his father. The child has a natural disposition to all the virtues and is not given to any vice. This makes me very fond of him.' Not surprisingly, however, this saintly disposition did not make for close relations between father and son.

Madame was even fonder of the duc de Chartres' half-brother, the twenty-year-old abbé de Saint-Albin, son of Florence. When the young man presented his thesis at the Sorbonne, Madame was present at the reading. Saint-Simon was profoundly shocked: 'Madame, such a foe of bastards and bastardy, has allowed herself to let her liking for this young man lead her to this scandalous spectacle ... everything passed as though it was the duc de Chartres who was reading the thesis. Madame went there in pomp, was received at her carriage door by cardinal de Noailles ... placed herself on a dais which had been made ready, in an armchair.' Philippe and his mother both liked Saint-Albin. Madame wanted Philippe to legitimise him, but Philippe was determined not to emulate Louis XIV in this regard; he had seen only too clearly the problems caused by the legitimising of the duc du Maine and the comte de Toulouse. Charles de Saint-Albin would remain a man of the Church.

Philippe saw his sister again that spring, for the first time in twenty years, when she and her husband, the duc de Lorraine, arrived in Paris for an extended visit. The pretty young woman had become a matron who had borne nine children and seen seven of them die, three within a week from smallpox. She was accompanied not only by her husband, but also by his mistress, Mme de Beauvau-Craon, and she probably hardly remembered the joys of her honeymoon, when she had told her mother how much she was enjoying the pleasures of the marital bed. The Duke was, as Madame delicately put it, 'excessively taken with this bagatelle'. He was, as she also related, particularly well equipped for such entertainment. 'The Duke was once taking a bath when the man washing him asked if "His Grace would move his arm so that I can wash His Grace?" It turned out, that it wasn't his arm that was in the way at all, but, by your leave, quite a different thing.'

The duchesse de Lorraine was eager to taste some of the Parisian amusements she had missed and, the night of her arrival, was taken to the Opéra ball. Unused to Paris customs, she was deeply shocked at what she saw. Observing 'ladies with great names sitting on the knees of gentlemen who seemed to be having a very good time', the Duchess could only exclaim, 'Madame, Madame!' When her mother replied that these were the manners of the times, the Duchess was clear: 'But these are ugly manners.' Her mother could not have agreed more.

There were great celebrations. The most splendid was at the Luxembourg where the duchesse de Berry gave 'a party which was as magnificent and tasteful as it is possible to be'. (Saint-Simon was not a dispassionate observer; it was his wife who was in charge of the evening.) Dinner was served in the Rubens gallery by two hundred Swiss Guards, and the menu was so breathtaking that it was celebrated in verse in the newspaper:

> Des filets minces d'aloyau
> Des gendarmes au jus de veau,
> Petits dindons aux ciboulettes,
> Et des anchois en allumettes ...
>
> (Thin slices of sirloin,
> Gendarmes in veal gravy,
> Little fowl with tiny onions,
> And anchovies ...)

and so forth for eight pages.

Philippe liked his sister; but the incessant festivities bored him. He expressed his ennui to the ever credulous Saint-Simon. As they walked in the little garden of the Palais-Royal, he told him that he was weary of this way of life, too old for late suppers and tired of wine and women. He would not break off his suppers until his sister left, as he would die of boredom supping every night with his wife and a troop of women. But when the Lorraines had gone he would give up his 'roués et putains', his own words, and lead a sage, reasonable life, suitable to his age and position. Saint-Simon congratulated him heartily, only to learn the next day that, later that evening, Philippe had regaled the company of 'roués et putains' with the conversation. Saint-Simon, although hurt ('this is the only time that he diverted himself at my expense'), did not let this disloyalty spoil their friendship. Knowing Philippe as he did, he simply shook his head at yet one more instance of his frailty.

The Lorraines did not leave empty handed; the duc de Lorraine gained the title of Royal Highness, and Philippe gave his sister an elegant present, described by Madame; 'it is called a *necéssaire*, that is, a rectangular box containing porcelain cups and everything that is needed for taking chocolate, coffee and tea. The cups are white, with a raised design in gold and enamel, and there is a little blue cushion with all kinds of gold objects underneath, needlecase, thimble, corkscrew-case, two golden boxes and some more things, all made of pure gold and finely worked.'

All this time Philippe was wrestling not only with *parlement*, but also with the British, over what terms should be offered to the recalcitrant King of Spain in order for him to be induced to join in the European peace.

Dubois was in London demanding, on behalf of the Regent, that Parma, Piacenza and Tuscany be handed over to Don Carlos, son of Elisabeth Farnese, Queen of Spain, on the deaths of their rulers. Philippe was unwilling to affront French public opinion by signing a peace treaty with the old enemy, Austria, without handsome concessions to the old ally, Spain. For his own survival, he could not be accused of pursuing a personal vendetta against Philip V.

The Emperor condescended to sign the Quadruple Alliance on 4 April. He would renounce his claims to Spain, and agree to Don Carlos inheriting the Italian duchies; in return he would receive Sicily, which had been awarded to the Duke of Savoy by the terms of the Treaty of Utrecht. (The Duke of Savoy received Sardinia in return for Sicily.) The British promised to consider handing over Gibraltar to Spain. As whole populations were thus shuffled from hand to hand, it remained only for Philip V to append his signature, and there would be peace in Europe.

Of course it was not the King of Spain who would make that decision, but the Queen and Alberoni. Philippe sent his old friend, the marquis de Nancré, to Madrid to try and persuade the Spanish court to see reason. Nancré dangled the proposition that the Spanish might recover Gibraltar if they signed the Quadruple Alliance and reported back that Alberoni seemed to want peace.

Alberoni might be talking of peace, but he was preparing for war. He had a vision of an attack on Hanover and England in league with the Russians; he hope to reignite the Jacobite cause. And he was furiously building ships and gathering provisions for another Mediterranean adventure. The King of Spain dreamed of retaking Sicily, perhaps using the island as a staging post for Naples; the Queen, even though temporarily indisposed with another pregnancy, was bellicose. Far from signing the Quadruple Alliance, Philip V was confident that the French themselves, in defiance of the Regent, would not sign it either. In Madrid the royal grip on reality was weakening.

Majestically, Philip V rejected Nancré's terms:

> Out of deference to my grandfather the King and in the interests of European peace I acquiesced in the Utrecht treaties which were dictated to me by a handful of private individuals. I have no desire to submit a second time to their dictation, since God has put me in a position of independence, where I need no longer bow under the yoke of my enemies, to the shame, scandal and utter indignation of my subjects.

Alberoni, for his part, complained that the European powers were 'cutting up and paring states and kingdoms as if they were Dutch cheeses...'

In this perilous situation, Philippe was deluged with conflicting advice. From London Dubois urged him to threaten Spain with force; from Madrid Nancré urged patience; in Paris Philippe was hearing the complaints of Huxelles, who wanted a full alliance with Spain and no part of the alliance with the Emperor. And the magistrates, the clergy, even the despised *nouvellistes* and pamphleteers, were joined with Huxelles in vocal opposition to the Regent's policy. Characteristically Philippe listened, weighed and waited.

Dubois was revelling in his role as chief negotiator with the British government. And he was putting together a network of men, and some women, who were at once couriers, facilitators and spies. These men and women were enterprising types who, without the benefits of birth, were ambitious for a career. Several of them were writers, including the playwright Destouches, who was Dubois' *homme de confiance* in London.

A little later Voltaire himself would join Dubois' service. But in the spring of 1718 he was simply relieved to be released from the Bastille, where he had spent almost a year. He was still the little Arouet, the brilliant and patronised son of a bourgeois notary, he was not yet Voltaire, and the Regent was determined to be strict with him. Although he was free, he was not allowed to return to Paris, being relegated to his father's house at nearby Chatenay. He made strenuous efforts to return to favour, assuring Machault, the Lieutenant of Police, somewhat unconvincingly, that 'I have only ever spoken of His Royal Highness to admire his wit . . . I have always had for him a veneration all the more profound inasmuch as I am aware that he hates praise as much as he deserves it.' He wrote to the secretary to the councils, La Vrillière, in the same vein: 'I beg you to let me have permission to come to Paris for two hours only: I only wish to have the honour of meeting you for a moment and throwing myself at the feet of His Royal Highness.'

Philippe hardly needed such an embarrassment. His daughter Charlotte-Aglaé, Mademoiselle de Valois, was proving a trial. She was eighteen, very pretty, if rather plump, a lively brunette with sparkling eyes. Madame, impossible to please, deplored 'her huge hawk's nose which has spoiled everything. I can guess what happened – she must have been allowed to take snuff, and that made her nose grow.' Regarding most of her grandchildren with a jaundiced eye, Madame took a particular dislike to this girl:

> she does not have a kind character, cares nothing for her mother and little for her father, except that she wants to rule him. Me she hates like the Devil and also hates all of her sisters. She is deceitful in all things, often

contemptuous of the truth, and dreadfully coquettish withal. In short, this girl is sure to bring us much unhappiness. I wish she were already married and living in a faraway country, so that we would not have to hear more about her.

When Madame wrote this, Charlotte was in the throes of a wild infatuation with the dashing young duc de Richelieu, causing vast embarrassment to her family. Richelieu (known in society as Fanfarinet) was, at the age of twenty-two, already an experienced seducer. All the young ladies of the royal family found him charming, even Mme de Maintenon once remarking that he was so sweet that she wanted to pat him under the chin. In fact no one was less sweet or more manipulative than Richelieu, who relished his reputation as a *dompteur de femmes*, and who all his life enjoyed ruining the lives of the women he seduced. He had already been sent to the Bastille twice, once for duelling and once for flirting with the duchesse de Bourgogne, but, nothing daunted, had taken up with Louise-Anne de Bourbon, Mlle de Charolais, a daughter of Madame la Duchesse. Louise-Anne was a free spirit, totally undisciplined, and had just had herself painted as a Franciscan monk, causing Voltaire to dub her Frère Ange de Charolais. Richelieu continued to see her that spring, even as he moved on to the conquest of Mlle de Valois herself. Using every weapon in the seducer's armoury, from disguise as a chambermaid to underground passageways, he succeeded in bending Charlotte-Aglaé to his will. The spectacle of these Princesses of the Blood quarrelling over the same man was a cause of mortification to Madam and to Philippe.

As for the duchesse de Berry, she was involving herself in politics, giving audience to several of her father's foes, and generally causing a stir in Paris. Her lady-in-waiting, Mme de Clermont, was so frustrated by the antics of her mistress that she resigned her post. Some time later the duchesse, seeing Mme de Clermont at the Opéra, demanded that she leave immediately. Mme de Clermont did so with dignity: 'I shall leave; I am delighted once again to have an opportunity to show Mme de Berry my submission and my obedience.' There was uproar. Mme de Berry was taking upon herself the prerogatives of the King, attacking 'la liberté publique'. Six weeks later the duchesse was compelled to apologise to Mme de Clermont.

The question of public liberty was the very issue being debated between Philippe and *parlement* that summer. The magistrates were increasingly upset at what they saw as the high handed attitude of the Regent, in everything from the Quadruple Alliance to John Law. They were particularly outraged by a recent devaluation of the coinage, about which they were not consulted. When they tried to remonstrate, the Regent issued letters de cachet forbidding other law courts to make common cause with parliament. The opposition of the magistrates seemed about to spread into the streets. When a disastrous fire erupted on the Petit-Pont, burning down all the houses between the Petit-Châtelet and the Hôtel-Dieu, a huge crowd came from miles around to watch the conflagration; there was such commotion, and the mood of the crowd was so volatile, that the gendarmes and musketeers were ordered to be ready to take horse.

The Regent adopted an increasingly authoritarian tone with *parlement*. When a delegation visited him to express their opposition to the devaluation, he was uncharacteristically overwrought, declaring that 'the *parlememt* could maintain its authority as it saw fit, but as for him, he had made provision with powder and lead to maintain his'. After further deputations and remonstrances, he went further, issuing a statement in which he stated, 'The laws both ancient and modern exist only at the will of the Sovereign and need only that will to be law; their registration in the courts to which their execution is entrusted adds nothing to the power of the legislator, that is only the promulgation and an indispensable act of obedience . . .' This was a very different position from the one he took in September 1715; after almost three years of governing, Philippe was beginning to feel that he would accomplish more without constant harassment from *parlement*. In particular, he was convinced that John Law knew how to make France rich and secure, and should be given the chance to prove himself.

In the summer of 1718 Philippe sensed that the time had come to take decisive steps to establish his position. His spies told him that the Spanish Ambassador, Cellamare, was involved in several nascent plots on behalf of Alberoni, plots designed to provoke a rebellion in France which would serve as a pretext to invite the King of Spain to intervene. Cellamare was in touch with many members of the *vieille cour*, with sympathetic magistrates, dissident Bretons, disaffected members of the nobility. The Regent's foreign policy, his backing of the dukes against the Légitimés, his support for the radical ideas of John Law, united these groups in opposition. *Parlement* was openly hostile and the mood in Paris tense.

The British were becoming concerned that the Regent was so preoccupied with *parlement* and with the growing hostility to his government that he was delaying, perhaps even reconsidering, having France sign the Quadruple Alliance. Stanhope himself came to Paris at the end of June to hurry matters to a conclusion. Although he was greeted at the Palais-Royal 'with much good sense and seeming frankness and sincerity', and despite a lavish party at Saint-Cloud, and a weekend at Lord Stair's country house at Montfermeil, the Quadruple Alliance remained unsigned. 'We found the Regent very upset by the views of the majority of his advisers and, so to speak, of almost all the Kingdom against the Treaty...'

Huxelles privately told Stair that the Regent was making a mistake isolating the King of Spain, that he would only succeed in ensuring Philip V's return to France as King. Stair replied that Huxelles would never dare confront the Regent himself with this view, adding that the British would prevent the King of Spain from thus reneging on his oath of renunciation with all the means at their disposal. Rashly, Huxelles boasted that he would rather cut off his arm than sign the Alliance.

Stair and Stanhope were aghast at Huxelles' open defiance. They were made still more uneasy by the news that a mighty fleet of forty-nine warships had set sail from Barcelona. The departure of the fleet was known to the British and French spies, but not their destination. The commander of this, the largest fleet launched by Spain since the Great Armada of Philip II, carried with him sealed orders, to be opened only at sea. As the armada disappeared into the Mediterranean, a British fleet under Admiral Byng set sail from Spithead, also sailing to the Mediterranean. While diplomacy faltered, navies advanced.

Before he knew of the departure of the Spanish fleet, Philippe had finally decided to call Huxelles' bluff. On 17 July, while Stair and Stanhope waited anxiously, the Regency Council approved the Quadruple Alliance, including a secret convention which called upon the Allies to attack Spain if Philip V did not adhere to the terms within three months. Only the duc du Maine spoke against it. Huxelles cravenly agreed to sign, thus inviting general contempt:

> Huxelles dit: 'Cette paix,
> Cette Quadruple Alliance
> Est la peste de la France.
> Je m'y souscrirai jamais.
> Contre ces projets iniques
> Je fus toujours indigné.'
> Après ces mots héroïques,
> Le maréchal a signé.

> (Huxelles says: 'This peace,
> This Quadruple Alliance,
> Is the scourge of France.
> I shall never sign it.
> To these wicked projects
> I have always been opposed.'
> After these heroic words,
> The maréchal has signed.)

'Tout est fini, Dieu merci!' exclaimed Philippe. Stanhope was exultant. 'We must do justice to the Regent, to whom this affair is entirely due. He has seen it through despite winds and waves, and against the inclination of the country.' The treaty was signed by Stanhope and Huxelles the next day and sent to London, where it was signed by Dubois, Lord Sunderland and the Emperor's representative, Pentenrieder, on 2 August.

Dubois was euphoric. 'I admit that I am happy that Providence has made use of me to obtain for the Kingdom, and for a master whom I have adored for thirty-five years, the greatest good for which one could hope in the present situation,' he told Saint-Simon. 'I beg you, Monsieur, to encourage the Prince, whom God seems to have destined for great things, to stay firm in his opinions and his confidence.'

Then, three days after the meeting of the Regency Council, on 20 July, the French heard the news that Alberoni's armada had arrived off Sicily and had disembarked thirty thousand men. There was shock and alarm; Lord Cadogan, dining with Stair in Paris, was so disturbed that he swallowed the contents of his snuff-box instead of his wine. Stanhope, thinking that the Spanish would back down, decided to go in person to Madrid. There, Nancré and the British Ambassador, Colonel William Stanhope (Lord Stanhope's cousin), warned Alberoni that the British fleet was approaching Sicily; to their astonishment, Alberoni's only response was, 'His Catholic Majesty has done me the honour to say that Admiral Byng is free to execute the orders he has received from his master.'

The British could not believe that the Spanish would reject their proposals; Lord Sunderland told Stair, as Stanhope was en route to Madrid, that 'though the Cardinal Alberoni has a good warm projecting head of his own, yet one can hardly imagine him mad enough to stand out against the whole world'. On his arrival in the Spanish capital on 12 August Stanhope presented Alberoni with a copy of the Quadruple Alliance and hinted once more that, if the Spanish signed, Gibraltar might be returned to them. But things were going well for Spanish arms in Sicily; Philip V refused to listen.

Stanhope knew that Admiral Byng's fleet had orders to attack the Spanish fleet. As it looked more and more likely that this would happen, and soon, and having no wish to be imprisoned in Spain a second time, he prudently withdrew to Bayonne. Somewhere off Sicily Byng's ships would accomplish what Stanhope's words had failed to do.

In Paris, as a heatwave oppressed the capital, the duchesse du Maine held secret meetings with the Spanish Ambassador, with the dissident Bretons, with sympathetic members of *parlement*. She had found a new and exciting hobby: fomenting a rebellion against the Regent in favour of the King of Spain. She had her first meeting with Cellamare at the end of May, going secretly through the gardens of the Arsenal to a little house on the river. Her lieutenant the marquis de Laval, a terrifying figure known as la Mentonnière for the black taffeta mask he wore to cover his disfigured jaw, arranged the tryst and kept lookout with the marquis de Pompadour. The duchesse referred to Laval as her Minister of the Interior, as he was the link with the Bretons and other disaffected provincials, and to Pompadour, who kept in touch with the Spanish Ambassador, as her Foreign Minister. They planned to distribute an appeal to the King of Spain, inviting him to take power in France.

The Spanish Ambassador played the Duchess like a fish. He assured her that her husband would be Philip V's principal lieutenant, the *de facto* ruler of France; Philippe d'Orléans would be executed for treason.

The maréchal de Villeroi, who might well have known what the duchesse du Maine was up to, let it be known that he considered the King's life at risk, inflaming the situation by claiming to have found a poisoned biscuit at the Tuileries. In the salons, everyone was discussing the recently published Memoirs of the cardinal de Retz, and their account of the Fronde. Another Fronde, the civil war which pitted magistrates and discontented nobles against the child Louis XIV and the Regent, Anne of Austria, was coming to seem a possibility.

In this quite literally overheated atmosphere, *parlement* struck another blow in its guerrilla war with the Regent. On 12 August the magistrates published a decree stipulating, among other attacks on Law's Bank, that no foreigners could administer the finances of the Kingdom. This was the last straw; Philippe decided that the time had come to act.

As always at moments of crisis Philippe turned to his most trustworthy ally. Although he had confidence in d'Argenson, and admired John Law, the Regent felt the need for Dubois' energy and readiness to take bold and dramatic action. These qualities would be indispensable in the coming confrontations. Dubois was summoned from London, arriving in Paris at one in the morning of 17 August, and was taken early the next day to Saint-Cloud for urgent discussions with his master.

The Regent summoned up his forces. Confiding only in Dubois, Law, d'Argenson and Saint-Simon, he decided to take on his enemies; he would stop *parlement* in its tracks, secure freedom of action for John Law, restore the royal authority. He first sent Saint-Simon on a crucial mission: to secure the support of Monsieur le Duc. This young man, insignificant in himself, was a crucial political player due to his rank as Prince of the Blood. He well knew how to use his power. The price he demanded for supporting the Regent's attack on *parlement* was not only a huge pension for himself and for his brother, the comte de Charolais, but also the position of Superintendent of the King's Education, the post currently held by the duc du Maine. The Regent consented. He had already decided that he must strike not only at *parlement*, but also against Maine, thus attacking both his enemies at once. He was more than happy to use Monsieur le Duc as his cover.

On 19 August Saint-Simon, relishing every moment, was given the task of preparing for a *lit de justice* at the Tuileries. (A *lit de justice* was an extraordinary session of *parlement* called to register great matters of state.) Preparations were to be made in the deepest secrecy. 'Everything was tending to the extremes,' he commented, 'and it was more than time for the Regent to awake from a slumber which had made him an object of scorn and had emboldened his enemies and those of the state.'

On 21 August Monsieur le Duc summoned Saint-Simon. This young man, very tall, thin like a twig, with a crooked walk, long legs like a stork, a very short body – in short extremely ugly ('I have never seen anyone as ugly,' was Saint-Simon's opinion) – was insisting that the duc du Maine not only lose his job as Superintendent of the King's Education, but be reduced in rank to duke. This was music to Saint-Simon's ears, although he protested vociferously that this might be going too far. Saint-Simon abhorred the fact that the duc du Maine held a higher rank than all the Dukes, and took it as a personal affront. But he did not wish to be as a leader in any anti-Maine party. As it happened, Philippe's move against one enemy, *parlement*, was becoming a full-scale assault on another, the 'Spanish party', as represented by the duc du Maine.

The next day there were manoeuvres on both sides. *Parlement* established a commission to enquire into the state of the finances; when Philippe received their delegation, he simply listened and turned his back. There was talk of a plot to take Law and hang him in the Palais de Justice. Law, fearing for his life, was advised to take temporary refuge in the Palais-Royal, where he lay low in the suite of Nancré, who was in Spain.

It was time to act. The Regent decided that the *lit de justice* would take place on 26 August. On the night of the 25th, Philippe, exhausted and tense, retired early, ostensibly with a fever; but he actually met until late in the night with the commanders of the household troops and the Musketeers. At four in the morning his faithful ally Contades went to the Tuileries to awaken the duc du Maine and tell him to have the Swiss Guard, whose commander he was, on the alert the next day. Maine was deeply alarmed by this mysterious visit.

On 26 August Paris woke to an atmosphere of siege. Troops guarded the Tuileries and were posted throughout the city; there were even soldiers under the arcades of the Saint-Germain fair. Several cavalry squadrons were in the courtyard of the hôtel de Soubise; the Grey Musketeers were ready in their barracks in the rue du Bac; the Black Musketeers, come from Charenton, were posted near the abbey of Saint-Germain-des-Prés. At six in the morning, Desgranges, the master of ceremonies, went to the Great Hall of the Palais to deliver a letter requesting that *parlement* convene at the Tuileries at ten o'clock. There all the trappings of the solemn ceremony, the throne, tapestries, hangings, were in place, installed overnight, to the stupefaction of the valets de chambre who had seen and heard nothing.

As the magistrates were being summoned, the Regency Council convened at nine o'clock in the King's room at the Tuileries. The Regent seemed relaxed and cheerful, chatting to Saint-Simon, who could hardly contain himself. When Maine and Toulouse arrived, Philippe took Toulouse aside and intimated that he and his brother should leave, as 'disagreeable' matters were to be discussed. The brothers, pale and anxious, left the room.

Then Philippe addressed the assembly. 'For today, Messieurs, I shall disobey my usual rule to hear your views; I thing it will be better if I speak for all.' A *lit de justice* was to be held immediately to bring the *parlement* to heel. *Parlement* could no longer be allowed to oppose his financial policies; its remonstrances must cease. At the same time another matter must be settled. The duc du Maine and the comte de Toulouse had lost their rank vis-à-vis the royal family in July 1717; now they must also lose it vis-à-vis the dukes. The Regent informed the Council of his decision to reduce them in rank from Princes of the Blood to dukes. Not only that, but they would take precedence only according to the date of their creation as dukes, and would therefore be outranked by all the other dukes. As the shock set in, Philippe immediately added that, in recognition of his service to his country, the comte de Toulouse would be allowed to keep all his rights for his lifetime. The duc du Maine alone was to be abased.

In the terrible silence that followed this announcement, Monsieur le Duc, his voice hoarse and grating, asked that the post of Superintendent of the King's Education be given to him, as the duc du Maine's rank was now too inferior for him to continue in the post. Only the maréchal de Villeroi himself dared speak: 'Voilà all the dispositions of the late King's will overturned; I cannot witness it without grief. M. du Maine is indeed unfortunate.' 'Monsieur,' responded the Regent with dignity, 'M. du Maine is my brother-in-law, but I prefer an enemy discovered to one that is hidden.'

Villeroi, Huxelles, Villars and the other allies of the duc du Maine on the Council said nothing. In total silence and in an atmosphere of trepidation, everyone waited for the *parlement* to arrive in procession from the Ile de la Cité. There was a rumour that the magistrates had refused to come. The minutes dragged by. Firmly the Regent refused to allow anyone to leave the Council chamber in order to prevent any communication between his enemies. Saint-Simon appointed himself monitor of those who wished to relieve themselves. After what seemed an eternity, there were shouts and the beating of drums. The magistrates, in red robes and black bonnets, were observed marching in double file towards the Tuileries.

In the chamber the heat was almost unendurable. Already deeply alarmed by the military presence and the air of crisis, the members of *parlement* perspired in their ceremonial robes. They listened to d'Argenson in silence as he condemned their political pretensions and their attempts to seize legislative power. They heard that the duc du Maine was now a junior member of the peerage, no longer responsible for the King's education. Two hours later all was accomplished. It had been the happiest day of Saint-Simon's life. All his hatred of the royal bastards and their lofty position, all his passionate attachment to his own rank as a duke, caused him practically to expire with joy. 'I was dying of joy. I was afraid of fainting; my heart, beating too fast, had no room to expand. The violence I did to myself in order not to let any detail escape me was infinite, and yet it was a delicious torment ... I triumphed, I avenged myself, I swam in my vengeance; I rejoiced in the complete realisation of my most heartfelt desires.'

On his return home to the rue des Saints-Pères, Saint-Simon found his friends, the duc d'Humières and Louville, gathered to congratulate him with all his family, including his mother, 'whom curiosity had brought from her room, which she had not left since the beginning of winter'. But then a messenger arrived with news that the Regent absolutely wished that Saint-Simon go to Saint-Cloud to break the news to Madame and the duchesse d'Orléans. Saint-Simon was horrified and somewhat chagrined, as he had wanted to savour his triumph in Paris. Gulping down some soup and an egg, he hurried to the Palais-Royal and found Philippe alone, striding round his *grand cabinet*. Saint-Simon congratulated him on his bearing at the *lit de justice*, his 'air of detachment, at once so businesslike and so majestic', and, after this shameless flattery, tried to avoid having to make the journey to Saint-Cloud. Philippe was implacable: 'One cannot refuse one's friends in such serious matters.'

At Saint-Cloud, Saint-Simon found first Madame, who remarked simply, 'At last!', adding that her son 'should have done all this a long time ago, but that he was too good'. The duchesse d'Orléans, on the other hand, wept bitterly, before rushing to Paris to commiserate with her brothers. She had always been on good terms with Maine and Toulouse, often more in sympathy with them than with her husband. She felt his disgrace keenly. There were tears of sorrow at the Palais-Royal, where Maine and Toulouse came to see their sister; when they left, there were tears between Philippe and his wife; when the duchesse de Berry joined them, also weeping, there was an emotional crescendo.

At the hôtel de Toulouse, where the duchesse du Maine had waited for the outcome of the *lit de justice*, there was anger and consternation. Mme du Maine's maid of honour, Rose de Launay, was hastily sent to Sceaux to burn papers and put things in order. She recorded in her memoirs what she found on her return to Paris: 'the Duchess's state cannot be described; there was a despondency like an entire deprivation of life, or a lethargic sleep from which one only wakes with convulsive movements'. The duchesse du Maine was paralysed with fury.

Across the river, at the hôtel de Condé, Monsieur le Duc was throwing a huge party in celebration of the day's events. Saint-Simon looked in there at the end of his tumultuous day, and received hearty congratulations. The next day Monsieur le Duc moved into Maine's rooms at the Tuileries.

Madame rejoiced at the blow against the Maines, but remained concerned. She quoted the duchesse du Maine as declaring, 'They say that I made the *parlement* rise up against the duc d'Orléans, but I despise him too much to take such noble vengeance, I would rather revenge myself otherwise.' Madame might tremble, but the general view of Mme du Maine was that of Lady Sandwich, who remarked, 'If Mme la duchesse du Maine had held a sceptre in her hand, she would have found the secret of transforming it into a baby's rattle.'

The magistrates, who had suffered the loss of all they had gained in September 1715, tried to regroup. But on 27 August at four in the morning the musketeers arrested three of the most outspoken. When a deputation from *parlement* hurried to see d'Argenson and protest, they were told that the arrests were affairs of state which required 'le secret et le silence'. D'Argenson added that 'the King has wished to have his authority respected; the conduct which his *parlement* adopts in these circumstances shall determine his disposition and his sentiments.' Philippe's comment was pithier: 'Quoi, those buggers still wish to meddle!' That was the end of *parlement*'s resistance. Philippe had won a great victory. He had surprised his enemies and gained the advantage. Now he could govern in the manner he chose.

The next day the news of the Spanish naval catastrophe at Cape Passaro arrived in Paris. Admiral Byng had destroyed the Spanish fleet to such effect that not a single ship could be found to take the news to Spain. The greatest armada since that of Philip II had met the same fate. It was left to Nancré to tell Alberoni the fate of his expedition. Nancré wept, Alberoni did not.

The news of Passaro, arriving in Paris on 30 August, and coming after the *lit de justice* of the 26th, placed Philippe in his strongest position since 1715. 'At this hour,' wrote Stair, 'fortune has turned in his favour, everything bends before him and he is absolutely the master.' However, as Saint-Simon observed, 'the plotters had gone underground, but they continued to plot'.

# ✺ 20 ✺

## CONSPIRACY

Philippe reacted to the tension of the previous weeks by falling into an apoplexy. But he was soon well enough a few weeks later to attend the wedding of his natural daughter, Philippe-Angélique. She was eighteen and a beauty, like her mother Christine Desmares. She married the comte de Ségur, receiving a large dowry; her husband, who was Master of the Wardrobe to the Regent, was given the *gouvernement* of the pays de Foix and the *lieutenance* of Brie. The comtesse de Ségur became a favourite of her father and was often at the Palais-Royal; she was an entertaining story-teller, much more fun than his legitimate children.

Philippe could take advantage of his victory over *parlement* to dismantle the council system, set up with so much fanfare in 1715. Ironically, the *parlement* had wanted him to do this very thing, complaining, with reason, that the councils were inefficient and expensive. But the magistrates had wanted more influence on affairs. Now they would have less. On 18 September 1718 Philippe abolished all the councils except for Finance, Commerce, Navy and the Regency Council itself. He firmly believed that he could run the government more effectively without the councils. He was also listening to Dubois, who had written, 'Suppress the councils if you wish to be indispensable, and replace the grands seigneurs with simple Secretaries of State who, *sans crédit et sans famille*, will remain your creatures.' Philippe agreed; he appointed Dubois himself Secretary of State for Foreign Affairs. The public mocked:

> Je ne trouve pas étonnant
> Que l'on fasse un ministre
> Et même un prélat important
> D'un maquereau, d'un cuistre;
> Rien ne me surprend en cela.

231

Eh! Ne sait-on pas comme
De son cheval Caligul
Fit un consul de Rome?

(I do not find it amazing
That they make a minister
And even an important cleric
Of a cad and a blackguard;
Nothing surprising there.
Eh! Do we not know that
Caligula made a consul
Of his horse?)

Philippe also recognised another talented newcomer when he appointed Claude Le Blanc Secretary for War. Le Blanc, nephew of the maréchal de Bezons, was 'very intelligent, capable, enterprising, very charming also' wrote Saint-Simon, 'a hard worker and a man who knew the world and who had always known how to please those who had business with him'. Philippe liked him. Le Blanc had had a successful career in the provinces, rising to the important post of intendant at Ypres, in charge of the logistics of the army in 1708. There he had played a large part in the French victory at Denain. In 1714 he had suggested the idea of building a port at Mardyck near Dunkirk, when Dunkirk's fortifications had to be dismantled under the terms of the Treaty of Utrecht. Philippe employed him 'en espionnages et en choses secrètes ... he was often very late at the Palais-Royal ... in the most strict intimacy ... he understood His Highness intuitively, and he was very loyal.'

Le Blanc brought with him on his ascent another ambitious young man, Charles Foucquet, comte de Belle-Isle. Belle-Isle had powerful connections, but had grown up in disgrace as grandson of the imprisoned Foucquet. He was intensely ambitious, supremely intelligent, but cold and vain, and rather terrifying. D'Argenson said of him much later, when he was the most powerful man in France, that 'one beholds him, upright and still as a statue, proposing the devastation of empires'. Philippe never really trusted Belle-Isle; but Dubois saw his talents and made full use of them.

After organising the government to his liking, with Dubois, Le Blanc, d'Argenson and John Law as his advisers, Philippe could now permit himself to relax somewhat and take up once more with Mme de Parabère and Mme de Sabran. He was also gratified to see the publication of the French translation of *Daphnis and Chloe*, complete with thirty engravings by Audran after his own original designs.

Madame could also turn to more tranquil pursuits. 'When ladies who aren't entitled to a tabouret do needlework,' she told Luise, 'they are allowed to sit in the presence of Mme de Berry and myself, and knotting counts as needlework, so when ladies come to call they knot.' She sent Luise a knotting kit – the bag which hangs from the arm with the shuttle and silks and cottons in it. She also found time to mention that 'it is quite true that women have their veins painted blue now, to make people believe their skin is so transparent that the veins show through'.

Mme du Maine was not knotting, nor painting her veins blue; she was too busy conspiring. Awash with invisible ink, disguises and secret codes, she had no idea that her every move was being carefully observed; even Madame knew a great deal about her activities:

> Their *cabale* is very strong, it has more than ten leaders, all of them among the richest and the greatest lords of the court; and what is even worse, they have a strong following among the wealthiest lords, all of whom favour the Spanish party, and hence the duc et duchesse du Maine, and want to bring the King of Spain here. My son is too clever for them; they want someone who can be manipulated to their advantage, and for that the King of Spain is a good choice.

Unsuspecting, the Duchess rented a house in the rue Saint-Honoré, better to pursue her secretive endeavours.

Monsieur le Duc, to celebrate the triumph of the houses of Orléans and Condé, gave a week-long party at Chantilly at the end of September in honour of the duchesse de Berry. It was an extravaganza; every day there was hunting, gambling, dancing, outdoor buffets, gondolas on the canal. Thirty thousand torches illuminated the forest, fireworks extinguished the stars. The only wrong note was struck by the escape of a tiger, 'grand et fort beau', from the menagerie and its irruption into the crowd of actors and musicians. No one was injured; but the symbolism of a savage beast disrupting the unsuspecting revellers no doubt strongly appealed to Mme du Maine, who had a taste for such conceits.

The Regent still had pressing foreign policy problems to resolve. Alberoni, seemingly unabashed by the disaster off Cape Passaro, was buying arms in the Low Countries, intriguing with the King of Sweden to invade Hanover, welcoming the Pretender to Spain, plotting with the Grand Vizier against the Emperor. A Spanish fleet arrived at Cadiz that September, bringing from America the gold and silver necessary for another military adventure. Alberoni was not for giving up.

Despite Alberoni's activities, Philippe still hoped that the King of Spain could be persuaded to make peace and join the Quadruple Alliance. He strongly believed that this was the only way to contain the real danger to the peace of Europe, the Emperor. 'I have had great reason to think of the Quadruple Alliance as a way of assuring the tranquillity of Europe,' he told the French Ambassador in Madrid, 'by limiting the House of Austria to a point beyond which she cannot pass; this has always been my point of view, far from working against the interests of France and Spain.'

But the King of Spain was determined on his 'honour', which meant continuing to make war. The Queen was obsessed with regaining territory in Italy for her sons; Philip V humbly put his country at Elisabeth Farnese's disposal. Under the terms of the Quadruple Alliance, Spain had until 2 November to join or risk war. Nancré, still labouring at the court of Spain, thought he had persuaded the King of Spain to accept the offers of Gibraltar and the Italian duchies for Elisabeth Farnese's son. The King and Queen went shooting at La Granja to consider the proposal. Nancré confidently expected success. But the next day, when summoned to the presence, he was disconcerted to hear Philip V say, 'It is extremely surprising that after all France has done to maintain me on my throne, exhausting her men and money, that the duc d'Orléans is going to take measures which will ruin both kingdoms.' He refused to sign the treaty; it appeared that the Queen had persuaded him that he must fight for his 'rights' in Italy. Nancré, shocked and disappointed, noticed that the Queen 'could not suppress a smile which I would qualify as malign, if respect permitted me'. The royal confessor, Père D'Aubenton, sighed, 'The night brought evil counsels; the alcove had triumphed over the prie-Dieu.' Nancré left Madrid, all his efforts brought to naught, his health fatally undermined.

With war against Spain looming, Dubois now infuriated the British by wanting to temporise. 'My lord,' complained Stair to Stanhope, 'our little abbé's head has turned . . . for some time I have found him obstinately and passionately contrary on all the points which can facilitate the execution of our treaty.' Dubois needed time for his own plans to mature – and time to convince reluctant French generals, who had fought side by side with the Spaniards, to rally against their old allies. Philippe spoke personally to his old comrade the marquis d'Asfeld. But Asfeld was determined. 'Monseigneur, I am French, I owe you everything; but', bringing out his Golden Fleece, 'what do you wish me to do with this, which I was awarded by the King of Spain, if I go to war?' The Regent was touched by this nobility and excused Asfeld from active duty. But he prevailed upon him to go to Bordeaux and take charge of the provisioning of the army there.

Before he had to turn his attention to war, Philippe was diverted by the irrepressible Voltaire, who thrust himself into his notice that October. The Regent received a letter from his would-be protégé;

A Philippe II, duc d'Orléans, Régent de France;

Monseigneur,

Poor Voltaire . . . flattered himself that after having sent him to Purgatory, you would remember him when you were opening the gates of Paradise to all the world. He takes the liberty of asking for two favours: the first, that he might have the honour of dedicating to you the tragedy he has just composed, the second, that you condescend to hear one day some pieces of an epic poem about the one of your ancestors [Henri IV] whom you resemble most.

    I am with profound respect
      Monseigneur
        Your Royal Highness's
          Most humble and very poor
            Secretary of inanities.

Philippe was amused. But he refused the dedication of the play, *Oedipus*, while allowing it to be dedicated to his mother. *Oedipus* was, after all, concerned with the theme of incest; that was a rather delicate subject for this Prince, given the rumours about him and his eldest daughter. But he did attend the play's première at the Comédie-Française on 18 November, taking the duchesse de Berry with him, and witnessing Christine Desmares in a triumphant performance. It was an evening full of delicious ironies. When an ovation greeted the lines,

> Et je me vois enfin, par un mélange affreux,
> Inceste, et parricide, et pourtant vertueux
>
> (And I see myself at last, in awful conjunction
> Incestuous, parricide and yet virtuous)

Philippe acknowledged the ironic cheers with an expansive gesture. Indeed he went further, offering the audacious author a pension, a suggestion which received the following response: 'I should appreciate it if Your Highness would take charge of my board. Yet I beg Your Highness to provide no longer for my lodging.' *Oedipus* was a huge success, running for forty-five performances, extraordinary for the time.

The Regent, realising that war with Spain was inevitable and that money would be needed, decided to press ahead with the 'royalisation' of Law's Bank. No doubt one of his reasons was that the Bank had already, despite its proclaimed rules, provided advances to the state; if the Bank were to become royal, those advances would continue and grow. But he also firmly believed in Law's ideas on the wide distribution of paper money and credit facilities and, having battled with *parlement* all year on the subject, could now move ahead without opposition. On 4 December d'Argenson brought to the Regency Council 'a proposal for a declaration making the general bank a royal bank. The project was approved by the Council, and was made ready to be sent to *parlement* for registration.

Before that happened, Philippe struck the second great blow of 1718. He still needed a coup to rally public opinion behind the unpopular course of war with Spain. He soon had what he needed. The schemes of the duchesse du Maine, Cellamare and the others were well known to Dubois and his spies. Since July Le Blanc had had a man in the Spanish Embassy who was employed as a copyist and furnished Le Blanc with copies of all confidential documents. Dubois watched and waited. At the beginning of December he learnt that two well-connected young men, the abbé de Portocarrero and the son of Monteleone, the Spanish Ambassador in London, were about to set off for Spain. When the travellers left Paris on 4 December they were carrying secret documents from Cellamare to Alberoni in the false bottom of one of their *chaises roulantes*. None of the documents was in code. Dubois first received word of the journey from the spy in the Embassy; his information was confirmed by the celebrated brothel-keeper, la Fillon, who reported that one of her clients from the Spanish Embassy had abruptly cancelled a date with one of her girls, claiming there were important dispatches for Spain which must leave that night.

In the evening of 5 December Portocarrero's party was stopped and arrested near Poitiers. As the police began to search their luggage, the young abbé managed to send a message to Cellamare, warning him of the impending disaster. But Cellamare, who received the bad news on the 7th, did not appear ruffled. He went straight to Dubois and demanded the return of all his papers. Dubois, who had not yet received the material and therefore did not know the extent of the windfall, was soothing. But when the papers arrived they were damning: lists of French officers who would fight for the King of Spain and a note from Cellamare himself which stated that, if Philip V should ever renounce his claims to the French throne, the little King of France would be dead within three months, a clear accusation against Philippe.

On 9 December Dubois roused the Regent at six-thirty in the morning. Shortly afterwards a troop of musketeers arrived at the Spanish Embassy in the rue Neuve-des-Petits-Champs and, under the direction of Le Blanc and Dubois, searched from top to bottom. More compromising documents were found. Dubois bore away heaps of paper, leaving the house sealed and the Ambassador guarded by a company of musketeers and by M. de Liboy, who 'possessed much wit and tact and was almost always chosen for such sad duties'.

Later that day Philippe summoned the Regency Council to the Tuileries. Saint-Simon remarked on his bearing that day: 'He had, better than any man I have ever known, the gift of eloquence, without needing any preparation. He said what he wished, no more, no less; his expressions were just and precise; a natural grace accompanied them, and an air of the greatest courtesy.' He informed the Council of the arrests at Poitiers and of the conspiracy 'of which the Spanish Ambassador was the principal promoter'. Two letters from Cellamare to Alberoni were read aloud. The Regent specifically exonerated the King and Queen of Spain from any part in the conspiracy, and stressed the importance of 'neglecting nothing to illuminate an affair so capital for the repose and tranquillity of the King-dom'. He ended by saying that he did not wish to name anyone yet who might be suspected; Villars, Villeroi and Huxelles sat like stones.

At the same time, at Sceaux, where the duchesse du Maine was enter-taining guests, a friend arrived. 'Interesting news! The Spanish Embassy has been searched and papers found. What on earth can be going on?' The duchesse du Maine practically fainted.

On 13 December, as Cellamare was taken away under guard to Blois, two hundred miles south of Paris, a few arrests were made in Paris, including the marquis de Pompadour, but mostly there was silence on the part of the government, and apprehension on the part of the plotters. On 14 December, Alberoni, in ignorance of events, sent Cellamare final instructions; 'Do not leave Paris until you are forced to do so, and do not depart before lighting the fuse to your mines.' 'Mines without powder,' snorted Cellamare when shown the missive. The Spanish court would not discover the arrest of their Ambassador for another week.

In the midst of the excitement, *parlement* decided to resist the regis-tration of the edict of 4 December on the Royal Bank. It asked the King to find 'other expedients more in keeping with his royal majesty and easier to execute'. That day Mesmes went to ask the Regent to revoke it, but received the reply that Philippe 'would let him know his will in the next few days'. In a few days Mesmes would be in no condition to resist.

On 25 December the Regent summoned Monsieur le Duc, Saint-Simon, d'Antin, d'Argenson, Torcy and Dubois for a secret meeting to discuss the plans for dealing with the King of Spain and the registration of the Bank. Philippe was calm and relaxed. When the meeting ended he asked Monsieur le Duc and Saint-Simon to stay behind, and, when sure that no one else was near by, told them that the duc and duchesse du Maine were deeply implicated in Cellamare's conspiracy and were to be arrested. As it was important that Monsieur le Duc be fully and publicly associated with the arrests, Philippe asked him, in his capacity as Governor of Burgundy, to accept responsibility for the captivity of his aunt at Dijon. Monsieur le Duc agreed. The arrests could proceed.

The duc du Maine was arrested at Sceaux at ten in the morning of 29 December as he returned from Mass. 'I was expecting you,' he told the officers meekly. His wife was much less co-operative when taken from her house on the rue Saint-Honoré. She demanded her jewels, complained of the modesty of the carriage sent for her, in short used all her well-known theatrical talents to the full. As she was escorted to the carriage taking her into captivity, her lady-in-waiting asked her where she was going. 'Que sais-je?' she declaimed. 'Peut-être au Mississippi!'

A few days after the arrest of the duc and duchesse du Maine, Saint-Simon recorded an odd incident. The président de Mesmes, alarmed and upset, pressed Mlle de Chausserais to obtain a private interview for him with the Regent. This she obtained. On the appointed day she let Mesmes in through one of the secret doors which led directly to the private apartments. Mesmes found Philippe cold and serious. To his protestations of loyalty, and lack of involvement in the conspiracy, the Regent made no response, until, drawing a letter from his pocket, he said, 'Monsieur, read this: do you recognise it?' On the instant Mesmes went down on his knees, embracing not only Philippe's legs, but his feet, and begged forgiveness. The Regent took the letter, pushed him away from his feet and left the room without a word. The letter was in Mesmes' own hand, and offered *parlement*'s support to the King of Spain.

Mlle de Chausserais followed Philippe from the room, finding him in the last extremities of indignation at Mesmes' wickedness, audacity, effrontery. He swore to have Mesmes arrested. La Chausserais knew the Regent well, however, and simply smiled: 'Bon, arrest him? He well deserves it, and worse; but with that letter in hand and his confession, behold a man whose fate is in your hands. From now on you can do what you will and he will not be able to breathe.' Philippe saw the wisdom of his old friend's advice; Mesmes went unpunished and in return became a pliant and amenable leader of a subdued *parlement*. For a long time he was 'dans les transes de la mort'. (How amazing, added Saint-Simon, that two years later Mesmes dared ask for 400,000 francs for his expenses and got them.)

The Regent had emasculated the *vieille cour* by disclosing the existence of the Cellamare conspiracy. He chose not to punish any of the old maréchaux, but concentrated his wrath, and the public ridicule, on the duc and duchesse du Maine. Villeroi, Villars, Huxelles and Tallard 'put away their pride', as Saint-Simon expressed it, 'became polite, agreeable, and ate from his hand'.

Armed with this coup, Philippe need delay no longer in waging war on Spain. The King of Spain, with his usual stupidity, issued a proclamation which caused grave offence to most Frenchmen:

> This detestable project [of an invasion of Spain by France] ... is the work of an individual whose premeditated designs have been only too well known to the world for a long time ... I am convinced that all good Frenchmen will have a horror of taking up arms ... If they present themselves in this spirit at my frontiers, as I do not doubt, I protest that I will receive them with open arms as my good friends and allies.

In response to this intemperate diatribe, Philippe issued a manifesto of his own, written by the distinguished Academician Fontanelle, known for the purity of his language. The wind changed: Philip V's manifestos, Alberoni's machinations, the ridicule of the Maines, all generated support for the Regent.

# ❧ 21 ❧

# DEATH OF A PRINCESS

On 9 January 1719 France declared war on Spain, six days after the British had done so. An army of thirty-six thousand men, under the command of the maréchal de Berwick, began to mass in the Pyrenees.

Rather than dwell on the forthcoming conflict, Philippe turned to the more enjoyable business of planning the improvement and modernisation of the University of Paris. He had already made provisions for free education there; the *Mercure de France* congratulated him, stating that 'this new arrangement should contribute substantially to the progress of letters and yield a greater number of subjects useful to the state'. He proceeded to discuss with the Rector proposals for the opening of new colleges on the right bank of the Seine, near the port Saint-Honoré, the place Royale and in the Marias. The Rector explained that these locations would be 'more convenient, for the youth of the nearby quarters, than the rue Saint-Jacques, the rue de La Harpe and other streets, the remoteness of which discouraged many families from sending their young children'. Middle-class life having moved to the new quarters across the river, the Rector wanted to move there too; unfortunately there was not enough money to embark on such an ambitious project. The University remained on the Left Bank.

Philippe needed the distraction of such pleasurable conversations, for the echoes of the Cellamare conspiracy were refusing to die down. Even with the duchesse du Maine far away in Dijon, the pamphleteers were having too much fun to stop. Three venomous odes, known as the Philippiques, were the talk of Paris. The Regent was compared to the licentious Romans, his eldest daughter to Messalina. Slurs of this kind had long since ceased to disturb him, but when he read the hateful accusations that he was about to poison the King, he wept.

Royal enfant, jeune monarque . . .
quand, par le secours de l'âge,
Tes yeux s'ouvriront davantage,
On les fermera pour toujours.

(Royal child, young monarch . . .
When, as you grow older,
Your eyes are opened wider,
They will shut them for ever.)

'Ah! this is too much,' he exclaimed to Saint-Simon, 'this horror is more than I can bear.' Saint-Simon was outraged. 'I have never seen a man so moved, so intimately touched, so overwhelmed by an injustice so enormous and so well publicised. I myself was beside myself. On seeing him, I was struck by his blaze of innocence and the horror of the crime which penetrated him. Let me simply say that I had trouble in regaining my own composure, and much more in helping him regain his a little.'

The author of these libels was a man called La Grange-Chancel, a well-known playwright and former maître d'hôtel to Madame. La Grange became a great favourite of the duchesse du Maine, but was exiled to Périgord in 1717. When the Philippiques began to appear, he took flight again, taking refuge in Avignon, where the Papal writ ran.*

Sensing that he might once more become a victim of the furore over the Philippiques, Voltaire, although basking in the success of *Oedipus*, decided to absent himself from Paris. Taking the opportunity to announce his new name, 'I have been so unlucky under the name Arouet that I have taken another . . . If you do me the honour of writing address your letter to M. de Voltaire . . .', he departed for the welcoming and luxurious châteaux of his noble friends. He progressed to Vaux-le-Vicomte, now the home of the maréchal de Villars, to Bruel with the duc de La Feuillade, to La Source near Orléans, where the exiled Bolingbroke lived with Mme de Villette. Everywhere he went he entertained his hosts by reading snippets of his epic poem, the *Henriade*. One evening at Sully, having received some criticism from his audience, he threw the manuscript into the fire; it was rescued by his friend and fellow playwright, Hénault, who said that Voltaire now owed him an epic and 'a nice pair of sleeve ruffles'.

One of Voltaire's greatest admirers was Lord Stair, who was determined that his own country should recognise the young genius. In April he wrote

---

* La Grange-Chancel was eventually taken prisoner and sent to the îles Sainte-Marguerite. Escaping from there in 1721, he became a refugee in Holland, and composed a fourth Philippique, and a fifth when he heard of Philippe's death.

to London, 'I hope ye King will make my little poet ye author of Oedipus a present. He's ye best poet maybe ever was in France; He is just now writing an Epic poem Henry le grand, he has read pieces of it to mee yt are most wonderfully fine.' George I, no doubt somewhat mystified ('I hate all Boets and Bainters,' he once sniffed.), obligingly sent a gold watch. Stair was gratified: 'I thank you for the present which the King wishes to give Arouet. I believe that a gold medal of the King, with a gold repeating watch, will be a more agreeable gift than giving him 100 guineas.'

Voltaire was in such good spirits that spring that he refused to take offence at the Comédiens-italiens for putting on *Oedipe travesti*, a parody of his celebrated play. 'I willingly pardon the rascals for their trivelinades, that is their métier, everyone should follow their own, mine is to scorn them.'

As Voltaire left the capital, a twenty-one-year-old beauty, destined to play a role in events, arrived. Agnès Berthelot de Pléneuf, marquise de Prie, was a woman of infinite seductiveness, driven by a boundless ambition. She impressed even the uxorious Saint-Simon, who called her 'extraordinarily pretty and well made, with a great deal of wit, surprisingly well read, with the figure of a nymph'; for d'Argenson she was 'the most heavenly creature, truly the cream of the crop'. Agnès de Prie had distinguished connections. She had just returned to Paris from Turin, where her husband had been the Ambassador. Her father, the rich businessman Pléneuf, remained there, having fled the attentions of the Chambre de Justice. Her mother held a salon in Paris to which Le Blanc and Belle-Isle were assiduous visitors. Mme de Pléneuf was not particularly pleased to see her daughter back in Paris; mother and daughter hated each other with a passion.

On entering the beau monde, Mme de Prie succeeded in captivating Monsieur le Duc. The young man might be ugly and crass, but he was a Prince of the Blood, rich and malleable. He soon became Mme de Prie's abject slave, throwing over his mistress, Armande-Félicité Mancini, marquise de Nesle.*

Mme de Prie found Paris bursting with energy. The war with Spain had little effect on the capital, where the pleasures of building, decorating, playgoing, lovemaking and gambling were being thoroughly indulged. The Regent attempted periodically to ban certain card games but to little effect. The duc de Tresmes, Governor of Paris, held a public gambling den in a house rented for the purpose, and was rewarded with a pension of

---

* Mme de Nesle turned her attention elsewhere. For the 'beaux yeux' of the prince de Soubise, declared the handsomest man of his time, she challenged her rival, Mme de Polignac, to a duel. Neither lady was hurt in the fracas, but Madame was astonished; all this for a man who 'isn't bad; but he looks like a calf who still sucks'.

twenty thousand livres for scaling it down. On the quai Malaquais the notorious hôtel de Transylvanie attracted young noblemen and ambitious provincials. There it was that the chevalier des Grieux took Manon Lescaut. Perhaps encouraged by the spectacle of the battling marquises, Philippe also tried to ban duelling; but that too failed.

As if to punctuate the end of one era and the blossoming of another, Mme de Maintenon died on 15 April at the age of eighty-four. Her dying words were suspiciously well turned, but characteristically opaque: 'Dying, it is the least important event of my life.' 'She was a woman of great merit,' intoned the diarist Dangeau, 'who had done so much good and prevented so much evil when she was in favour, one could not speak of her highly enough.' When Saint-Simon read this passage in Dangeau's journal he was so infuriated that he noted in the margin in his own hand, 'Behold how tastelessly, dirtily and stinkingly he lies in his teeth.' Mme de Maintenon was one subject upon which Saint-Simon and Madame could agree. Madame was succinct; 'La vieille gueuse', she wrote piously, 'est crevée...' (The old whore has kicked the bucket...).

Far away in Spain, the King and Queen paraded in front of their army of thirteen thousand men, awaiting invasion by forty thousand French. On 20 April the French army advanced across the Bidassoa and attacked the new naval base of Passage, where they burnt six great ships still in the process of construction. At the end of May Berwick began the siege of Fuentarrabia. There was so little opposition that Berwick found his main problems in his own ranks rather than in those of the enemy. His cavalry commander, the prince de Conti, 'showed himself wholly unlike his distinguished father, with no trace of Bourbon blood. All the men were scandalised by him.' Haughty and impetuous, suspicious and a great drunkard, he did not impress the cold and pragmatic Berwick; but the King of Spain saw him as an opportunity. Philip V offered Conti Sicily if he deserted, and the Prince's loyalties were considered so fragile that he was hurried home. Undaunted, the King of Spain then offered the Regent Burgundy and Flanders if he accepted the sons of Philip V on the throne of France. When this offer was met with silence, the King returned to Madrid and abandoned himself to his wife and his confessor, incredulous that God seemed to have deserted him.

Conti was not the only French commander whose loyalty was considered suspect. At the end of March the troublesome duc de Richelieu was arrested, the Regent saying that he had enough evidence in his pocket to try him for treason; the evidence was four letters from Richelieu to Alberoni discussing handing over the city of Bayonne to the Spanish, in return for which Richelieu would be made Captain of the Guards in the new regime.

'If he had four heads I could cut them all off,' threatened Philippe. At the Bastille for a third time, Richelieu made himself as comfortable as possible; he was allowed a valet de chambre as well as books, games and a bass-viol. Although it seemed clear that Richelieu had dallied with the enemy, many suspected that his open affair with the Regent's daughter Charlotte was a further reason to have him removed.

For the Regent, however, all annoyances, even war itself, paled besides the excitement of Law's Bank. The Parisians were also fascinated, in particular by the new banknotes which made their appearance at the beginning of 1719 in denominations of ten thousand, one thousand, one hundred, and ten livres. For the first time they were equivalent not to a piece of metal, but to paper. It was a great simplification for business, as the public no longer needed to convert sums of money from livres to louis d'or or écus.

Law's campaign to entice the public into exchanging their gold and silver for them was gaining momentum. In April an edict was issued making it clear that banknotes would not be affected by the devaluations of the coinage. A week later another edict devalued the louis d'or from thirty-six to thirty-five livres. More and more people were persuaded to hasten to the Bank to hand over their precious metal. Law foresaw that the Bank's offices in the Marais would not be large enough for the great schemes he had in mind; on 10 May he bought the hôtel de Nevers on the rue de Richelieu and prepared to open the Bank's offices there, right in the middle of town, and very close to the Palais-Royal.

At the same time Law's Compagnie de l'Occident was gradually absorbing the other trading companies, of the East Indies, China and Africa. Large vistas were opening for a company which had only a few ships but seemingly boundless prospects. In May the Compagnie d'Occident became the Compagnie des Indes, and Law was authorised to create fifty thousand new shares at a nominal price of five hundred livres each.* The operation was a great success. Demand for shares went through the roof.

The people who bought the shares were not particularly interested in the territory of Louisiana itself, or, as it was generally known, the Mississippi. It was, they assumed, a land where gold and silver would be found in such profusion that French commerce would be transformed, as that of Spain had been in the previous century with the discovery of the New World. The real excitement of the Mississippi lay in the novelty of making profits from paper money and the appetite for speculation. There were two

---

* Holders of the former shares had preferential treatment when it came to buying new ones; for four former shares ('mères'), one acquired one new one ('fille').

Mississippis: the fabled land of wealth, repository of money and dreams, and the miserable patch of land on the Gulf of Mexico. The two never coincided. The French had over the years made efforts to sail down the Mississippi from Canada, hoping to extend their possessions in a great arc from Montreal to the Gulf of Mexico and stop the British moving inland from the eastern seaboard. But the odd combination of Jesuit missionaries and fur trappers (coureurs des bois) never inspired the government in Paris with much confidence. (Nor did the missionaries and the trappers have much time for each other; the Jesuits accused the trappers of being disruptive and of giving the Indians brandy. The trappers argued that, if they did not do so, the English would give them rum and turn them into Protestants.)

The first settlement founded by the French on the Gulf of Mexico was at Biloxi, established in 1699 by a daring explorer called Pierre Le Moyne d'Iberville. The early years were desperate. The local water supply was poor, the ground subject to flooding and the Indians unfriendly. The settlers, not farmers but soldiers of fortune, found only poor-quality pearls, extraordinarily long reeds and woolly buffalo hides. In 1702 Iberville decided to move the colony to Mobile, which remained the administrative capital until New Orleans became so in 1722. By 1710 the colony was on the verge of collapse; the population was still less than two hundred souls. There was not a single good harbour; the low coastline with long shifting sandbars was treacherous to navigate. Nothing worth exporting seemed to exist. The terrain consisted of snake-filled swamps, semi-tropical jungle and mosquitoes. There were long, hungry intervals between the arrival of supply ships from France.

Despite this unpromising start, the Secretary for the Navy, Jérôme de Pontchartrain, struggled to interest French merchants in investing in Louisiana. He resorted to subterfuge, recruiting a man called Lamothe Cadillac, the former commandant of Detroit, to extol the virtues of Louisiana to Antoine Crozat, the richest man in France. Crozat had taken the bait in 1712, and was granted a fifteen-year monopoly on trade, which was exempted from customs duties, as well as perpetual ownership of any lands, bodies of water or industries improved or created during the fifteen-year period of proprietorship. He was required to send two ships a year, ten emigrants of either sex and twenty-five tons of goods. Crozat flagrantly ignored the provision to establish farmers; the tiny colony struggled to survive; but he gambled millions in the hope of finding rich mines.

When Crozat extricated himself from Louisiana in 1717, he no doubt heaved a sigh of relief and concluded that he had done a good piece of business. The Regency Council might have been excused for thinking that good money should not follow bad into the swamps of the Mississippi delta, but Philippe was personally interested in the ways in which science could help the purposes of exploration, and still had faith in colonies as a means of strengthening the Kingdom. Despite everything he still believed in Louisiana, whose vast spaces he hoped to settle and whose mineral wealth he hoped to exploit. So the vast Louisiana territory was farmed to the Compagnie d'Occident, and the Mississippi was born. By July 1719, John Law was master of France's foreign trade. Shares in the Compagnie des Indes stood at three thousand livres.

Throughout this period the duchesse de Berry was treading the primrose path. At her father's supper parties at the Palais-Royal she laughed and drank as the men did; they called her 'Princess Joufflotte' (chubby) and the 'beautiful peacock'. But the laughter had become hysterical, the wit addled. Besotted with her lover Rions, Mme de Berry had lost all semblance of self-control; she became pregnant by him that spring, while continuing to indulge in suppers 'fort arrosés de vins et de liqueurs les plus fortes'.

One day in April Mme de Saint-Simon found her in a little room at the Luxembourg, in bed, suffering from the vapours and convulsions. It was clear that she was in labour. Languet de Gergy, the stern curé of Saint-Sulpice, came to the palace but, realising the situation, refused the Sacraments, and demanded that her friend Mme de Mouchy and Rions leave. Thinking that the Duchess was dying in mortal sin, Mme de Saint-Simon hurriedly sent for the Regent. He in turn sent for the cardinal de Noailles, hoping that he would compel the curé to give the Sacraments. However, when the Cardinal arrived he strongly approved of the actions of the curé. And he was not alone; according to Saint-Simon, 'the most fashionable bishops, the grandest ladies, even the libertines, not one of them blamed the curé nor his cardinal'. The duchesse de Berry had forfeited the respect even of the most cynical. Philippe, in desperation, called through the bedroom door, begging la Mouchy to explain to the Princess her perilous position. The duchesse de Berry, in agony, refused to send her companions away. After two fruitless hours of such farcical antics, the Cardinal left; but the curé planted himself by the door to stop the Sacraments being clandestinely administered and he stayed there for four days and nights. Then the danger passed; the duchesse de Berry gave birth to a still-born daughter.

After this unedifying spectacle, the Duchess made the gesture of opening her gardens to the public again; she vowed to wear white for six months (and had a carriage made of silver to match her outfits); she gave money to the building works at Saint-Sulpice. But her health had been fatally undermined. After Easter she left Paris for Meudon. She was now in disgrace with her father; for almost the first time she failed to bring him round with her overtures of remorse. When he ordered Rions to report to his regiment immediately, she threatened to marry her lover and make it public; the scenes with her father grew even more violent. In the end Rions was sent away to fight in the war against Spain. The Duchess, trying to make amends, and very frightened, gave her father a supper on the terrace at Meudon, but it was not a success and she caught a chill from the night air. 'The air of Meudon is very changeable,' noted Madame, 'as it is on a hill; it was still extremely cold. When one is recovering from a grave illness like Mme de Berry, one is more susceptible to the air; but the season was advanced, and she was already taking quinine, so we can hope that this fever will not last long.' But she did not improve. Wrapped in blankets, she was taken to La Muette, her house in the Bois de Boulogne. All through June and July she was ill with fevers.

While the duchesse de Berry was worn out by excess, her second sister was advancing in the religious world. Louise-Adélaïde had surprised everyone by not starting her holy life at the top, but going to Chelles as a simple nun, taking the name Sister Bathilde. Soon enough a difficulty arose. Louise-Adélaïde was after all a princess of the Blood Royal and quickly found it disagreeable to show obedience to the Abbess of Chelles, Mme de Villars. She decided that Mme de Villars must step aside.

Agnès de Villars was a pious and, more important, well-connected woman. She had been a model abbess for twelve years, was now sixty years old and wanted to stay where she was. She refused to move aside. Displeased, Sister Bathilde moved out of the Abbey to another Benedictine community at Val-de-Grâce in Paris, where she took up residence in the beautiful apartment of the late Queen Mother, Anne of Austria. There she waited for Mme de Villars to take the hint. Six months went by; finally Mme de Villars realised that she had no choice. In May she gave up and retired. Her family protested loudly.

Madame was not sympathetic to Mme de Villars: 'She is going to get an annual pension of eighteen thousand livres and she will have the next abbey which comes free. But she still complains, she and her brother, as if my son had done them the greatest injustice in the world, as if my granddaughter and she were equal. People are really too insolent here in France.' Saint-Simon was not so tolerant. 'Louise-Adélaïde could only stay in the abbey, where she had gone to obey, as its absolute ruler.'

Louise-Adélaïde returned triumphantly to Chelles on 25 May, having dined with her parents at Bagnolet, the country house her mother had recently bought near by. That evening she gave a fireworks display in the park for her sister, Mlle de Valois, still pining for her lover, the duc de Richelieu, imprisoned in the Bastille.

These festivities were soon followed by graver news. The duchesse de Berry was still at La Muette, her health fatally impaired. During the stormy night of 14 July she worsened dramatically and word was sent to the Palais-Royal. Mme de Saint-Simon was summoned and found the danger great. They bled the duchesse from the arm and then the foot and sent for her confessor. She received the Sacraments in the presence of her parents, and then, when the priest had left, congratulated herself on her courage. It was her last act of bravado.*

Saint-Simon, alerted by his wife that Philippe was alone at the deathbed, arrived to be with his friend at his hour of need. A heartbroken Philippe charged him with the details of the funeral. They walked together, Saint-Simon trying to lead Philippe away from the bedchamber but, as the evening advanced, Philippe went inside to be with his daughter for the last time. Having made his farewell, he walked out on to the balcony of the little room next door, sobbing until his friend thought he would suffocate. When he recovered his composure, he started to talk of 'the misfortunes of this world and the short duration of everything which is agreeable'. Saint-Simon, deeply moved, spoke 'the words God gave me, as gently, soothingly and tenderly as I could'. The two men talked for more than an hour before Mme de Saint-Simon quietly told them that the time had come to depart. The only way out was through the bedchamber; Philippe said one more farewell and took his leave, overwhelmed by the most bitter grief. Saint-Simon, who was at his very best that night, prevented his wife from going into the bedchamber 'où il n'y avait plus que de horreur'.

The duchesse de Berry died at midnight on 21 July. She was almost twenty-four years old. Her family was sorrowful; even Madame's heart was moved. 'I have wept a great deal over the death of my granddaughter. It is an awful spectacle to see someone one loves die so young.' As for Philippe, he was in such affliction, said his mother, it would melt a rock. 'He does not wish to weep and he tries to hide his grief, and yet at every minute the tears come to his eyes ... I am in terrible anguish, he cannot endure this, he will fall ill.' Following the immutable custom, Mme de Berry's heart was taken to Val-de-Grâce the next day, accompanied by Mme de Saint-

---

* Two days later Monsieur Garus, inventor of a famous elixir, arrived with medicine which seemed to help her, but the famous doctor Chirac insisted on giving her a purge, after which she immediately weakened. As she lay dying, Chirac made an insolent bow, wished her bon voyage and left for Paris. (Chirac did not have the bedside manner. When Mme de Prie lay dying in agony a few years later, he refused to visit her at all, remarking 'she's only an actress'.)

Simon. Her body was carried to Saint-Denis; but the funeral service did not take place until September and there was no funeral oration. She had already become an embarrassment.

Saint-Simon, who knew Mme de Berry well, summed her up thus:

> Born with superior intelligence, and, when she wished, agreeable and amiable, with a pleasing figure which became too stout, she talked with singular grace and a natural eloquence which was all her own. What could she not have done, but for the vices of her heart and soul, her violent temperament? There was something in her eyes which made you afraid. Her faults were legion; her pride was immense, she lied, she believed in nothing. She read advanced books and listened to her father too much. She got drunk and she was a glutton. She had no self-control.

She was a witty, if crude, conversationalist. She made her father roar with laughter, partly at her jokes and partly at her outrageousness. She was brave and bold. She was a child when she married, and had received no training to prepare her for becoming the grandest lady in the land. She was reminiscent of her grandmother Madame de Montespan in her eloquence, her embonpoint, her drinking, her sexuality, her fear of death. Was there worse? Some have thought her capable of poisoning the Dauphin and Dauphine, as her grandmother was alleged to have used love philtres and poisoned Mme de Fontanges. But she was only seventeen when they died. She remains a troubling shadow.

As Philippe wept for his 'beautiful peacock', the public mocked:

> Là pleures-tu comme mari,
> Comme ta fille ou ta maîtresse?
>
> (Do you weep for her as a husband,
> For your daughter or for your mistress?)

# ✖ 22 ✖

# THE MISSISSIPPI

S eeking escape from his sombre reflections, Philippe plunged into his meetings with John Law, stimulated by the dazzling prospects of the wealth and prosperity which lay ahead. He recalled Law telling him that he could 'restore the Kingdom ... re-establish order in the finances, undertake and augment the number of the population and the revenues, pay off useless and burdensome charges, augment the King's revenues while looking after the population, diminish the state's debts without injuring creditors'. It was his dearest wish.

That summer both Law's ventures, the Bank and the Company, seemed to be flourishing. The Compagnie des Indes had an almost complete monopoly of French maritime trade. And, after a slow start, it was becoming a magnet for investors. Between May and October 1719 there were five issues of shares in the company, each abundantly subscribed, even though the cost of a share with a face value of five hundred livres went up to five thousand livres by the end of the year.

In July of that year the Regent accorded Law the sole right to coin money. Law was now the director of the Bank which issued paper money and the director of the Company which had control of French foreign trade. He controlled almost all aspects of the economy, taking in gold and silver, handing out paper money, printing more paper money, which was used to buy shares in the Company. He seemed to be capable of taking the prosperity of France to new heights. In London Stanhope was so impressed that he wrote to Dubois, 'I cannot finish without rejoicing with you on the happy state of your finances. Their prompt and surprising re-establishment is the talk of Europe.' Voltaire, still leading the *vie de château*, was more sceptical about the new frenzy:

It is good to come to the country when Plutus is turning all heads in the city. Have you really all gone mad in Paris? I only hear talk of millions. They say that everyone who was comfortably off is now in misery and everyone who was poverty-stricken bathes in opulence. It this a reality? Is it a chimera? Has half the nation found the philosopher's stone in the paper mills? Is Law a god, a rogue, or a charlatan who is poisoning himself with the drug he is distributing to everyone?

Most people did not stop to ask such questions. They simply accepted the idea that money was somehow gushing forth from a mysterious spring, and they hastened to spend. Country houses, town houses, estates were bought and sold; then the furniture, mirrors, *objets de luxe* necessary to fill them, not to mention new carriages and horses, and liveries for the new servants. From the Princes of the Blood to the bourgeoisie, the urge to acquire comfort and luxury became a passion. Madame la Duchesse, older and settled with the marquis de Lassay, began to build an enormous house on the Seine, calling it the Palais-Bourbon; next door she built a smaller palace for her lover. The wits commented on how her palace seemed to lie on top of his. Her son began the marvellous stables at Chantilly, remarking that he hoped to come back in the afterlife as a horse. The hôtel de Matignon, perhaps the most beautiful of all, began to take shape in the rue de Varenne; the comte d'Evreux, son-in-law of Antoine Crozat, made his new hôtel along the rue du Faubourg-Saint-Honoré a showplace of the fine arts. The Parisian businesses of furniture-making, silversmithing, gilding, portrait-painting and manufacture of articles *de luxe* received an immediate and lasting boost.

During that hot summer, the wealthy moved out to the country. Pierre Crozat, younger brother of Antoine, took his salon of artists and musicians to his château at Montmorency; long summer evenings passed in music-making, dancing and the pleasures of the table. Watteau was sometimes there, suffusing his paintings of these *fêtes galantes* with an insistent melancholy. Philippe, acutely aware of the fragility of life and the pain of loss, attended the parties, hoping for solace, finding 'Joy, whose hand is ever at his lips Bidding adieu'. He took consolation where he could. With the economy seemingly in such a healthy state, commerce revitalised and money available, Philippe felt himself the beneficent father of a happy country.

This was the moment at which John Law's 'System' was actually born. In August the Compagnie des Indes took over the tax-raising responsibilities of the *fermes générales*, adjudged only the previous year to the Paris brothers. In return it took over the national debt, buying out the government investments and offering the investors Company shares, initially at the same rate of interest, 4 per cent. Finally, on 12 October, the Company was charged with the task of raising direct taxes. Thus all the fiscal apparatus of the Kingdom passed from the hands of the old regime of tax-farmers and the like into those of Law. To complete Law's ambitions, all that remained was to unite the Bank and the Company, which was done in February 1720. Financial speculation became a frenzy, caused partly by the fact that buyers need pay only a relatively small premium for a share, the balance in instalments. As the shares became more expensive and ever more sought after, this was an evident encouragement to speculate. By October original shares, bought for the premium of fifty livres on the price of five hundred, were trading for three thousand livres, by the end of the year for ten thousand livres.

There being no such place as a Stock Exchange, the trading took place in the narrow rue Quincampoix, to the east of Saint-Eustache, and in the adjoining rue des Ours. The tumult was such that security patrols were stepped up and the street closed at night. Large crowds continued to flock there, however, mostly eager provincials, avid to get rich, and the city was full of stories of the fabulous profits which could be made in a day. The dame Chaumont, arriving in Paris with a few notes received in payment of a former debt, amassed 'une soixantaine de millions' in a few days. She promptly bought the hôtel de Pomponne, and the château of Ivry, where she gave splendid parties. According to Barbier, 'she consumed every day a cow, two veal calves, six sheep, not to mention chickens and game, with a great deal of Champagne and Burgundy. Benefactor of the arts, she commissioned the Gobelins to make her superb tapestries of a new design.' Mme Chaumont showed more aplomb in dealing with her wealth than the nameless lackey who, newly enriched, bought himself a carriage and horses. When his carriage arrived, he forgot that it was his own, and got up behind. 'Eh, Monsieur, what are you doing?' the coachman called. 'This is your own carriage!' The owner sheepishly clambered down. There were many such stories.

Madame was bemused: 'Mlle de Chausserais used to be very poor, but she placed everything she had into the Mississippi bank that was founded by Monsieur Law ... in this way she has made a million and is now rich instead of poor. One of these days she will buy a fine domaine.'

With all the excitement in the capital, it was hard to realise that France was at war that summer, her army fighting in Spain. But that war was in reality a series of easy victories for Berwick, who exerted himself only sporadically to swat the inept Spanish forces. Philippe could concentrate fully on his new age of gold. He was delighted to be able to act as generously as he had always wanted. Pensions, favours, gifts of all kinds flew from his hands. There seemed no end to the Regent's generosity. Mme de Parabère, living in splendour at 20 place Vendôme, bought property from the comte de Toulouse for 300,000 livres, and the estate of Blanc en Berry for 1,500,000 livres, all in the space of two months. Law himself bought the palais Mazarin, on the corner of the rue des Petits-Champs and the rue Vivienne, for a million livres; he planned to install the Compagnie des Indes there, next door to the Bank, which he had just installed at the hôtel de Nevers.

Philippe increased his mother's pension and gave her two million livres in shares for her household. All the royal households received shares, as did all the officers who had served in Spain. For his son, the duc de Chartres, he bought the governorship of Dauphiné; not only did he buy it from his old enemy La Feuillade, but he paid 'this gallant gentleman, the most corrupt and despicable I have ever known', according to Saint-Simon, over a million livres, and made him Ambassador in Rome. All this for a son whom he already considered a failure, and who was more interested in sowing his wild oats than governing a province. 'He has fallen into the hands of the girls at the Opéra,' clucked Madame, 'and you can scarcely believe what they have been able to teach him.'

Chartres' half-brother, the chevalier d'Orléans, Philippe's son by Mme d'Argenton, was named Grand prieur when the dissolute Philippe de Vendôme stepped down. (Vendôme spent the rest of his life searching for a wife, but 'no one wanted an old drunk of sixty-four, rotten with the pox, whose only merit was his extreme impudence'.) The Grand prieur was the head of the Knights of Malta in France; in that position he ruled his domain of the Temple, near the Bastille, almost as a sovereign ruler. Fugitives could not be arrested there, nor warrants issued. Under Philippe de Vendôme, brother of the celebrated Duke, the Temple had been a place of joyous riot where a certain raffish world convened to drink and versify. Qualifications for the post of Grand prieur were somewhat odd, including the ability to swim, as well as proof that one had made one's 'caravanes' to Malta; the chevalier d'Orléans had met those requirements, although perhaps not that of celibacy, but, notwithstanding, the young man entered into his small kingdom unopposed.

His half-sister Louise-Adélaïde was solemnly installed as Abbess of Chelles, six weeks after the death of her sister the duchesse de Berry. The ceremony, attended by Philippe and his mother, was of an astonishing sumptuousness. Hundreds of candles illuminated the chapel, the marble walls were hung with purple velvet, the musique du Roi sang motets especially composed by Delalande, the cardinal de Noailles said Mass. Two by two, the sixty-six nuns of the convent came to make the act of sub-mission to their Abbess, who was seated on a dais covered with fleur-de-lys. A lady from the provinces, overcome by the spectacle, cried, 'Is this not Paradise?' 'Eh non, Madame,' she was told, 'there would not be so many abbesses nor so many bishops.' After the service, six hundred people sat down to dine, the new Abbess presiding over a table of fifty while Philippe ate 'in private with some ladies whom he had brought with him'. Altogether it was a strange and somewhat discomfiting occasion for the gentle Benedictines.

While one daughter entered the cloister, another was being uncer-emoniously propelled into marriage. The scandal of Mlle de Valois' affair with the duc de Richelieu moved Philippe to action. He extracted a promise from his rebellious daughter that, if he released Richelieu from the Bastille, she would go through with a marriage to Francesco Maria d'Este, the Hereditary Prince of Modena, and leave the country. He had in fact already offered the girl to his half-sister, Anne-Marie, now Queen of Sardinia, for her son; but Madame, who was fond of the Queen, made sure that she knew what a 'mauvais présent' Charlotte would be. 'I have a horror of that girl ... My stomach turns when-ever I have to look at the little fool.' Anne-Marie politely turned her down. Now her father was desperate. The Modena marriage was not a brilliant one, but 'anything will do', said Philippe, 'as long as I get rid of her'.

News of the marriage was public at the end of October; as were the Princess's reservations. 'The fiancée is in despair,' wrote Madame, 'she would have preferred Charolais, the brother of M. le Duc; but he did not wish to take the bait as all these cousins of the Blood hate each other like the Devil ...' Charlotte's despair grew when she learnt that Richelieu, released from the Bastille, had taken up with her rival, Mlle de Charolais. But by the beginning of December Madame noted that, 'Mlle de Valois is beginning to console herself a little as she has seen her beautiful gowns. Further, they have sent some fine diamonds from Modena, that's another consolation.'

Madame was happy to see that her granddaughter's departure was imminent. But she had started to worry about the excesses on daily view in Paris.

What six ladies of quality did from pure greed is really too shameless. They had waylaid Monsieur Law in the courtyard and surrounded him, but he begged them to let him go. They did not want to do it, and he finally told them, 'Ladies, I beg your pardon a thousand times, but if you do not let me go I will burst, because I need to piss so badly that I cannot hold out another minute.' The ladies answered, 'Well then, Monsieur, go ahead and piss, just so long as you will listen to us.' He did, and they stayed right with him; this is disgusting, but he himself nearly died laughing. Here you see, dear Luise, what point avarice and greed have reached in this country.

Law was now so clearly in charge of the finances of the nation that the natural step was for him to become Controller of Finances. D'Argenson was head of the Finance Council, so any such move would entail his demotion; but d'Argenson was too perceptive and had too much knowledge of the world not to realise that, if he fought Law's promotion, he would lose not only the Finance Council, but also his job as Chancellor. He therefore ceded to Law, but not before taking the opportunity to advance both his sons, the elder to be intendant of the town of Maubeuge, the younger to be lieutenant of the Paris police. The only remaining difficulty was Law's religion; he would have to convert to Catholicism in order to be appointed Controller. Dubois had just the man to accomplish a quick and easy conversion.

The abbé de Tencin, a native of Grenoble, had, according to Saint-Simon, 'a bold and enterprising spirit ... infinitely supple, discreet, gentle or harsh depending on his need ... proud or abject depending on the person and the circumstances ... an unbounded ambition'. He had two sisters in Paris, Mme de Ferriol, a hostess and social figure, and Claudine-Alexandrine, Mme de Tencin, his *alter ego* and promoter. Now in her thirties, Mme de Tencin had already made a name for herself as a wit and an adventuress. In 1717 she had given birth to a son by the chevalier des Touches and had abandoned the child on a church doorstep; he became the mathematician d'Alembert. She had briefly shared the Regent's bed; it was she he had in mind when he remarked that he 'never discussed politics with a whore between the sheets'. Having gravitated from the bed of the Regent to that of Dubois, where she presumably was able to raise political issues, among other things, she was perfectly placed to put her brother on the road to fortune by suggesting him as John Law's mentor in the Catholic faith. The abbé de Tencin took the Scotsman in hand.

Law seemed triumphant. On 30 December, at the annual meeting of the Compagnie des Indes, attended by the Regent, the duc de Chartres, M. le Duc, all the maréchaux and dukes of the Regency Council and twelve hundred shareholders, the Regent himself distributed a dividend of two hundred livres per share. But the fissures under the System were deepening. The wealth expected from the Compagnie des Indes' colonial ventures would, Law believed, produce the means to offer security for the additional paper money, but he needed time for that wealth to be acquired. He also needed a calm atmosphere in which the operation could unfold. He had neither. Things were going too fast; there were only a few hundred settlers in Louisiana, the eye of this speculative storm. Law decided on the use of coercion to increase their number; from September to December young men and women were forcibly married, sent to La Rochelle and thence to Louisiana. At the same time, at the instigation of the Regent, the port of Lorient in Brittany began to be developed as a base for Law's operations. By the end of 1719 the Compagnie des Indes had thirty large ships, more than the British East India Company. But the pace of the colonial enterprise was ominously slow.

Inflation took hold. From July 1719 the price of food and other necessities began to climb steeply, with a huge increase in December and January 1720. Wages, which had been rising, did not do so during these months. When prices began to rise, due to the over-issue of banknotes, the low interest rates, which were essential to Law's view of the System, added impetus to the inflation. But even as the crisis deepened, and the speculation in shares became more frenzied, Law achieved his dream. On 5 January 1720 he became Controller General and undisputed master of the finances of France; and at that moment some speculators began to sell their paper holdings for gold and silver, the first warning sign of the collapse of everything for which John Law had worked.

# ❧ 23 ❧

# THE ROOT OF ALL EVIL

As Law triumphed, Alberoni fell. He had continued trying to foment revolt in France, sending six ships to Brittany to help the rebels there. The ships were dispersed by contrary winds; the revolt failed and its leaders were arrested. This reverse caused the duchesse du Maine to give up all hope of victory and humble herself before the Regent. From captivity in Burgundy she begged Philippe for 'the goodness to accord me the absolution which you had the grace to promise me'. She insisted that her husband knew nothing about her activities. ('It's possible that this is true, although it's difficult to believe,' remarked Madame.) Most people who knew the duc du Maine agreed with the marquis de Lassay, who described him as 'more feeble than one can imagine, shy, timid, devout, and expressly made to be ruled; and so he was, completely, by his wife'. Mme du Maine did not scruple to name her fellow conspirators, desperate to return from Burgundy to her beloved Sceaux.

Alberoni also faced cold reality. The Spanish had fared disastrously in the war; the French were in the Pyrenees, poised for invasion. There were no more resources. Alberoni was given the *coup de grâce* by his former ally, the Duke of Parma, who was so alarmed by the advancing Imperial forces in Italy that he demanded that his step-daughter, Elisabeth Farnese, make peace. He dispatched an emissary who succeeded in convincing the Queen that all would be lost if Spain continued to fight. Alberoni must be made the official scapegoat.

On 5 December 1719 Alberoni received a note from the King; it ordered him to leave Madrid within a week. Indignant, but resigned, the Cardinal left Madrid with a large entourage of friends and servants. They were searched by soldiers and attacked by bandits, but struggled on to Italy through southern France. Along the way, he regaled his French escort with salacious stories of the King and Queen of Spain. The Queen, he said, had the 'diable au corps': 'If she finds a good general she will trouble Europe. It is easy for her to govern her husband, who, despite whispering "It is I who wish to be the master," always obeys, and who needs only a prie-Dieu and a woman's thighs.'

Philippe, delighted that the war was over, immediately congratulated the King and Queen of Spain on being delivered of a man who was 'not only the enemy of their glory, but of the peace of Europe'. Everything could be blamed on the Cardinal. Spain would be warmly received into the European peace. On 17 February 1720 Philip V signed the Quadruple Alliance. The settlement reached at Utrecht was finally confirmed, in particular the guarantee of the orders of succession to the crowns of France and Great Britain; if Louis XV died, Philippe d'Orléans would succeed to the throne of France; Don Carlos, the son of Elisabeth Farnese, would eventually inherit Parma and the Italian duchies.

The Regent had secured his position; but he was exhausted, 'almost finished as far as women were concerned, although not so for wine'. His fervent hope was that John Law would continue his magical ways and that he, Philippe, would be able to bask in the dawning age of peace and prosperity. He saw himself within reach of his most cherished goals.

But with the triumph in Spain came the first signs of the disintegration of the System. People were becoming anxious at having so much paper money; they were beginning to go to the Bank to exchange it for gold, making significant withdrawals. Attempting to staunch the flow, Law, five days after taking over both the Bank and the Company on 22 February, forbade anyone to keep gold or silver coins of more than five hundred livres on pain of confiscation or a fine. Inspectors from the Bank were given the right to enter private homes to search for the forbidden coins. These actions worked for a time, but there was much grumbling that such repressive measures were necessary; and rapidly rising prices caused additional discontent.

Law was showing signs of stress. He quarrelled bitterly with his former friend Lord Stair, who was talking of leaving his post. Their disagreement was symptomatic of the deteriorating relationship between France and Britain. The Regent believed that the British had given their word that Gibraltar would be restored to Spain; he in turn had given his word to Philip V. Now to his fury he learnt from Destouches, Dubois' man in London, that Gibraltar was not to be given back after all. Philippe received this blow on 12 February, just as he was preparing to attend the proxy marriage of his daughter Charlotte to the Prince of Modena. His bad temper only accentuated the general gloom; neither he nor his wife had bothered to invite any guests, the bride was more than reluctant, and the whole ceremony was rushed through in a most unseemly way.

When the marriage had been performed at the Tuileries, the King escorted the bride to her carriage, saying, as was the custom, 'To Modena!'; but Charlotte actually returned to the Palais-Royal and promptly fell ill with a timely case of measles. She seemed destined never to leave Paris. Madame la Grande-duchesse, the bride's ancient great-aunt, who had herself been sent to an unhappy marriage in Tuscany, but had made sure to return to Paris, said, 'Go, my child, and remember to do as I did; have a child or two, and then come back to France; that is the only proper course.' Charlotte took this advice closely to heart.

Finally, a month after her proxy marriage, following complaints from Modena, and under pressing orders from her father, in storms of tears, she set off for Italy.* 'I am giving you a greater proof of my love,' she wrote piteously to her faithless lover Richelieu, 'than I have ever given you before, for, judging from the state of my affairs at present, this will be the greatest misfortune of my life. But since nothing can increase that of being separated from you, I do not fear any unhappiness sufficiently to weigh it for a moment against the chance of giving you pleasure ...' Richelieu, back in Paris and fully engaged with other women, made no response.

Throughout February the young King Louis XV danced at the Louvre to music by Delalande. He became so bored and tired of it that he declared a lifelong aversion to all fêtes and public appearances. In his dealings with the world, the boy was resorting more and more to the only weapon he had, silence. He did everything he was asked, but mutely and with a certain sullenness. It was hard to know how to divert him; only horseriding and shooting seemed to give him any pleasure. He had started attending meetings of the Regency Council, bringing his cat, Pasca, for company. One day Pasca, no doubt as bored as her master, jumped on to the table, frightening the duc de Noailles, who had a phobia about cats. 'Let the cat stay,' remarked Saint-Simon, 'she will make the seventeenth member.' On this occasion, Louis XV, usually so morose, permitted himself a smile.

Surly as the boy was, he was charmed by Philippe. In their sessions together the Regent would choose his words with care: 'Are you not the master? I am here only to explain, propose, receive your orders and execute them.' This gentleness, so different from the posturing of the maréchal de

---

* Even for those days of leisurely journeys, that of the Princess of Modena was noteworthy; it took her three months to reach her husband. At Moulins she played at cards for seventeen hours at a stretch. She stayed nine days at Lyon, then sailed down the Rhône to Marseille, escorted by galleys under the command of her half-brother, the chevalier d'Orléans, embarking at Antibes on 1 June. She did not meet her husband until 20 June.

Villeroi, won the boy over. And Philippe was one of the few people with whom he could have a little fun.

Later in February, the duchesse du Maine arrived at Sceaux after her brief but humiliating exile. Her husband was at Clagny with their sons and, summoning up all his courage, stubbornly refused to see her. Finally, after four months of separation, the Duchess's mother arranged a meeting with her son-in-law at Vaugirard, and brought her daughter with her. In the presence of his wife, the Duke was cowed; the couple returned to Sceaux together, and the Duchess took up her accustomed way of life as if nothing had happened. The duc du Maine spent his time at prayer or amiably greeting his guests. He had become completely irrelevant.

While Law's system consumed Paris, Dubois was pursuing a delicate course. Having supported Law and his financial schemes, he was now realising that the Scotsman was becoming a threat to him in the political arena. Law, flushed with success, was promoting a pro-Spanish, anti-British party; the Regent, infuriated by the British volte-face on Gibraltar, was listening. Dubois told Destouches that 'M. Law is very changed in his views on England. He has made Le Blanc share them. They attack me for being biased and in favour of England. His Royal Highness is very irritated.'

Dubois saw his life's work undone. He strongly believed that the alliance with Great Britain was still essential for France, and he deeply resented Law's manoeuvres – all the more so, as he himself was coming to believe that Spain must be more closely associated with France, and that a move towards Spain would be wise. But this should not be at the expense of peace with Great Britain; and certainly not at the initiative of Law. The ebullient Scot was threatening all the delicate underpinnings of European diplomacy. The fuss over Gibraltar had to be defused.

Once again, Dubois summoned Stanhope to Paris. Stanhope found that Law, together with the new Spanish Ambassador, Don Patricio Laulès, and the diehard *vieille cour*, were active in proposing to the Regent a new foreign policy. 'For several weeks we have been two fingers from defeat,' he wrote back to London. 'This court believed itself assured of being able to dispose of Spain as it wished. A *cabale* which was the strongest a fortnight ago and could become so again in another has not equivocated in proposing to the duc d'Orléans to make war upon ourselves and the Emperor. M. l'abbé Dubois believed himself lost, cried for help and made me come here.'

Once again it was the stupidity of the King of Spain which ensured that France would remain firmly allied to Great Britain: he forbade his commander in Sicily, the marquis de Lede, to evacuate the island as required by the terms of the Quadruple Alliance. Irritated, Philippe referred the matter of Gibraltar to the Congress of Cambrai, a gathering of the Allies just getting under way, and closed the door, for the time being, on a closer relationship with Spain. In attempting to undermine Dubois, Law had overreached himself and also made a formidable enemy. Dubois, however, made no move against Law just yet. Law was still dazzling the Regent with his financial wizardry, and was – for the time being – too influential to topple. The abbé turned to an equally important affair, that of his own career, which he was determined would culminate in a cardinal's hat.

Cambrai, the richest archbishopric in France, had become vacant in January, on the death of cardinal de La Tremoille in Rome. Dubois archly told the Regent that he had had a beautiful dream, in which he, Dubois, was the Archbishop of Cambrai. Philippe, 'sensing where this was leading, *fit la pirouette*', and made no reply. Dubois persevered. Predictably, Philippe gave in, partly because he truly admired Dubois' handling of the relation-ship with Great Britain, but also because the idea of such a man, with such beliefs, as Archbishop of Cambrai, where the saintly Fénelon had sat, was just too amusing to contemplate. 'I don't think God will be very pleased with me,' he mused, 'as I have named the greatest knave, the greatest atheist, the greatest rogue and the worst priest in the world.' When the usually imperturbable Nocé was moved to make known his surprise, 'Comment, Monseigneur, Dubois Archbishop? Only the other day you said he was a worthless dog,' Philippe had his answer ready. 'Ah, yes; and that is why I have named him, so that he will have to take his first communion.'

Dubois hurtled through all the stages of priesthood in eight days, 'Just like Saint Ambrose!' he said, and, immediately starting work on a solution for the most intractable problem in the Church, the acceptance of the Bull *Unigenitus*, Dubois did work a miracle; he set himself to impose a solution to this intractable problem, now at an impasse. The Pope required *par-lement* to register the Bull: *parlement*, opposed to certain parts of the Bull, were determined to uphold the rights of the French Catholic church against the Pope. When, in March, ninety-five prelates agreed to adopt a compromise, known as the Corps de Doctrine which accepted the Pope's position with certain qualifications, there was at least a basis for nego-tiation.

But *Unigenitus*, Gibraltar, Cambrai, all paled in the public mind beside the prospect of so much easy money being made in speculation. With money so available to the well connected, the taste for luxury was every-where indulged. Even Philippe, who was among the least extravagant of his family, embarked on an ambitious redecoration of the state rooms at the Palais-Royal. Everything was to be in the latest taste. Oppenord used no marble; wood panelling was adopted throughout, carved with exuberant Rococo curves in sparkling white and gold.

The most famous room of all, the Lanternon, was also finished that spring. This grand salon was projected on consoles over the rue de Richelieu and rose through two floors. At the higher level was a balcony where musicians could sit; around the walls were statues in niches, alternating with trophies. The gilded sculptures, the panelling and crimson silk hangings, the rare marbles and huge mirrors gave an effect of overwhelming luxury. All the stools and benches were covered in gold-embroidered Gobelins tapestries, a twelve-branched chandelier of rock crystal illuminated the green Campagna marble tables, encrusted with violet Brescia. There were no fewer than twenty-seven paintings hung here, including works by Veronese, Titian and Rubens.

Mme de Parabère was also decorating. She bought from John Law 22 place Vendôme, at the north-east corner of the square, letting number 20, where she had been living since 1718, to her good friend Charles de Nocé. Boffrand was soon working on the decoration of her new house; one can still see, although installed elsewhere, her beautiful panelling, sculpted with small baskets of fruit on delicate stands, twined with exquisite tendrils. Her salon boasted all that was elegant in Paris, mirrors, richly gilded commodes, tapestries, silk and damask armchairs, and from candelabra, chandeliers and wall-sconces hundreds of candles glowed and were reflected in the mirrors, producing dazzling effects.

Mme de Parabère entertained lavishly, inviting all the prettiest girls in Paris, hoping perhaps to help stimulate her lover's jaded appetite, and also distract him from her own increasingly frequent infidelities. She gave a particularly splendid party after the performance of Philippe's opera *La Suite d'Armide*, which made its debut at the Opéra that March.

In Paris, there was a feeling of giddiness, of events spiralling out of control. The city was crowded with tourists and provincials, most betting on getting rich as quickly as possible. Madame, paying her calls, was not pleased with the resulting traffic jams: 'At the moment there are so many coaches and such crowds in Paris that when I came back from a visit to Mme la Duchesse it took me three-quarters of an hour to get from the Pont Neuf to the Palais-Royal because of the traffic.'

An engagement announced that spring epitomised the mood. The thirty-three-year-old marquis d'Oise, son of the duc de Brancas, signed a marriage contract with Mlle Marie-Charlotte André, not yet three, daughter of the financier André, who had made millions in the Mississippi. The actual marriage would be celebrated when the girl was twelve; in the meantime André agreed to pay a deposit of one hundred thousand écus to the Brancas family, with the promise of twenty thousand livres per year until the marriage, then millions on the consummation. The engagement was the talk of the town: 'None of the little girls want dolls any more and ask for a marquis d'Oise to play with.'*

Saint-Simon, years later, still felt a frisson on recollecting the mood in Paris at that time: 'Who could recount the effects, the transmutations of paper, the incredible bargaining, the several fortunes in their immensity, and still more their unbelievable rapidity, the quick fall of most of the enriched through their extravagance and dementia . . .' In fact the whole delicate mechanism of Law's System was about to be fatally undermined. The contemptible prince de Conti now 'held a knife to the throat of John Law'; he decided simply to steal what he could. On 2 March he brought three covered wagons into the courtyard of the Bank, presented fourteen million shares at the counter, demanded their reimbursement in gold, and disappeared with his loot. The next day Monsieur le Duc brought a mountain of claims and plundered twenty-five millions. Philippe was outraged. 'It appears, Monsieur, that you take pleasure in destroying in a moment that which we have had so much trouble in establishing . . . is it not exhausting the Bank to draw twenty-five millions, as you have done these last four days, you and M. le prince de Conti, who had drawn fourteen millions? What are you each going to do with such a great amount of money?'

By his action, and that of Monsieur le Duc, Conti fully exposed Law's vulnerability. There was simply not enough gold and silver to cover further large withdrawals such as these. It was rumoured that the Pâris brothers and Samuel Bernard, jealous of their rival's success, had suggested the idea to the princes; but neither the prince de Conti nor Monsieur le Duc needed any prompting to expose their greed. Madame hung her head over this new disgrace for the royal family.

Already alarmed by these withdrawals, and desperate to combat the fall in share prices, Law opened an office at the Bank for the buying and selling of shares in unlimited amounts, at the fixed rate of nine thousand livres. He believed that this automatic convertibility simply proclaimed that coin and shares were equivalent, and therefore that people would buy and sell at the same rate. But it was a disastrously wrongheaded move. Predictably, there were many more sales of shares than purchases, the bank was con-

---

* The marriage never took place, the contractual points being argued in law courts for years; Marie-Charlotte André never married.

demned to print more paper money to satisfy the demands, and inflation roared ahead.

At the same time Law felt compelled to reduce the interest on the Company's shares from 4 per cent to 2. Those who had invested in government stock at 4 per cent, and had had their stock replaced with company shares, following the latter's takeover of the national debt, now saw their interest summarily reduced. *Parlement*, the voice of the rentiers, was outraged at the reduction of interest rates, and on 18 April presented remonstrances noting that, as the clergy, the magistrates and the nobility were excluded from commerce, they should be entitled to the higher rate. But on the 22nd the Regent ordered the immediate registration of the edict; he was uncharacteristically overwrought, telling the deputation of magistrates, 'these are not remonstrances, this is sedition'.

In truth, civil disorder was increasing that summer, not only in Paris, where murders and robberies were rampant, but in Amiens, Lille, Montpellier and elsewhere. The most celebrated crimes occurred in the capital. Madame was horrified by the outbreak of murder and lawlessness she saw around her. 'I believe that the Devil is altogether out of hand this year with all these assassinations; lately not a night passes but that one finds people murdered for the sake of banknotes.' The age of gold was turning into an age of blood.

The most celebrated crimes occurred in the capital. On 22 March the young comte de Horn, son of a princely family in the Low Countries, murdered a broker in the tavern of the Épée-de-Bois, off the rue Saint-Martin. Horn was arrested on the spot and sentenced to be broken on the wheel. His noble relations begged first for mercy, and then, when the Regent stood firm, for a less ignominious punishment, such as beheading. Philippe majestically quoted Corneille: 'La crime fait la honte, et non pas l'échafoud'. (It is the crime which is the shame, not the scaffold.) Horn was duly taken to his execution on 26 March and died after an hour on the wheel.

Madame supported her son absolutely on the matter of the comte de Horn. 'Today in the carriage my son told me something that has touched me so much that it brought tears to my eyes. He said, "The people are saying something that quite touches my heart; I am very happy about it." When I asked what they had said he replied that when the comte de Horn was broken on the wheel, they said, "Whenever someone does something against the Regent personally, he forgives everything and does not punish him; but when something is done against us, he takes it very seriously and does it justice, as you can see by this comte de Horn."'

Throughout this time unfortunates were being picked up and sent to

Louisiana. By an edict of 10 March able-bodied vagabonds were ordered to be deported to the colonies. At the end of April 'they have begun to pick up in the streets all the beggars, men and women ...' Freelance vigilantes roamed the streets, arresting honest workmen and the sons of the bourgeoisie, and making them buy their freedom. There were riots on the pont Notre-Dame, in the rue Saint-Antoine and the rue du Roi-de-Sicile. This could have been a useful measure, said Saint-Simon, and have relieved the city of a useless and often dangerous burden, but it was carried out with such inhumanity that people were revolted. Indeed, people were very upset at the treatment of the pressed, who were not fed en route to the coast and were often left in barns and ditches to die. Fortunately, the experiment was short-lived; an edict of 3 May ordered that 'only vagabonds with criminal records would be sent, no longer to Louisiana, but to other colonies'. But the unsavoury episode, and the resulting exaggerations and embellishments, have lived on, in the novel *Manon Lescaut*. Manon became and remains an enduring symbol of the period.

Manon perished in the 'burning sands of Biloxi'; many other real-life settlers perished in similarly desperate circumstances. The real Louisiana, not the mythical Mississippi, comprised a tiny group of souls trying to survive in wild, unhealthy conditions. Supplies were almost non-existent, sedition was rife, poverty endemic. The hopes of gold and precious stones being mined had proved illusory. By December 1719 those investors who knew anything at all about the colony were withdrawing. And yet, despite floods, lack of drinking water and fever, the settlement of New Orleans was becoming established. In 1719 the first shipment of four hundred and fifty Negroes had been brought in. More were on the way. But it was no Eldorado.

In this febrile atmosphere, a financial crisis erupted. The pegging of the price of the shares at nine thousand livres had not worked. Shareholders were dumping their shares for cash, and few were buying. It was a haemorrhage. Law decided to meet the crisis with a policy of massive deflation. On 21 May an edict was published slashing the value of shares and notes in a staggered 50 per cent devaluation. Shares would pass from nine thousand livres to five thousand in December; notes of ten thousand livres would be reduced to five thousand, one thousand to five hundred, and so on, with stages of devaluation on the first day of each month. There was shock and consternation; 'every rich man thought himself ruined without resource', noted Saint-Simon, 'and every poor man saw himself a beggar'. But it was the Pentecost holiday and *parlement* was not in session. The streets remained calm.

On Monday, 27 May the magistrates returned to Paris, and wasted no time in remonstrating against the devaluation. But Philippe was ahead of them; he had already convinced himself that the edict of 21 May was a mistake, and that it was better to retreat when there was still time, even if one had to go back on one's word. At midday he sent word to the magistrates that the edict was being revoked, that shares and notes would revert to their former levels, and that he wished to re-establish the interest rate at 2.5 per cent. In order to calm things down further, it was announced that it would again be legal to keep gold and silver, and that all searches would be stopped. The effect was not exactly the one desired; Barbier's comment was acid: 'There is an edict permitting everyone to have as much money as they wish. This comes when no one has any.'

The issuing and revoking of the edict of 21 May had undermined confidence; the work of two years was destroyed. And yet Law did not seem defeated. He appeared at the Palais-Royal with more ideas for retrieving the situation; but Philippe was ill at ease with him, would not meet his eye. That night Le Blanc went to Law's house and told him he was dismissed as Controller. An officer of the Swiss Guard and sixteen of his men arrived to protect him and his family. At the same time the Bank was closed and three commissioners sent there to verify the accounts.

With the Bank ceasing to buy back shares at the fixed price of nine thousand livres, the speculators, already driven from the rue Quincampoix to the place des Victoires, from there to the palais Mazarin, set themselves up in the place Vendôme. There they carried on a raucous business in both shares and notes. The whole scene was satirised as an army commanded by Monsieur le Duc, with Law as second-in-command, and Mmes de Prie, de Sabran and Parabère as camp followers.

On 30 May the commissioners started work at the Bank. That same day Law was let in through a back door of the Palais-Royal. The next day he met Monsieur le Duc for a long time. Then, abruptly, the work of the commissioners at the Bank was suspended. Whatever had transpired between Philippe, Monsieur le Duc and Law, the result was the ending of the enquiry into the Bank, and the return to favour of Law. The commissioners, it seems, were about to unearth some details which would embarrass the Regent; the evidence suggests that Philippe had authorised the printing of notes beyond what was permitted with back-dated decrees of the Council. Rather than have these details exposed, Philippe decided to curtail the investigation. Monsieur le Duc, who would also have been implicated in these shady dealings, was clearly of the same opinion. Both men were persuaded of the wisdom of sitting tight and waiting for the storm to blow over.

As for John Law, it is possible that his dismissal as Controller was intended by Philippe as a temporary gesture designed to appease *parlement*, and that his return was always anticipated. The investigation into the Bank reinforced the mutual dependence of Philippe and Law; the Regent determined that Law should return to the stage. On 2 June the Swiss Guard were removed from Law's house and he himself reappeared at the Council, to the astonishment of the participants. He was not named to his former job of Controller, but given the titles of 'conseiller d'epée et intendant général du commerce'. Many who had thought him finished were confounded. D'Argenson, in particular, who had wanted to send the Scotsman to the Bastille, was taken completely by surprise. Now he was the one to fear retribution, for Law claimed to believe that it had been d'Argenson himself, with his friends the Pâris brothers, who had orchestrated the disastrous edict of 21 May.

Four days after his return, Law, with a great show of secrecy, went out to Fresnes to see the former Chancellor, Daguesseau, who had been languishing there since his removal from office two years before. Law talked of what needed to be done to restore the System, and asked Daguesseau to return to help him with *parlement*. Daguesseau, who was dying of boredom, accepted with alacrity.

Meanwhile d'Argenson, whose job they were discussing, was puzzled and suspicious. He knew of Law's journey to Fresnes and decided to confront the Regent with his knowledge. Philippe feigned astonishment. D'Argenson offered to follow Law, and make sure that he was not fleeing the country. Philippe was bland: 'Do not trouble; I take all that on myself.' D'Argenson saw the light; when Dubois arrived the next day to remove the seals, he was ready and resigned to his fate. He went in person to the Palais-Royal, handing the seals to Philippe in the kitchen courtyard as the Regent left for Saint-Cloud. Then he retired to his dear priory in the faubourg Saint-Antoine, perhaps a little relieved to be out of the fray; he was no longer young, had made his fortune and had established his sons. The wits were unkind to him: 'Do you believe that you are seeking the rat run back into his Dutch cheese?' The public were blasé. Placards soon appeared: 'Reward. Twenty million livres. Lost a large black dog with a red collar, in the faubourg Saint-Antoine. Anyone who finds him return to Madame l'abbesse de Trainel.' His younger son lost his job of lieutenant de police, but remained philosophical: 'I don't know why they gave me this job, and I don't know why they took it away.'

Philippe might have thought that banishing d'Argenson, whom *parlement* hated, and replacing him with their ally, Daguesseau, would ensure the magistrates' support. Unfortunately for Philippe, there was little enthusiasm for Daguesseau either.

In the midst of all this turmoil, Dubois had taken a back seat. He was no doubt pleased enough that Law was having problems with the finances, but he did not wish to appear too hostile. His instincts were to keep away from the battle; and he had a perfect reason to do so. He was about to be consecrated Archbishop of Cambrai, and was having some difficulty learning his lines. He was also aware that many of Philippe's friends, including Saint-Simon, were advising the Regent not to attend the ceremony. On 8 June, the day before the consecration, and the day after Dubois had taken the seals from d'Argenson, Saint-Simon thought he had persuaded Philippe not to go. That night at the Palais-Royal the following conversation took place between Philippe and Mme de Parabère as they lay in bed.

Mme de Parabère coyly remarked that Philippe ought not to go to the Sacre, as Saint-Simon advised, but that she knew that he would go. 'But this is wonderful; you say that M. de Saint-Simon is right, so why therefore shall I go?' 'Because I wish you to.' 'Why would you wish me to go? What folly is this?' 'Why? Because.' 'Ho! Because; because, that means nothing; tell me why, if you can.' 'Do you really want to know? You are aware that the abbé Dubois and I had a row four days ago and that the matter is not finished yet. He's a devil who puts his nose into everything; he will know that we have slept here tonight together. If you do not go tomorrow to his Sacre he will certainly believe that it was I who prevented you; nothing could then get that out of his head; he will never forgive me; he will make trouble for me and blacken my name with you, and in the end will break up apart. And so, as I do not wish us to part, I wish that you go to the Sacre, even though M. de Saint-Simon is right.' (Mme de Parabère related this whole story word for word to her *greluchon* – a lover who was kept secret because other men were paying for her favours). The 'greluchon', possibly Charles de Nocé, related the conversation to Biron, thence it reached Saint-Simon.

The Regent was duly present at the magnificent ceremony at Val-de-Grâce the next day, watching his 'petit faquin' (little scoundrel) consecrated by the cardinal de Rohan. After the ceremony Philippe went off to join Mme de Parabère at Asnières, while a splendid dinner for sixty was given at the Palais-Royal. He clearly felt a certain reticence before public opinion, which was having a field day with the new Archbishop. In Paris the Sacre was known as the massacre.

Dubois himself had no hesitation about taking advantage of his new position. Four days after his consecration, he informed the Spanish Ambassador, Laules, that the Regent desired an entente with Spain. Laules was surprised; this was a definite change in the wind. Dubois, now in pursuit of a cardinal's hat, was eager to make an arrangement with Spain. The Regent was already inclined to make an approach to his old enemies in Madrid.

With d'Argenson gone, Law demanded next the exile of the Pâris brothers. These four brothers had been supported by d'Argenson and given the privilege of directing the tax forms. With d'Argenson's fall, Law wished them dismissed, for he knew them to be hostile to his System. Philippe was reluctant: the brothers were energetic and capable. Sons of an innkeeper from Grenoble, they had made their fortunes supplying the armies, and had arrived at the pinnacle of French financial circles. When Monsieur le Duc joined Law in pressing for their exile, Philippe wearily conceded. 'Monsieur, what you ask is unjust. These men have always served me well and, far from deserving exile, are worthy of recompense. You force me to do violence to my feelings in order to oblige you.' At the end of June the Pâris brothers were exiled to their native Dauphiné.

Law might still have the Regent's ear, but his System was mortally wounded. He attempted to reduce drastically the circulation of paper money, and cut the number of shares. But it was to no avail. The Bank was forced to shut due to lack of gold and silver. 'No one in France has a sou,' wrote Madame; 'but with your permission and in good Palatine, we have toilet-paper in plenty.'

To calm her nerves, Madame turned to the theatre. She went to see her favourite actor, the aged Baron, play opposite Christine Desmares and took Desmares' daughter, the comtesse de Ségur, with her. 'Desmares has a daughter by my son. He has not legitimised her but he is very fond of her. He married her off to a man of quality, Ségur, who used to be a page to the late King. When this lady is in our box the Desmares can't stop gazing at her, and one often sees tears of emotion in her eyes.'

Philippe had more serious concerns. When a deputation from *parlement* complained to him about the lack of currency, he promised he would see to it, but when asked when that might be, snapped, 'Ah, when, when, when, I do not know; when I can!' The irritability was brought on by his awareness that the revocation of the edict of 21 May, the return of Daguesseau, all the other measures he had taken, were failing to restore calm or confidence. Daguesseau hurried between the Palais-Royal and the Ile de la Cité trying to keep a dialogue going with *parlement*. But by this stage *parlement* wanted only one thing, the departure of John Law.

The Bank had closed for five days at the end of May, then reopened. Because of the throng of people trying to exchange their notes for coins, it was forced to operate limited hours and exchange only notes of small denominations. There was so much commotion that it closed again for four days in early June. And so, when the Bank announced on 8 July that it would start to pay in cash for a ten-livre note, huge crowds gathered in the rue Vivienne, waiting for the doors to open. For a week there were daily disturbances in the crowd.

During the night of 16 July several thousand people began to gather as usual. The gates were opened at five in the morning; on that day the crush was such that twelve or so people were trampled underfoot and suffocated. An angry procession swept into the streets, carrying several of the bodies towards the Palais-Royal. There they demanded to see the Regent and massed in the square in front of the palace. They were addressed by Le Blanc and La Vrillière, and finally after some tense hours the crowd began to disperse. But then a carriage was observed making its way through the throng; as it entered the Palais-Royal, the people recognised that it was Law himself and hurled themselves upon it. One woman clung to the bridle of one of his horses, screaming, 'Bastard, if there were only four other women like me, you would be torn to pieces.' Law managed to get into the courtyard, and, having gained the sanctuary, did not leave it for a week. His coachman, trying to return home to the rue Neuve-des-Petits-Champs, had his coach overturned in the street and its windows broken.

Philippe witnessed the disturbance from his window. Saint-Simon, who was with him that day, described him as 'fort tranquille' (although Barbier, who was not, claimed that he was 'as white as his cravat'). In any event he acted decisively, summoning the troops stationed around Paris into the city, and sending gold out to Gonesse, where Paris' bread came from, to ensure that the bakers would not have the opportunity to refuse notes, and would deliver the next day's supply. Finally he announced that the Bank would not convert any more notes 'jusqu'à nouvel ordre' (in fact it never did so again), and crowds were forbidden from assembling in public places.

Madame had come from Saint-Cloud that morning to the Carmelites in the rue de Grenelle and was having a peaceful time with the old duchesse du Lude when she was told of the riots in the streets. She went to the King as usual, however, and claimed that 'I heard the people grumble, but only about Law. I didn't hear a word against my son.'

A semblance of calm returned; but it had been a narrow escape. The next day, 18 July, the Regent decided to punish *parlement*, which he held responsible for fomenting disorder by its refusal to co-operate, exiling them to Blois. He was determined that any joining of forces between the magistrates and the people must be prevented and, to ensure that the Council would approve his drastic action, hinted at shadowy plots to declare the King's majority and usurp his government. The Council agreed to the exile without demur; though when everyone else had left, Philippe allowed Daguesseau to persuade him that the magistrates should not be exiled as far away as Blois, but Pontoise, much closer to Paris.

The next day was quiet. Troops were in evidence all over the city, but bread arrived and there were no disturbances. The orders for exile were delivered to the magistrates during the night of 20 July and 'tout se passa poliment de part et d'autre'. *Parlement* was given four days to make its arrangements, and Philippe thoughtfully sent over two hundred thousand livres to cover the expenses of the move. The population remained at best indifferent, at worst hostile, to *parlement*'s fate. But it was another matter as far as the Regent was concerned.

'Save the King, kill the Tyrant . . .' – the pamphlets were everywhere. It was impossible for Philippe to remain unaffected by the hatred; at the end of July he fainted at a meeting of the Council. But that was the only sign of weakness; otherwise he kept his nerve.

Paris was seething. The middle class had no money, prices were high, edict after edict failed to clarify or alleviate matters. Madame spoke for many that summer: 'I am as tired of all this bank business be it the Mississippi or the South Sea as if I had been stuffed with it by the spoonful. I do not understand any of this, and I certainly do not like to see little scraps of paper instead of money and gold.' *Parlement*, in Pontoise, assumed the role of martyr, while indulging in an orgy of reciprocal entertaining.

Away from the madness, Voltaire congratulated himself and his host, the duc de Sully, on their wisdom in staying out of the capital:

> Que dans votre charmant séjour,
> Je me fais un plaisir extrême
> De parler sur la fin du jour
> De vers, de musique, d'amour,
> Et pas un seul mot du Système!

> (In this charming place of yours
> I find enormous pleasure
> In talking to the end of day
> Of verse, of music and of love,
> With no word of the System!)

Those who could afford to do so diverted themselves at the Comèdie-Italienne, where a play by a new author, *Arlequin poli par l'amour* by Marivaux, was a hit, running for twelve performances. Philippe, who loved his Harlequins and Colombines, would certainly have attended; but one of his favourite projects, building a new theatre for the Italian troupe, had had to be abandoned in the financial squalls.

Outside the theatre, there was a frightening anger in the air. 'The rumours that are spread around Paris are a thousand times worse even than what can be read in the newspapers,' reported Madame. 'This very morning I received an unsigned letter saying that next month I am to be burnt with all my household here at Saint-Cloud and my son in Paris, so that nothing will be left of him. These are cheery and clever billets-doux as you can see, dear Luise. I am not afraid for myself, but very much for my son, for these people are just too vicious and hateful . . .' On 1 September Barbier went out to the Etoile with all the fashionable men and women of the city, to see the return of the fair from Bezons; 'I went to walk there; when Law's daughter arrived in a carriage with six horses and seven windows, she was injured when the carriage was stoned.' And to add to the alarm, bubonic plague was just beginning its onslaught on Marseille, which would leave hundreds of thousands of dead in its path. 'One dies here without the time to recognise oneself,' wrote an Oratorian priest from the devastated city. 'I go to do battle with Death, for, in all likelihood, I shall not return.' The epidemic would last for almost three years; the Parisians found it one more cause for satire:

> Que la peste soit en Provence,
> Ce n'est pas notre plus grand mal,
> Ce serait un bien pour la France,
> Qu'elle fut au Palais-Royal.

> (That the plague is in Provence,
> Is not our greatest problem,
> What a blessing for our France,
> If t'was at the Palais-Royal.)

John Law was still determined to save his System. But his incessant activity was making a bad situation worse. Abruptly, he decided that banknotes of ten thousand and one thousand livres would be withdrawn from circulation almost immediately, with those of smaller denominations following in six months' time. Then the value of all current accounts in the Bank was reduced by three-quarters with immediate effect. In October Law announced that banknotes could not be used in any transaction; Voltaire remarked that paper money was being reduced to its intrinsic value. These edicts caused confusion and fury. Bankers and merchants complained. Holders of current accounts presented demands for reimbursement en masse. Suddenly, as Mathieu Marais remarked, it was the end of 'the system of paper money which has enriched a thousand beggars and impoverished a hundred thousand honest men'.

Ironically, as the Bank collapsed, the affairs of the Company were flourishing. Several dozen ships were active in colonial commerce. The Mississippi was also attracting more explorers and adventurers, particularly brave Jesuit priests, who were as much agents of the crown as of Rome. Father Laval left Toulon that summer to make mathematical observations. 'This country will be good when it is cultivated,' he reported on his arrival. 'There is not, I think, as yet either sugar or indigo or tobacco or vines or mulberry trees. But the colony is just begun.' Father Charlevoix, on the Regent's orders, sailed down the Mississippi from Canada and saw Law's abandoned concession and the spiritual distress of the colonists in 1721. Philippe was much interested in a route to the western ocean, and encouraged researches in geography. The Council of the Marine sent instruments for hydrography to Dauphine Island. Even when the Mississippi was an abandoned dream, these scientific enterprises continued.

Law's attempts to stay afloat on the rough waters of Paris were causing the Regent a great deal of anxiety. He had invested so much in this man and his System that it was acutely painful to contemplate its failure. But Philippe, above all else, was a pragmatist and a realist. If Law's System was leading to civil strife and endangering the stability of the government, then Law would have to be sacrificed. 'My son was much beloved,' complained Madame, 'but since the confounded Law has come here he is becoming more and more hated.' Meanwhile Law continued with his unpopular policies. There were new and sinister developments; it was announced that everyone who wished to leave the country needed a special passport. The names of those requesting such a passport would be sent to the directors of the Company. Law seemed to think that proscriptions, searches, fines and manhunts would succeed where his theories had failed. Philippe grew extremely uneasy. He himself was certainly capable of authoritarian behaviour, but he had no taste for mass repression.

Dubois observed Law's struggles with a cold eye. He decided that the moment was approaching when he himself must intervene to prevent the Scotsman bringing down the Regent, and with him Dubois' dreams of a cardinal's hat. He saw the opportunity to make use of his superb negotiating talents and reconcile the Regent with *parlement*. Of course, any such reconciliation would entail the fall of John Law, which was the magistrate's dearest wish. Dubois perceived that if he could offer *parlement* the head of Law, he would be in a position to demand a *quid pro quo*. And that would be *parlement*'s agreement to register the unpopular Bull

*Unigenitus.* Once the Bull was registered, a grateful Pope would have every reason to make his servant Dubois a cardinal.

Dubois' energy was formidable when he had something at heart. He threw himself into the complicated negotiations with all his wonted gusto. When the British Ambassador, Robert Sutton, who had replaced Lord Stair, wrote that 'The Archbishop of Cambrai neglects totally every other affair which does not involve his hat for which he is dying of desire,' he was not quite correct. The truth was that for Dubois everything came together with the fall of Law, and perhaps especially the salvation of his master the Regent.

While Dubois wheeled and dealt, Philippe watched intently. He saw that Law was exhausted, his head spinning, his ideas ever more extravagant. And he saw that the Treasury was empty and bills falling due. He made his decision. He set Dubois to work even harder to strike the deal; *parlement* would register *Unigenitus* in return for the dismissal of Law.

For diversion from the drama, Philippe turned to a pretty new face. Mme de Parabère was too strident, too interested; she was becoming Philippe's worst nightmare, a woman who talked about politics. And she was distressingly unfaithful. On 1 December the duchesse de Falaris appeared on Philippe's arm at a public ball at the Palais-Royal. Marie-Thérèse Blonel d'Haraucourt was twenty-three, an entertaining young woman who, according to Marais, 'indulges in three or four lovers at a time, does not lack beauty, nor a certain seductive allure'. Abandoned by her disreputable husband, who had left her to fend for herself when he escaped to Spain for non-payment of debts and 'friponnerie', she had spent some time in a convent before being recognised by the duchesse d'Olonne as a distant relative, and introduced into society. She had impressed the wily Mme de Sabran, who had seen a chance to make use of the frequent infidelities of her rival, Mme de Parabère, and who had presented her to Philippe. No doubt due to her varied love life and her vanished husband, she was said to be 'spoilt'; but Philippe was insouciant: 'I do not worry; if she gives me the peas, I shall give her the beans.' He found Mme de Falaris diverting, but he was not in love with her. When she charmingly told him that she would be happy simply to keep him company, he accepted. They became close friends.

Mme de Falaris' appearance heralded a quickening of the pace of events. On 3 December Philippe went in person to the Bank for a crisis meeting; the ships of the Company had not arrived, there was not enough money in the Treasury to pay the monies due, there were no coins, banknotes had no currency. It seemed that the Treasury was insolvent. This was the end of the adventure.

The next day *parlement* registered the declaration on *Unigenitus* at Pontoise. 'The Bull is accepted with explanations which explain nothing,' scoffed Marais, 'and the registration is made as if it was not being made.' Marais was unaware of the chain of events which the registration would set in motion. He preferred to speculate upon the Regent's mistresses; one might easily believe that Philippe's behaviour was designed specifically to divert attention from the bigger drama unfolding around Law. In the days between the registration of the Bull and the fall of John Law, Philippe appeared to have nothing on his mind but women. On 5 December 'the good fortune of the duchesse de Falaris has passed like a shadow. Mme de Parabère's star shone brighter than hers. The Regent supped with Mme de Parabère tonight, telling la Falaris and Mme de Sabran, who came together to sup with him, that he was ill.' On the 6th, the duchesse de Falaris, 'whom one thought drowned, has reappeared in the water'.

Then on 9 December Law resigned. There are no witnesses to the conversation between him and Philippe. But Law seems to have been given the impression that he need not flee, he was not to be exiled, perhaps he even understood that he might be needed again, as he had been in June. He remained in Paris for five days, at his house near the Palais-Royal, watching events unfold.

Five days later, on 16 December *parlement* returned to Paris. Mesmes was congratulated by the public on his 'courageous conduct and mag-nificent table'. Mesmes was complacent. Although they had bowed to the Regent over the Bull, the magistrates had unquestionably gained more than they had lost. Their position at the centre of law-making was reinforced. For the first time since August 1718, Philippe would have to deal with them on almost every issue.

On that same day Law and his family finally left Paris, going first to his château at Guermande in Brie seven leagues away. He probably thought he could sit out the hostility; he would wait in the wings for his luck to change. He had always been a great believer in luck. His instincts were still those of a gambler.

In Paris, life went on with brio. 'People are well accustomed to luxury and pleasure in this city! Despite the general misery, I have never seen a spectacle more crowded or more superb than at the Opéra yesterday,' marvelled Marais. 'It is impossible that the Regent, on seeing this, does not repent nor be touched by all the ills he has caused; there is not a sol in the best houses, and the circulation of essentials is only done by credit.'

Philippe was not the repenting sort; but he realised that Law could not return, at least not in the foreseeable future. He asked Monsieur le Duc to see that Law got away safely. And so John Law left Saint-Cloud on 20

December with a passport supplied by the Prince, and passed by Paris on his way to the Low Countries. He was so certain that he would return that he took only thirty-six thousand livres and one or two diamonds. 'Monseigneur,' he wrote to Philippe, 'time will show that I have been a good Frenchman. The establishments which I have set up will be attacked, but they will survive, and posterity will render me justice.' Law blamed Dubois, Mme de Parabère and Nocé for his downfall. All three believed that Law should go; but it had been Philippe who, in the end, had made the decision.*

On 29 December, at an assembly of the Compagnie des Indes, the Regent announced his plan to dissociate the 'affaires du roi' from those of the Company. A few days later the Company lost its lease of the Mint, the tax farms and the management of direct taxes. Forty new tax-farmers were named; the Pâris brothers were summoned back; all the old apparatus of fiscal management was reintroduced. The Compagnie des Indes was obliged to assume the debts of the Bank and went into a slow decline.

The Mississippi bubble had burst. Law had been too impatient, taken on too much, failed to allow his fragile mechanisms time to work. He had helped instigate a recovery in commerce and agriculture, but he had gone too fast, and had imperilled his own success. In the process he had made the notion of paper money feared in France, hindering economic reform in the future. As for the terrible social dislocation described by the writers of the day, this was in all probability not as wrenching nor as widespread as it must have appeared to those who witnessed the distressing scenes at the Bank in July 1720 or whose friends and family suffered losses. The fact that most of the contemporary chroniclers came from the milieu of the rentiers, those worst affected by the System, can easily mislead. On the whole, after all the upheaval, the country benefited from Law because he gave the impetus for commerce, within and without France. Voltaire's view, in this regard, is accurate. 'Enfin, s'il y est beaucoup de fortunes particulières detruites, la nation devint bientôt plus commerçante et plus riche.' (In the end, although many private fortunes were destroyed, the nation soon became richer and more mercantile.)

Perhaps, if Philippe had been king, he would have persevered with Law. But, as Regent, he decided he could not take the risk. He resolved to forget the daring new ideas and return to the unsatisfactory past.

---

* Law left Brussels on 24 December, making his way to Innsbruck. He then resided for some time in Venice, where he died in 1729. Mme Law and her daughter stayed in Paris, in reduced circumstances. At the beginning of 1722 Philippe accorded her a pension.

# ☙ 24 ☙

# DISILLUSION

Philippe faced the wreckage of his dream with gloom. The Mississippi was finished; the reputation of America as an Eldorado irretrievably tarnished; the interest of the French in colonial commerce stalled. After the heady excitement of Law's enterprise, he now had to face a resurgent *parlement* anxious to reassert its power, and the old corrupt faces of the financial establishment, as well as the hostility of the streets and the insolence of Monsieur le Duc, the prince de Conti and the maréchal de Villeroi. He lacked the energy, tired and disappointed as he was, to fight. But Dubois was at hand, tireless and avid, ready to make all the moves Philippe could not. Dubois could claim that he had never been associated too closely with Law, that he had always respected the Pâris brothers and their allies, that he was now rather against the British and rather pro-Spanish. He bore no animosity towards the *parlement*. Philippe allowed himself to be pushed aside, taking refuge in wine and women.

On 1 January 1721, at a sombre meeting of the Regency Council, the Regent wearily revealed the extent of the ruin. He sat passively while Monsieur le Duc brazenly criticised him for his weakness in allowing Law to flee, while the maréchal de Villeroi blustered and rejoiced. He admitted that there had been some illegal printing of notes to cover expenses. He accepted that he would not intervene in the activities of the commissioners appointed to liquidate the bank; Monsieur le Duc wanted the King to make public the fact that he had forbidden the Regent to do so. It was a humiliation.

The Pâris brothers started a long and detailed certification process of all notes and shares. Gradually order emerged from chaos. But there was widespread bitterness over what had occurred. In Paris the middle class, who were the worst affected by the System, were desperate. 'Despair is in all the good families; there are no more profits or revenues,' wrote Barbier.

'One is charged with notes and shares which are worth nothing. Every day one hears new stories of men dead in desperation or reduced to the charity of their parishes. France has never been in such a state, and all for having believed that miserable Englishman.'

Philippe was mercilessly satirised as the Emperor Nero, fiddling while Paris burned:

> Parabère fait tous tes plaisirs,
> Personne n'en ignore:
> Sabran contente tes désirs;
> Ce n'est pas tout encore.
> Ton Sénèque est le Daguesseau
> Et Law est ton Narcisse.

> (Parabère gives you all your pleasures,
> As everybody knows:
> Sabran fulfils your desires;
> And yet that is not all.
> Your Seneca is Daguesseau
> And Law your Narcissus.)

The hostility affected his temper, all the more as he thought it unjust. In his heart he still believed in Law, and he watched the destruction of his work with frustration. Haunted by a sense of failure, he quarrelled with Mme de Parabère, accusing her of infidelity with the chevalier de Beringhen. They argued constantly.

He was momentarily diverted by the abbé de Broglio, who sent him three hundred bottles of wine, hoping he could influence him to grant him the abbey of Mont-Saint-Michel. Philippe said he wished to pay for the wine. So the abbé sent a bill: wine, bottles, corks, string, sealing-wax, crates, carriage, and at the bottom added, 'Total: the abbey of Mont Saint-Michel.' Broglio got his abbey, and the malcontents said that favours were only granted to those who 'told good jokes and those who played good tricks'.

But, amid the furore, Mathieu Marais, commenting on Philippe's ill-health, spoke for many when he remarked, 'One is obliged to pray for his preservation, for what happens after him is worrisome, the public does not wish to fall into the hands of Monsieur le Duc, who knows nothing and has never known anything except for the hunt.' Even with the government in turmoil, Marais and the majority of the middle class felt that Philippe, imperfect as he was, was the best safeguard France had. The prospect of Monsieur le Duc, the duc de Chartres or the prince de Conti was alarming. 'The Regent and Mme de Parabère are getting along better. This affair is necessary to his health and his repose and even to matters of state which proceed more smoothly when he is not quarrelling. They presented Mme de Pramnon, but although she is beautiful she did not please. The Regent took her once to his little box at the Opéra and she had all the shame without the pleasure.'

While the bourgeoisie struggled to recover from financial catastrophe, the nobility, its coffers full, was left relatively untouched. But their morals did not match their fortunes. The loftier the rank, the more depraved. 'The grand seigneurs, that is the Princes of the Blood or dukes, all of that is a bunch of good-for-nothings,' was the opinion of Madame.

And yet, at this very moment, one of the greatest masterpieces of art was being created in Paris. At the beginning of 1721 Watteau was staying with his dealer Gersaint, at the sign of the Grand Monarque on the pont Notre-Dame, and painting a sign for his shop. The sign, *L'Enseigne de Gersaint*, said to have been painted in eight days, is perhaps Watteau's greatest work.

In a shop open to the street, paintings are arranged on the walls, portraits, still lifes, pastorals, above all nudes. A spectator is watching two young men packing a portrait of Louis XIV into a crate; the straw for the packing lies on the cobblestones. Glancing at the portrait of the Grand Monarque, an elegant young woman is helped up the step into the shop by her companion. We see only her back, her rose-pink gown cascading from its lace collar, her hair swept up with a ribbon, revealing an adorable neck. On her feet are high-heeled shoes, there is a glimpse of green silk stocking. Within the shop an older couple are examining a large oval painting of naked goddesses and nymphs, shown to them by Gersaint himself; the man kneels down with his lorgnette, the better to inspect the details. Again, we see only their backs, and every detail of their soberly coloured but richly textured clothing. At the counter sits a woman in a wide skirt of luminous silver silk striped in palest green, a lace fichu around her throat. She regards a toilet set and a mirror shown her by Mme Gersaint, more modestly dressed in a tobacco-coloured robe with a pink scarf. Two fashionable young gentlemen look at the objects, but they also look at Mme Gersaint. At the far right a dog scratches itself for fleas.

A moment is suspended; life in Paris on a spring day in 1721 is captured and held. And at the very moment of doing so, Watteau transforms this ordinary subject into a reflection on the fleeting nature of each human experience and the uncertainty of happiness. It was a feeling fully shared by the Regent, who often spoke of the 'misfortunes of this world, and the short duration of everything which is agreeable'. In Watteau's case that duration was short indeed; his tuberculosis was gaining on him. That spring Pierre Crozat, perhaps wanting a memorial of his friend, commissioned Rosalba Carriera to paint his portrait. She portrayed a young man already slipping away, his regard still piercing, as if to take a last look at life. In May Watteau moved to Nogent; he died there on 18 July, in the arms of Gersaint, at the age of thirty-six.

There would be no more *fêtes galantes*, although Lancret and Pater would try and recreate the vanished world of Watteau. Now the mood had swung to satire, the audience more cynical, the world more brittle. As Watteau died, Paris was caught up in a new book. The *Persian Letters* had appeared in Amsterdam and became a sensation in Paris. Its author, the baron de Montesquieu, a sober magistrate from Bordeaux, offered a vision of Paris as seen through the eyes of two Turkish visitors, and the salons were thrilled to find themselves so accurately depicted. And to complete the fun, the Turkish Ambassador, Mehmet Effendi, arrived in the city to congratulate Louis XV on his coming majority in February 1723. One could watch his fantastic cavalcade parade through the streets and feel the book had come to life. In fact, the book was far more stimulating than the real life visitor.

In London, in the tumult of the South Sea Bubble, Philippe's old colleague Stanhope dropped dead on 16 February, in the heat of an argument in the House of Lords. The rise and fall of the South Sea Company in London had closely paralleled that of the Mississippi. It too had experienced a dizzying boom at the end of 1719. When news came to London in the summer of 1720 of Law's troubles, stock in the South Sea Company rapidly declined. At the beginning of 1721 the city of London was 'a scene of iniquity and corruption' and the leaders of the government stood accused of taking bribes. In the midst of the crisis Stanhope collapsed. A link between France and Great Britain which went back almost two decades was severed. Philippe, still bruised by the British perfidy over Gibraltar, felt able to authorise Dubois to undertake a rapprochement with Spain. On 27 March, therefore, France and Spain signed a defensive alliance; the French received favoured commercial status, and in return promised to use their good offices to have Great Britain return Gibraltar. This treaty cemented French ties with Spain without loosening those with Britain. It was a typically skilful negotiation by Dubois, who now looked on the improvement of relations with Spain as another step towards his cardinal's hat.

It was all very vexing therefore when Pope Clement XI died in March without agreeing to Dubois' nomination. Cardinal de Rohan was hastily dispatched to the conclave to vote for Cardinal Conti, the candidate of Dubois. Rohan, divinely pretty, completely empty-headed, was assured by Dubois that he would be made Prime Minister if he proved useful in the matter of the hat. The abbé de Tencin also went to Rome as Dubois' agent, with large amounts of gold and silver. Nothing was left to chance. Conti was duly elected and became Pope Innocent XIII. Tencin remained in Rome to bribe, cajole and beg. His master in Paris, while awaiting anxiously for news, was also taking the opportunity of Philippe's retreat to consolidate his position. Dubois had no time for the conventional methods of diplomacy. He was an opportunist, and liked others of the same temperament. He preferred to employ outsiders, men from the provinces or even writers like Destouches, men who owed their loyalty to him and were prepared to use any means to achieve their end. He encouraged espionage, ruses and deceptions. Dubois' most important operatives were Le Blanc and Belle-Isle; these three men spent most evenings alone together, discussing and resolving many affairs of the day.

Their work accomplished a masterpiece; on 13 June a triple defensive alliance was signed between France, Spain and Great Britain. Dubois had managed to keep France allied with both Great Britain and Spain, and had further isolated Austria. The price they paid was extensive trade privileges for the British. The Regent and Dubois were not unaware of the commercial implications of the treaty. Dubois' view was that 'this treaty is so good and advantageous on the whole that one must console oneself that it lacks complete perfection'. But he acknowledged that 'it gives the English privileges and exclusive advantages, contrary to the interests of the King's subjects'.

The population of Paris was less interested in foreign treaties than in continuing high prices and increasing disorder. At the opening of the Saint-Germain fair there was a brawl between the pages of the King and those of the ambassadors. The former prevented the latter from going into a performance of acrobats, and fighting broke out. Soldiers had to be called in; six lackeys were arrested, and the whole of the quartier Saint-Germain was in uproar. On another occasion there was a riot in the rue des Grands-Augustins when the owner of a fleet of hired carriages had his coachman condemned to be flogged and branded for stealing an iron bar. When the owner's wife, who was present at the punishment, called for the wretch to be flogged harder, a mob entered her house in a fury, broke the windows, took two carriages from the stables, set fire to them and dragged them as far as the rue Saint-André. Shortly afterwards there was another riot, this time at the church of Saint-Nicolas-du-Chardonnet, where the funeral of d'Argenson, the former Chancellor, was taking place. This time, in a scene the wily old man would have appreciated, the mob threatened to make off with his coffin.

Perhaps seeking solace from these outrages, the Regent performed his Easter devotions at Saint-Eustache and then went to the Temple to hear the fine voices of the musique du Roi sing a Miserere by Delalande which was considered a masterpiece. Loving music as he did, perhaps Philippe drew some consolation from the performance; but he had other consolation at hand.

Mme de Parabère had been the favourite for five years. Her position seemed secure. She had just received a new house at Argenteuil, 'a sumptuous hermitage', and she and Philippe had just been painted as the happy couple of Greek mythology, Vertumnus and Pomona. But she was openly unfaithful. Madame worried that her son would contract 'quelque chose de laid du commerce-là', and her suspicion seems not to have been unfounded. The Prussian envoy recounted the story that Mme de Parabère had acquired some little creatures in her private regions, allegedly from the Regent; Philippe's response was that, as M. de Nocé also slept with her, one could not know where the little things came from. 'After all, they do not wear livery.'

Philippe continued to associate with Mme de Parabère; Marais saw him just after Easter at 22 place Vendôme, 'in a room all lit up, with all the doors open'. But he had fallen for a new face, or had persuaded himself that he had. Sophie de Brégy, comtesse d'Averne, was a young woman highly on view in Paris. She was the mistress of the marquis d'Alincourt, Villeroi's grandson, a young man about town and a *mauvais sujet*. Smitten, Philippe had offered Mme d'Averne 100,000 écus in return for her favours, and her husband a regiment. But Mme d'Averne did not succumb immediately. 'The terms have been proposed, but not yet accepted,' observed Marais. Sophie went to her country estate for the summer, whither Philippe sent jewels, and even arrived one night, uninvited, for supper.

Convincing himself that he was passionate about Sophie d'Averne, he resolved to dismiss Mme de Parabère. He was most uncharacteristically brutal. One evening he took her aside and whispered, 'What a beautiful head, I could have it cut off whenever I wished.' Mme de Parabère, as startled as if her lover had turned into a rabbit, fled. It was, indeed, the end of the 'belle illusion'.

Mme d'Averne let herself be taken to La Roquette; the next day Philippe told his friends that he had achieved his heart's desire. D'Alincourt, the rejected lover, was in despair, claiming that 'The whore had promised me that she would rather sleep with a chimneysweep than with him.' D'Alincourt's grandfather, the maréchal de Villeroi, presented his compliments to the Regent, and told him he would now send d'Alincourt back to his wife, thus mending one ménage while breaking up another. Marais had another reason to sigh. 'Behold how the court diverts itself with *débauche*.' Sophie was the Regent's last adventure. And like most of its kind, it was not a dignified spectacle. Philippe seemed obsessed with proving that he was still a great lover. He took his new mistress to Saint-Cloud and escorted her round the gardens in an open carriage, under the windows of Madame. He showed her off in his box at the Opéra. He gave a masked ball at the Palais-Royal. 'We are ruined and we dance,' murmured Parisians.

As Philippe dallied, he was forced to take note of the antics of his ever troublesome daughter Charlotte. He might have thought that, away in Modena, she was safely out of mischief. But she had taken an immediate dislike to her Italian home; the court of France and that of Modena were very different. Lonely, bored and restless, she had not settled to marriage at all well. 'Odd things are happening in Modena,' noted Madame, 'the couple live together like cat and dog and quarrel all the time. This does not surprise me, as I know only too well how wild, ill brought up and spoilt my granddaughter is.'

In Paris there was an ominous atmosphere. The plague, having killed hundreds of thousands in Marseille, was spreading through Provence and Languedoc; the inhabitants of Paris were forbidden to keep pigs, pigeons, hens, rabbits or hares in their houses, on the grounds that 'the stench is liable to corrupt the purity of the air and to cause pestilential illness'. At Philippe's instigation, a 'conseil de santé' was set up in June to discuss ways of preventing the spread of the disease; but everyone acknowledged that they were in the hands of God and fate. There was great apprehension. And there were other worries. There was an epidemic of venereal disease among the young fast set in Paris. 'Of nine young people of quality who dined with my grandson a few days ago,' wrote Madame, 'seven had the French malaise.'

In this atmosphere, the news of Dubois ascending to cardinal evoked only ennui and sarcasm. Dubois himself was radiant with joy; he hastened to present himself to Philippe in his new dignity, causing the Regent some chagrin with his speech: 'I would blush with embarrassment at appearing thus before Your Royal Highness if what I am was not your own work.' The wags said that the cardinal's hat had cost the Regent four million livres; and they had much else to say:

Or, écoutez, petits et grands,
Un admirable événement,
Car l'autre jour notre Saint-Père
Après une courte prière
A par un miracle nouveau,
Fait un rouget d'un maquereau.

(So listen, rich and poor,
To this admirable story,
When the other day our Holy Father,
After saying a brief prayer,
Made as in a new miracle,
A mullet from a mackerel.)

(A mullet is a red fish, hence a cardinal; a mackerel another word for pimp.)

The sober magistrate, Barbier, did not find the news amusing: 'this does a great deal of wrong to religion to see a man known for being without faith and without religion placed in one of the first positions in the Church'. Neither did Philippe's entourage. 'You can make a cardinal from a cad,' was Nocé's comment, 'but you cannot make cardinal Dubois an honest man.'

As for Torcy, the distinguished minister, he had been treated to a display of the Regent at his most disingenuous. Torcy learnt from his officials at the Postes, whose job it was to open and read any interesting looking mail, that Dubois was intriguing for his hat, and went to Philippe for clarification. Philippe laughed: 'Cardinal! That little scoundrel! You are making fun of me; he would never dare think of it.' When Torcy persisted, showing Philippe certain letters, the Regent became angry. 'If the little impudent has gone so far in folly, he will be punished.' A day later the Regent called Torcy into a corner at the Palais-Royal: 'A propos, monsieur, we must write on my behalf to Rome for the hat of Monsieur de Cambrai; see to it, there is no time to lose.' Torcy stood speechless as Philippe hurried away.

The Regent had never flaunted his mistresses in public. They were an integral part of his life, necessary and valued, but they had not so far been celebrated in an ostentatious way. Perhaps in an indication of how disoriented he was that summer, he now proceeded to make an extravagant declaration of his love for Sophie d'Averne. On 30 July he threw a party at Saint-Cloud, not at the château, but at the house which had belonged to the Elector of Bavaria, on the river, near the bridge. The party was ostensibly for the maréchale d'Estrées, the delicious Lucie-Félicité de

Noailles, who had entertained the Regent a short while before. But it was Mme d'Averne to whom the spectacle was dedicated.

The party was select; twelve men and twelve women, in smart new clothes, dined and danced in the gardens by the river. There were twenty thousand lanterns in the trees, and all the fountains played. At fifteen minutes after midnight fireworks burst out over the river. To watch the show, 'all the carriages of Paris were in the bois de Boulogne at Passy and Auteuil and one saw on every side 'the delights of Capri'. On both sides of the Seine, the night passed with revelry and carousing. The next day the peasants petitioned at the Palais-Royal for recompense for the damage done to their crops and vines by the carriages. The man in the Parisian street complained that such goings-on, publicly celebrating adultery and vice, were contrary to religion and decency. And the heroine of the evening was, according to Barbier, not even pretty: 'she has too much bosom, dark and pendulous, and her only éclat comes from her pink and white complexion'.

As Philippe returned to Paris from this ill-considered jaunt, he heard the news he had always expected and dreaded. The King had fallen seriously ill. Having woken up with a sore throat and a headache, he had been sent back to bed, shivering and feverish. Villeroi was in panic, all the King's doctors were summoned, the duchesse de la Ferté was in the antechamber screaming that the boy had been poisoned. The illness lasted five days, until Helvétius cured him; he alone of all the doctors kept his head and prescribed an emetic, at which the King 'made a charming evacuation'. When the boy recovered there was an explosion of joy in Paris, sedulously encouraged by Villeroi. Throughout the month of August there were church services, fireworks, deputations, speeches, dancing in the Tuileries gardens. La Motte read verses of celebration at the Académie in the presence of the Regent. There was a huge celebration in the place du Carrousel which Villeroi forced the King to watch, dragging him to the balcony while declaiming, 'Look at this, my master, all these people, all these crowds are yours, all of them belong to you, you are the master ...' The boy shrank into himself in panic.

During this anxious time, Philippe behaved perfectly. 'M. le duc d'Orléans conducted himself so sensibly and prudently that he greatly benefited,' said Saint-Simon:

> He showed a reasonable anxiety and worry but he was restrained, used a great reserve in his speech, and paid an exact and sustained attention to what he said and did, so that nothing escaped him that implied that he thought he would soon be the master. Above all, he left people no reason

to think that he either feared the King's recovery, or hoped for him to worsen. His entire household down to the valets never said anything to which any suspicion could be attached.

But the contrast between the delirious joy of the people at the King's recovery and the unpopularity of the Regent was clear. 'Vive le Roi et la régence au diable!' The explosion of joy was a cry of hate.

When Louis XV recovered, the Regent and Dubois decided that the time was ripe to unveil the results of their long negotiation with Spain. This time, the matter concerned not a new treaty, but two marriages, that of Louis XV with the three-year-old Infanta Maria Anna Victoria of Spain, daughter of Philip V and Elisabeth Farnese, and that of the Regent's eleven-year-old daughter, Mlle de Montpensier, with the thirteen-year-old son and heir of the King of Spain, the Prince of the Asturias.

Philippe could not resist breaking the news to Saint-Simon, who arrived one day at the Palais-Royal to be greeted by the Regent in a state of euphoria. 'Ho çà!' he exclaimed, taking his friend's hand. 'I cannot keep secret from you a thing which I desire most in the world, and which matters to me the most, and will bring you the same joy; but I ask for your discretion.' Saint-Simon's first thought, like everyone else's, was to wonder at the length of time they would have to wait for the Infanta to reach maturity. 'One is astonished that the King will not be able to have children until twelve years from now, and that they have thus put off his posterity.'

Philippe fully expected Saint-Simon's reaction, and knew that it would be the reaction of most Frenchmen and women. For that reason he would have to finesse the announcements of the two weddings. The King's wedding would be announced first and, once that had been accepted, that of Philippe's daughter. It was critically important that the marriages be seen as the first results of the Franco-Spanish rapprochement, not as a deal made to keep the Regent in power in France and his daughter on the throne of Spain. To those who complained, Philippe was trenchant: 'What? I should wish that my son should rule to the prejudice of this adorable child who today is my natural master? Ah! How different are my prayers!' The denial was firm, if not comprehensive. The marriages were seen as a triumph for the Regent. There would be no dauphin in France for many years, and therefore, if Louis XV were to die, Philippe d'Orléans would be king. The Regent's opponents were furious. They attributed it all to his and Dubois' Machiavellian tactics. Indeed Philip V had been manoeuvred into suggesting them by the diplomacy of Dubois.

The King of Spain, in one of his periods of religious fervour, had taken a vow to abdicate before 1 November 1723; it was therefore important this his son and heir marry. Philip V first thought of some Austrian archduchesses; but he was told that Louis XV was about to marry Mlle de Montpensier. How could he allow his old enemy the Regent to score such a victory? He would have to put forward his own daughter. Poor befuddled Philip V tried to forget how much he feared and distrusted the Regent. He duly offered the girl, and accepted the Regent's daughter for his son. But he gained something too. He, no more than the duc d'Orléans, wished to see a dauphin in France in the near future. If Louis XV died without a son, he still had hopes of the succession. The fact that the lives of four children were thus sacrificed to royal ambition was never considered for a moment. Philippe and Dubois were jubilant. Their enemies, the *vieille cour*, all pro-Spanish, were confounded. The Cardinal, remarked the Regent, 'had the Devil's own energy when it came to things he wanted so badly'.

Then came the difficult task of telling the eleven-year-old King of his three-year-old bride. The Regent, taking Monsieur le Duc, Villeroi, Fleury and Dubois for support, plucked up the courage to tell the boy the news. Predictably, Louis XV turned red and began to cry. 'Come now, my master,' encouraged Villeroi, 'we must accept the thing with a good grace.' The boy still wept, tears of rage and frustration. Only Fleury could calm him. When he was a little quieter, they immediately brought him before the Regency Council. 'Behold, Sire, your marriage approved and consented to, and a great and happy deed accomplished,' declared the Regent, all smiles and very nervous. The King stared sullenly into space; it was a lugubrious session. The next day the boy still could not summon up any cheerfulness, but he was soon less sombre and then seemingly back to normal. Philippe hastened to write to his old foe, the King of Spain. 'Monseigneur ... I find, in the re-establishment of the union between the King and Your Majesty and the return of the trust and friendship with which Your Majesty honours me, the greatest satisfaction of my life...'

The reward for Dubois had already arrived. A courier from Rome had brought the cardinal's biretta to Paris on 12 September and the King presented it on the 21st. A few days later cardinal Dubois paid a ceremonial visit to Madame at Saint-Cloud. Madame was not looking forward to it:

Everybody here is *en grand habit*; because I have a ceremony at three o'clock, that is the reception of this accursed cardinal Dubois. The Pope has sent him his biretta, and I must salute him, invite him to take his place and converse for some time. This will be a trial for me, but trials and annoyances are my daily bread. But here is our Cardinal who is advancing;

I must therefore break off ... The Cardinal prayed that I forget the past; he made the finest speech it is possible to hear. It is evident that this man has a great deal of wit; if he was as good as he is intelligent, he would leave nothing to be desired.

Dubois moved to the Tuileries, to the apartment of the duchesse de Ventadour, who was moving to the Louvre to be with the Infanta, and began attending daily meetings with the King and the Regent. Villeroi was horrified.

Two weeks after the announcement of the King's marriage, that of Mlle de Montpensier was also announced. As Philippe expected, the news attracted less attention in the hullabaloo over the King. Madame was naturally pleased with the honour to her granddaughter, but she was not particularly fond of the girl herself:

> She came to see me some days ago in a Spanish gown; it suited her much better than the French. Her gown was of green and gold brocade; she wore no bonnet, but a little black hat with a white feather. This get-up seemed to me very pretty and suits Mlle de Montpensier all the more as she has a long face ... What is so surprising is how Spanish she seems. She is very serious and never laughs and speaks very little. She is brunette and her eyes are almost black. You couldn't call Mlle de Montpensier ugly ... But with all this she is the most unpleasant child I have ever seen, so far as her manners go: the way she talks and eats and drinks makes one lose one's temper just to look at her.

The Parisians took a cynical view of the marriage. 'The Spaniards, who are proud, could they like to have as their Queen the daughter of Mme le Régente?' wondered Barbier. 'There will always be something to say about her birth ... this scheme is from the boutique of cardinal Dubois, who must be a great politician; as there is nothing finer for M. le Régent than to make his daughter Queen of Spain.'

At the end of September it was announced that the duc de Saint-Simon would be sent to Spain as envoy of the court of France, charged with the signing of the marriage contract of Mlle de Montpensier. It was the proudest moment of his life, and in order to acquit himself as a duke and peer of France should, he indulged in so many extravagances that he ruined himself for life. But, at the time, the preparations for departure, the establishment of the correct etiquette, the promise of the Order of the Holy Ghost for one of his sons and a Grandeeship of Spain for the other, had Saint-Simon dazzled and elated.

As Philippe prepared to bid farewell to Saint-Simon, another old friend announced his departure. The duc de Brancas, constant companion at the Regent's supper parties, retired to a monastery at the beginning of October. According to d'Argenson, he was tormented by his taste for boys and by the fact that, being no longer young, he had to pay for his pleasures. Then 'God touched him', and he made the decision to enter a monastery. On their last night together he was so cheerful and amusing that Philippe had twice to leave the table in tears, and later wrote him a tender and pressing letter asking him to change his mind.

> Reviens, Philis, en faveur de tes charmes,
> Je ferai grâce a ta légèreté.

> (Return, Philis, on account of your charms,
> I shall pardon your frivolity.)

But Brancas was adamant. He suggested that Philippe join him; Philippe declined. They never saw each other again.*

Philippe was consoled on Brancas' defection by the arrival at the Palais-Royal of the fabled art collection of Queen Christina of Sweden. He had spent several years negotiating for these paintings; two hundred and sixty, including forty of the very best quality. As the collection was unwrapped, Philippe could feast his eyes on such masterpieces as Raphael's *Holy Family*; Titian's *Allegory of Human Life* and *Venus in her Shell*; luscious Veroneses; *Io, Leda* and *Danaë* by Correggio; *The Continence of Scipio* by Rubens; and a Tintoretto, an Andrea del Sarto, a Michelangelo (*Ganymede*) and so on. Philippe sold several diamonds in Holland to pay for all this. He owed the success of the negotiations to his friend Pierre Crozat who had gone to Rome for the purpose. Crozat undertook the production of bound volumes of prints of the paintings and drawings in the collections of the crown, the Regent and a number of private individuals. Philippe, who already allowed parties of students to visit the Palais-Royal and view his collection, was eager to see these beautiful works of art disseminated as widely as possible.†

On 17 November the marriage contract for Mlle de Montpensier was

---

* Brancas stayed at the abbey for ten years; we catch a glimpse of him, characteristically dining well on shrimp bisque, a 'pretty sole, and a bottle of Burgundy which cost fifty sols'. In 1731, at the death of his wife, he returned to Paris where he lived at the Oratory. He stunned his family by marrying again, at the age of seventy-five, but died the next year, 1739.

† These paintings are now dispersed to St Petersburg, Edinburgh, Boston, Washington, Vienna. Philippe's son sold many of them, in particular the nudes, which he found disturbing and offensive. He personally attacked Correggio's *Io*, which superbly depicts 'the lineaments of gratified desire', striking it with a knife and cutting it to pieces. Luckily Charles Coypel collected the fragments and put together all but the head which was repainted by Prud'hon.

signed by Louis XV at the Tuileries. Everyone then proceeded to the Opéra for a performance of Lully's ever popular opera, *Phaeton*. The Spanish Ambassador, the duc d'Ossuna, sat between Madame and the Regent in Madame's box. As he passed, Philippe bowed courteously to Mme de Sabran, who was with some of her friends. 'Monseigneur,' she called, 'stay a little with your old harem.' The performance was followed by a superb ball in the Gallery of Aeneus at the Palais-Royal attended by the King. All the nobility were 'in cloth of gold or silver; this is the fashion at present'. The veteran diplomat, Amelot, remarked on the 'surprising magnificence, all the court dressed up, and the clothes so rich that one would have thought there had never been more money around'.

The next day Philippe drove out two leagues from Paris with his daughter and her entourage, and then left her to make her slow and splendid way to Spain. Knowing the court of Spain as he did, he must have wondered what awaited his daughter in that gloomy, over-heated atmosphere. Perhaps he gave a thought to his half-sister, Marie-Louise, who had made the same journey so many years before, and had found nothing but sorrow. But such was the lot of princesses. He turned back to Paris. For her part, Madame had no regrets: 'I assure you I shed no tears at saying adieu, and nor did she.'

Philippe found time to advance another child, his favourite, Charles de Saint-Albin, son of Florence, promoting him to Archbishop of Laon. Saint-Albin was, said Saint-Simon, 'extremely handsome, but perfectly ignorant'. The Regent was very fond of him, and told the cardinal de Rohan that he had hesitated a long time over this promotion, 'in the fear of being seduced by the tender feelings I have for him . . .' Having overcome his scruples, Philippe had to contend with an embarrassing uproar over the nomination when it was realised that Saint-Albin's official father was listed as Coche, valet de chambre to the Regent, and thus the young man could not be received as a Peer of France. After much dispute, he did become Archbishop of Laon, but could not be thus registered at *parlement*, due to the irregularities of his birth.

In October the famous burglar, Cartouche, was finally arrested, having terrorised the wealthy quarters of Paris for months. Cartouche was taken in his bed, six pistols by his side, betrayed by an informer. He was interrogated by Le Blanc, and then conducted on foot to the Châtelet, followed by a huge crowd. The notorious bandit turned out to be such a charming young man that he became a sort of hero. Actors from both the Comédie-Française and the Italienne rushed to visit him in prison and plays about him were presented, to popular acclaim, before his execution.

Cartouche was sentenced to be broken on the wheel. The spectacle was witnessed by thousands, who filled the square and observed by those who had rented every window with a view. The young man retained his sang-froid; when offered a cup of coffee as a last supper, he drank it but then politely asked if he might have a glass of wine and a little bread. He remained composed even on beholding the fearsome scene at the place de Grève and 'his courage and spirit made everyone pity him'. Nevertheless, throughout December they hung and broke forty of his accomplices, including young Balagny, son of a gilder who worked on the pont Notre-Dame, 'la grande Jeanneton', a flower-seller, and Touton, son of a candle-maker. They were all dispatched in the dead of night, their last words unrecorded. Only the awful death of Cartouche's fifteen-year-old brother caused comment; condemned to the galleys for life, the youth was also to be punished by being taken to the place de Grève and suspended from his wrists for two hours. He cried out that he was dying, that all his blood was draining out of his head. Then he could cry no more. He died as the onlookers mocked.

## ❧ 25 ❧

# CORONATION

The Regent took little consolation from the new year, 1722. Bored to death with everything other than work, he still could not summon up the energy to return to affairs. Dubois was in command of every detail. Listlessly, Philippe had allowed himself to be pushed aside. Mme d'Averne did not have the resources to keep him amused. Perhaps he found some fun in the new titles promised in the Bibliothèque Satirique: *The Art of Leading Husbands by the Nose* by the Queen of Spain; *The Pleasures of Married Life* by the Prince of Modena; and, particularly, *The Art of Dividing Men to the Infinite and the Secret of Profiting from their Division* by the duc d'Orléans. But he was tired, and watching the antics of the younger generation made him feel his age.

The duc de Chartres was suffering from a venereal disease contracted from the actress Maria-Anne Quinault, known as La Mignonne, the eldest of three celebrated sisters. She had already been the mistress of Samuel Bernard, who had bought her virginity for fifty thousand livres, and then passed her on to the marquis de Nesle, and thence to Chartres.*

As for Philippe's daughter Montpensier, he received a hopelessly misspelt note, scribbled in large, childish handwriting as she progressed over the Pyrenees to Spain; 'Permete mon cher papa que j'aie l'honnoeur en vous souhaitent davance une bonne ane de prendre encore conge de vous' ('Allow me my dear Papa to have the honour to wish you in advance a good year and to take my leave of you once more'). One wonders what her father thought of this pathetic reminder of his sacrificed little girl.

He soon heard more from Saint-Simon, who met the Princess at Cogollos, a little town near Lerma. Saint-Simon had had an uncomfortable

---

* She lived to be almost a hundred, having become the idol of the duc de Nevers and a brilliant social figure. She was followed to her grave by all France in 1791.

journey to Spain; and an equally uncomfortable meeting with the King of Spain. He had been astonished at his first glimpse of the grandson of Louis XIV. 'He was very bent, shrunken, his chin poked far in advance of his chest; he planted his feet straight, touching one another, and though he moved quickly enough, he crossed them as he walked; his knees were more than a foot apart. His speech was so formal, his words so drawled, his expression so vacuous, that I was quite unnerved.' As for Elisabeth Farnese, 'I was deeply shocked by her face, all pock-marked and scarred by the ravages of smallpox . . . but she had beautiful shoulders, and a plump white bosom, with pretty hands and arms.'

Worn out by receptions and ceremonies, Saint-Simon had contracted smallpox himself and spent a month in some danger. Barely recovered, he rose from his bed and rode on mule back eight leagues to greet the Princess. It was a mortifying encounter. 'Her ladies did everything they could to have her say one word to us, without any success.' The girl was clearly uncooperative. In Madrid she fell ill with erysipelas and the King and Queen were convinced that she had a venereal disease, credulous as they were about the Regent's debauches. They forced Saint-Simon to go to her bedside and observe the suspicious glands. Saint-Simon told Philippe that he had reassured the King, and had even expressed some reassurances on the Regent's own behaviour, 'which Your Highness will pardon me saying that Your Highness has not always merited in this regard'. The Princess soon recovered her health, but not her manners. She refused to leave her room and attend the ball prepared for her. 'I, go there? I refuse. The King and Queen should go, if they wish; they like balls, I do not like them at all; they like to get up and go to bed late, I like to go to bed early. They will do what they like and I shall do what I like.' In the end the King and Queen held a little ball without her, and the King wore the famous pearl La Pellegrina on his hat.

Saint-Simon was wishing he was home. But he was perfectly happy to have missed the drama of cardinal Dubois' entry into the Regency Council, which caused a furore. Saint-Simon had had a good relationship with Dubois in the early years of the Regency, but as Dubois' power increased, so did Saint-Simon's horror at the spectacle of one of such low birth ascending to the highest offices of Church and State. They had recently quarrelled bitterly over Saint-Simon's embassy to Spain, which Dubois thought a waste of time and money when there was a perfectly capable Ambassador in Madrid available to do the honours of the royal marriage. Now Dubois was in the process of inflicting a blow on Saint-Simon's most cherished possession, his rank as Duke.

Dubois was not satisfied with being the most influential man in France;

he wished to take his seat on the Regency Council in his rank as cardinal, thus taking precedence over all the dukes and peers. But first he sent his dupe, cardinal de Rohan, ahead. Rohan had been in Rome, where he had worked hard on Dubois' account, and where he had caused great amusement when it was known that he bathed in milk to preserve his fine soft skin. Dubois encouraged Rohan to think that, in return for his pains, he would be named Prime Minister on his arrival in Paris; now Rohan was back, and eager for glory. Dubois sat back to watch the fun.

On 8 February 1722 the cardinal de Rohan entered the Regency Council, taking precedence over the Chancellor, the dukes and the marshals. Rohan, ever gullible, had no idea that he was being used by Dubois to establish his own pre-eminence. Two weeks later, Dubois himself took his place immediately after Rohan, and therefore ahead of everyone else. In a startling affront, the Chancellor, Daguesseau, left the room. 'You cannot deny, M. le Cardinal,' intoned Noailles, 'that the day of your entry into the Council will be a day well known in our history, since this will be the day on which the high nobility of the kingdom leaves it.' Philippe, putting the best face on this lack of respect, said he had saved as much as twenty thousand francs in pensions now that all these members had left. But Belle-Isle told Saint-Simon that the Regent was extremely annoyed at this blatant lack of respect for his, and therefore the King's, authority, especially on the part of the Chancellor, and resolved 'to conduct himself with the necessary firmness'. Dubois told Saint-Simon that Noailles was behind the walk-out, and was leading a *cabale* against him; Dubois was obsessed with *cabales*. But Saint-Simon felt as outraged as the offended dukes that the wily Cardinal had made use of the foolish Rohan to vault over their dignity.

The public were profoundly uninterested. They were flocking to La Motte's tragedy *Romulus* at the Comédie-Française, starring the ageless Baron, and then running to the marionettes to see *Pierrot Romulus* by Lesage and Fuselier, a hilarious skit.

At the end of February Philippe took his revenge on the Chancellor. For the second time Daguesseau was relieved of the seals. Once more he took the road to Fresnes. D'Armenonville took over the job and his son Morville became Navy Secretary. D'Argenson the younger, Philippe's protégé, who had briefly been Lieutenant of the Paris police when his father was Chancellor, took up his post again.

Government reshuffles were not as interesting to the Parisians as the arrival of the little Infanta, the three-year-old future Queen. The talk was all of dancing, of balls and fireworks and celebrations. She arrived on 2 March in a magnificent procession over the pont Notre-Dame and along the rue Saint-Honoré to the Louvre. Five triumphal arches were erected along the way, beneath which passed companies of musketeers, the maison du Roi, grenadiers, gendarmes, pages, valets de pied, the Spanish Ambassador, the magistrates of Paris. There were seats along the rue Saint-Jacques, but as Barbier noted, 'a telling sign of the times, so many windows with to let signs and yet not let'.

The Infanta was an adorable little girl. On her way into Paris she had called to the Captain of the Guards, in French which she had learnt on the way from Bordeaux, 'Ah, do not hit those poor people who want to see me!' Madame thought she was the prettiest and sweetest child she had ever seen. When she visited the little girl at the Louvre, 'the dear child put down her doll and ran towards me with open arms; she showed me her doll and said with a laugh, "I tell everyone that this doll is my son, but I can tell you, Madame, that he's only a wax model"'.

On 8 March there was a great ball at the Tuileries at which fifteen young men and women of the court danced. The men wore gold or silver with Spanish lace and shoulder knots. All the women sparkled with diamonds. Then the King and the Infanta went to watch fireworks in the place du Palais-Royal; the place was illuminated on every side and decorated with arcades and singular structures which attracted all Paris. In the midst of all the rejoicing, there were several disobliging signs and many satirical verses.

The little girl charmed the Parisians, but unfortunately her charm did not infect the King, who remained horribly embarrassed by this clinging child. Shortly after her arrival, the Duke of Ossuna gave a fireworks display on the river between the Pont-Neuf and the Pont-Royal. Bérain designed the spectacle, with fireworks bursting from boats arranged in an octagon. The Regent was not present; he 'has fallen ill, for overheating himself at the fireworks at the Palais-Royal, and, as others say, overheating himself with his mistress, whom he saw the very same day he was purged and after getting drunk'. As the King and the Infanta watched the fireworks from the Louvre, 'the Infanta pulled the King several times by the sleeve, because he was not talking to her at all, and asked him, "Monsieur, do you not find this beautiful?" Finally he said "Yes"; at which she clapped her hands and waved to her attendants, "He spoke to me! He spoke to me!" Every day one admires her vivacity and charm.'

Madame tried to help the King to relax:

The King had colic the day before yesterday, and yesterday I gravely went up to him and put a little piece of paper into his hand. Maréchal de Villeroi asked me in a pompous voice, 'What is that note you give the King?' I answered, equally seriously, 'A remedy for the colic.' The maréchal: 'Only the King's physician may prescribe for the King.' I answered, 'As for that, I'm sure that M. Dodart will approve of it. It's even written in verse.' The King grew embarrassed, read it secretly and began to laugh. The maréchal said, 'May I see it?' I said, 'Of course, there is no secret,' and he found the following words: 'Fart, fart, you cannot do better, Fart, it will make you feel better, etc.' Everyone laughed so hard that I was almost sorry to have played the joke. The maréchal de Villeroi was quite out of countenance.

The King would be thirteen, and therefore reach his majority, in February 1723. But he would still require guidance. The Regent's illness had alarmed *parlement*, what if Philippe died and Monsieur le Duc claimed the Regency? Suddenly the magistrates looked more fondly at their old nemesis. They knew him, they respected him, they could deal with him. But the strange, violent, cruel Condé? Now there were secret meetings about how to circumvent Monsieur le Duc, perhaps by declaring the King major before his thirteenth birthday. As Philippe's health failed, the joke was that shares in Mme d'Averne were falling, those in Mme de Prie rising. But Philippe recovered, and Mathieu Marais breathed a sigh of relief: 'he ate a little in public, and one was very relieved to see it, out of fear of something worse'.

In fact, Philippe was exhausted. He had handed the initiative over to Dubois. And Dubois knew how to use it to strengthen his own position. In April Charles de Nocé was exiled, Dubois demanding that a man who so publicly insulted the Foreign Minister must be punished. (Nocé had been Dubois' most unsparing and public critic.) Nocé, on hearing the whispers, had gone to Philippe and begged him not to make such a mistake, and exile a man who had been loyal for so many years. 'How can you believe that I would do that, knowing me as you do?' asked Philippe. Nocé came to the point: 'It is because I know you as I do that I believe the stories absolutely.' Nocé was sent away to Tours with his sister Mme du Tort, 'a great enthusiast for modern words and for metaphysical sentiments in conversation'. Broglio was sent further away. Dubois feared Nocé's freedom of speech and Broglio's bold ways, and both their liberty and familiarity with the Regent. Philippe acquiesced. It was easier.

As the Regent declined, so too did the tone of the society around him. Everyone had been disoriented by the upheavals of the System, some overwhelmed with new wealth, others completely ruined. The moment of equilibrium and harmony, the moment enshrined in the luminous *fêtes galantes* of Watteau, was already passing into history, replaced by a vicious, greedy frenzy.

In Paris there was a mood of depravity. Mme de Sandricourt circumcised her lover 'in order to increase her pleasure', and almost killed him. It was said that Mme d'Ussé had an ass at her service. Mlle le Maze, 'fille de l'Opéra, très-jolie', ruined by the System, drowned herself in the Seine, 'wearing red, with her beauty spots, and flesh-coloured silk stockings, like a bride'. The body of Sandrier de Mitry, an official at the War Ministry, was found in the river near Marly with two stab wounds in the stomach, wearing a black coat and no trousers. It was thought that he had been killed to silence him as he knew too much about his superiors' embezzling. There was an epidemic of insulting pamphlets. A commission was established to judge those who engraved, printed and distributed libels against the government. But, a ray of light in the gloom, young Marivaux, also ruined by the System and constrained to earn a living by his writing, produced a success at the Comédie-Italienne with *La Surprise de l'amour*, which ran for thirteen performances. He had found his métier and was launched on his long and sprightly career.

Saint-Simon arrived back in Paris in April after an absence of almost six months. His leave-taking of the Princess of the Asturias had been a surprising experience. The Duke advanced, bowed three times and made his compliment to the Princess, who stood upon a dais with her ladies. In the ensuing silence the Princess issued a resounding fart. 'I was so surprised that I stood confounded.' Then came a second fart, then a third, even louder than the others. The company fled in disarray; 'all their Spanish gravity was completely disconcerted'. Thus the Duke took his leave with some relief.

He had been briefed on the situation in Paris by Belle-Isle, who had come out to Etampes to meet him. His wife had also come to his side, and his good friends, the duc d'Humières and Louville. Belle-Isle told Saint-Simon of the *cabale* against the Regent and about the danger posed by the duc de Noailles. Clearly Dubois, through Belle-Isle, wished Saint-Simon to be aware of the fact that he, Dubois, was now the master and that *cabales*, whether of the duc of Noailles or the duc de Saint-Simon, would not be tolerated.

Voltaire, who was always alert to which way the winds of patronage were blowing, had no doubts about how to advance in this new world. Perhaps conscious of the example of the playwright Destouches, who had served Dubois as secretary in London and was now a member of the Académie française, Voltaire wrote to Dubois offering his services as a spy:

I can go to Germany more easily than anyone in the world under the pretext of seeing Rousseau, to whom I wrote two months ago that I wished to show my poem to Prince Eugène and to him. I even have letters from Prince Eugène, in one of which he does me the honour to say that he will be very pleased to see me. If these considerations persuade Your Eminence to employ me in some capacity, I beg him to believe that he will not be dissatisfied with me...

Dubois, who always admired spirit and enterprise, promised to consider him.

And so in July Voltaire left for Cambrai and then Brussels and The Hague with Mme de Rupelmonde, a thirtyish redhead with a penchant for intrigue. As he left, Voltaire reminded Dubois that his illustrious predecessor, the cardinal de Richelieu, had offered protection to the poet Vincent Voiture. 'I beg you, Monseigneur, not to forget that the Voitures were always protected by the Richelieus.' To which Dubois replied, 'It is easier to find Voitures than Richelieus.' These two men with their sly, knowing features and their sceptical souls were a match for each other. Whatever Voltaire was doing on his trip to the Low Countries is impossible to discover.

Rumours started at Easter that the court was going to move to Versailles. It was not a popular idea with Parisians. The King's surgeon, La Peyronie, a blunt-spoken Languedocien, tried to tell the boy that he should not leave Paris, quoting the words of François Premier to the Emperor Charles V: 'Do you have a Paris?' But Louis XV was eager to go. In Paris he spent his time avoiding the little Infanta, 'la reine future' as she was known, and sulking. His favourite pastime was riding out to hunt; he quite obviously disliked city life. When he was warned of the expenses the move would incur, he said simply and royally, 'Bagatelle, bagatelle.' And so it was decided. Most people believed that Dubois had persuaded the Regent to the move in order to remove him from his 'roués et favoris'; it was said that the Regent had been exiled to Versailles on the orders of cardinal Dubois. Perhaps Philippe was worried by the disturbances in Paris due to the Mississippi scandal and thought the move would enhance the King's safety. Perhaps he was convinced that Versailles was the proper dwelling for the King of France, whatever its unhappy memories for him.

There is no doubt that Louis XV was delighted to be back at the beautiful palace. As soon as he arrived, he ran all over the grounds, the exhausted Regent in tow. He ended his day by lying on the floor of the Hall of Mirrors the better to admire the ceiling, and thus giving his weary uncle Philippe the chance to go and change his shirt.

The court moved into their uncomfortable quarters; the old etiquette was imposed. Philippe chose to inhabit the rooms formerly lived in by Monseigneur, on the ground floor looking out on to the parterre de Midi. Dubois took over the hôtel de la Surintendance near the Orangerie. There was need of extraordinary reparations, at huge cost. Philippe ordered a comfortable armchair of red leather; for the Infante-Reine there was 'a little stair of pine wood like a footstool covered with red damask' to allow her to climb into bed. Glumly, Philippe settled into this place so full of hateful memories. He probably did not appreciate that the garden was probably never as beautiful as it was that summer. The hornbeams, elms and limes had filled out, escaping the strict palisades, blurring the green geometry, adding a new and subtle touch of poetry to Le Nôtre's classical vision.

As the court moved, there were more banishments. Dubois demanded the exile of the duc de Noailles and of Canillac. Saint-Simon watched Philippe walking furiously round his *petit cabinet*, exclaiming, 'The wine is drawn; one must drink it.' Dubois had convinced his master that these men were his enemies, and that they had always to be on the lookout for enemies. In fact these men were dangerous, by virtue of their prestige, their ambitions, their independence, but only to Dubois, never to Philippe. It was a sad spectacle.

At Versailles Philippe was lonely and bored. He did not find Mme d'Averne as diverting as his old girlfriends, particularly in the gilded tedium of the palace. There was no Opéra, no suppers – and, even if there had been, there were very few of his old group still there to enjoy them. Every Thursday he went to Paris to find solace with such friends as remained, returning to Versailles on Saturday mornings.

He had ceded so much to Dubois, even allowing his oldest friends to be sent away in order to protect the Cardinal's position. More and more he saw his main task as that of perfecting the education of Louis XV. Saint-Simon has left a charming description of their sessions together:

When he worked with the King, he did so with a light touch, showing him that nothing was being done without an explanation, speaking briefly and at the level of his age, but always with the air of a minister at his command. He discussed the governances, benefices, pensions, described them, and the reasons why people wanted them, proposed the person he wanted, never neglected to add that he gave his opinion as he was obliged to do, but that these choices were not for him to make, that the King was the master and he had only to choose and to decide. If, rarely, the King seemed to prefer someone, and was too proud and too shy to say so, the duc d'Orléans would pay great attention and say with grace that he had some doubts, but then: 'But are you not the master? I am here only to explain, propose, receive your orders and execute them.' This conduct in public and in private, above all this way of working with the King, charmed the little monarch; he thought himself a man; he intended to reign, and felt a liking for the man who in this way let him reign.

These sessions were threatened by the officious behaviour of the maréchal de Villeroi. The old man was constantly interposing himself between the Regent and the King; he made it quite clear that he still suspected Philippe of nefarious designs and saw himself as the King's protector against his sinister uncle. Such an attitude was insulting and intolerable. Philippe foresaw that, at the King's majority, Villeroi would pose even more of a problem. Luckily, Villeroi himself handed Philippe an opportunity to act. Unable to conceal his loathing of Dubois, he got into a furious shouting match with him. 'You are all-powerful,' cried Villeroi. 'Everything bows before you. What are the greatest in the land compared to you? Use your power, put yourself at ease, have me arrested, if you dare. Who could stop you? Have me arrested, I say; that is all you need to do.' He had gone too far.

On Monday, 10 August towards midday the Regent went to work with the King after his walk. This day, when work was over, the Regent asked the King to accompany him into a little back room where he had a word to say tête-à-tête. Villeroi immediately objected. The Regent politely asked him not to hinder their confidential exchange. Villeroi huffed and puffed and demanded to be present. The Regent gave him a hard look and said, with ominous disdain, that the maréchal was forgetting himself and should think over his words. With a profound bow to the King, he left. Villeroi followed him, muttering and gesticulating, without the Regent giving a sign that he saw or heard.

A little later Villeroi, 'avec son fracas accoutumé', came to the Regent's *grand cabinet*, a large room with four windows looking on to the gardens. Having made a dramatic entrance, he asked to see the Regent but was told that he was working. Then, quietly, a group of men detached themselves from the walls and surrounded the maréchal. La Fare, the Regent's Captain of the Guards, demanded his sword; there was confusion and alarm. Suddenly the indispensable Le Blanc appeared outside the window with a sedan-chair. The maréchal was planted within it and, escorted by La Fare and d'Artagnan, Captain of the Grey Musketeers, hustled down the steps of the Orangerie, on the garden side, and pushed through the open gate where a carriage with six horses was waiting. Twenty musketeers surrounded the carriage. Then 'Touché, cocher!' and the maréchal de Villeroi was bowling down the road to exile.

The Regent went immediately to the King. Louis XV was yet again presented with unwelcome news. When Philippe told him that his governor was gone in disgrace, Louis turned red, his eyes grew moist, he put his face against the back of a chair and said nothing. He was perfecting his deep retreat into himself. That night he scarcely managed to eat his supper, wept and did not sleep at all. It was perhaps not so much from affection for his governor; Villeroi had continually told him that he alone protected his life and that without him he was in danger; the boy was terrified.

And then a week later his tutor, the abbé Fleury, his most reassuring ally, disappeared. Fleury claimed he had promised to leave the court when Villeroi did, but this was a cruel and cunning move on his part; he fully understood how important he was to the King and he wanted to make that perfectly clear to the Regent in order to protect and strengthen his own position. The boy was distraught; Philippe embarrassed. For a whole day no one knew where Fleury had gone; then he was located at Courson near Arpajon, a château belonging to the Lamoignon family. The Regent wrote him a pressing letter: 'I share your concerns, Monsieur, and nothing is more unjust than to involve you in the slightest way with what the maréchal de Villeroi has done . . .' Fleury returned the next day; the King's tears ceased. The old man's power was clear to all.*

Villeroi was sent to Lyon, accompanied by the inevitable Liboy, the same man who had accompanied the duc du Maine into exile, known for his qualities of tact and discretion. The maréchal behaved with dignity, after the first shock, and received visits from his family. Unfortunately his relatives, far from providing consolation, were a considerable embarrassment. His grandsons, the duc de Retz and the marquis d'Alincourt, had been discovered with the young duc de Boufflers and the marquis de Rambure playing homosexual games in the *bosquets* at Versailles. D'Alincourt was sent away with his wife to Joigny; the duc de Boufflers and his wife, d'Alincourt's sister, to Picardy. When the King asked why they had been sent away, they told him they had torn up the railings in

---

* Fleury had made his reputation when in 1707, as Bishop of Fréjus, he had successfully roused the population at the siege of Toulon, and personally negotiated with the Duke of Savoy, convincing him to spare the city. Back from Fréjus in January 1715, he was given the abbey of Tournus and designated tutor to the King in a codicil of Louis XIV's will. In 1722 he was almost seventy and seemed frail. Philippe would have been astonished to learn that Fleury lived until 1743, dying at the age of ninety, having ruled France for almost twenty years.

the park. From then on, 'arracheurs des palissades' became the accepted term for homosexuals at Versailles.

After the turmoil the Regent announced the engagement of his eight-year-old daughter, Mlle de Beaujolais, to six-year-old Don Carlos, eldest son of the King of Spain and Elisabeth Farnese. This was no doubt the news that Philippe was attempting to tell the King when prevented by Villeroi from doing so. Madame was pleased: 'she is a beautiful and pleasant child, well mannered, cheerful and funny; this one I like with all my heart. She will be quite intelligent one day.' With some tact she told the Queen of Spain that she would find Mlle de Beaujolais 'more cheerful than her elder sister. She is more like our charming Infante-Reine.'

But Philippe could not rejoice in this distinguished marriage; he was agonising about naming Dubois Prime Minister, making official what was already the case. Saint-Simon, who opposed this action with all his heart, found his friend troubled:

> He was distracted, preoccupied, making me repeat everything, he who had always been so ahead of one, and who liked to mix some jokes in with business, especially with me to make me impatient and have some fun at my expense. This distraction and seriousness were new. It was to do with making Dubois premier ministre. He said he was tired of politics and of the constraint of being at Versailles. At least in Paris he could relax with suppers with all his friends at hand . . . but here, when his head was splitting, he only had boring evenings. It was too much for him and he wished to pass the stress on to a prime minister.

As Philippe listened, his elbows on his desk and his head in his hands, Saint-Simon asked him what pleasure he found in these suppers except noise. Philippe shrugged. 'Very well! I shall go and plant cabbages at Villers-Cotterets.' Then after a silence: 'You know, Dubois persecutes me every day. What the devil more does he want? To make himself God the Father, if he could.' Then after a long silence: 'But why wait, I shall declare it immediately!' Horror from Saint-Simon. Once more Philippe hesitated. 'Very well, come back here tomorrow at exactly three o'clock to discuss this matter further, and we will take our time.' But the next day, after listening to another lecture from Saint-Simon, Philippe had heard enough. 'I must get this over with; it only remains to declare it as soon as possible.' Admitting defeat, Saint-Simon withdrew not only from the presence, but also from the close friendship of a lifetime. From now on he stayed at Meudon or in Paris. He could not be reconciled to this low-born upstart ruling France.

The news of Dubois' ascension was made official on 23 August. Philippe kept only the presidency of the Regency Council and the supervision of public expenditures. He composed an address to the King which was a summation of his achievements; interestingly, the only reference to Law was oblique: 'During your minority various means have been employed to escape from the debt left by Louis XIV ... and to support the indispensable expenses of the state, but since the chief means have not succeeded, the immediate task is to pay off the remainder of these debts and make up what is lacking in funds to provide for current and necessary expenditure.'

Dubois was all-powerful, but found he had even more foes with whom to contend. One of them was the Regent's son, the duc de Chartres, who disliked Dubois intensely and refused to work with him. Chartres was not highly regarded, least of all by his father, so his bluster had little effect. But he continued to irritate Dubois, sending his father's old girlfriend, Mme du Deffand, to ask for the release of Nocé from exile. Mme du Deffand, who later became a celebrated salonnière and writer, had had an affair lasting a fortnight with the Regent and was part of the circle at his suppers. She succeeded only in having Dubois allow Nocé to move nearer to Paris, to Beaumont-sur-Oise, near Mme de Parabère, but no closer. For her efforts, Mme du Deffand received six thousand livres of annuities.

There were other, more serious intrigues against the Cardinal. He had learnt that a party was forming around Monsieur le Duc, being informed by one of his spies that 'Belle-Isle is the conductor, chief and engine of this machine ... he supports the shaky M. Le Blanc alone with his intrigues.' Dubois, who had sacrificed so many people to his ambition, found himself faced with the prospect of doing the same to his oldest colleagues and associates, Le Blanc and Belle-Isle. They had turned against him, that was unforgivable. In September he set up a commission to investigate Le Blanc's financial affairs.

Philippe kept apart from his Prime Minister. He threw himself into preparations for the coronation of Louis XV. The ceremony was to be held at Reims on 25 October and there were to be triumphal processions, fêtes, fireworks and all kinds of celebrations. Although most of the dukes boycotted the ceremony out of pique at the reduced role they were assigned, Philippe was determined to lay on a splendid occasion, with all the more pleasure in that he truly liked and respected the boy in whose honour the celebrations were to be held.

The King left Versailles on 16 October for the Tuileries, then processed to Soissons, where he climbed all the way up the tower of the cathedral, which is very high, shouting to the courtiers with a smile, 'Gare les gras!' (Beware the fat ones!) Thence to Reims and the imposing ceremonial.

There was hardly a dry eye at the coronation itself. 'Everyone remembered for a long time', noted the unemotional d'Argenson, 'how he looked like Love itself the morning of his coronation at Reims, with his long habit and his silver hat. I have never since seen anything so moving; one's eyes were moist with tenderness.'

The King wore a chemise of holland cloth and a tunic of crimson satin over a robe of silver, with a hat of black velvet studded with diamonds. He entered the cathedral in a procession of Swiss Guards, to the music of oboes, trumpets and tambours. Heralds of Arms in white velvet and four chevaliers of the Holy Spirit preceded him, then came the duc de Charost, the grand écuyer, the capitaine des gardes, the garde des sceaux, the grand maître de la maison du Roi, the grand chambellan, the premier gentilhomme de la chambre and the gardes du corps.

The King made his vows to the Archbishop of Reims and received the seven unctions. The prince de Turenne presented the tunic, dalmatic and manteau royal. Then the eighth unction and the crown of Charlemagne was held above his head. Louis XV mounted the throne with sceptre and *main de justice*, the maréchal de Villars carrying the sword before him, the comte de Charolais the train. Then the people entered, medals were distributed, bells sounded, guns roared. There followed a Te Deum, Mass, Confession, Communion. And then, after a ceremony lasting six hours, the crown, specially made by the royal jeweller, Laurent Ronde, was placed on his head. Long live the King!

In the following days Louis XV paid visits of ceremony to various abbeys, touched the scofulous, freed prisoners, heard endless Masses. Eventually, a week after his coronation, he arrived at Philippe's nearby estate of Villers-Cotterets. There, in the newly renovated château and the newly pruned gardens, Philippe hosted a *fête villageoise*, with stag and boar hunting, a fair with puppets, harlequins and lotteries, and a buffet which lasted for forty-eight hours and at which thirty-six thousand eggs, eighty thousand bottles of burgundy and champagne, and sixty-five thousand lemons and sweet oranges were consumed on thirty thousand dessert plates of fine Oriental porcelain. Two days later there was another party at Chantilly. Then the procession of exhausted King and nobility marched to the abbey of Saint-Denis, where the King kissed the cross of Philippe-Auguste, and heard a De Profundis at the tomb of Louis XIV. Finally everyone returned to Versailles on 10 November, after almost a month of religious devotion and worldly excess.

Philippe was tired but uplifted. All his plans had been carried out to perfection. He seemed to have found new appetite to continue playing his part. The minute he arrived at Versailles, he sent Mme d'Averne away; he told her gently that it was not appropriate for her to stay there as she set a bad example, she should go to Paris where he would sup with her and sleep with her too if she wished. Sophie was not best pleased; she was heard to remark that all she had got from supping with the Regent was indigestion; and when someone remarked that there was about to be a great void in her life, she said that totally the opposite would be the case. Her reign had lasted for a year and a half.

On 20 November the duc and duchesse du Maine returned to live in Paris in their new house in the rue de Bourbon. Philippe had forgiven and forgotten; his dislike and distrust of Monsieur le Duc was growing to the point that Maine, feeble as he was, might be useful as a counterweight. As for Dubois, he was looking to a possible future without the duc d'Orléans when he might need the protection of a prince other than Monsieur le Duc. So the duc du Maine came back; but he never showed any interest in playing a larger role. He settled down to a quiet, retired life while his wife continued to run off to Sceaux at every opportunity, preferring to play her literary games than meddle in any more politics. Both had aged, but only one of them had matured.

As the year drew to its close, Voltaire returned from his secret mission in the Low Countries and went to spend some time with Bolingbroke and his wife at their comfortable house at La Source near Orléans. There he met Canillac, visiting from his exile at Blois. Voltaire, never one to miss an opportunity, gave him a copy of his newly finished epic poem, the *Henriade*, the subject of which had been chosen to flatter the duc d'Orléans. Perhaps Canillac would one day be back in favour and be able to help. 'As I write, M. de Canillac is reading my poem and judging it.'

Philippe prepared to bid farewell to another daughter. Little Mlle de Beaujolais was to depart for Spain on 1 December. Before she left, she paid a visit to Madame, who was at Saint-Cloud and unwell. Madame had made the arduous journey to Reims for the coronation, and had been rewarded with the joy of seeing her daughter and grandchildren; but her appearance had shocked the duchesse de Lorraine, who had not seen her mother for more than three years. 'When she saw me, she was so shocked that tears came to her eyes: I felt sorry for her.' When Madame left Reims, mother and daughter both knew that they would never see each other again.

Returning to Saint-Cloud on 3 November, the old lady found herself weak and lethargic. Although it was winter, and Saint-Cloud unsuitable for cold weather, that was where she wanted to be. Having bade farewell to Mlle de Beaujolais, she wrote to Luise on 3 December, 'I am getting more miserable day by day, but I am, thank God, ready for anything and only beg God Almighty to give me patience in the great pain I must suffer day and night ... Whether I will get out of this God alone knows; time will tell, but I have never been as sick as this.' She faced death with courage and dignity, telling Mme de Châteautiers, her devoted lady-in-waiting who tried to kiss her hand, that she might embrace her, and she was going to a place where all was equal. It had always been her hope that she would not have to see the death of her son. This she would be spared.

On 7 December, at eleven in the morning, she received Extreme Unction. Philippe was at her bedside. 'You weep, my son. Did you think I was immortal? Eh, do you not know that a Christian should only wish to live in order to learn how to die?' He stayed with her until late in the evening when she lost consciousness. At three-thirty the following morning she died.

Saint-Simon, who knew how close Philippe had been to his mother, made the effort to go to Versailles the next day and found his friend weeping bitterly. They spent several hours alone together until Philippe was able to face the day. He would have agreed with the verdict of Mathieu Marais: 'Behold a loss for all Europe. We lose a good princess and that is a rare thing.'

## ҂ 26 ҂

# MASTER AND MAN

Philippe's relationship with his mother was, arguably, the most important of his life. Mistresses had come and gone, friends had proved dispensable, his beloved daughter had died, but, through the years, he had always known that he would find in his mother, if not soft words of solace, at least a source of encouragement. She had never failed him and, up to her final day, had remained the 'eternal rock beneath'.

Her death seemed to bring home to him the notion that he must try to lead a more orderly life. With Mme d'Averne gone, he took to spending more time with his wife, who patiently welcomed him back, and seeing more of his daughter the Abbess, whose beliefs he could not share, but whose conversation he enjoyed. He was aware that his health had been undermined by his excesses; a mood of reflection came over him. Even in Paris, he was enjoying his paintings and the meetings of the Académie des Sciences more than the nightly suppers. But he was no recluse; he still loved the Opéra, and gossip, and jokes. There was no Nocé, no Brancas, no Canillac, no Mme de Parabère; but Mme de Sabran and Mme de Falaris still entertained him, and his daughter Mme de Ségur was proving to be a delightful companion.

He missed his mother; but he was not one for public displays of grief. On 5 February 1723 Madame's funeral service was held at Saint-Denis. 'M. le duc d'Orléans was not at his mother's service,' noted Barbier, 'that day he had been busy with affairs, and in the evening he went to the Opéra ball.' He had already said his farewells; he did not wish to endure the pious platitudes he considered inevitable at these occasions. And he was in the midst of preparations for the official majority of Louis XV, which took place on 15 February, the King's thirteenth birthday.

Philippe might have been tempted to retire from the fray on seeing his royal pupil reach this milestone. But he really had no choice; it was far too

307

risky to allow the boy to fall into the hands of his enemies. And educating the boy was a surprisingly pleasurable activity. Philippe was determined to remain as *de facto* Regent, although he would lose the title and revert to duc d'Orléans once again. In order to bolster his position in the majority, he prepared a long memorandum to read to the King, explaining why he should remain as chief adviser, and justifying his action in having Villeroi removed: 'I am still able to help Your Majesty in the maintenance of foreign alliances and the restoration of the finances; but I did not know how to live with M. de Villeroi. I am not at all vindictive or angry, everyone knows that; but I am incompatible with M. de Villeroi, because M. de Villeroi is incompatible with the good of the kingdom.' Despite the fact that Louis XV had reached the age at which he could, in theory, make all his own decisions, Philippe and Dubois had no intention of retiring the ground.

On 19 February the King received the respects of the duc d'Orléans and the court at Versailles, then the next day came in pomp to Paris. He caused some anxiety when he fell ill again; he had been shooting rabbits at La Muette, got wet in the streams and in the woods, would not change his stockings when he came back; the next day he fainted at Mass and was put to bed. Having recovered, he was allowed to go on to the roofs and gutters of the Louvre, but was put on a diet of bouillon; when the bowl was ceremoniously presented to him, and he grumbled that he would prefer a good piece of beef, word of his wit spread through Paris.

The Parisians wanted to love Louis XV, and they wanted him to love them. His passion for hunting and shooting, and his dislike of the opera and theatre, worried them, as it meant he did not like to come to the city. Feeling rejected, the scribbling classes looked for stories of the King's failings; they recorded that he was cruel to his dogs and horses, sulky and morose. The courtiers too were becoming somewhat alarmed by the boy; they were shocked when he called the marquis de Nesle a coward in public. Nesle was no paragon of courage, but it was considered unseemly to insult him so crudely.* The King did indeed have a sharp tongue, but he used it rarely. For the most part he remained silent, confiding only in Philippe, and in the marquis de Nangis; the courtiers said that he inherited this trait from his late mother, who had had a flirtation with Nangis years earlier.

The *lit de justice* held on 22 February to mark the King's official majority was a formality. The King attended the session in the splendidly redecorated Great Hall of the Palais de Justice; there were endless speeches, but, in the event, nothing much changed, exactly as Philippe intended. The

---

* Nesle lived to see three of his daughters in succession mistress to the grown-up Louis XV.

maréchal de Villeroi, the duc de Noailles and Daguesseau remained in exile. A Conseil d'En-Haut replaced the Conseil de Régence, comprising the duc d'Orléans, the duc de Chartres, Monsieur le Duc, Dubois and Fleury. Le Blanc remained Minister for War and Morville for Foreign Affairs. A new era opened, in name at least. The King ruled, there was no Regent, simply a council of advisers of whom the duc d'Onais was one. In fact, the State was governed in the same way as it had been for the previous seven years, Philippe and Dubois continued to make the decisions. Only the outward forms had changed. Philippe's first act in his new role as ex-Regent was a benevolent one. The royal library was about to move into its new home on the rue de Richelieu and the duc d'Orléans had the pleasant duty of approving the details. He had always taken a strong personal interest in the library, ever since 1716 when he approved the decision to move it from cramped quarters in the rue Vivienne to a part of the hôtel de Nevers on the rue de Richelieu. He had asked the Librarian, the learned and pleasure-loving abbé de Bignon, to have all the books and documents properly classified before the actual move. Now the task was almost accomplished, and the library could be formally established in its new home. That winter he approved the rules governing the institution; every book printed there needed prior authorisation, from the lieutenant of police or the bureau de la librairie, the workshops of the library were limited to a restricted area, and the printers were supervised by the University. Philippe was clearly not a believer in a free press; he had been gravely wounded by anonymous attacks and still bore the scars. For the epoch, he was not unusual; what was unusual was his interest in and support for the library, and his decision to allow free study there. The Bibliothèque Nationale is very much his creation.

While Philippe enjoyed the pleasure of benevolence, Dubois, all-powerful but increasingly manic and obsessive, was pursuing a punishing schedule. He woke at five to deal with his correspondence and arrange his dossiers before attending the King's Lever. He met the duc d'Orléans every day, sometimes with the ministers, sometimes in private, and attended thrice-weekly sessions with the King. Then more meetings with his premiers commis, in particular Couturier, his chief assistant, and with the ministers, the Controller of the Finances, and the Lieutenant of Police. He devoted four days a week to foreign dispatches, each country having its own day, and every Wednesday he gave audience to the ambassadors and foreign ministers. He was obsessed by plots. He feared the influence of anyone close to Philippe. At the same time the Cardinal, all too aware of his master's precarious health, tried to protect himself in any future government of Monsieur le Duc by obliging the prince and his mistress,

Mme de Prie. Le Blanc, Philippe's intimate friend and Mme de Prie's determined foe, was destined to be the next victim of Dubois' paranoia. It seemed that Le Blanc was doomed; but, unexpectedly, Philippe turned a deaf ear to Dubois' demands. Philippe liked le Blanc and trusted him; having sat by as so many others were purged, he asked this time for hard evidence of guilt and forced Dubois to provide it. Of course, what Dubois could not provide, he could manufacture. But it took him until July to gain Le Blanc's dismissal.

Mme de Prie, for her part, was looking to a future in which she would be pre-eminent. She was already assuming the role of protector of the arts, devoting herself to promoting Italian artists and musicians familiar to her from her years in Turin. She also patronised the young artist, Lancret, and Marivaux, whose play *La Double Inconstance* opened at the Comédie-Italienne that April and was a great success. The hit of the theatrical season, however, was *Inès de Castro*, a sentimental drama by La Motte, which was playing triumphantly at the Comédie-Française. Adrienne Lecouvreur played Constance 'avec dignité et délicatesse'. Voltaire came to Paris specially to see it and met the ancient comte de Verdun in the intermission. The old man declared that the play was not as good as *Le Cid*, the best play about Spain ever written. 'And yet it seems to me', remarked Voltaire, 'that at the first performance of *Le Cid* (more than eighty years ago), which you attended, you said you found the first two scenes rather dull.'

Dubois, in agony from a retention of urine, was constantly being bled and purged. Moreover, his most trusted assistant, Pecquet, had died and Dubois was drowning in detail. He had always been prone to rush around a room at full speed, stepping on chairs and tables in his excitement. Now he was so irritable and unpredictable that people were terrified to approach. Mme de Conflans was persuaded to visit him at Versailles, but before she could say anything more than 'Monseigneur,' Dubois exclaimed, 'This cannot be, by all the devils, when I tell you it cannot be, it cannot be,' and promptly seized her by the shoulders, turned her around, pushed her with his fist and cried, 'Go to all the devils and leave me in peace.' When Mme de Feuquières came to ask a favour, he snapped, 'I am overwhelmed with work, and yet I must deal with these whores who come to disturb me.' With some dignity, she replied, 'Monseigneur, let us not speak of the past, for you would lose more than I.'

Every evening the Cardinal ate a chicken for supper; one evening the servants forgot the chicken. Dubois thundered and screamed. They calmly told him that he had already eaten it. 'Comment? J'ai mangé mon poulet?' The steady insistence of the staff convinced him that he had indeed done so. He felt himself losing his grip.

The Irish adventuress, the princess d'Auvergne, the former Olive Trant, complained to the duc d'Orléans about the Cardinal's rudeness, but Philippe only shrugged: 'It is true that he is a little lively, but he sometimes gives good advice.'

Dubois was in fact working on a significant project, that of a new alliance with Peter the Great. The duc d'Orléans had always been consistent in his view that Austria was the most dangerous power in Europe, and should be isolated by every means possible. He was now fully engaged with Dubois' negotiations. 'If I can consummate my negotiations with the Czar,' Dubois told his colleague Chavigny, 'I will have put enormous obstacles in the way of the house of Austria.' Such a treaty would have changed the course of Europe if it had been accomplished; but neither Philippe nor Dubois had time to execute it, and Russia turned to Austria.

At the end of April the duc du Maine and the comte de Toulouse were re-established with the intermediate rank between Princes of the Blood and dukes. This was not done out of any urge to advance the two men personally, but rather as a counterbalance to Monsieur le Duc. It was an echo of the situation at the death of Louis XIV, when the old King wished Maine to be a counterbalance to Philippe. Philippe must have pondered the fact that such manoeuvrings occurred when a death was expected; Dubois clearly expected that of Philippe, and was taking precautions for his own future. Events were very soon to turn out differently.

The early summer was extraordinarily dry. It hadn't rained in two months. There was no hay, very few oats, and the vines and wheat were endangered. There was also an epidemic of smallpox. A certain lethargy pervaded the Palais-Royal. 'The duc d'Orléans hardly works at all any more,' Voltaire wrote to a friend, 'and although he is even more useless to women than to business, he has taken a new mistress who is called Mlle Houel.'

After Sophie d'Averne, Philippe had renounced a maîtresse en titre. Close friendships, such as that with Mme de Sabran, family ties, as with Mme de Séger, gossip with Mme de Falaris satisfied him, with the occasional peccadillo, like Mlle Houel.

She was sixteen, came from Provence and was the niece of Mme de Sabran. She was a brunette, tall and well made, not particularly pretty, but with fine teeth. She arrived in Paris without a chemise to her name, but, as soon as her aunt realised her value, and introduced her at the Palais-Royal, she was seen to have the finest outfits in the world. Mme de Sabran was of the same eighteenth-century school of thought as the marquise de Merteuil in *Les Liaisons dangereuses*. Both ladies would have agreed with Marmontel when he wrote, 'What! I have a pretty sister and see all the others making their fortune from their little second cousins!' What were relatives for?

Mlle Houel remained charmingly naive; as she and Philippe walked in the gardens of the Palais-Royal one day, they met Monsieur Mitton, the intendant of Toulon; 'You must salute him,' exclaimed the girl, 'he is our intendant!' The gossips reported that Philippe only slept alongside Mlle Houel, not with her. They sniggered at him taking her to Saint-Cloud to see the paintings the chapter of Reims had given him, a Titian, a Corregio and others. 'One does not know which is the stronger passion,' sniffed Marais, 'that for his paintings or for his women. But he has no taste for arrangement; he hangs a religious painting near a nude, an architectural drawing next to a landscape. His main pleasure comes from amassing so many.' One cannot quite accept the notion that Philippe saw himself as a kindly uncle escorting his pretty niece around his art collection; but Mlle Houel was perhaps more of a surrogate daughter than a new passion. The Parisians poured scorn on the couple, and yet the duc d'Orléans, so clearly battling ill-health and a ruined constitution, also aroused admiration for his courage and for his refusal to change his ways. 'He is a Proteus,' was Marais' verdict, 'a fabulous divinity who takes on all kinds of personalities, today the lover in transports, tomorrow the gallant husband, and always out of the reach of all the courtiers who surround him and cannot penetrate him.'

Dubois watched his master's health with care, to the extent of neglecting his own. Inevitably, however, his own sufferings began to overwhelm him; he was more brutal, more impatient, more irritable than ever. In June he installed himself at Meudon, rather than at Versailles, so that he could be closer to Paris, and need suffer less on the road to and from the capital. Under the pretext of cleaning Versailles, but really to accommodate the imperious Cardinal, the King and court all moved to Meudon that month. It was there that Dubois finally prevailed upon Philippe to exile Le Blanc. Perhaps it became easier to cut off one's friends the more often one did so. At any event Philippe performed the melancholy ritual with his accustomed grace. Le Blanc, like the others, left for his country estate, pained but forgiving. When Belle-Isle suffered the same fate a fortnight later, neither he nor Philippe realised that this was the last exile.

Through the month of July, Dubois' condition worsened. On 6 August the regular meeting of the Council had to be held in his bedroom at Meudon. Two days later, he was in agony. Reluctantly, he decided to return to Versailles for an operation, and on Monday the 9th was carried over to the palace, lying on a mattress hung on cords. He arrived at Versailles about midday, escorted by three carriages, one containing almoners, one with doctors and one with surgeons. On his arrival, he changed his mind about the operation, saying he wanted to be left alone to die in peace; it was clear that he was mortally afraid. Philippe hurried in to see him and to persuade him that the operation was absolutely necessary. 'You must have more courage,' he told him, before leaving with tears in his eyes. But Dubois still could not face the inevitable. He insisted that there was a special procedure for cardinals receiving the Viaticum and had messengers sent to Paris to find the ceremonial. Everyone knew he was delaying. Finally, in unspeakable pain, he confessed and allowed La Peyronie to use his knife. Three or four men held him down; he swore like a madman. As soon as the surgeon had made the cut, it was clear that there was no hope. Gangrene had already set in. Outside a thunderstorm broke.

The next day Hénault went to visit the dying man. He found him 'on his back, suspended between two valets who supported his groin, with an apothecary who held a spoon to his mouth, and a priest in a surplice who prayed in front of a crucifix'. Philippe could only hope that the suffering would soon be over. 'I hope that this stormy weather will help the rascal on his way,' he sighed, not without tenderness.

Cardinal Dubois died at about four o'clock in the afternoon of 10 August. The great nobles cheered the end of this upstart; Saint-Simon spoke for his class when he called Dubois a bigamist, a paid spy for Great Britain, a congenital liar, the man who corrupted the mind and morals of the young duc d'Orléans. But opinion in Paris was more charitable. 'He did no great harm' said the lawyer Barbier, 'but he was little liked, haughty, unpleasant and arrogant. Perhaps he did achieve some good by his negotiations in foreign countries to avoid war.' In fact he was a remarkably able man, a skilled diplomat, with profound intelligence, a vision and a lucid mind. He was, like his master, disingenuous and evasive, unscrupulous and manipulative. His ascension to cardinal was extraordinarily cynical, even for his age; his hat was an insult to the pious. But most of the hatred he engendered came not from those who despised his acts, but from those who despised his birth. Born into another class, he may have been hailed as a second Richelieu; instead he was vilified and called a pimp.

When Philippe became Regent he turned more and more to Dubois to carry out his wishes. The two of them were very finely tuned to each other. 'Dubois was one of those men of whom one could say much bad, all of which would be true, and of whom however there could be some good to say,' wrote the marquis d'Argenson, son of Philippe's friend; 'he put himself at the head of an infinite number of intrigues which had for object only the private interests of the duc d'Orléans.'

D'Argenson added that Dubois was to be most reproached with the fact that he persuaded his Prince that, in the world, real piety and probity were worth nothing, and that merit lay in accomplishing one's ends while concealing one's game. The only decent people in the world were stupid, ran the gospel according to Dubois, the rest were rogues. Better to be a knowing rogue than an uncomprehending fool, so he seems to say, as he regards us from his monument, in the church of Saint-Roch in Paris, his wily eighteenth-century face sardonic and unsurprised. His look reminds one of Voltaire; they were both completely of their time and place.

# ✖ 27 ✖

# CAPAX IMPERII

The death of Dubois awoke Philippe from his lethargy. He recognised that it was his duty to assume the burden of governance once again. To do so, he would need the support of all the old colleagues whom Dubois had banished. Saint-Simon was the first to return, rushing back from La Ferté where he had been for two months. 'As soon as Monsieur le duc d'Orléans saw me,' he recorded, 'he ran to me and asked me insistently whether I wished to abandon him. I told him that, while the Cardinal lived, I had felt I could be of no use to him ... but now I was his most humble servant.' Philippe immediately began to talk of the new Company of Ostend just established by the Emperor, and the risks it posed to France. He seemed eager to wrestle with such pressing matters, pleased to have another chance to use his mind and stretch his capacities.

One hour and a quarter after the death of Dubois Philippe had sent a courier to Charles de Nocé in Senlis. The message was simple: 'Morte la bête, mort le venin. Je t'attends ce soir à souper au Palais-Royal' (Dead the beast, dead the poison. I await you this evening for supper at the Palais-Royal). When Nocé arrived Philippe was disarming: 'Let us not talk about the past; I could not have acted differently; but, for now, ask me what you wish, I shall grant it you.' 'I ask only my life,' smiled Nocé, 'for, as surely as you granted my exile to the Cardinal, you would give my life to the first one who asks.' Philippe laughed heartily, and presented Nocé with a pension of two thousand écus and a gift outright of fifty thousand livres.

Canillac and Broglio appeared soon after, and then the duc de Noailles. Philippe, who had heard that Noailles had become very devout in exile in Auvergne, took the duke's head in his hands and kissed it seven or eight times, intoning, 'Pax vivis, requies defunctis.' Then he carried him off to see the King, who had his cat Charlotte with him and asked Noailles if he still feared cats. Everyone was delighted at all the reunions. Philippe felt himself the 'père de famille'. All the friends were quite giddy at seeing each other again; they were so pleased to be back that no one felt like holding a grudge against the man who had sent them away.

The duc d'Orléans rallied all his strength. He declared himself Prime Minister, in place of Dubois: 'Me voilà premier ministre de France malgré moi!' He rededicated himself to the education of Louis XV; Saint-Simon found him content, cheerful, taking up his work with pleasure. So easily bored, he was now stimulated and happy. 'Although he talks of learned matters it is easy to see that they bore rather than please him,' his mother had once remarked. 'I have often taxed him about this and he has told me that it was not his fault, that as soon as he understood something it ceased to give him any pleasure.' The more new and difficult matters arrived at his desk, the more fun he had. Philippe wished to prove he was not finished. Morville, d'Argenson fils, Dodun were his loyal seconds. They were all young men: Morville was thirty-three, Maurepas, the Minister for the Navy, twenty-two, d'Argenson, son of the late Chancellor and 'l'homme du Régent', twenty-seven. There was a new feeling of energy and even optimism. France was at peace and secure abroad; but at home the legacy of the System had to be dealt with. All the problems which the System had tried to address remained unsolved; there was still the spectre of bankruptcy, abuse of privileges, corrupt officials. Perhaps Philippe thought once more of Law.

On rediscovering the pleasures of work, Philippe tired of those of Mlle Houel. He ordered Mme de Sabran and her niece to leave their house at Sèvres, saying they were costing him too much. Mme de Sabran made fun of the order and said she would wait until the guards came to arrest her. But Mlle Houel vanished from the scene.

In mid-October Philippe made a *grande nomination* to vacant arch-bishoprics and abbeys. His son Saint-Albin, Bishop of Laon, was named to Cambrai, the richest see in France. The saintly Bishop of Marseille, Belsunce, who had heroically tended his flock during the plague there, refused Laon in order to stay in his devastated diocese. Philippe's daughter, the Abbess of Chelles, who was again living at Val-de-Grâce to be nearer her father, complained about many of the new bishops, writing sternly to her father and warning him that God would not be mocked. Philippe read and reread her letter; he told Saint-Simon he admired her position on abuses within the Church. 'He was moved enough to talk of it and even to let her see that he had paid attention, but I do not know if he profited by it. He didn't have the time.' (It was rumoured that Louise-Adélaïde was trying to persuade her father to see a priest.) This daughter had something of her father's spirit, and a taste for matters of the mind. Philippe went to see her every Tuesday. Despite their different modes of life, for most of the time they got along splendidly. They shared interests in painting, music, science and philosophy. And although Philippe never understood his daughter's passion for her religion and her ardent embrace of Jansenism, he respected her views.

Philippe had rarely been more engaged in his life. But his willing spirit could not overcome the weakness of his flesh. One morning in November Saint-Simon came to Versailles with the duc d'Humières, who wanted to thank the duc d'Orléans for giving him a lodging at Meudon. On being ushered into the presence, they found Philippe sitting on his *chaise percée* with his valets and two or three officers standing around. Saint-Simon was frightened at what he saw:

> His head was bowed, he was purple in the face, he seemed stupefied and did not notice our arrival. When they told him I was there, he turned his head towards me slowly, almost without raising it, and asked me with a thick tongue what brought me. He greeted the duc d'Humières with an air of befuddled surprise, and he, who was always gracious and polite with everyone, and who knew so well how to speak *à propos et à point*, could scarcely reply to Humières' compliments. I took Simiane into a corner and asked him what was the matter. Simiane said that he had been like this for a long time in the mornings, that there was nothing extraordinary about this morning, that I was only surprised because I never saw him at this time and that he would be all right when he had shaken himself and dressed.

Philippe had told Saint-Simon that his doctor, Chirac, was purging him ceaselessly; that he had completely lost his appetite and took nothing all day except for a cup of chocolate at midday. Chirac bluntly told Philippe that if he continued to attend his late-night suppers in Paris, he would either fall into a sudden apoplexy or suffer a slower, but deadly, constriction in his chest. At this Philippe protested; he was afraid of a slow, suffocating death, he preferred apoplexy, which would take him by surprise and kill him at once, without giving him the time to think. Saint-Simon sadly remarked that any other man, on hearing Chirac's words, would have decided then and there to lead a sober, sane and decent life. Philippe, however, knew it was far too late for that. He was not blind to the dangers, but recognised, accepted and perhaps even welcomed them. 'If you do not change your ways,' said his doctor, 'you will die at the moment you least expect.' His reply was perfectly clear: 'That is what I wish.'

On 1 December d'Argenson met the duc d'Orléans in the park of Versailles as he was coming back from L'Etoile, his wife's little house. 'The weather was awful and the Regent had the beginnings of a cold … He was wearing a huge red overcoat and coughing a great deal; he was short of breath, his eyes puffy and all his face swollen; his mind seemed to show the effects of his physical infirmity: he had to search for what he wished to say. He gave me his orders, and I spent half an hour with him, then he wished me farewell.'

The next day Philippe departed from his usual habit and had lunch with his wife before he took his public cup of chocolate. Having exchanged polite pleasantries with those in attendance, he took Saint-Simon into his *cabinet* for a tête-à-tête, which lasted for three-quarters of an hour. Saint-Simon found him somewhat slow and laborious, as was his wont these days, but his mind was clear and his reasoning as sound as usual. But he remarked that he had a headache, and that his stomach was charged. As Saint-Simon left, Philippe was awaiting the arrival of Couturier, the official who briefed him on current affairs.

Couturier was late. Philippe used the time to tell his son, the duc de Chartres, who was on his way to Paris, that he had decided not to go himself because of his cold. He put together the bag of documents he would take to the King later in the afternoon. At five o'clock Couturier arrived at last and the two men worked for about an hour. Then Philippe called Mme de Falaris into his *cabinet* for a little relaxing gossip. His bag all ready to go to the King, he was chatting with the young woman when he suddenly slumped over in his chair. To her horror, she saw that his eyes were fixed, his mouth open. Running for help, she found the anterooms deserted, as this was the time when the duc d'Orléans would normally be with the King, and the courtiers had gravitated upstairs to the staircase down which he would come when the meeting was over. Mme de Falaris had the greatest difficulty finding anyone to come to her aid, but finally she encountered Chirac, who rushed to the scene and discovered Philippe unconscious, still in his chair. They placed him on the floor and bled him, but it was too late. Philippe d'Orléans never regained consciousness.

Calumny followed him even at the moment of his death. It was recorded that Mme de Sabran, on arriving at the ghastly scene, cried, 'You must not bleed him, he has just come from his whore.' Then a grislier story circulated: when his body was being opened, one of his dogs, a Great Dane, sprang up and ate three-quarters of his heart. (Neither story seems based on fact.)

As soon as the news of the death of the duc d'Orléans reached Monsieur le Duc, he hastened to the King, who was with Fleury, and demanded the post of Prime Minister. Louis XV, as we might have expected, was 'very sad, his eyes red and moist'; he did not respond to Monsieur le Duc, but turned mutely to his tutor, who nodded assent. Knowing the precarious state of Philippe's health, the two men had already agreed on their strategy. When the duc de Chartres arrived back from the Opéra, he found his father dead and his job taken. As he alighted from his carriage, there was no crowd to meet him, only the duc de Noailles and the duc de Guiche, who offered him their services. He received them as importunates whom he hastened to get rid of before he rushed away to see his mother. There he remarked that he had met two men who had wished to lead him into a trap. 'This great mark of judgement and policy', noted Saint-Simon sardonically, 'gave promise of everything this prince has done since.'

Saint-Simon, informed of his friend's collapse, heard the news of Philippe's death as he travelled from Meudon to Versailles. After the courier departed he had to seclude himself in his carriage for half an hour, 'absorbed in grief and reflection'. Quite apart from his sorrow, he realised at once that for him every vestige of influence would disappear with the duc d'Orléans. He emerged from his carriage with sufficient dignity to withstand the humiliations to come.

At Versailles Philippe's coterie of loyal friends mourned. His wife, self-absorbed as ever, was too lazy to grieve. The courtiers had new idols to worship. Even as the body of the duc d'Orléans was being taken to Saint-Cloud, Monsieur le Duc and Mme de Prie were receiving the homage of the court.

The body lay in state until 16 December, when it was taken on its final journey to Saint-Denis, making its way through Paris 'avec la plus grande pompe'. The populace had their last chance to deliver their opinion, and did so with gusto:

> Philippe est mort à la sourdine;
> Il est descendu dans l'Enfer;
> C'est pour enlever Proserpine
> Ou pour détrôner Lucifer.

> (Philippe is dead without a word
> And when he gets to hell,
> He's sure to rape Proserpine
> And dethrone Lucifer as well.)

The suddenness of his death, without time to recognise himself and repent, terrified all those who believed in the fires of Hell. Saint-Simon was frozen with horror, shuddering to the marrow of his being, at the thought that God had granted Philippe his wish for a sudden death, in order that his unshriven soul be delivered to the Devil. Many sermons were delivered on the theme of Divine vengeance. There were also many more frivolous anecdotes. Marais reported that, when Philippe's papers were opened, they found that his code for foreign affairs used 'all the dirtiest and most obscene words in the language', adding that this was typical of the Regent, who had loved 'dirty, filthy words'.

The magistrates, who had viewed the adventure of John Law with horror, were pitiless: 'He died eight or nine years too late for the good of the state and the people; everyone is delighted at his passing, and with reason; he was a wicked prince.' But there was also a sense of sadness and loss. Montesquieu, enjoying the success of the *Persian Letters* in Paris, was eloquent: 'The death of M. le duc d'Orléans made me regret a prince for the first time in my life. He had a thing hard to express in French and which Tacitus called "imperii facilitatem"; as long as one must have princes, they should all be like him.'

'I must render justice to the truth,' declared Barbier. 'Except for the System, there has never been such a great prince; he had received a fine education and understood everything; he could paint prettily, understood music perfectly, engineering, chemistry, history, ceremonial, public law. He talked like an angel, and had all the qualities of a Prime Minister ...' Voltaire, who had been sent to prison by the Regent, nevertheless always admired him and his achievements: 'Of all the race of Henri IV, Philippe d'Orléans was the one who was most like him; he had the courage, the good nature, the tolerance, the gaiety, the intelligence, the plain speaking, but he had a more cultivated wit. His expression, although incomparably more gracious, was that of Henri IV ...' Voltaire also noted that: 'He left the country better, richer and happier than it had been under Louis XIV, and even quite considerable sums in the King's coffers.' D'Argenson, who predictably lost his job as Lieutenant of Police to a cousin of Mme de Prie, continued to serve Philippe's son, saying, 'If they made me dishwasher to the son of M. le duc d'Orléans I would be content. I have too many obligations to the late Regent not to abandon everything for his son.'

The contrast between the tributes of those who knew him, and the insults of the majority, who did not, is somehow indicative of the man. He was a slave to pleasure and chained to his desk; grossly indecent, with a delicate sense of refinement; a great prince and a low fellow. He saved France from war; and ensured her weakness with regard to Great Britain. He tried to make France wealthy, and ruined the bourgeoisie. He mocked God and worked for reconciliation in the Church. He took nothing seriously and dedicated himself to serious pursuits. He was a scholar and a drunk. One thinks of Prince Hal, another prince who had a rebellious youth and who became a great king. And there's the rub: Prince Hal had the opportunity to rule and show his genius, Philippe did not. He was a most unlucky man; and yet he was of course lucky enough to watch his relations fall dead, leaving him a path to the throne. There is no end to the paradox.

One man who worked closely with him, Angrand de Fontpertuis, an officer of the Compagnie des Indes, delivered a particularly penetrating analysis:

> he was pliant and they thought him weak, as indeed he appeared to be in trivial matters, though always very strong in important ones; he was a man of great intellect, penetrating, rational, profound, and they thought him superficial and frivolous ... they did not believe that he possessed any of the qualities necessary to govern yet he had almost all of them: an elevated and fertile mind, the ability to dissemble, shrewdness, consistency, the ability to work quickly; they took him for an adventurer.

Philippe d'Orléans would have wanted his epitaph to be his concern for the well-being of the nation and its people. But he was too wordly-wise not to realise that the stories of his excesses, repeated and embellished for years, would leave a stronger mark. Historians have argued since the day of his death about the real nature of his personality and achievements. He himself chose to project an image which invited caricature. From an early age he had enjoyed shocking people. It was one of the great complaints against Dubois that he had encouraged his pupil in this course of conduct. 'He flaunts his vices,' complained Louis XIV.

After the humiliation of 1709, when he stood accused of treason, and of 1712, when he was called a murderer, the duc d'Orléans added to this bravado a general contempt for his fellow men. The lesson he took from his experience was that he could trust no one. More than ever he subscribed to the theory that all men were either gullible idiots or scoundrels. Mme du Deffand, who knew him well, later remarked that she was 'like the late Regent, I see only fools and rogues'. In the belief that he was usually dealing with knaves, he liked to manipulate, to bribe if he had to, to listen, always with a hidden agenda of his own, telling people what they wanted to hear, seeming to agree, and pursuing his own course. This left friends and enemies discomfited. 'He broke so many pledges', wrote Saint-Simon, 'that his word ceased to have any meaning ... in the end no one believed him even when he spoke in good faith and his glibness in speech greatly discredited him.' Saint-Simon had to resort to foreign terms to describe the Regent's behaviour: 'mezzo termine', 'sproposito', 'divide et impera'.

Finally he had to admit, 'although I had known him intimately for many years ... yet I still did not know him'.

Philippe certainly provided a great deal of material for stories of his bad faith and deviousness; he also made his private excesses the stuff for public gossip; but he was not a wicked man 'Of few scruples, but incapable of crime,' was the considered verdict of Voltaire.

The black legend of his orgies, his talent as a poisoner, his thirst to kill, was sedulously manufactured in his lifetime, ably disseminated by the allies of Madame la Duchesse and the King of Spain.

Mme de Caylus was Mme de Maintenon's niece and dependent on her goodwill to retain her place at court. She was also a close friend and admirer of Madame la Duchesse and the mistress of the duc de Villeroi. Her view reflects her affiliations. 'To describe M. le duc d'Orléans, one must use a singular and terrible paintbrush.' She believed that he had squandered the benefits of a good education and ruined his character; he certainly had intelligence, discernment, eloquence and a good mind, she said, but he had come to believe that there was no such thing as goodness, that, the world being divided into fools and 'gens d'esprit', virtue and morality were the lot of fools and that 'gens d'esprit' merely affected to possess these qualities as it suited them. 'When he was young,' Mme de Caylus went on, 'the qualities of his mind concealed the defects of his heart. They conceived great expectations of him. But when he was married and master of himself, he adopted tastes he had not possessed; he courted all the women, and the freedom he gave himself repelled the *dévots* who had founded great hopes on him.' This was what Mme de Maintenon thought.

The view of Philippe as poisoner, traitor, unnatural father, has an equally untenable counterpart, that he was simply an amiable drunk who presided over a giddy, tarnished slice of history, a sort of extravagant Rococo curve away from the straight line from Louis XIV to Louis XVI. 'Everything turned to gaiety and amusements in the Regency,' remarked Montesquieu. 'It was the age of bons mots; the Regent conducted himself with a bon mot, and they ruled with a bon mot.' But again the men and women who knew him do not bear this out. There were plenty of bons mots; Philippe d'Orléans was the wittiest of men. He could never resist a joke. But the fundamental quality he brought to his position was that of diligence. He was, by every contemporary account, a *grand travailleur*. Neither vile debauchery nor vacuous bonhomie was a hallmark of the man.

His achievements were solid. He succeeded in his primary tasks: handing over royal authority intact to the King; keeping France at peace; and increasing prosperity. He tried but failed to do more dramatic things, but he was Regent, not King, and, after the failure of Law's System, he opted to play a role more transitional than dynamic.

He saw himself a reforming Bourbon like Henri IV. If he had been King himself, perhaps he would have made the monarchy more like the British, 'constitutional' model; Saint-Simon records that 'he praised England one day to me on this point, a country where there are no exiles, no *lettres de cachet*, and where the King cannot forbid entrance to his palace nor keep someone in prison'. But, although he ruled France, he was not King, and that crucial distinction made it difficult for him to effect the changes he assuredly wished to make. If he had lived, perhaps he would have persuaded Louis XV to move more decisively in modernising France; under his influence, Louis XV might have done great things. But his fate was otherwise, leaving us to paraphrase Tacitus: he would have been a great ruler if only he had been allowed to rule.

> For he was likely, had he been put on,
> To have prov'd most royal.

# AFTERWORD

Louis XV was ruled by Fleury until the Cardinal's death in 1743. In 1745 Mme de Pompadour became his mistress, and thereafter he was ruled by her. When she died in 1764, he took up with Mme du Barry. He died in 1774, unregretted.

The duchesse d'Orléans outlived all her children, except for her son and the Duchess of Modena. D'Argenson said she was very like her mother, Mme de Montespan, but also had Louis XIV's orderly mind with his failings of injustice and harshness. She ruled the Palais-Royal until her death in 1749 at the age of seventy-two.

The Duchess of Modena gave birth to a son in 1727. She and her husband fled to Genoa in 1728 and she returned to France in 1733. In France Charlotte found herself unwelcome; her mother, who had never liked her, was cold; her closest friend in the family was her half-brother, the chevalier d'Orléans. In 1739 she reluctantly returned to Modena, which for a few years she made rather fashionable. But in 1743 she returned to Paris with her daughter. She was now a stout, red-faced woman, looking rather like her father. She lived on the rue de Grenelle in the faubourg Saint-Germain, was a friend of the King's mistress Mme de Châteauroux, and close again with Richelieu. She intrigued successfully to marry her daughter to the richest man in France, the duc de Penthièvre, son of the comte de Toulouse. But her influence at court ended with the arrival of Mme de Pompadour in 1745. She returned to Italy, then led a wandering life, dying in 1761. Her granddaughter married Philippe-Égalité and was the mother of Louis-Philippe, King of the French.

The Abbesse of Chelles left Chelles in 1734 for a more secular life at the Benedictine convent of La Madeleine de Trainel in the rue de Charonne; there she had a studio in which to paint and a laboratory, with an apothecary cabinet, a good number of precious bibelots, rings, porcelain snuffboxes, screens, chandeliers, a tea-set, a chocolate-set, pipes, microscopes, compasses, and so on. Her library had two thousand books, including the works of Newton and Montaigne, volumes of history and geography, travel, medicine and mathematics. Here the abbess gave good parties for Christmas, Epiphany, Easter, Ascension. 'She is my brother's daughter!'

said her aunt the duchesse de Lorraine. Mme de Chelles died of smallpox in February 1743, aged forty-four. She had become an edifying personage 'quoique en princesse', and the only one of Philippe's children to have inherited his pleasure in matters of the intellect.

The duc d'Orléans, son of Philippe, continued his disappointing life. He married a princess of Baden, but when she died in 1726, he became more and more reclusive and pious. He retired in 1740 to the abbey of Sainte-Genevieve in Paris where he died in 1752.

Jean Philippe, chevalier d'Orléans died the same year as his mother, Mme d'Argenton. He was wounded in 1744 on the Rhine and commanded galleys in the Mediterranean in 1746. He died in 1748, covered with debts, to the tune of almost a million livres.

Charles de Saint-Albin, archbishop of Cambrai, son of Florence, became a Jesuit Ultramontane. He died in 1746 in the rue de Bourbon.

Philip V of Spain died on July 9 1746 'of chagrin and corpulence'. He was sixty-three.

Elisabeth Farnese did not die until 1766 aged seventy-four. Her eldest son, Don Carlos, became King of Naples and Sicily and then King of Spain. A younger son, Don Felipe, became Duke of Parma and married the eldest daughter of Louis XV.

The Prince of the Asturias was briefly King Luis of Spain but died in 1724 aged seventeen.

The Princess of the Asturias, formerly Mlle de Montpensier, briefly Queen of Spain, was sent back to France on the death of her husband, a fifteen-year-old Dowager Queen. She held a little court at Vincennes where there were odd goings-on. 'She was fat, gluttonous, ate with both hands; she never reads or works, seldom plays cards, and cuts her hair like an English schoolboy.' She died in Paris in 1742 aged thirty-three.

Mlle de Beaujolais, who never married Don Carlos, was sent back with her sister and died in 1734 aged twenty.

The Infante-Reine was sent back to Spain in 1725 when Monsieur le Duc decided to marry Louis XV to Marie Leczynska, a candidate of his own choosing. She married King Joseph-Emmanuel of Portugal and lived until 1781.

Monsieur le Duc was premier ministre for only three years before losing to the influence of Cardinal Fleury. He then retired to Chantilly, where he finished the magnificent stables, and married a princess of Hesse-Rheinfeld who gave him one son.

Mme de Prie was exiled to Courbepine in Normandy in June 1726 where she went accompanied by Mme du Deffand. She died there in 1727 aged twenty-nine, in mysterious and terrible circumstances, a possible suicide by poisoning.

The duc du Maine lived quietly at Sceaux. He never wished for any further participation in public life and died of throat cancer in 1736 aged sixty-six.

The duchesse du Maine continued to entertain at Sceaux, where Voltaire visited in 1747. After her husband's death she bought the hôtel de Biron in the rue de Varenne, now the Rodin museum. She died in 1753 aged seventy-seven.

Mme de Parabère returned to the place Vendôme, her parties and her lovers. She died rich and sated in 1759.

Mme de Falaris lived a long life and was gracing Paris society where she was known as Madame Jezebel until her death in 1782 at the age of eighty-five.

The duc de Noailles became maréchal de France and died in 1766.

John Law died in poverty in Venice in 1729 aged fifty-eight.

Alberoni was absolved of charges brought against him by France and Spain in September 1723 and lived in Rome. In 1733 he started to build a college outside his native Piacenza for aspirants to the priesthood. (The seminary, still known as the Collegio Alberoni, displays the Cardinal's collection of superb Flemish tapestries.) He died there at the age of eighty-eight in 1752, having outlived the Regent, Dubois and Philip V.

# ACKNOWLEDGEMENTS

I would like to thank the following for their help and support; Joan Bingham, Bill Hamilton, Michaela Phillips, Ion Trewin, Lois Wallace, Alan Williams, Charles Woods, Rebecca Wilson and Paulette Zabriskie.

# BIBLIOGRAPHY

## CONTEMPORARY SOURCES

Alberoni, Cardinal, *Lettres intimes ... au comte Rocca, ministre des Finances du duc de Parme*, ed. E. Bourgeois, Paris, 1893.

D'Argenson, Réné Louis de Voyer, marquis de, *Journal et Mémoires*, ed. J. B. Rathery, Paris, 1859.

D'Aumale, Mlle, *Souvenirs de Mme de Maintenon*, ed. d'Haussonville, Paris, 1902–5.

Balleroy, marquise de, *Les correspondants de la marquise de Balleroy*, ed. Barthelemy, Paris, 1883.

Barbier, E.-F.-J, *Journal d'un Bourgeois de Paris sous le règne de Louis XV*, Paris, 1857.

Bossuet, *Oraisons funèbres*, ed. Velat et Champailler, Paris, 1961.

Buvat, J, *Journal de la Régence*, ed. Campardon, Paris, 1865.

Caylus, Marthe Marguerite Le Valois de Villette, comtesse de, *Souvenirs*, ed. Noel, Paris, 1910.

Choisy, abbé de, *Mémoires*, Paris, 1966.

Dangeau, Philippe de Courcillon, marquis de, *Journal*, ed. Firmin-Didot, Paris, 1854–60.

Duclos, Charles, *Mémoires secrets sur les règnes de Louis XIV et Louis XV*, Paris, 1829.

Félibien, A, *Description du château de Versailles ...* Paris, 1696.

Law, John, *Oeuvres complètes*, ed. Harsin, Paris, 1934.

Madame Palatine, Letters. (In various collections: Bodemann, *Aus den Briefen der Herzogin Elisabeth Charlotte von Orléans an die Kurfürstin Sophie von Hannover*, Hanover, 1895. Brunet, *Correspondance complète de Madame duchesse d'Orléans*, Paris, 1855. Jaeglé, *Correspondance de Madame Duchesse d'Orléans*, Paris, 1890. Van der Cruysse, *Lettres françaises*, Paris, 1989. Also, in translation, M. Kroll, *Letters from Liselotte*, New York, 1971. E. Forster, *A Woman's Life in the Court of the Sun King, Letters of Liselotte von der Pfalz*, Baltimore, 1984).

Maintenon, Mme de, *Lettres inédites ... de la princesse des Ursins 1705–15*, Paris, 1826.

Maintenon, Mme de, *Après sa correspondence authentique*, ed. Geffroy, Paris, 1887.

Maintenon, Mme de, *Lettres*, ed. Langlois, Paris, 1935–39.

Marais, Mathieu, *Journal et Mémoires*, ed. M. de Lescure, Paris, 1863–68.

Marlborough, John Churchill, First Duke of, *Letters and Despatches*, ed. Murray, London, 1845.

Marlborough-Godolphin Correspondence, Oxford, 1975.

Montesquieu, baron de, *Oeuvres*, ed. Masson, Paris, 1950–55.

Narbonne, P, *Journal des règnes de Louis XIV et Louis XV de 1701 à 1744*, Paris, 1777.

Pollnitz, baron de, *Mémoires contenant les observations . . . Europe*, London, 1735.

Primi Visconti, *Mémoires sur la cour de Louis XIV*, ed. Lemoine, Paris, 1908.

Saint-Simon, Louis de Rouvroy, duc de, *Mémoires*, 42 Vols, ed. A. de Boislisle, Paris, 1879–1928.

Saint-Simon, Louis de Rouvroy, duc de, *Mémoires*, 8 Vols, ed. de la Pléiade; ed. Y. Coirault, Paris, 1983–88.

Sevigné, Mme de, *Correspondance*, ed. de la Pléiade, Paris, 1972–78.

Spanheim, E, *Relation de la cour de France en 1690*, Paris, 1973.

Staal-Delaunay, Mme de, *Mémoires*, ed. Barrière, Paris, 1846.

Stair, Lord, *Journal*, Hardwicke State Papers, London, 1777–78.

Théâtre du XVIII siècle vol. 1; ed. de la Pléiade. ed. Truchet, Paris, 1972.

Torcy, marquis de, *Journal inédit pendant les années 1709, 1710, et 1711*, Paris, 1884.

Voltaire, *Correspondance* vol. 1; ed. de la Pléiade; ed. Besterman, Paris, 1977.

Voltaire, *Oeuvres historiques*, ed. de la Pléiade; ed. Pomeau, Paris, 1957.

## OTHER WORKS

Aligre, président d', *Rélation de ce qui se passa au parlement de Paris a la mort de Louis XIV*, Revue retrospective, 1836.

Barker, Nancy Nichols, *Brother to the Sun King*, Baltimore, 1989.

Baudrillart, A, *Philippe V et la cour de France*, Paris, 1890–98.

Bluche, François, *Louis XIV*, New York, 1986.

Bosher, J. F., *French Finances 1707–1795: From Business to Bureaucracy*, Cambridge, 1970.

Bourgeois, E, *La diplomatie secrète au XVIII siècle*, Paris 1909–10.

Braudel, Fernand, *Civilisation and Capitalism*, 3 vols., London, 1981–84.

Cermakian, Marianne, *La princesse des Ursins, sa vie et ses lettres*, Paris, 1969.

Champier, V. and Sandoz, G, *Le Palais-Royal*, Paris, 1900.

Clark, Sir George, *The Later Stuarts*, Oxford, 1934.

Cobban, Alfred, *A History of Modern France*, 2 vols., London, 1957.

Cole, Hubert, *First Gentleman of the Bedchamber*, New York, 1965.

Crow, Thomas E, *Painters and Public Life in Eighteenth Century Paris*, Yale, 1985.

Dunlop, Ian, *Royal Palaces of France*, New York, 1985.

Elias, N, *The Court Society*, New York, 1969.

Erlanger, Philippe, *Le Régent*, Paris, 1938.

Faure, Edgar, *La Banqueroute de Law*, Paris, 1977.

Gay, Peter, *The Enlightenment: An Interpretation*, 2 vols., New York, 1966 and 1969.

Goubert, Pierre, *Louis XIV et vingt millions de Français*, Paris, 1966.

Harcourt Smith, Simon, *Cardinal of Spain*, New York, 1944.

Hauser, Arnold, *The Social History of Art*, New York, 1958.

Hazard, Paul, *The European Mind*, New York, 1990.

Hyde, H. M, *John Law*, London, 1948.

Kalnein, Wend von, *Architecture in France in the Eighteenth Century*, Yale, 1995.

Kimball, Fiske, *The Creation of the Rococo Style*, New York, 1980.

Kunstler, C, *La Vie Quotidienne sous la Régence*, Paris, 1960.

Lablaude, Pierre-André, *The Gardens of Versailles*, Paris, 1995.

Le Nabour, Eric, *Le Régent, libéral et libertin*, Paris, 1984.

Lewis, W. H, *The Splendid Century*, London, 1953.

Lewis, W. H, *The Sunset of the Splendid Century*, London, 1954.

Levey, Michael, *Painting and Sculpture in France 1700–89*, Yale, 1993.

Levey, Michael, *Rococo to Revolution*, London, 1966.

Lough, John, *France Observed in the Seventeenth Century by British Travellers*, London, 1985.

Lynch, John, *Bourbon Spain 1700–1808*, Oxford, 1989.

Macdonald, Robert R. (ed.), *The Sun King: Louis XIV and the New World*, New Orleans, 1984.

Magne, E, *Le Château de Saint-Cloud*, Paris, 1932.

Massie, Robert K, *Peter the Great: His Life and World*, New York, 1981.

Meyer, Jean, *Le Régent*, Paris, 1985.

Meyer, Jean, *La Vie Quotidienne en France au temps de la régence*, Paris, 1979.

Michel, Marianne Roland, *Watteau*, London, 1984.

Mitford, Nancy, *The Sun King*, London, 1966.

Orieux, J, *Voltaire*, Paris, 1970.

Perkins, James B, *France under the Regency*, London, 1892.

Petitfils, Jean-Christian, *Le Régent*, Paris, 1986.

Roche, Daniel, *The People of Paris*, Paris, 1981.

Seilhac, comte de, *L'abbé Dubois, Premier ministre de Louis XV*, Paris, 1862.

Shennan, J. H, *Philippe, Duke of Orléans, Regent of France*, London, 1979.

Solnon, J.-F, *La Cour de France*, Paris, 1987.

Thaddeus, Victor, *Voltaire: Genius of Mockery*, New York, 1928.

Van der Cruysse, Dirk, *Madame Palatine*, Paris, 1988.

Verlet, Pierre, *The Château of Versailles*, Paris, 1985.

Weigley, Russell F, *The Age of Battles*, Indianopolis, 1991.

Wiesener, L, *Le régent, l'abbé Dubois et les Anglais d'après les sources britanniques*, Paris, 1899.

Williams, Basil, *Stanhope*, Oxford, 1932.

Wolf, John B, *Louis XIV*, New York, 1968.

# SOURCE NOTES

NB SS refers to the *Mémoires* of the duc de Saint-Simon. Edition de la Pléiade. Ed. Coirault. Paris 1983–8.

CHAPTER ONE:  The Son of Monsieur and Madame

p.10    'Their Majesties . . . the world has to offer', Félibien.

p.11    'In a gown . . . to make the ambassadors gasp', Mme de Sévigné to Mme de Grignan, 29 July 1676.

p.13    'It can . . . of others,' Louis XIV, *Mémoires*, pp.102–3

p.13    'Fait comme on peint les anges', Abbé de Choisy, *Mémoires*.

p.15    'She had an open and easy air . . . gentleness', Spanheim, p.75.

p.16    'O! comment . . . avec elle?', Primi Visconti, pp.29–30.

p.16    'You do not persuade me . . . virginity', Madame to the Princess of Wales, 18 October 1720.

p.16    'When Monsieur . . . scolded', Madame to Sophie, 21 January 1703.

p.17    'I'm very much afraid . . . Antichrist', Madame to Sophie, 16 November 1674.

p.17    'Un tour, un sel . . . inimitable', SS, vol. viii, p.552.

p.18    'I very much hope . . . as beautiful as these', quoted in E. Magne, *Le Château de Saint-Cloud.*

p.18    'The first you enter . . . very ordinary,' Martin Lister, 'A Journey to Paris in the year 1698,' from *A General Collection of the Best and Most Interesting Travels in All Parts of the Worlds*, ed. Pinkerton (London 1809).

p.19    'Palais des délices', SS, vol. ii, p.8.

p.19    'Between . . . shadier', Madame to Sophie, 23 August 1691.

p.19    'Madame . . . again in France', Mme de Sévigné to Mme de Grignan, 27 September 1679.

p.21    'Never have . . . the King', Louis XIV, *Mémoires*, p.141.

CHAPTER TWO:  The Little Prince

p.23    'Monsieur le duc de Chartres . . . character', Dubois quoted in V. de Seilhac, *L'abbé Dubois, Premier ministre de Louis XV.*

p.25 'Fame, fortune ... our pleasures', Saint-Evremond, letter to the comte d'Olonne, 1656, reproduced in *Receuil des textes littéraires françaises: XVII siècle.* ed., Chassang et Senninger. Paris p.429.

p.25 'I would like to see ... no such man', La Bruyère, *Les Caractères*, ch. 16.

p.26 'I greatly need strength ... happiness', Mme de Maintenon, *Lettres*, vol. ii, ed. Langlois.

p.27 'He took me for ... lofty things', *Souvenirs sur Mme de Maintenon*, Mlle d'Aumale, ed. Haussonville, p.55.

p.27 'It would be ... by her', *Souvenirs de Mme de Caylus*, ed. Noel, p.42.

p.27 'Parfaitement ... toutes choses', Mme de Sévigné to Mme de Grignan, 20 March 1680.

p.28 'How original ... how varied', Mme de Sévigné, 22 July 1685.

p.29 'I do not hate ... as Monsieur', Madame to Sophie, 4 July 1686.

p.29 'Although ... kick the bucket', Madame to Sophie, 8 February 1690.

p.29 'Some hate ... numerous', Madame to Ameliese, 3 December 1705.

p.30 'I get annoyed ... eyes', Madame to Sophie, 8 October 1688.

p.30 'I engaged ... given it up', Madame to Luise, 22 April 1706.

p.30 'It doesn't seem ... notion', Madame to Sophie, 26 August 1689.

p.31 'A red so perfectly placed ... artificial', *La vie de Philippe d'Orléans*, attrib to P. de la Motte (London 1736).

p.31 'If you ... poor country', Madame to Sophie, 26 September 1688.

p.32 'I am a tougher nut ...', Madame to Sophie, 8 February 1690.

p.33 'I have ... with mine', Madame to Sophie, 14 April 1688.

CHAPTER THREE: Royal Wedding

p.34 'They want ... the fear of exile', Primi Visconti, p.250.

p.35 'It is as ... black spots', Madame to Sophie, 6 July 1702.

p.36 'Marly ... Versailles', Mme de Maintenon, quoted in *Royal Palaces of France* by I. Dunlop (London 1985), p.159.

p.37 'As long as ... at Saint-Cyr ...', Madame to Sophie, 30 June 1691.

p.37 'M. le duc de Chartres ... marvels', quoted in *The Sunset of the Splendid Century* by W. H. Lewis, p.115.

p.38 'Never has a young man ... obstacles ahead', the maréchal de Luxembourg to Louis XIV, 31 May 1691, quoted in *Le Régent* by J.-C. Petitfils, p.39.

p.38 'I hope the beautiful weather ... most tenderly', Madame to her son, 19 March 1691, reproduced in *Lettres françaises* ed. Van der Cruysse.

p.38 'I did not plan ... my dear child', Madame to her son, 24 March 1691. As above.

p.38    'He was gallant . . . all the men', SS, vol. iii, p.368.

p.39    'I had been . . . close friends', SS, vol. i, p.20.

p.40    'My eyes . . . all night', Madame to Sophie, 10 January 1692.

p.40    'So far above . . . held', SS, vol. ii, p.32.

p.41    'I don't care . . . marries me', Mme de Caylus, *Souvenirs*, p.109.

p.42    'I put . . . far from feeling', Madame to Sophie, 21 February 1692.

p.43    'Tristes réjouissances de commande', SS, vol. i, p.46.


CHAPTER FOUR: War and Peace

p.45    'It's all . . . disappeared', Madame to Sophie, 12 April 1692.

p.45    'They say . . . ill', Madame to Sophie, 28 June 1692.

p.47    'You are at . . . a perfect prince', 10 August 1692, Archives du château de Chantilly, reproduced in *Lettres françaises*, p.108.

p.47    'All the gilt . . . beautiful', Madame to Sophie, 7 December 1692.

p.47    'Let off . . . laughed', Madame to Sophie, 1 January 1693.

p.48    'So much wind . . . musical', Madame to Sophie, 18 January 1693.

p.48    'He has led . . . still alive', Madame to Sophie, 23 August 1693.

p.48    'I could not be . . . energy', Louis XIV to Philippe, 10 July 1693, quoted in Petitfils, p.61.

p.48    'I often say . . . about', Madame to Sophie, 24 March 1695.

p.49    'My son . . . look easy', Madame to Sophie, 6 May 1700.

p.49    'The girl . . . already', Madame to Sophie, 8 November 1696.

p.51    'The thing . . . a decent life', Madame to Dubois, 3 June 1696.

p.52    'With my son . . . looks', Madame to Luise, 19 January 1719.

p.52    'It's true . . . chaise-percée', Madame to Sophie, quoted in Petitfils, p.74.

p.52    'Once could write . . . crimes', SS, vol. iv, p.7.

p.54    'I am sure . . . condemn me', SS, vol. i, p.781.

p.54    'People . . . duc d'Anjou', Madame to Sophie, 13 November 1701.

p.54    'I see that . . . here I am', SS, vol. i, p.785.

p.55    'Without reason . . . treated so', SS, vol. i, p.874.

p.56    'I passionately desired . . . amusing himself', SS, vol. ii, p.6.

p.56    'Monsieur . . . du Trevou' and 'No convent . . . convents', SS, vol. ii, pp.9 and 10.

p.57    'Ah! Sire . . . love me', SS, vol. ii, p.11.

p.57    'Eh bien . . . could do', SS, vol. ii, p.9

p.57    'Cards! . . . example', SS, vol. ii, p.11.

p.57    'It was a terrible . . . princess', SS, vol. ii, p.17.

p.58    'It is rare . . . may think', Madame to Ameliese, 15 July 1701.

p.58    'The King . . . waterfall', Madame to Sophie, 28 July 1701.

## CHAPTER FIVE: War Again

p.59 'And so ended ... with it', SS, vol. ii, p.151.

p.59 'I should have ... so good', Madame to Sophie, 26 January 1702.

p.60 'Pretty ... air', SS, vol. ii, p.755.

p.61 'He was ... devoured everything', SS, vol. ii, p.693.

p.62 'The company ... embarrassment', SS, vol. ii, p.218.

p.62 'Everything passed ... Palais-Royal', SS, vol. ii, p.220.

p.63 'God has given ... subjugated one', Louville to Torcy, 15 August 1703. Boislisle, vol. xi, p.526.

p.63 'Cold ... courtier', SS, vol. ii, p.540.

p.63 'The ... nightingales', Madame to Sophie, 26 April 1704.

p.64 'I have not ... coach', *Dispatches of the First Duke of Marlborough*, ed. Murray.

p.64 'One can judge ... prisoner', SS, vol. ii, p.491.

## CHAPTER SIX: Italy

p.66 'Généraux de gout ... de cabinet', SS, vol. ii, p.714.

p.67 'We could not reap ... success', SS, vol. ii, p.718.

p.67 'Monsieur le maréchal ... our age', Louis XIV to Villeroi, Archives du Ministère de la Guerre, quoted in *Louis XIV* by J. Wolf.

p.67 'An old burst balloon ... out', SS, vol. ii, p.765.

p.68 'Buffoon ... strange stews', SS, vol. ii, p.696.

p.68 'I was enjoying myself ... Villcroi', SS, vol. ii, p.734.

p.69 'Feeling less ... all hope', SS, vol. ii, p.754.

p.70 'I admit that ... to think about', Madame to the duc de Lorraine, 3 July 1706, reproduced in *Lettres françaises*, p.294.

p.71 'The length ... time is', La Feuillade to Chamillart, Archives du Ministère de la Guerre, quoted in Wolf.

p.71 'Eh bien! ... Piedmont', SS, vol. ii, p.763.

p.72 'If we ... l'ennemi' and 'Comme un prince ... général', Voltaire, *Le Siècle de Louis XIV* and *Oeuvres historiques*, p.843 and 844.

p.73 'It is not fitting ... course we take', Philippe to Louis XIV. As above.

p.73 'He performed miracles ... courage', SS, vol. ii, p.778.

p.74 'The duc d'Orléans ... stayed with her', SS, vol. ii, p.780.

p.75 'I find here nothing ... bread', Philippe to Chamillart, 21 September 1706, quoted in Boislisle, vol. xix, p.510.

p.75 'I found His Royal Highness ... grapes', Albegotti, quoted in Petitfils, p.116.

p.75    'A mediocre priest ... good man', SS, vol. ii, p.787.

p.75    'I do not believe ... complete defeat', SS, vol. ii, p.787.

p.75    'If my son ... size', Madame to Dubois, 3 September 1706. Archives du château de Chantilly. Fourteen letters from Madame to Dubois, from 12 July to 25 October, are reproduced in *L'abbé Dubois* by Seilhac, pp.236–45.

p.75    'I would far rather die ... my dear child', Madame to her son, September 1706, Boislisle, vol. xiv, pp.505–6.

p.75    'I have wept ... dangerous', Mlle d'Orléans to Philippe, 18 September 1706, Boislisle, vol. xlv, p.508.

p.76    'This ridiculous journey ... scandal', SS, vol. ii, p.791.

p.76    'I must beg ... King's service', Philippe to Chamillart, Boislisle, vol. xiv.

p.76    'Only as ... for consolation', Philippe to Chamillart, Boislisle, vol. xiv, p.518.

p.76    'His poor wounded hand ... pain', Madame to Luise, 11 November 1706.

p.76    'Since he started ... the flute', Madame to Luise, 2 December 1706.

p.77    'It's true ... mistake?' SS, vol. ii, p.792.

p.77    'Monsieur ... the two of us!', SS, vol. ii, p.794.

p.77    'The duchesse de Bourgogne ... dull', Mme de Maintenon to Mme des Ursins, 23 December 1706. Receuil Geffroy, p.287.


## CHAPTER SEVEN: Spain

p.80    'Comment! ... take him with you', SS, vol. ii, p.869.

p.80    'Yesterday ... time for peace', Madame to M. Polier de Bottens, 25 March 1707, reproduced in *Lettres françaises*.

p.81    'Chairs ... fire-irons', Mme des Ursins to the duc de Gramont, 18 March 1707, quoted in *La Princesse des Ursins* by M. Cermakian.

p.82    'Gendre ... connaître', quoted in *Aus den Briefen der Herzogin Elisabeth Charlotte von Orléans an die kurfürstin Sophie von Hannover*, ed. Bodemann (Hanover 1895).

p.82    'On a mule ... ears', Mme des Ursins to Mme de Maintenon, Receuil Bossange, vol. iii, p.454.

p.83    'I have had the misfortune ... as complete as he did', Philippe to Louis XIV, 27 April 1707, quoted in Boislisle, vol. xix, p.625–6.

p.83    'I wasn't there ... I wasn't there', Philippe to his mother. Madame sent Sophie extracts from seven of her son's letters dating from May to September 1707. They are reproduced in *Correspondance de Madame Duchesse d'Orléans*, ed. Jaeglé (Paris 1890).

p.84 'The city ... here', Philippe to his mother, 8 May 1707.

p.85 'Yesterday I was ordered ... not to give in', Philippe to his mother, 12 August 1707.

p.85 'When the Devil ... old woman', Madame to the duc de Gramont, 1 August 1707, reproduced in *Lettres françaises*.

p.85 'A saint ... a saint', Philippe to his mother, 8 May 1707.

p.86 'A pious old lady ... honourable than another', Mme de Maintenon to Mme des Ursins, September 1707, quoted in Cermakian.

p.86 'His natural manner ... successful', SS, vol. ii, p.917.

p.86 'Everyone just eats away ... a neighbour', Madame to Ameliese, 3 February 1707.

p.87 'I always distrust ... neither side', Philippe to Louis XIV, archives nationales, Série KK 1321–2.

p.87 'His reception ... campaign', SS, vol. iii, p.64.

p.88 'My son ... of Lerida', Madame to Sophie, 19 January 1708.

p.88 'Great esteem ... tenderness', Mme de Maintenon to Mme des Ursins, Receuil Bossange.

CHAPTER EIGHT: Danger in Spain

p.90 'I am ... here at all', Marquis de Sourches, *Mémoires*, xi, p.68.

p.90 'Has she not already a son? ... rest', SS, vol. iii, p.113.

p.90 'He has had a cruel journey ... out of nothing', Madame to the duc de Gramont, 26 March 1708, reproduced in *Lettres françaises*.

p.91 'A little tipsy ... supplies', SS, vol. iii, p.182.

p.91 'Fine speeches ... another time', Philippe to Mme des Ursins, 19 September 1708, quoted in Petitfils, p.145.

p.91 'I cannot understand ... troubles he has', Madame to the duc de Gramont, 4 June 1708, quoted in *Lettres françaises*.

p.92 'I wish you could ... my own joy', and 'The King ... with joy', Madame to Sophie, 11 August 1708.

p.93 'I see, messieurs ... already', SS, vol. iii, p.194.

p.93 'I could never have believed ... an opera', quoted in Boislisle, vol. xvi, p.561–3.

p.93 'M. de Vendôme ... than before', 23 July 1708, quoted in SS, vol. iii, p.197, n. 2.

p.93 'Since the monarchy ... ignominious campaign', Maréchal de Tesse to Mme des Ursins, quoted in SS, vol. iii, p.325, n. 8.

p.94 'Why was not ... prisoner?', Mme des Ursins to Chamillart, 16 July 1708, Receuil Geffroy, p.342, quoted in Cermakian.

p.94   'Worries . . . our affairs', Mme des Ursins to the duc de Noailles, 17 August 1708, quoted in Cermakian.

p.94   'Stanhope . . . d'Orléans', Archduke Charles, Journal, 22 August 1708, quoted in Baudrillart, vol. ii, pp.89–90.

p.95   'They wish that . . . kingdom', quoted in Baudrillart, vol. ii.

p.95   'They knew . . . peace of Europe', quoted in Petitfils, p.156.

p.95   'I wish that this prince . . . appropriate', Mme des Ursins to Mme de Maintenon, 9 December 1708, quoted in Cermakian.

p.95   'I have always . . . affairs permits', Louis XIV to Philip V, November 1708, Archives du Ministère de la Guerre, quoted in Wolf.

p.95   'As handsomely . . . deserved', SS vol. iii, p.302.

p.96   'I cannot thank . . . he has passed', Madame to M. Polier de Bottens, 7 December 1708, reproduced in *Lettres françaises*, p.395.

CHAPTER NINE: The End of the World

p.97   'There . . . the cold', Madame to Ameliese, 19 January 1709.

p.98   'The King's views are . . . of our enemies', Philippe to Mme des Ursins, quoted in Petitfils, p.148.

p.99   'If Philip V . . . without hope of return', SS, vol. iii, p.550.

p.99   'The Duke of Orléans . . . permission', reproduced in *The Marlborough-Godolphin Correspondence*, vol. iii, 1200 and quoted in Shennan, p.20.

p.99   'The judgement . . . King of Spain', reproduced in *Letters and Dispatches of the First Duke of Marlborough*, ed. Murray, vol. iv, p.409 and quoted as above.

p.99   'With evil intentions . . .', Mme des Ursins, 26 January 1709, quoted in Cermakian, p.392.

p.99   'Many malversations . . . crown', Boislisle, vol. xviii, p.56.

p.99   'A character . . . intelligent', SS, vol. iii, p.542.

p.99   'HRH would be . . . felt for him', Mme des Ursins to Mme de Maintenon, 1 March 1709, Receuil Bossange, vol. iv, p.225.

p.100  'Here you . . . hunger', Madame to Ameliese, 19 January 1709.

p.100  'The ill-will . . . . to ignore', Philip V to Louis XIV, April 1709, reproduced in *Philippe V et la cour de France* by A. Baudrillart, vol. i, p.340.

p.101  'Messieurs . . . in my name', Philippe's lettre de créance to Flotte, 5 May 1709, reproduced in *Une mission en Espagne* by A. Baudrillart, p.83.

p.101  'I have asked . . . in Spain', Louis XIV to Phil V, 2 June 1709, reproduced in Baudrillart.

p.102  'Criminel d'Etat', Madame to Sophie, 11 July 1709.

p.102 'I believe ... against you', the duc de Bourgogne to Philip V, quoted in Petitfils, p.154.

p.102 'His idleness ... the King', SS, vol. iii, p.450.

p.103 'His explanation ... to know', SS, vol. iii, p.550.

p.103 'Very reassured ...' Dangeau, *Journal*, 2 August 1709.

p.103 'Not only ... harm', Louis XIV to Philip V, 5 August 1709, Baudrillart, vol. ii, p.95–6.

p.103 'What really concerns ... permission', Philip V to Louis XIV, 12 August 1709, Baudrillart.

p.103 'These enquiries ... bad effect', Louis XIV to Amelot. As above.

p.104 'The respect ... the world', Mme de Maintenon to Mme des Ursins.

p.104 'The King ... imposes secrecy', Torcy, *Journal*, 30 November 1709.

p.104 'Under ... in the back', SS, vol. iv, p.462 and *passim*.

p.104 'He started ... chemistry', Madame to Sophie, June 1709.

p.105 'The French ... order', Madame to Sophie, 29 September 1709.

p.105 'Never in my ... all that', Madame to Luise, 14 September 1709.

p.106 'All are ... bad company', Madame to Sophie, 28 September 1709.

p.107 'Amoureux ... eclat', SS, vol. iii, p.234.

CHAPTER TEN: Disgrace

p.108 'A peasant ... huge wig', SS, vol. iii, p.651.

p.109 'There is only one ... must go!', SS, vol. iii, p.666.

p.109 'You are regarded ... for nothing ...', SS, vol. iii, p.664.

p.109 'You wish ... nothing to do?', SS, vol. iii, p.668.

p.110 'Toujours gaie ... malade', Madame to Luise, 23 November 1719.

p.111 'Desperate ... even criminal', Mme de Maintenon to Mme des Ursins, Receuil Bossange, vol. i and vol. iv, p.269.

p.111 'My son ... he has won', Madame to Sophie, 5 January 1710.

p.112 'The splendid diamond ... split our sides', Madame to Sophie, 29 June 1710, tr. Kroll.

p.113 'The effect ... above ...', SS, vol. iii. p.994.

p.113 'If it took ambition ... nose', SS, vol. iii, p.784.

p.114 'Preparons ... percée', quoted in *Cardinal of Spain* by S. Harcourt-Smith, n. p.73.

p.115 'Villaviciosa ... Europe', Torcy, *Journal*, 24 December 1710, p.322.

p.115 'Provided ... commerce', quoted in Wolf, p.576.

p.115 'All ... admonitions', Madame to Luise, 14 December 1710.

p.115 'My son has such a passion ... to home', Madame to Sophie, 23 December 1710, tr. Kroll.

p.116 'Paris did not ... desolate', SS, vol. iii, p.1043.

CHAPTER ELEVEN: Deaths

p.117 'The most beautiful ... in the world' and 'he had no ... in his own fat' and 'he would sit ... no thoughts', SS, vol. iv, pp.78–96, *passim.*

p.118 'Le spectacle touche' and 'I know ... won't last' and 'A thing ... my own eyes', SS, vol. iv, p.69.

p.118 'She sought ... succeeded', SS, vol. iv, p.198.

p.118 'With the face ... made', SS, vol. iv, p.52.

p.119 'What a ... will tell', Madame to Sophie, 26 April 1711.

p.119 'I trust her ... important things', SS, vol. iii, p.1039.

p.120 'The misfortune ... a girl', Madame to Luise, 14 August 1711.

p.120 'I hope ... I do', Madame to Sophie, 15 November 1711, tr. Kroll.

p.120 'One must expect ... years of age', Mme de Maintenon to Mme des Ursins, 11 January 1712, Receuil Geffroy, vol. ii, p.96.

p.120 'My son ... new books', Madame to Sophie, 11 August 1711.

p.121 'En déshabilée ... shawl', SS, vol. iv, p.397.

p.121 'She has convulsions ... intervals', Mme de Maintenon to Mme des Ursins, 7 February, Receuil Geffroy, vol. ii, p.298.

p.122 'Princess today ... forgotten', quoted in *The Sunset of the Splendid Century* by W. H. Lewis, p.186.

p.122 'With her ... worthy to be so', SS, vol. iv, p.408.

p.122 'Everything has gone ... pointless', Mme de Maintenon to Mme des Ursins, 27 March 1712, Receuil Geffroy, vol. ii, p.303.

p.122 'A spectacle ... shuddering', Sourches, *Journal,* vol. xiii.

p.123 'Here they play ... poisons', Madame to Sophie, 27 March 1712.

p.123 'What do you mean ... ashamed yourself', SS, vol. iv, p.465.

p.123 'Profoundly outraged and defeated', SS, vol. iv, p.463.

p.124 'When my heart ... lady', Madame to Sophie, 20 February 1712.

p.124 'When the ... was wrong?', Madame to Sophie, 8 June 1712.

p.125 'Monseigneur ... Bastille', D'Argenson, *Mémoires,* vol. i, p.183.

p.125 'I do not know ... the accused', D'Argenson.

p.125 'Thanks be to God! ... over here!', Madame to Luise, 5 May 1712.

p.125 'I have been ... in the succession', Louis XIV to Philip V, quoted in Wolf and cited in Baudrillart.

p.126 'The King of Spain ... the duc d'Orléans', Bonnac, quoted in Erlanger, p.115.

p.126 'The prince ... sole support', Alberoni to the Duke of Parma, quoted in *Cardinal of Spain.*

p.126 'It was purely ... chance', SS, vol. iv, n. p.520.

p.128 'In a word ... Mme de Maintenon', SS, vol. iv, p.464.

p.128 'They already ... to the court', Madame to Sophie, 8 June 1712.

p.128    'I will give him ... advice', Madame to Sophie, 14 April 1712.

p.129    'He does not miss ... kisses her hand', Pollnitz, vol. i, p.211.

p.129    'The King ... His Majesty', Madame to Sophie, 14 April 1712.


CHAPTER TWELVE:  Ends and Beginnings

p.130    'In veritable towers ... of their body', SS, vol. iv, p.592.

p.131    'There is something ... coiffure', Mme de Sévigné to the duc de Chaulnes, 15 May 1691.

p.131    'Like a fine set ... porcelain', SS, vol. iv, p.593.

p.132    'Who from then on ... the people', SS, vol. iv, p.628.

p.133    'I shall neither gain ... faster', Madame to Luise, 30 April 1713, tr. Kroll.

p.133    'Because ... sleep', Madame to Sophie, 24 November 1713, tr. Forster.

p.134    'They are wrong ... theirs', SS, vol. iv, p.797.

p.135    'Ce garçon-la ... de l'esprit', SS, vol. v, p.291.

p.135    'Dubois is the greatest scoundrel ... he tells him', quoted in Erlanger, p.155.

p.135    'My son ... everything', Madame to Sophie, 24 November 1713, tr. Forster.

p.135    'I am reaching ... weakness', quoted in Cermakian, p.492.

p.136    'They are ... see anyone', Receuil Geffroy, vol. ii, p.339.

p.136    'Esprit de cabale', Philip V to Mme de Maintenon, 8 March 1714, AEM, Espagne 99, f. 46–7.

p.136    'I have very strong ... like this', Brancas to Torcy, quoted in Boislisle, vol. xxiv, p.441.

p.137    'To warm ... cabale', Philip V to Mme de Maintenon, 29 March 1714, AEM, Espange 99, f. 51–2.

p.137    'I will have ... Madrid', quoted in *Vie du Dauphin père de Louis XV* by abbé Proyart.

p.138    'Now you are all I have', SS, vol. iv, p.437.

p.138    'If my son's ... unhappiness', Madame to Sophie, 15 June 1714.

p.138    'What is then ... play with us!' Henry St John, Viscount Bolingbroke, letter of 3 August 1714.


CHAPTER THIRTEEN:  The End of a Reign

p.140    'You have wanted this ... if you can', SS, vol. iv, p.838.

p.141    'Un idiot ... esprit', SS, vol. v, p.120.

p.141    'Everyone became alarmed ... duc d'Orléans', Mme de Maintenon to Mme des Ursins, 5 August 1714, Receuil Bossange, vol. iii, p.95.

p.141    'Messieurs, here is my will ... rest thus', SS, vol. iv, p.837.

p.141 'Everything . . . duc d'Orléans', F. Bluche, *Louis XIV*, p.595.

p.142 'I have told you . . . dexterity', Alberoni to the Duke of Parma.

p.143 'This alas . . . with it', Madame to Luise, 20 October 1714, tr. Kroll.

p.143 'I never get used . . . diminish at all', Mme de Maintenon to Mme des Ursins, 10 November 1714, Receuil Bossange, vol. iii, p.136.

p.143 'Guzzling . . . wolf', Madame, 2 December 1714.

p.143 'Do you know . . . criminal', SS, vol. iv, p.904.

p.143 'Le théâtre des folies . . . grandeur', SS, vol. iv, p.918.

p.144 'The Queen . . . desire', D'Aubigny to Torcy, 14 December 1714, quoted in Baudrillart, vol. i, p.602.

p.144 'Two bottles . . . may happen', Alberoni to the Duke of Parma.

p.144 'She has a pious . . . sheets', Alberoni to the Duke of Parma.

p.144 'Our great Queen . . . services', Alberoni to the Duke of Parma.

p.144 'Behold a Queen . . . personage', quoted in Cermakian, p.531.

p.145 'I avow . . . masters', quoted in SS, vol. v, n. 2, p.163.

p.145 'Took the prize . . . taste', SS, vol. v, p.170.

p.145 'Très méchant visage', SS, vol. v, p.170.

p.145 'M. le duc d'Orléans . . . insulting her', 24 February 1715, Receuil Geffroy, vol. ii, p.362.

p.146 'She is virtually . . . presence', Abbé de Mascara to Philip V, 29 June 1715, reproduced in *Vieilles histoires, vieilles enigmes* by L. Hastier.

p.146 'M. le duc d'Orléans . . . as possible', 24 February 1715, Receuil Geffroy, vol. ii, p.362.

p.147 'I can tell you . . . comte d'Uzès', Voltaire to Mme de Mimeure, *Correspondance*, vol. i, p.31.

p.147 'Under the pretext . . . serve his master', SS, vol. v, p.762.

p.148 'Dangerous creature . . . intrigues', SS, vol. ii, p.879.

p.148 'Supple wit . . . fortune', SS, vol. vii, p.515.

p.149 'If I continue . . . September', SS, vol. v, p.208.

p.149 'Assez laconique', Boislisle, vol. xxvi, p.514.

p.149 'Fire took . . . was ill', SS, vol. v, p.402.

p.150 'Serve the Dauphin . . . do it well', SS, vol. v, p.460.

p.150 'He gave up . . . ever see', Dangeau, *Journal*, vol. xvi.

## CHAPTER FOURTEEN: Taking Power

p.151 'The death of the King . . . foreseen', SS, vol. v, p.619.

p.151 'People were . . . laughing', Voltaire, *Le Siècle de Louis XIV*, ch. xxviii, p.366.

p.152 'As the first . . . subjects', Dangeau, *Journal*, 1 September 1715.

p.152　'The Duke of Orléans ... troops', Lord Stair, 26 August 1715.

p.152　'Bantering ... smiling', Abbé Mascara, *Correspondance*, quoted in Petitfils, p.235.

p.155　'With all his ... nobility', M. D'Aligre, *Revue retrospect*, vol. vi.

p.155　'Messieurs ... laws of the Kingdom', speech of the duc d'Orléans, reproduced in Marais, vol. i, p.173.

p.157　'Without the duc d'Orléans ... Regency council', testament of Louis XIV reproduced in Isambert, *Anciennes lois françaises*, vol. xx.

p.158　'The guardian ... troops', Marais, vol. i, p.165.

p.158　'Ravie de joie', SS, vol. v, p.638.

p.158　'The duc d'Orléans ... fox', P. Narbonne, *Journal des règnes de Louis XIV et Louis XV de 1701 a 1744.*

p.158　'This astute prince ... public liberty', Montesquieu.

p.159　'Earning countless ... humanity', SS, vol. v, p.643.

p.159　'Appeared handsome ... a little pale', Marais, vol. i, p.192.

p.159　'I have come ... my intentions', Buvat, *Journal*, vol. i, pp.58–74.


CHAPTER FIFTEEN: Philippe d'Orléans

p.164　'He talked eloquently ... forgot nothing', SS, vol. v, p.233. and *passim*.

p.164　'I am terrified ... around me', quoted in *The Age of Louis XIV* by Durant, p.619.

p.164　'I never saw    too far', SS, vol. v, p.234 and *passim*.

p.165　'For who better ... other sciences', quoted in *Le Palais-Royal* by Champier and Sandoz.

p.167　'The garden ... good company', Martin Lister, *A Journey to Paris.*

p.168　'I would not know ... the moon', Marivaux, *La Vie de Marianne.*

p.170　'Monseigneur, Dufresny ... absolument', quoted in *La Vie Privée sous la Régence* by C. Kunstler.

p.171　'Everyone wants to judge ... religion', Mme de Maintenon.

p.171　'Many government ... settle elsewhere', quoted in *The People of Paris* by D. Roche, p.15.

p.171　'The petit peuple ... reason', Fontanelle. As above, p.36.


CHAPTER SIXTEEN: Power

p.173　'I see my son ... like this', Madame to Luise, 24 September 1715, tr. Kroll.

p.173　'Many reasons ... Marly', Madame to Harling, 12 October 1715.

p.174　'I must stay ... for each other', Madame to Luise, 8 October 1715.

p.174　'I have kept ... spoil it', Madame to Luise, 1 October 1715.

p.174 'He told me ... even more', Mlle d'Aumale, *Souvenirs sur Mme de Maintenon*, p.207.

p.175 'Infinite quantity ... to smoke it', quoted in F. Braudel, *Civilisation and Capitalism 15th to 18th Century: Vol. 1 The Structures of Everyday Life*, p.262, *Mémoires de M. de Montsegur*.

p.176 'Monsieur le duc d'Orléans ... amazed', SS, vol. vi, p.35.

p.176 'Veille-je ... gentilhomme', B.N. F. fr. n. a. 9680. fo. 71.

p.177 'They drank, the next day', SS, vol. v, p.824.

p.178 'Gracious ... a woman', SS, vol. iv, p.363.

p.178 'Jeunes valets faits', SS, vol. ii, p.303.

p.178 'Cet homme ... vivant', Madame to Sophie, 29 September 1709.

p.180 'Tormented ... ambition', SS, vol. v, p.667.

p.180 'There are no ... calculate them', quoted in Shennan, p.99.

p.181 'The most courteous man ... impenetrable', Lord Stair, *Journal*.

p.182 'Never lost his sang-froid ... courtesy', SS, vol. vii, p.767.

p.182 'He was well resolved ... looking for', SS, vol. v, p.769.

p.183 'On a footing ... the Regent', SS, vol. v, p.770.

p.183 'I must ... too late', Madame to Luise, 15 November 1715.

p.184 'So then ... proof of it', Philippe to Lord Stair, quoted in *Cardinal of Spain*, p.140.

p.184 'I must say ... my son', Madame to Luise, 21 February 1716.

p.184 'Monsieur ... with patience', quoted in Petitfils, p.400.

CHAPTER SEVENTEEN: Une Année Folle

p.187 'If my son ... ladies', Madame to Leibniz, 21 November 1715.

p.188 'A short, chubby ... abscess', SS, vol. v, p.819.

p.188 'I think you a saint ... spoken of', SS, vol. v, p.821.

p.188 'I have brought ... bourgeoises', SS, vol. vi, p.505.

p.188 'La ... putain', reproduced in *Voltaire* by J. Orieux.

p.189 'My son ... pays them well', Madame to the Princess of Wales, 13 March 1716, tr. Kroll.

p.190 'There was hearty ... land lay', Madame to the Princess of Wales, 13 March 1716, tr. Kroll.

p.190 'It is pure ... armchair', Madame to Luise, 17 April 1717.

p.190 'You observe ... respond', Dangeau, *Journal*, 29 August 1716.

p.191 'A very tall ... broad and low', quoted in *John Law* by H. M. Hyde.

p.191 'They mentioned him ... Louis XIV', SS, vol. v, p.883.

p.192 'The bank ... credit', John Law, *Mémoire sur la Banque*, reproduced in *Oeuvres complètes*, ed. Harsin, vol. i, p.214.

p.193 'I have said ... kind of thing', SS, vol. vii, p.730.

p.193 'Arouet ... certain people', SS, vol. v, p.888.

p.194 ' "His Royal Highness" ... satire', Chaulieu to Voltaire, 16 July 1716, conserved in *A World Biography of Biographies*, ed. Besterman.

p.194 'Malgré ... m'ordonne!', Voltaire to Chaulieu, 20 July 1716, *Correspondance*, vol. i, p.36.

p.194 'It would be ... to leave', Voltaire to Mme de Mimeure, summer 1716, *Correspondance*, vol. i, p.42.

p.194 'You would perhaps ... trone des rois', Voltaire to unknown, September 1716, *Correspondance*, vol. i, p.48.

p.195 'The year 1716 ... Une année folle', Jean Meyer.

p.197 'We negotiated ... nightcaps', quoted in Wiesener.

p.197 'At a time ... canal'. As above.

p.197 'The King ... finishing it', quoted in *Cardinal of Spain*, p.185.

p.197 'When our negotiations ... generosity', quoted in Bourgeois.

p.198 'Remember ... scorched', quoted in Petitfils, p.412.

p.198 'This alliance ... miss it', quoted in Petitfils, p.413.

p.198 'I signed ... anxiety', quoted in Erlanger, p.202.

p.198 'Your journey ... tranquillity', quoted in Petitfils, p.415.

p.198 'I am Regent ... only of myself', quoted in Shennan, p.64.

p.199 'Their Royal Highnesses ... the same', Buvat, vol. i, p.243.


## CHAPTER EIGHTEEN: The Czar in Paris

p.200 'As for Voysin ... le maréchal?', D'Argenson, vol. ix, p.139.

p.200 'His stomach ... every morning', SS, vol. vi, p.145.

p.200 'Monseigneur ... perfect health', Dangeau, *Journal*, vol. xvii.

p.201 'Eyes as black ... every day', Madame to Luise, November 1717.

p.202 'No doubt ... God', quoted in Pollnitz, *Mémoires*, vol. i, p.326.

p.202 'To the Opéra! ... tomorrow', SS, vol. vi, p.221.

p.202 'And making a ... at the spectacle', SS, vol. vi, p.221.

p.203 'With your spirit ... Jesuits!', SS, vol. vi, p.232.

p.203 'Assez sombrement', SS, vol. vi, p.234.

p.203 'Well, ... son-in-law', Duclos, *Mémoires Secrets*, vol. i, p.336.

p.203 'My heart beats ... keep them', Madame to Luise, November 1717.

p.203 'A boy reigning ... Perish!', reproduced in *Voltaire* by J. Orieux, tr. *Voltaire; Genius of Mockery* by V. Thaddeus, p.40.

p.204 'I have seen ... and rage!'. As above, p.41.

p.204 'Monsieur Arouet, already seen!', quoted in Thaddeus, p.44.

p.204 'Two copies ... geroufle', Voltaire to M. de Bernaville, 21 May 1717, *Correspondance*, vol. i, p.50.

p.205 'Homme de grand train', SS, vol. vi, p.352.

p.205 'Majestic . . . frightening', SS, vol. vi, p.353.

p.206 'Yesterday . . . a belt', Madame to Luise, 14 May 1717, tr. Kroll.

p.207 'The Czar . . . virgin', the duc d'Estrées to the comte de Toulouse, 17 May 1717.

p.207 'Temple de la pruderie', SS, vol. vi, p.358.

p.207 'Toujours le même', SS, vol. vi, p.361.

p.207 'He said . . . found there', *Mémoires de Louville*, vol. ii, p.240.

p.207 'They . . . my son', Madame to the Queen of Prussia, 16 September 1715.

p.208 'These troubles . . . duc d'Orléans', SS, vol. vi, p.509.

p.209 'When one has . . . give it up', SS, vol. vi, p.244.

p.209 'You know me . . . to do so', SS, vol. vi, p.285.

p.209 'I don't care . . . father', SS, vol. v, n. 1, p.877.

p.210 'I feel real joy . . . interests', Alberoni to Philippe, quoted in *Cardinal of Spain*, p.195.

p.210 'There must be . . . into prison', Lord Peterborough to Philippe, 17 September 1717, Archives du Ministère des Affaires Etrangères.

p.210 'The lion . . . good deed', Dubois to Philippe, November 1717, quoted in Erlanger, p.212.

p.210 'After all . . . foreign powers', Philippe to Dubois, quoted in *Cardinal of Spain* by Harcourt-Smith, p.202.

p.211 'A hundred . . . conversation', quoted in Petitfils, p.435.

p.211 'He had been . . . lose it altogether', Madame to Luise, 28 November 1717, tr. Kroll.

p.211 'It is . . . really love them', Madame to Luise, 9 December 1717.

p.211 'He was not one . . . mistress', SS, vol. vi, p.621.

p.212 'Charming at table', SS, vol. vi, p.622.

p.212 'No one was as handsome . . . good heart', SS, vol. vi, p.621.

p.212 'Race de chien . . . Adieu, chien', Mme de Sabran to Philippe, *Chansonnier de Clairambault*, p.41.

p.212 'Regarde-toi . . . d'affaires', Duclos, *Mémoires secrets*, p.538.

p.212 'Beau marbre . . . s'y tromper', from *Sur Trois Marches de marbre rose* by Alfred de Musset.

## CHAPTER NINETEEN: Coup d'Etat

p.215 'As long as I am . . . abased', Shennan, p.136.

p.215 'Do you ask . . . of it', SS, vol. vi, p.595.

p.216 'He was of cheerful . . . conceivable', D'Argenson, vol. i, p.172

p.216 'I have never . . . great fruit', SS, vol. vi, p.601

p.216  'A nice boy . . . fond of him', Madame to Luise, 31 March 1718, tr. Forster.

p.217  'Madame . . . in an armchair', SS, vol. vi, p.602.

p.217  'Excessively . . . different thing', Madame to Sophie, 25 October 1698, tr. Kroll.

p.217  'Madame!' Madame quoted in Holland *Briefe der Herzogin Elisabeth Charlotte von Orléans*, vol. iii, pp.204–5.

p.218  'Des filets . . . allumettes', *Nouveau Mercure*, quoted in Dangeau, vol. xvii, p.254.

p.218  'This is the only time . . . expense', SS, vol. vi, p.619.

p.218  'It is called . . . worked', Madame to Luise, 24 March 1718, tr. Kroll.

p.219  'Out of deference . . . my subjects', Philip V. May 1718, quoted in *Cardinal of Spain*, p.206.

p.219  'Cutting up . . . cheeses', Alberoni to Bubb, quoted in *Cardinal of Spain*, p.207.

p.220  'I have only ever . . . His Royal Highness', Voltaire to Machault. April 1718, *Correspondence*, vol. i, p.50.

p.220  'Her huge . . . grow', Madame to Luise, 18 July 1715, tr. Kroll.

p.220  'She does . . . about her', Madame to Luise, 31 March 1718, tr. Forster.

p.221  'I shall . . . obedience', SS, vol. vi, p.649, n. 5.

p.222  'The parlement . . . maintain his', SS, vol. vii, p.111.

p.222  'The laws . . . obedience', SS, vol. vii, p.113, 2 July 1718.

p.222  'With much good sense . . . sincerity', quoted in *Cardinal of Spain*, p.212–13.

p.222  'We found the Regent . . . Treaty', Stair and Stanhope quoted in Wiesener.

p.223  'Huxelles dit . . . a signe', quoted in SS, vol. vii, p.9, n. 1.

p.224  'Tout est fini!' and 'We must do justice . . . country'. As above.

p.224  'I admit . . . confidence', quoted in SS, vol. vi, p.155, n. 7.

p.224  'His Catholic . . . his master', quoted in Erlanger, p.223.

p.224  'Though the Cardinal . . . world', Sunderland to Stair, 25 July 1718, quoted in *Cardinal of Spain*, p.214.

p.226  'Everything . . . State', SS, vol. vii, p.119.

p.227  'For today, Messieurs . . . for all', SS, vol. vii, p.234.

p.227  'Voilà . . . unfortunate', and 'Monsieur . . . hidden', SS, vol. vii, p.244.

p.228  'I was dying . . . desires', SS, vol. vii, p.263.

p.228  'Whom curiosity . . . winter', SS, vol. vii, p.269.

p.228  'Air of detachment . . . of majestic', SS, vol. vii, p.270.

p.228  'One cannot . . . matters', SS, vol. vii, p.272.

p.228  'At last! . . . should good', SS, vol. vii, p.277.

p.229  'The Duchess's . . . movements', Mme de Staal, *Mémoires*, p.119.

p.229  'They say . . . otherwise', Madame to Sophie, 25 August 1718.

p.229 'If Madame la duchesse ... rattle', quoted in *Mémoires of Cardinal de Bernis*, vol. iii, p.66.

p.229 'Le secret et le silence', Barbier, *Journal*, September 1718.

p.229 'Quoi, the buggers ... at it!' Barbier, *Journal*, September 1718.

p.230 'At this hour ... master', Lord Stair to Craggs, 31 August 1718.

p.230 'The plotters ... plot', SS, vol. vii, p.300.


CHAPTER TWENTY: Conspiracy

p.231 'Sans crédit ... creatures', Dubois to Philippe, quoted in Petitfils, p.472.

p.231 'Je ne trouve ... de Rome?', quoted in *La vie quotidienne ... Régence* by J. Meyer, p.278.

p.232 'Very intelligent ... with him', SS, vol. v, p.657.

p.232 'En espionnages ... very loyal', SS, vol. v, p.539 and vol. viii, p.528.

p.232 'One beholds him ... empires', D'Argenson, *Mémoires*, vol. iv.

p.233 'When ladies ... knot', Madame to Luise, 19 June 1718, tr. Kroll.

p.233 'It is quite true ... show through', Madame to Luise, 29 September 1718, tr. Kroll.

p.233 'Their cabale ... good choice', Madame to Harling, 21 September 1718, tr. Forster.

p.233 'Grand et fort beau', SS, vol. vii, p.307.

p.234 'I have had ... France and Spain', Philippe to Saint-Aignan, 4 September 1718, quoted in Petitfils, p.479.

p.234 'It is ... both kingdoms', declaration of Philip V, copy at Archives des Affaires Etrangères, Corr. pol., Espagne 275.

p.234 'Could not ... permitted me', Nancré quoted in Petitfils, p.480.

p.234 'The night brought ... prie-dieu', Daubenton quoted in Erlanger, p.243.

p.234 'My lord ... treaty', Lord Stair to Stanhope.

p.234 'Monseigneur ... go to war?' SS, vol. vii, p.318.

p.235 'A Philippe II ... inanities', Voltaire to Philippe, November 1718, *Correspondance*, vol. i, p.55.

p.235 'Et je me vois ... vertueux', Voltaire, *Oedipus*, Act V, Sc. IV.

p.235 'I should appreciate it ... lodging', quoted in *Voltaire; Genius of Mockery* and elsewhere.

p.236 'A proposal ... Royal bank'. *Procès-verbal du Conseil de Régence*, 4 December 1718, B.N.F. fr. 23673, fo. 107.

p.237 'Possessed much wit ... sad duties', SS, vol. vii, p.336.

p.237 'He had ... courtesy', SS, vol. vii, p.336.

p.237 'Neglecting nothing ... Kingdom', SS, vol. vii, p.337.

p.237 'Interesting ... going on?' Mme de Staal, Delaunay, *Mémoires*.

p.237  'Do not leave ... powder', Madame to Luise, 5 January 1719.

p.237  'Would let ... few days', Dangeau, *Journal*, 1447, p.889.

p.238  'I was expecting you', SS, vol. vii, p.347.

p.238  'Que sais-je? ... Mississippi', SS, vol. vii, p.348, n. 9.

p.238  'Monsieur ... recognise it?' SS, vol. vii, p.599.

p.238  'Put away ... from his hand', SS, vol. vii, p.364.

p.239  'This detestable ... allies', Philip V, Archives du Ministère des Affaires Etrangères, Corr. pol., Espagne 285 and 293.


## CHAPTER TWENTY-ONE: Death of a Princess

p.240  'This new ... useful to the state'. *Mercure de France*, April 1719, quoted in Shennan, p.144

p.240  'More convenient ... children',

p.241  'Royal enfant ... toujours', *Philippique Ode 1*, quoted in Buvat, *Journal*, vol. ii, pp.126–54.

p.241  'Ah! this is ... I can bear', and 'I have never ... a little', SS, vol. vii, p.384.

p.241  'I have been ... M. de Voltaire', Voltaire to J. B. Rousseau, *Correspondance*, vol. i, p.57.

p.242  'I hope ye king ... guineas', Lord Stair to Craggs, 2 and 24 April 1719. *Annals and correspondence of the first and second Earls of Stair*, vol. ii, pp.128–30.

p.242  'I willingly ... scorn them', Voltaire to Thieriot, *Correspondance*, vol. i, p.102.

p.242  'Extraordinarily ... nymph', SS, vol. vii, p.92.

p.242  'Truly ... crop', D'Argenson, *Mémoires*.

p.243  'Dying ... of my life', quoted by Madame to the Princess of Wales, 12 May 1719.

p.243  'She was ... highly enough', Dangeau, *Journal*, 15 April 1719, vol. xxxvi, p.241.

p.243  'Behold ... teeth', as above.

p.243  'La vieille ... crevée', Madame to Ameliese, 16 April 1719.

p.243  'Showed himself ... by him', SS, vol. vii, p.372.

p.244  'If he had four ... off', SS, vol. vii, p.410.

p.246  'Fort arroses ... plus fortes', SS, vol. vii, p.411.

p.246  'The most ... cardinal', SS, vol. vii, p.413.

p.247  'The air ... last long', Madame to Luise, April 1719.

p.247  'She is going ... France', Madame to Luise, 14 May 1719.

p.247  'She could stay ... ruler', SS, vol. vii, p.425.

p.248  'The misfortunes ... as I could', SS, vol. vii, p.455.

p.248 'Ou il n'y ... horreur', SS, vol. vii, p.455.

p.248 'I have wept ... so young', Madame to Luise, 23 July 1719.

p.248 'He does not ... ill', Madame to Luise, 23 July 1719.

p.249 'Born with ... self-control', SS, vol. vii, p.449 and *passim*.

p.249 'Là pleures-tu ... maitresse?', quoted in Erlanger, p.263


CHAPTER TWENTY-TWO: The Mississippi

p.250 'Restore the kingdom ... creditors', John Law, *Oeuvres Complètes*, ed. Harsin.

p.250 'I cannot finish ... of Europe', Stanhope to Dubois.

p.251 'It is good ... to everyone?' Voltaire to M. Lefèvre de La Faluere, July 1719, *Correspondance*, vol. i, p.61.

p.252 'Eh, ... carriage!' Madame to the Princess of Wales, 21 October 1719.

p.252 'Mlle de Chausserais ... domaine', Madame to Luise, 7 October 1719.

p.253 'This gallant ... ever known', SS, vol. v, p.787.

p.253 'He has fallen ... teach him', Madame to Luise, 8 December 1719.

p.254 'Eh! non ... Bishops', quoted in *Madame Palatine* by D. Van der Crusse, p.576.

p.254 'In private ... ladies', SS, vol. vii, p.494.

p.254 'I have a horror ... fool', Madame to Luise, 13 May 1719.

p.254 'The ... the Devil', Madame to the Princess of Wales, 15 December 1719.

p.254 'Mlle de Valois ... consolation', Madame to the Princess of Wales, 9 November 1719.

p.255 'What six ladies ... country', Madame to Luise, 23 November 1719, tr. Forster.

p.255 'A bold ... ambition', SS, vol. vii, p.509.

p.255 'Never discussed ... sheets', Duclos, *Mémoires Secrets*.


CHAPTER TWENTY-THREE: The Root of All Evil

p.257 'The goodness ... me', quoted in SS, vol. vii, p.1311, note B.

p.257 'It's possible ... believe', quoted in SS, vol. vii, p.1312, n. 1.

p.257 'More feeble ... his wife', SS, vol. vii, p.462, n. 3.

p.258 'Diable au corps ... thighs', Duclos, *Mémoires Secrets*, p.556.

p.258 'Not only the enemy ... Europe', quoted in Baudrillart.

p.258 'Almost ... wine', Voltaire, *Correspondance*.

p.259 'Go, my child ... course', SS, vol. vii, p.604.

p.259 'I am giving ... pleasure', quoted in *First Gentleman of the Bedchamber* by H. Cole, p.54.

p.259 'Let the cat ... member', SS, vol. vii, p.611.

p.259 'Are you not ... execute them', SS, vol. vii, p.563.

p.260 'M. Law ... extremities', Dubois to Destouches, 24 February 1720, quoted in Petitfils, p.575.

p.260 'For several ... come here', Stanhope, 1 April 1720, quoted as above.

p.261 'Sensing ... fit la pirouette', SS, vol. vii, p.611.

p.261 'I don't think ... in the world', Barbier, *Journal*, July 1720.

p.261 'Comment ... communion', Barbier, *Journal*, July 1720.

p.261 'Just like ... Ambrose!', SS, vol. vii, p.614.

p.262 'At the moment ... traffic' Madame to Luise, 28 January 1720, tr. Kroll.

p.263 'None of the ... play with', Marais, vol. i, p.266.

p.263 'Who could recount ... dementia', SS, vol. vii, p.605ff.

p.263 'Held a knife ... Law', SS, vol. vii, p.578.

p.263 'It appears ... money?', Buvat, Journal de la Régence, vol. ii.

p.264 'I believe ... banknotes', as above.

p.264 'Today ... comte de Horn', Madame to Luise, 31 March 1720, tr. Forster.

p.265 'They have begun ... women', SS, vol. vii, p.644.

p.265 'Only vagabonds ... colonies', Dangeau, *Journal*, 12 May 1720.

p.265 'Every rich man ... beggar', SS, vol. vii, p.667.

p.266 'There is an edict ... any', Barbier, *Journal*, May 1720.

p.267 'Do you believe ... cheese?' quoted in *Les Correspondants de la marquise de Balleroy.*

p.267 'Reward ... Trainel', Marais, vol. i, p.320.

p.267 'I don't know ... away', D'Argenson, *Mémoires.*

p.268 'But this is wonderful ... is right', SS, vol. vii, p.618.

p.269 'Monsieur ... oblige you', quoted in Boislisle, xxxvii, pp.478–84, appendix reproducing a passage from a *Discours à ses enfants* by Paris de La Montagne.

p.269 'No one ... in plenty', Madame to the Princess of Wales, 21 June 1720.

p.269 'Desmares ... her eyes', Madame to Harling, 4 July 1720.

p.269 'Ah, when ... when I can!' Marais, vol. i, p.317.

p.270 'Bastard ... to pieces', Barbier, 18 July 1720.

p.270 'Fort tranquille', SS, vol. vii, p.669.

p.270 'As white ... cravat', Barbier, 18 July 1720.

p.270 'I heard ... my son', Madame to Luise, 18 July 1720.

p.271 'Tout se passa ... autre', SS, vol. vii, p.695.

p.271 'Save the King ... Tyrant', Barbier, vol. i, p.50.

p.271 'I am as tired ... gold', Madame to Luise, 2 November 1720.

p.271 'Que dans votre ... Systeme!' Voltaire to the duc de Sully, 18 August 1720, *Correspondance*, vol. i, p.67.

p.272 'The rumours ... hateful', Madame to Luise, 24 August 1720, tr. Forster.

p.272    'I went to walk ... stoned', Barbier, 1 September 1720.

p.272    'One dies here ... return', letter of Père Gauthier, quoted in Buvat, *Journal*, pp.167–9.

p.272    'Que la peste ... Palais-Royal', Marais, vol. i, pp.413–14.

p.272    'The system ... honest men', Marais, vol. i, p.386.

p.273    'This country ... just begun', Father Laval.

p.273    'My son ... hated', Madame to the Princess of Wales, 4 October 1720.

p.274    'The Archbishop ... desire', Wiesener.

p.274    'Indulges ... allure', Marais, vol. ii, p.2.

p.274    'I do not worry ... beans', Marais, vol. ii, p.8.

p.274    'The Bull ... made', Marais, vol. ii, p.4.

p.275    'The good fortune ... ill, Marais, vol. ii, p.6.

p.275    'Whom one thought ... water', Marais, vol. ii, p.8.

p.275    'Courageous ... table', SS, vol. vii, p.695.

p.275    'People are well ... credit', Barbier, 22 December 1720.

p.275    'Monseigneur ... justice', Law to Philippe, *Oeuvres complètes*.

p.276    'Enfin ... riche', *Précis du siècle de Louis XV*, Voltaire, Pléiade Ed. p.1307.

## CHAPTER TWENTY-FOUR:  Disillusion

p.277    'Despair ... Englishman', Marais, vol. ii, p.59.

p.278    'Told good jokes ... tricks', Marais, vol. ii, p.61.

p.278    'One is obliged ... the hunt', Marais, vol. ii, p.57.

p.279    'The Regent ... the pleasure', Marais, vol. ii, p.57.

p.280    'A scene of ... corruption', Cambridge Modern History, vol. vi, p.181.

p.281    'This treaty ... subjects', quoted in Baudrillart, vol. ii, p.463.

p.282    'Quelque chose ... la', quoted in Petitfils, p.260.

p.282    'After all ... livery', quoted in *Les Maîtresses du Régent* by Lescure.

p.282    'In a room ... open', Marais, vol. ii, p.119.

p.282    'The terms ... accepted', Marais, vol. ii, p.157.

p.282    'What a beautiful ... wished', Marais, vol. ii, p.157.

p.282    'The whore ... with him', Marais, vol. ii, p.160.

p.283    'Behold ... debauche', Marais, vol. ii, p.160.

p.283    'We are ruined ... dance', Marais, vol. ii, p.167.

p.283    'Odd things ... granddaughter is', Madame to the Queen of Prussia, 12 April 1721, reproduced in *Lettres françaises*, p.690.

p.283    'The stench ... illness', Marais, vol. ii, p.140.

p.283    'Of nine ... malaise', Madame to Luise, 26 April 1721, tr. Kroll.

p.283    'I would blush ... own work', SS, vol. vii, p.804.

p.284    'Or, écoutez ... maquereau', quoted in Marais, vol. ii, p.180.

p.284 'This does ... Church', Barbier, 22 July 1721.

p.284 'You can make ... honest man', quoted in Marais, vol. ii, p.273.

p.284 'Cardinal! ... to lose', SS, vol. vii, p.765.

p.285 'All the carriages ... Caprée', Marais, vol. ii, p.182.

p.285 'She has too much ... complexion', Barbier, 26 July 1721.

p.285 'Has made ... evacuation', Buvat, i. p.146.

p.285 'Look at this ... master, SS, vol. vii, p.809.

p.285 'M. le Duc d'Orléans ... attached', SS, vol. vii, p.810.

p.286 'The explosion ... hate', *Le Régent* by P. Erlanger, p.312.

p.286 'Ho ça! ... discrétion', SS, vol. vii, p.794.

p.286 'One is astonished ... posterity', Marais, vol. ii, p.191.

p.286 'What! ...prayers!' D'Argenson, vol. i, p.192.

p.287 'Had the Devil's ... badly', SS, vol. vii, p.794.

p.287 'Come now ... grace', SS, vol. vii, p.838.

p.287 'Monseigneur ... of my life', Philippe to Philip V, quoted in Baudrillart, vol. ii.

p.287 'Everybody ... desired', Madame to Luise, 25 September 1721, tr. Kroll.

p.288 'She came to ... look at her', Madame to the Queen of Prussia, 13 November 1721.

p.288 'The Spaniards ... Queen of Spain', Barbier, vol. i, p.160.

p.289 'God touched him', SS, vol. vii, p.828.

p.289 'Reviens ... légérete', D'Argenson, vol. i, p.192.

p.290 'Monseigneur ... harem', Marais, vol. ii, p.217.

p.290 'In cloth of gold ... money around', Boislisle, vol. xxxiv, p.445.

p.290 'I assure you ... did she', Madame to Luise, 21 November 1721.

p.290 'Extremely handsome ... ignorant', SS, vol. vii, p.830.

p.290 'In the fear ... for him', letter quoted in Boislisle, vol. xxxviii, p.478.

p.291 'His courage ... pity him', Barbier, 29 November 1721.


CHAPTER TWENTY-FIVE: Coronation

p.292 'Permete ... conge de vous', SS, vol. ii, p.908, n. 2.

p.293 'He was very bent ... unnerved', SS, vol. viii, p.19.

p.293 'I was deeply shocked ... arms', SS, vol. viii, p.19.

p.293 'Her ladies ... success', SS, vol. viii, p.303.

p.293 'Which Your ... regard', letter of 2 February 1722, reproduced in SS, vol. viii, p.880, n. 5.

p.293 'I, go there? ... I like', SS, vol. viii, p.362.

p.294 'You cannot deny ... leaves it', Narbonne, *Journal*, p.74.

p.294 'To conduct himself ... firmness', letter reproduced in Boislisle, xi, p.349–52.

p.295 'A telling . . . not let', Barbier, March 1722.

p.295 'Ah, do not . . . see me!' Madame to Harling, 5 March 1722.

p.295 'The dear child . . . wax model', Madame, April 1722, quoted in *Madame Palatine* by D. Van der Cruysse, p.611.

p.295 'Has fallen ill . . . drunk', Marais, vol. ii, p.260.

p.295 'The Infanta . . . charm', Marais, vol. ii, p.266.

p.295 'The King . . . countenance', Madame to Luise, 26 March 1722.

p.296 'He ate . . . worse', Marais, vol. ii, p.268.

p.296 'How can you . . . absolutely', Marais, vol. ii, p.273.

p.296 'A great enthusiast . . . conversation', Marais, vol. ii, p.273.

p.297 'In order to increase . . . pleasure', Marais, vol. ii, p.274.

p.297 'Fille . . . jolie', Barbier, April 14 1722.

p.297 'I was so . . . disconcerted', SS, vol. viii, p.437.

p.297 'I can go . . . with me', Voltaire to Dubois, *Correspondance*, vol. i, p.1378.

p.298 'I beg you . . . Richelieus', Marais, vol. ii, p.358.

p.298 'Bagatelle', Marais, vol. i, p.316.

p.299 'The wine is drawn . . . it', SS, vol. viii, p.466.

p.299 'When he worked . . . reign', SS, vol. vii, p.563.

p.300 'You are . . . need to do', SS, vol. viii, p.473.

p.300 'Avec . . . accoutumé', SS, vol. viii, p.486.

p.301 'I share . . . has done', letter reproduced in Appendix of Boislisle, vol. xli, pp.375–8.

p.302 'She is a . . . one day', Madame to Luise, 31 March 1718.

p.302 'More cheerful . . . Infante-Reine', Madame to the Queen of Spain, 15 August 1722, *Lettres françaises*, p.741.

p.302 'He was distracted . . . Prime Minister', SS, vol. viii, p.499.

p.302 'Very well! . . . soon as possible', SS, vol. viii, p.505.

p.303 'During your minority . . . expenditure', *Arsenal*, ms. 4492, p.351, tr. and reproduced in Shennan, p.125.

p.303 'Belle-Isle . . . intrigues', letter of Rémond, reproduced in Boislisle, vol. xli, p.387.

p.303 'Gare les gras!', Marais, vol. ii, p.365.

p.303 'Everyone remembered . . . tenderness', D'Argenson, vol. i, p.193.

p.305 'As I write . . . it', Voltaire to Thieriot, December 1722. *Correspondance*, vol. i, p.96.

p.305 'When she saw me . . . for her', Madame to Luise, 5 November 1722.

p.306 'I am getting . . . sick as this', Madame to Luise, 3 December 1722.

·p.306 'You weep . . . how to die?' quoted in Saint-Géry de Maynas, *Discours prononcé dans l'église de Saint-Denis* and *Mercure Galant*, January 1723, pp.90–101.

p.306 'Behold a loss . . . rare thing', Marais, vol. ii, p.377.

## CHAPTER TWENTY-SIX: Master and Man

p.307 'M. le duc d'Orléans ... Opéra ball', Barbier, vol. i, p.255.

p.308 'I am still able ... kingdom', quoted in Petitfils, p.613.

p.310 'And yet ... dull', Marais, vol. ii, p.441.

p.310 'This cannot be ... in peace', SS, vol. viii, p.603.

p.310 'I am overwhelmed ... than I', Marais, vol. ii, p.398.

p.310 'Comment? ... poulet', SS, vol. viii, p.604.

p.311 'It is true ... advice', P. Narbonne, *Journal*, pp.76–7.

p.311 'If I can ... Austria', Dubois to Chavigny, Archives du Ministère des Affaires Etrangères, quoted in Shennan, p.74.

p.311 'The duc d'Orléans ... Mlle Houel', Voltaire to Mme de Bernières, *Correspondance*, vol. i, p.107.

p.311 'What! ... cousins!' Marmontel, *Mémoires*.

p.312 'You must ... intendant!' Marais, vol. ii, p.477.

p.312 'One does not ... so many', Marais, vol. ii, p.465.

p.312 'He is a Proteus ... penetrate him', Marais, vol. ii, p.368.

p.313 'You must ... courage', SS, vol. viii, p.593.

p.313 'On his back ... crucifix', Henault, *Mémoires*, pp.64–6.

p.313 'I hope ... way', quoted in *Le Régent* by Erlanger, p.334.

p.313 'He did no ... avoid war', Barbier, *Journal*, vol. i, pp.186–7.

p.313 'Dubois ... duc d'Orléans', D'Argenson, vol. i, p.29.


## CHAPTER TWENTY-SEVEN: Capax Imperii

p.315 'As soon as ... servant', SS, vol. viii, p.606.

p.315 'Morte ... Palais-Royal', *Journal de la Régence*, ed. Campardon.

p.315 'Let us not ... asks', Marais, vol. iii, pp.7–8.

p.315 'Pax ... defunctis', Marais, vol. iii, p.45.

p.316 'Although he talks ... pleasure', quoted in *Correspondance complète de Madame duchesse d'Orléans*, ed. Brunet, vol. i, p.306.

p.316 'He was moved ... the time', SS, vol. viii, p.612.

p.317 'His head was ... dressed', SS, vol. viii, p.613.

p.317 'If you do not ... expect', SS, vol. viii, p.614.

p.317 'The weather ... farewell', D'Argenson, vol. i, p.195.

p.318 'You must not ... whore', Marais, vol. iii, p.50.

p.318 'Very sad ... moist', SS, vol. viii, p.647.

p.319 'This great mark ... since', SS, vol. viii, p.647.

p.319 'Absorbed ... reflection', SS, vol. viii, p.645.

p.319 'Avec ... pompe', SS, vol. viii, p.656.

p.319 'Philippe ... Lucifer', B.N. F. fr. 12699, pp.59–80.

p.320 'All the dirtiest ... words', Marais, vol. iii, p.56.

p.320 'He died ... wicked prince', Delisle, *Journal*, Archives nationales.

p.320 'The death ... like him', Montesquieu.

p.320 'I must render ... Prime Minister', Barbier, 3 December 1723.

p.320 'Of all the race ... Henri IV', Voltaire, *Précis du Siècle de Louis XV*, Oeuvres historiques, ed. Pomeau, p.1313.

p.320 'He left the country ... coffers', D'Argenson, vol. i, p.23.

p.320 'If they made me ... his son', Marais, vol. ii, p.73.

p.321 'He was pliant ... adventurer', Angrand de Fontpertuis, Arsenal, Ms. 3857, p.67.

p.321 'Like the late ... rogues', Mme du Deffand, quoted in *Correspondance complète* ... ed. Lescure.

p.321 'He broke so many ... discredited him', SS, vol. v, p.246.

p.322 'Although ... know him', SS, vol. v, p.232.

p.322 'To describe ... hopes on him', Mme de Caylus, *Souvenirs*, ed. Noel, p.109.

p.322 'Everything ... bon mot', Montesquieu, *Mes pensées*, p.1024.

# INDEX